THE POWER
OF SYSTEMS

THE POWER OF SYSTEMS

How Policy Sciences Opened
Up the Cold War World

Eglė Rindzevičiūtė

CORNELL UNIVERSITY PRESS   ITHACA AND LONDON

Copyright © 2016 by Cornell University

All rights reserved. Except for brief quotations in a review, this book, or parts thereof, must not be reproduced in any form without permission in writing from the publisher. For information, address Cornell University Press, Sage House, 512 East State Street, Ithaca, New York 14850.

First published 2016 by Cornell University Press

Library of Congress Cataloging-in-Publication Data

Names: Rindzevičiūtė, Eglė, author.
Title: The power of systems : how policy sciences opened up the Cold War world / Eglė Rindzevičiūtė.
Description: Ithaca ; London : Cornell University Press, 2016. Includes bibliographical references and index.
Identifiers: LCCN 2016002042 |
ISBN 9781501703188 (cloth : alk. paper)
Subjects: LCSH: Policy sciences. | Political science—Methodology.
Classification: LCC JA80 R635 2016 | DDC 320.6—dc23
LC record available at http://lccn.loc.gov/2016002042

Cloth printing   10 9 8 7 6 5 4 3 2 1

ISBN 978-1-5017-8220-6 (pbk.)

For Francis

Contents

Acknowledgments	ix
Abbreviations	xi
Introduction: The Rise of System-Cybernetic Governmentality	1
1. Gray Eminences of the Scientific-Technical Revolution	24
2. Bridging East and West: The Birth of IIASA	52
3. Shaping a Transnational Systems Community (1): Networks and Institutions	73
4. Shaping a Transnational Systems Community (2): Family versus War Room	94
5. The East-West Politics of Global Modeling	129
6. From Nuclear Winter to the Anthropocene	150
7. Acid Rain: Scientific Expertise and Governance across the Systemic Divide	181
Epilogue: The Avant-Garde of System-Cybernetic Governmentality	204
Notes	219
Bibliography	267
Index	287

Acknowledgments

It is a pleasure to be able to acknowledge all the people who played a significant role in the writing of this book. The original idea of this project emerged more than a decade ago, in 2004, and was developed during six years of postdoctoral research. Thanks to a generous scholarship awarded by the Tore Browaldh Foundation, Handelsbanken, Sweden, I was not only able to conduct my fieldwork at the International Institute of Applied Systems Analysis (IIASA) in Laxenburg, Austria, but also to develop my ideas while working alongside some of the finest minds in organization studies at Gothenburg Research Institute (GRI), School of Business, Economics and Law at Gothenburg University, Sweden. I thank Barbara Czarniawska, Rolf Solli, Ulla Eriksson-Zetterquist, and Sten Jönsson for inviting me to become part of the unique research community at GRI, and I am particularly grateful to Barbara for her insightful comments on my ongoing work, as they helped enormously to attune my historical analysis and understanding of organizational life.

At Centre d'études européennes (CEE) of the Paris Institute of Political Studies (Sciences Po) in France, my work was supported by a generous grant from the European Research Council, awarded to Jenny Andersson, which enabled me to carry out my fieldwork in Moscow, plunging into the archives and interviewing scientists involved in East-West cooperation. I thank Jenny and the team at the project Futurepol, particularly Vítězslav Sommer, Pauline Prat, and Sibylle Duhautois, for reading and commenting on my work at Futurepol meetings. Paris proved to be conducive for intense engagement with both French and US academia and I thank S. M. Amadae, Olivier Borraz, Marie-Laure Djelic, Matthew Evangelista, Gabriella Hecht, Paul Edwards, Paul Josephson, Tatiana Kasperski, Dominique Pestre, and Leena Riska-Campbell for support and constructive comments. I also thank CEE and its director, Renaud Dehousse, for hosting my project and providing both a stimulating intellectual environment and the most efficient administrative support that can exist. Thanks to Linda Amrani, Silvia Duerich-Morandi, Assya El Mahnaoui, Katia Rio, and Samia Saadi.

Parts of this book have been discussed at many research meetings, and I wish to particularly thank Centre de Sociologie des Organisations (CSO), Sciences Po, Nicolas Guilhot at CIRHUS at New York University, Susanne Bauer and Tanja Penter at Ruprecht-Karls-Universität in Heidelberg, the German History Institute

(DHI) in Moscow, and the London-based Foucault Political Life and History group, particularly Colin Gordon, Patrick Joyce, and David Edgerton.

Special thanks go to my former PhD supervisor, Irina Sandomirskaja, who encouraged my interest in the history of Soviet cybernetics and provided continuous support to my postdoctoral work, guiding me in the conceptual and institutional labyrinths of doing research into Soviet history. Concerning the latter, practical tips from Sari Autio-Sarasmo on how to survive as a researcher in Moscow were simply indispensable.

This study would have been impossible without the friendly help of many people who opened up their institutions for my scrutiny. I thank the Swedish Research Council FORMAS, particularly Uno Svedin, for facilitating my access to the IIASA archives. The IIASA administration and library staff were the kindest and most efficient help possible and I thank Aviott John and Michaela Rossini for opening the archives for me and arranging for the interview meetings. My work in Moscow was enormously helped by the archivists at the Russian State Archive of the Economy (RGAE) and the Archive of the Russian Academy of Sciences (ARAN), where Irina Tarakanova was of great help. I also thank Vanessa Voisin and the staff at the French-Russian Center for Humanities and Social Sciences for the remarkable reduction of red tape relating to my trips to Moscow.

I just cannot thank enough my interviewees for sharing their memories, ideas, and materials with me. It was a privilege to meet you all and although I do not expect you to agree with everything that I propose in my book, I hope that you will at least find it an interesting read.

At Cornell University Press, Roger Haydon was an inspiring guide in the publishing process and I thank the two anonymous reviewers for their generous and constructive comments, which were extremely helpful in revising the final manuscript. I also thank the production team at Cornell, particularly Susan C. Barnett and Emily Powers, and Michelle Witkowski and Carol Noble at Westchester Publishing Services.

Finally, I thank my family, especially my parents, who outlived the Soviet regime and, regardless of all the hardships of post-Soviet transition, always supported my interest in science. This project could have never been completed without Francis Dodsworth, whose gentle and patient support to my international career has simply been unique and stands as proof that life does not have to be limited by national boundaries.

Abbreviations

ARAN	State Archive of the Russian Academy of Sciences
CERN	European Organization for Nuclear Research
CoCom	Coordinating Committee for Multilateral Export Controls
FRG	Federal Republic of Germany
GDR	German Democratic Republic
GKNT	State Committee for Science and Technology
GOELRO	State Commission for the Electrification of Russia
Gosplan	State Planning Committee
IAEA	International Atomic Energy Agency
ICSU	International Council of Scientific Unions
IIASA	International Institute of Applied Systems Analysis
IKSI	Institute for Concrete Social Research
IMEMO	Institute of World Economics and International Relations
ISA	Institute of Systems Analysis
MGIMO	Moscow Institute of International Relations
NAS	National Academy of Science
NATO	North-Atlantic Treaty Organization
NKVD	People's Commissariat of Internal Affairs
OECD	Organization for Economic Co-operation and Development
OGAS	All-Union Automated System
OMENTO	GKNT Department for International Economic and Technoscientific Organizations
OR	Operations Research
PPBS	Planning-Programming and Budgeting System
RGAE	Russian State Archive of the Economy
STR	Scientific-Technical Revolution
UN	United Nations
UNACASTD	United Nations Advisory Committee on the Application of Science and Technology to Development
UNITAR	UN Institute for Training and Research
VNIISI	All-Union Scientific Institute of Systems Research
VNIPOU	All-Union Institute for Problems of Management of National Economy
WHO	World Health Organization

THE POWER
OF SYSTEMS

Introduction
THE RISE OF SYSTEM-CYBERNETIC GOVERNMENTALITY

If the reader could step back in time and peer through the door of any Moscow institute of mathematics in the late 1940s or early 1950s, she would perhaps be surprised to see scholars wearing a military *kitel`*, the jacket of a Red Army officer's uniform. If she guessed that these were Soviet Cold War warriors crafting algorithms and strategies for defense against the West, she would not be entirely wrong: many of these researchers would go on to work in the fields of operations research, systems analysis, and computer science. However, this particular wardrobe choice was both symbolic and pragmatic: the uniforms were worn not only to signify military preparedness in the context of the escalating Cold War, but also because it was cold and researchers could not afford proper suits, which were enormously expensive at that time. Decorations were kept on not only out of pride, but because they left unseemly holes in the material when removed.[1] Later in the 1950s, *kitel`* jackets would be replaced by smarter dress as Soviet scholars, then better off, strove to keep pace with US professors in fashion as well as in bomb technology and computer science.[2] This shift from a *kitel`* to a suit is a sign of the ambiguous character of the Soviet technoscience that spanned military and civil applications. It also points to the ambivalence of Soviet technocracy, a mode of government that derived its authority from professional expertise. Soviet technocrats, just like US technocrats, gained authority from their military success during World War II, but they also selectively discarded this military legacy. A couple of decades later, Soviet scientists would turn into smart, suit-wearing scientific experts, able to mediate between academic research institutions, industries, and the government, and between East and West. Far from being Cold War warriors, they harnessed the Cold War divide to channel political priority, funding, and policy, with the aim of developing new intellectual technologies, by which I refer to forms of scientific expertise dedicated to aiding policy and management decisions, enabling them to define and govern the world as a mesh of intertwined systems, and not as a Modigliani-style assemblage of territorial states.

This book is about science and power. It is a historical sociology of the forging of scientific governance across the Iron Curtain in the 1960s–1980s. The idea for this volume began when I encountered a puzzling question: how is it possible that both Soviet and US governmental elites embraced the same scientific methods of governance, gathered under the umbrella names of cybernetics, systems analysis, and, later, policy sciences, and, moreover, closely cooperated in development of these methods during the Cold War? Surely, one would think, government of communist and capitalist societies could not be amenable to the same techniques of discipline and control? But this was the case when the science of governance, cybernetics, and its sibling, the systems approach, circulated between East and West, beginning in the 1950s. As is so often the case, an apparent paradox suggests a complex mechanism at work that we do not yet understand. This book seeks to unravel and explain this paradox, introducing a more nuanced understanding of the history of scientific governance in the late twentieth century. In the opening paragraph, I use the example of the polyfunctionality of Soviet military uniforms as a metaphor to show that scientific governance and its international transfer can be guided simultaneously by different rationales. Nowhere were political symbolism and pragmatic, utilitarian rationales so tightly intertwined as in the development and international transfer of system-cybernetic sciences of government.

What is system-cybernetic governance? Cybernetics and the systems approach, which includes but is not limited to operations research (OR), systems theory, systems analysis, and, at a later stage, policy analysis, constitute a hybrid field of science and technology that emerged from innovations in mathematics and electronic engineering during World War II, to become part of the academic establishment during the late 1940s. "Cyborg," "cyberpunk," and "cybersecurity" are just a few of the terms that originated from this field, spreading widely through public discourse. But the field of system-cybernetic, computer-based science originated as a resource for both formulating and solving governmental problems. As such, system-cybernetic sciences were part and parcel of the late modern worldview (although not necessarily high modernist, as I explain later), according to which societies, economies, and nature were so highly complex that neither common sense nor sector-specific knowledge was sufficient to govern them.

We already have groundbreaking work emerging which has attempted to place cybernetics and the systems approach at the center of the scientific and governmental epistemology of the twentieth century.[3] However, most of these studies focus mainly on US and West European developments and only a few engaged with the Soviet or, indeed, transnational side of the development of these sciences.[4] One of the tasks of this book, therefore, is to introduce the transnational dimension of these extraordinary policy sciences, the uses of which stretched beyond mere utility, facilitating the building of alliances in world and institutional politics, and to discuss some of important transformative moments in the Soviet system-cybernetic governance.

The reader, accordingly, should not expect to find a comprehensive history of the systems approach in this volume. There remains to be written, for example, an exciting history of the system-cybernetic governance embracing the global South. Rather, the intellectual journey that I propose is a first step in the direction of a transnational history of system-cybernetic governance, involving encounters with a few, but highly important moments when the systems approach traveled across the Iron Curtain in the 1960s–1980s. At the center of my story is the International Institute of Applied Systems Analysis (IIASA), which was anything but an arcane academic institute. IIASA was an extraordinary creation of scientific and policy elites, an organization, the history of which not only provides a fascinating angle on East-West relations, but also reveals the late Soviet engagement with governance as an intellectual project, an aspect which tends to be neglected.

What was this institute? Nicknamed "the East-West Institute" and "East-West RAND," IIASA was initiated by Lyndon B. Johnson's administration in the mid-1960s. It was founded in 1972 by the Soviet Union and the United States, along with ten other countries from Eastern and Western blocs. Since then IIASA has been luxuriously accommodated in a baroque palace, Laxenburg Schloss, a dozen kilometers from Vienna, Austria. With a location fit to shoot an episode of a James Bond movie and the unlikely rationale of bringing the best men (they mainly were men) in East-West policy sciences to work together, IIASA might appear, on the surface, to be an extravagant quirk of Cold War diplomacy, an impression registered in fiction writing about IIASA.[5] In reality, however, IIASA scholars in policy sciences spent lengthy periods of time not so much spying on each other—the use of classified data was excluded by house rules—as developing scientific expertise for what were defined as global and universal problems: world food supplies, water, energy, transport, and the environment. To be sure, the East-West geopolitical tension lingered in the atmosphere, especially during the 1970s, but it is precisely to cope with this geopolitical tension that highly sophisticated organizational and discursive techniques were used to frame activities at IIASA as apolitical.

Although the original idea of the international think tank which would become IIASA was part of a US foreign policy initiative, the intellectual rationale of this institute was formulated by a particular and increasingly transnational community of systems scholars, seeking to solidify their networks and promote their epistemological agenda. These two strands, foreign diplomacy and academic politics, intertwined: there are extensive studies on how the United States assumed a leading role in developing management and policy sciences and disseminating them internationally during the 1950s and 1960s. Historians of Cold War science, such as Theodore Porter, Giuliana Gemelli, Nicolas Guilhot, Philippe Lafontaine, and Jenny Andersson, to mention just a few contributors to this quickly expanding field, detailed the spread of American methods of policy-oriented quantification in Western Europe.[6] Along with this, a particular US form of the organization of scientific expertise through think tanks was disseminated. US think tanks, according to Diane Stone, were highly diverse organizations, which espoused an entrepreneurial spirit seeking to produce policy- or management-relevant scientific expertise and dated back to the interwar period; however, the real explosion of the think-tank population took place during the 1950s and 1960s.[7] It is remarkable, though, that the first international think tank, IIASA, would be established by opposing super powers, the Soviet Union and the United States.

In this context, it is difficult to understand how the East-West Institute managed to escape the attention of Cold War historians and sociologists, and political scientists studying globalization. Also, given IIASA's diplomatic origins and scientific agenda, and its research on what was called universal and global problems, it is surprising that, so far, IIASA has been overlooked in studies of globalization, appearing only in a few, recent works.[8] True, case studies of IIASA surface occasionally in work on environmental history, because IIASA hosted many pioneering studies on global climate change, on globalization, and, more recently, on East-West cooperation under the Johnson administration.[9] But the burgeoning field of Soviet studies tended to completely overlook this case of East-West cooperation.

Perhaps it was the elite character of IIASA, a certain curtain of discretion, and the Cold War legacy of keeping its profile rather low that kept it obscure.[10] The in-house history explains that the cryptic name of IIASA was intentionally chosen to fend off unnecessary political scrutiny: posing as a technocratic, narrow, specialist, and obscure institution was thought to be a good strategy. The acronym, indeed, managed to protect the intention of IIASA's leaders to forge a discrete gate between East and West, a laboratory where a new worldview could be developed. Thus one of my goals is to argue that this institute should not be considered a mere stage for diplomatic rituals. Neither was it limited to dissemination of US science as a way of expanding US hegemony globally. In contrast, IIASA enabled the spread of system-cybernetic policy sciences through East-West *coproduction*, where the receiving end (East) was as active as the sending end (West) and the traffic was not unidirectional.[11]

I also want to use the case of IIASA to demonstrate how the new transnational, system-cybernetic governmentality was forged in the postwar period.[12] In doing this, I pursue two inter-related arguments. First, I argue that IIASA should be understood as both a cause and a symptom of the emerging system-cybernetic governmentality, where, second, I posit the importance of the Soviet contribution. Indeed, I use the IIASA case to examine the transformation of late Soviet governance. How did the systems approach rise to prominence as a policy science in the Soviet Union? How and why did the systems approach serve as a channel for international transfer? And, most importantly, what kind of social and institutional settings enabled all these processes? To answer these questions I go beyond the internalist history of science and technology to study the wider institutional context, but also to focus on trajectories of distinct personalities, whose contribution should not be reduced to their impact on the advance of science (albeit this impact was significant). Their life trajectories have much to reveal about the link between social settings and intellectual agendas, as they used their intellectual entrepreneurship and transnational sociality to navigate geopolitical undercurrents, producing new conceptual and institutional frameworks for government.[13] I thus offer a study of IIASA as host to a set of extraordinary scientific communities, a node where loosely coupled networks intersected, linking nascent global thinking with emerging policy sciences, and seeking to harness rather than exacerbate the Cold War divide by channeling the geopolitical will for competition into technoscientific and governmental innovation.[14]

The reader can choose between two ways of reading this book: the first one following East-West relations in the development of global, system-cybernetic governance; the second one focusing on the transformation and globalization of late Soviet governance. Both tracks seek to contribute to the relevant literatures on the subject, which I discuss briefly in the remaining part of this introduction.

For a System-Cybernetic Governmentality

The themes of complexity and informational and network control have been discussed among policy scientists since the 1960s, and in the late 1980s became objects of both theoretical and critical writing in the humanities and social sciences.[15] While there are several histories that explore the governmental implications of cybernetics and feedback-based control in the United States and the Soviet Union, the transnational history of the systems approach remains to be written. Existing case studies of the systems approach tend to focus on US actors, both individuals and institutions, the most studied ones being nuclear strategists at RAND, the postwar think tank in Santa Monica, California. Such studies were part of wider liberal intellectual criticism of the US military and top-down, technocratic elite governance, established during the Cold War. However, we do not know much about the other side of the systems approach, where it served as a source of avant-garde ideas on governability. This is where the studies of systems analysis and cybernetics part, as cybernetics has been widely analyzed as a governmental technology and intellectual experiment.

Thus scholars like Robert Kline and Slava Gerovitch recognized the power of cybernetics to revolutionize traditional notions of control in the United States and the Soviet Union in their respective studies. However, few have attributed a similar power to the systems approach, although many applications of the systems approach significantly modified, if not undermined, the existing structures of state centralist power. When such arguments were proposed, they were mainly confined to the internalist literature of systems theorists. A recent breakthrough is Hunter Heyck's study of US systems thinking, which registers the transformative effect that the systems approach had on postwar social sciences in general, arguing that the systems approach could be described as a Cold War epistemology, one that not only shaped administrative practices but also significantly influenced what he called the "high modern" governmental imagination by providing new technologies, a new language, and new visions of governability, thus expanding the horizons of governmental ambitions.[16] While Heyck usefully points out the centrality of the systems approach to both modern social science in general and organizational science in particular, he does not explicate how exactly this scientific epistemology was translated into governmental practice. Furthermore, as Heyck focuses exclusively on US science, he leaves out the transnational side of the systems approach.

On the other hand, we do have some studies of the international impact of the systems approach on governance, particularly the ones produced by Sovietologists since the development of the field in the 1960s.[17] However, a thorough assessment of the impact of the systems approach on emerging global institutions, discourses, and practices is missing. One should not generalize from the US experience with system-cybernetic policy sciences: as a field, cybernetics and the systems approach were forged transnationally and had highly diverse impacts on local practices in different contexts. I posit this point as both empirical and theoretical: a full-fledged sociology of system-cybernetic governance that only focuses on national cases is bound to miss its target. This is not least because the very roots of the field were international, and lay not just in military conflict and Cold War competition. In addition, if we assume that there exists a pure, objective science, which is structurally separate from (national) political power frameworks, there is a risk of misunderstanding much of what has been done in the name of system-cybernetic research.

One way to approach this complex phenomenon is to treat it as a "system-cybernetic governmentality," a particular mode of scientific governance that emerged after World War II and that led to different outcomes in different contexts. I define "system-cybernetic governmentality" as an assemblage of discourses, state and nonstate organizations, technologies, and social networks, a complex that is best understood through a combination of insights derived from the ideas of Michel Foucault and from science and technology studies. It is important to note that the study of "governmentality" involves a different analytical angle than traditional political history or sociology. Instead of focusing on formal state organizations, the governmentality perspective examines a wide range of practices of sense-making and regulation that forge governmental subjects and objects.[18]

Here a few words on this are due. Michel Foucault introduced his idea of the art of governance as a combined intellectual and technical activity, or *gouvernmentalitè*, in his lecture at the Collège de France in February 1978. The French word was translated into Anglophone discourse as "governmentality" in 1979.[19] The governmentality perspective emphasizes that government is not limited to legalistic practices and state departments, but can instead be practiced through many different interventions in the "conduct of conduct."[20] In his lectures, Foucault argued that the word "government" historically referred to rule over the population rather than "a state, a territory, or a political structure"; "to govern" meant to regulate behavior, to take care of self-regulating processes. "Being able to hold on to one's principality," observed Foucault, "is not the same as possessing the art of governing," where government is not so much about imposing law, as about disposing things "to their own suitable goals," an activity that is best described as tactical.[21]

Another important feature of the governmentality perspective is its focus on the historical variation of meanings or rationalities of governance. "Governmental rationality," however, may be a somewhat misleading term, especially in the context of the history of Cold War science, which has predominantly focused on the forging of a rational actor in line with rational choice theory, where rationality is defined as a feature of individual decision makers, set to maximize their own interests.[22] Instead, and following Foucault, I define "governmental rationality" as any systematic way of sense-making and/or articulation of a rationale of governance. Accordingly, rational choice theory can be understood as a particular governmentality, but I want to emphasize that system-cybernetic governance can entail different governmental rationalities, ones that are not limited to rational choice.

There is also an important and serendipitous relationship between Foucauldian governmentality theory and the object of my study, the system-cybernetic governance. As Ian Hacking notes, scientific theories are not abstract constructs but products of their time, dependent on such factors as knowledge-generating devices, and social and politico-economic structures, and so is the governmentality theory.[23] Indeed, there might be more than just a parallel between Foucault's notion of governmentality, which discerns the historical development of an "art of government," involving skills and craft, and the claim of policy scientists to develop "an art of systems analysis."[24] According to McKinlay and Taylor, Foucault borrowed the term "governmentality" from Roland Barthes, who coined this intentionally awkward word in 1957 to describe the ongoing technocratization of French state government and what he understood as its depoliticization. Although Foucault might have been introduced to the term "governmentality" at Barthes's seminars in the late 1950s and early 1960s, it has to be noticed that Barthes did not use this term in his later writings.[25] At precisely this time system-cybernetic ideas were being employed to rethink managerial and political practices, and the exchange between East and West in the policy sciences began. The articulation of governance as an intellectual and policy category was isomorphic: thus, when the term "governmentality" began to circulate in the early 1980s, the notion of systems analysis as *an art of governance* was being widely promoted in management education. The system-cybernetic perspective constructed the world as a set of complex and dynamic systems, consisting of different geological, biological, and technical phenomena, which were subject to tactical regulation in the same way as population was for Foucault. Also, I want to add that the world according to cybernetics was defined as a network of human and nonhuman actors well before actor-network theory was formulated in the 1980s.

My point is not, however, that Foucault himself recycled system-cybernetic ideas in his intellectual project of rethinking the changing nature of governance in the modern state (although he might have done so), but rather that the very emergence of governmentality studies could be understood as an outcome of registering the actual changes in governance that are analyzed in this book.[26] Furthermore, I suggest that the analytical project of governmentality studies shares some basic principles with the policy sciences, in particular the systems approach: namely, they both approach governance as an activity of sense-making, which draws upon technoscience for the meanings and instruments enabling action, particularly action-at-a-distance. My study, therefore, offers a journey on a Möbius strip, where the Foucauldian governmentality perspective might be seen as a part of the system-cybernetic world of governance. The role of history here is to enhance our reflexivity by revealing the specific political and technical contexts that generated our current inquiry into ourselves.

Soviet Scientific Governance Revisited

When it is applied to the Soviet case, the governmentality perspective enables a genuinely innovative take on the character of late modern scientific governance. Students of Soviet governance have long designed their studies as either inquiries into ruthless, personalist rule or as studies of misconceptions and ill-qualified beliefs in scientific rationalization, planning, and management. That the Soviet elites held certain types of science and technology in high regard has been duly registered by the historians of Soviet science; yet Soviet studies rarely posed research questions from a framework other than the "use or abuse of science." Only rarely was Soviet technoscience approached like Western technoscience, as an intellectual, technical, and institutional resource for innovation and change, and when that did happen, the stories revolved around the struggle between the dominant system (the Party and bureaucracy) and resistance (the scientists).[27]

One exception is the groundbreaking study on Soviet cybernetics by Slava Gerovitch, which demonstrates that cybernetics was not just a technical science of control, its uses limited to the fields of computer technology and automation and making the existing control processes more efficient. Instead, Gerovitch shows how Soviet cybernetics shaped an entirely new way of thinking, a rich semantic resource which supplied Soviet—just like Western—intellectuals, managers, and policy makers with new terms—such as feedback, self-regulation, complexity— to describe governmental relations. And yet there is a certain pessimistic note to Gerovitch's story of Soviet cybernetics. In his study, Gerovitch traced this spillover of cybernetics into Soviet governance, particularly economic planning, as a process that saw an incremental deterioration of the intellectual potential of this theory. The problem was that Soviet ideologues adopted the cybernetic language as part of their official jargon, something that Gerovitch calls "cyberspeak," a ritualistic language that acquired a popular appeal and, consequently, rendered void the revolutionary aspect of cybernetics.[28]

Gerovitch's argument undoubtedly captures a very important side of the development of Soviet cybernetics. However, I suggest that the revolutionary potential of Soviet cybernetic governance was not entirely lost in the 1970s: indeed, it was continued under the conceptual umbrella of the systems approach. Furthermore, to fully appreciate the impact of Soviet system-cybernetic governmentality, I suggest that we should go beyond the interpretation of the "correct" and "distorted" uses of a scientific discourse of cybernetics, for the impact of cybernetics is not limited to linguistic expression. The development of a new language, especially a scientific language, requires extensive organizational resources and, in turn, generates new practices and institutions. This is illustrated by my case of East-West coproduction of system-cybernetic governmentality: this was not just a language, a new way of speaking about old things, such as order and control, but a performative intellectual technology. Systems scholars did produce new descriptions or texts, in the form of stories, statistics, images, and maps, but texts were not their only end products. It was the new practices and institutions that counted.

It is true that early systems analysis was intended to be a utilitarian instrument, serving managers and governments, a "social technology," to put it in Karl Polanyi's terms.[29] The systems approach created an illusion of control by making previously opaque or large-scale categories, such as world population and world energy, especially their future states, visible, thus creating an impression that they could be acted upon. One example of a large-scale control application is the computer-powered "social technology" of surveillance, which was put to use by the Soviet State Security Committee (KGB) in the late 1980s.[30] However, state surveillance and control were not the sole uses of the social technology of systems analysis, which is evident in cases where systems analysis evolved into a more ambitious intellectual enterprise. Yet to appreciate this we need to adopt a particular theoretical stance toward scientific governance in general and Soviet governance in particular.

We are informed by historians and sociologists of science and technology that technoscience operates as a performative assemblage, that is, that scientific theories and instruments do not merely reflect societal and cultural norms, but actually embody and directly shape them by constituting material settings for action.[31] We also know from recent social histories of computer-based technologies that such performative assemblages generate not only new notions of governance, but also new institutions and practices.[32] I propose that the system-cybernetic sciences can be understood as an increasingly reflexive, performative, and hybrid enterprise, which was driven by multiple, sometimes inconsistent rationales and which found diverse areas of application, thus leading to different sociopolitical effects. Here the performative character of the system-cybernetic approach is of key significance: these policy sciences are not so much concerned with generating an internally consistent "truth regime," as interested in "what works," putting emphasis on analytical approaches and methods developed to enable governmental action. Another important feature of system-cybernetic governmentality, in this way, is its high tolerance of "unknowns": the aspiration for total knowledge and perfect representation was suspended; the scientific expertise fulfilled its promise as long as "it worked." The outcomes of this work, then, were diverse and, as I show in this book, not reducible to the question of the validity of knowledge.

This is an important distinction between system-cybernetic governmentality and modern positivist science or governance by numbers that fostered an excessive belief in human knowability and controllability. For instance, for the systems analyst the task of scientific governance was not to base authority on some underlying truth, or to attempt to discover and harness the laws of nature, but to construct, assemble, and mobilize links between data, technology, people, and organizations. I use the term "assembling" in a way similar to the way Bruno Latour uses it in *Reassembling the Social*, pointing to the process of putting together, intertwining, and stabilizing concepts, language, technologies, practices, and organizations that hang together, constituting a particular setting for action.[33] I prefer the term "assemblage" to Michel Foucault's term "apparatus" (in French, *appareil*), because "apparatus" suggests a greater degree of internal order and a machine-like operational mode than "assemblage," which can be haphazardly put together, and remain open and unfinished. An assemblage is always a project-in-the-making; therefore I also place a heavier emphasis on assembling as a continuing process. At the analytical level, I use this terminology as a way of placing people, organizations, material devices, and settings at one analytical level, for all of these perform important roles in forging a system-cybernetic governmentality. Approached from this perspective, system-cybernetic science can be understood as a particularly important intellectual resource which enabled East-West managers, policy makers, and politicians to forge new links among governments, industries, and societies, leading to an incremental transformation of the social and political order.

These performative and reflexive dimensions need be taken into account in order to appreciate the innovativeness of the system-cybernetic sciences in the Soviet context. Indeed, as I show in this book, some prominent practitioners of the systems approach rejected the notion of positivist science, discarded the search for the truth, and postulated instead that different data and solutions may be valid depending on the pragmatic situation, that is, on reflexive interaction among the decision makers, experts, and the context. Of course, this tolerance of the unknown was not always shared by the clients of these policy sciences: many of the governmental elites, representatives of what is called "technocracy," did dream about total or perfect control.[34] My story is thus one of incremental change, where new epistemologies and modes of action emerged and developed in certain pockets of Soviet governance, sometimes, however, spilling over into wider agendas.

East-West Coproduction of Global Governance

The importance of Cold War competition as a source for extensions of militarized notions of behavior, reason, and order into civil governance, where such notions were deemed inadequate at best and often damaging, has been widely studied by urban, economic, and intellectual historians.[35] However, there were also some productive and innovative aspects of East-West competition and cooperation.[36] I show that East-West cooperation had some important outcomes in the development of global governance as an intellectual and socio-technical project. There was a particular transnational community of policy scientists emerging during, and partially because of, the Cold War. Historians have revealed that Cold War policy scientists, in particular those based in the United States, benefited from the divide, because the struggle between the great powers involved massive investment in the military-industrial complex. In turn, many branches of policy sciences were regarded as an extension of Cold War competition.[37] New institutional spaces emerged that could best be described as transnational organizations, that is, organizations whose constituents were not sovereign governments, but lower-level organizations. Importantly, the agenda of these transnational organizations was increasingly set independently from national interests.[38]

Furthermore, if the development of system-cybernetic governmentality is approached as a transnational process of coproduction, this has some important implications for the debate on the relation between liberal and authoritarian governance within governmentality studies. Let me dwell on this for a moment. Governmentality scholars have long analyzed "soft power" mechanisms in liberal democratic contexts, but their interest has also extended to colonial and postcolonial studies, and has begun to be applied to authoritarian regimes.[39] On the one hand, beginning in the 1990s, governmentality studies registered the problem-oriented, calculation-based, decentered character of advanced modern governance, debating whether they were witnessing the emergence of a distinct, neoliberal statecraft. On the other hand, in 1999 Mitchell Dean wrote that governmentality was equally applicable to the study of (neo)liberal and authoritarian regimes, noting that certain governmental techniques can be shared by liberal democratic and illiberal states. Dean extended his observation to identify authoritarian components that are inherent to liberal governmentality—for instance, in the procedures used to govern welfare dependent subjects.[40]

But the relationship between liberal and authoritarian governmentalities is more complex than a classification into liberal and authoritarian modes of government. In this book I show that some key technoscientific approaches enabling *liberal*, limited governance at a distance, its conceptual framework, techniques, and institutions, were *coproduced* through direct interaction between the liberal West and authoritarian East. I use the term "coproduction" to refer to the programs of cooperation between East-West scientists and policy makers, but also to the dynamics of a simultaneous forging of natural and social orders.[41] As Sheila Jasanoff has put it,

> scientific knowledge . . . is not a transcendent mirror of reality. It both embeds and is embedded in social practices, identities, norms, conventions, discourses, instruments and institutions—in short, in all the building blocks of what we term the *social*. The same can be said even more forcefully of technology.[42]

Thus defined, coproduction is not so much a theory as a perspective that helps us to avoid omissions, which tend to occur in a singular focus on "just science" or "just politics," something which is particularly important when we approach science in dictatorships. Importantly, Jasanoff points out the ability of technoscience not only to serve, but also to subvert or transform the governmental authority of the state.[43] I show that system-cybernetic governmental techniques were adopted by the authoritarian Soviet regime because they appeared to promise *more* control, yet, in contrast to the expectations of Soviet administrators, the system-cybernetic approach transformed the very character of control.

This happened in the following way. The system-cybernetic approach was framed to suit the requirements of East-West transfer, accordingly, being depoliticized, declared a universal, value-free technology of governance. However, this political maneuver was but a superficial one: the very point of the system-cybernetic approach was to underscore a new, postpositivist notion of the human and nonhuman systems, which were intertwined and the understanding of which required global and long-term analysis. Although it was deemed to be a value-free technology, the system-cybernetic approach ultimately required a new politics, where scientific expertise and intellectual technologies played an increasingly important role.

Governmentality studies have been long engaged in analyzing the "governmentalization of the state," which in principle signifies the reorientation of the modern state away from the political struggle for sovereignty to the art of the governance of the population. Part of this process involved the (liberal) state devolving authority to other agencies and individuals through the encouragement of self-regulation and strategies of responsibilization. This process maps in a curious way onto an authoritarian regime, such as the Soviet Union, where the introduction of system-cybernetic policy sciences, as an institutionalized sphere of scientific expertise, testified to a certain governmentalization. I suggest approaching the role of technoscience in the governmentalization of the Soviet regime through Bruno

Latour's concept of hybridization and purification as a dialectical, simultaneously ongoing process. According to Latour, there are ongoing processes of political purification, defining certain activities as nonpolitical, which contrast with the opposite efforts to politicize them.[44] I detail the ways in which systems analysis was carefully depoliticized as an art of governance, but the story does not stop here. As noted by Thomas Gieryn, any claim to "real science" in fact constantly produces counterclaims, such as pseudoscience, lay knowledge, and politics. This process, explains Gieryn, can be understood as a form of boundary work, separating science and nonscience, politics and nonpolitics. This kind of boundary work was of fundamental importance in the development of system-cybernetic governance across the Iron Curtain. Importantly, this boundary work—just like my example of the use of *kitel`* jackets described earlier in this chapter—served both symbolic and pragmatic functions.[45] The development of the system-cybernetic governmentality relied on the intertwining of purification, hybridization, and boundary work.

In this respect, my study of East-West co-production of the systems approach confronts some of the key questions asked by the humanities and social sciences: namely, whether societies are becoming prisoners of their own tools of control by building and relying on formal methods of governance. Nikolas Rose has argued that freedom is a disciplining construction. According to Rose, freedom is not the mere absence of control, but rather a particular distribution of techniques and mechanisms of regulation and control.[46] There is, therefore, a complex dynamic between freedom and control, and it would be premature to dispose of the technocracy debate as a simple issue of delegation, as well as to discard the management and policy sciences as tools of subjugation in the hands of elites, be they communist or neoliberal.

This dynamic becomes particularly clear in the context of the Soviet Union, where the system-cybernetic sciences of control often had a strong liberalizing effect. With their roots in quantitative methods and computer technology, system-cybernetic sciences constituted an alternative to the personalist rule of the Communist Party, which operated on the basis not only of formalized and bureaucratic planning, but also on the distribution of personal favors and penalties. According to Theodore Porter, the production of impersonal numbers served as an important source of credibility in democratic systems. Whereas Porter bases his argument on the French, British, and US cases, Loren Graham proposes a similar argument, writing that numbers played a comparable role in the Soviet Union, but not exactly as one would presume. Although Soviet statistics were subject to notorious manipulation, quantification and technoscientific rationalism also constituted a space for reform. The growing institutional power of scientific governance had a corrosive effect on the largely irrational Stalinist system.[47] Graham, to be sure, argues that the outcomes of the rationalization of Soviet governance were severely limited because the Soviets were preoccupied with what he called "technological fixes," that is, solutions that were solely technical and disregarded economic and social issues.[48]

While agreeing with Graham's thesis that post-Stalinist technoscience corroded the Soviet bureaucratic Party centralism, this study shows that there were attempts to go beyond technical fixes in Soviet technoscience, namely through the policy sciences. Economic and social issues were assessed in the systems approach that gained prominence in the Soviet Union from the early 1970s and which was developed as an international field par excellence, thus undermining not only the departmentalist mentality, but also the Iron Curtain itself. As Soviet scientific governance was entrenched in East-West transfer, it helped to disperse the authority and power to heterogeneous actors, enabling their mobility and stimulating institutional reform.[49]

We can now begin to understand the revolutionary effect of Soviet systems analysis as a policy science, which emerged in the symbiotic relationship between technoscience and state governance. The East-West policy scientists, active between the 1950s and the late 1980s, were acutely conscious that they were forging more than just an instrument for policy decisions. As I show, East-West policy scientists intentionally coproduced governmental techniques and the world for which these techniques were intended, the world which governmentality scholars have been attempting to grasp. That these scientists resorted to different discursive strategies for the depoliticization of both science and governance, was, in many cases, a strategic move enabling them to work toward a change in political values.

In this book I show that the purification of systems analysis as a governmental technique was also a politically driven project, which was embedded in a Cold War diplomatic agenda at the crucial moment of its development as a discipline, the 1960s. This moment had a lasting, complex legacy. The systems approach was intentionally and carefully construed as a universal, nonpolitical science of governance in different ways, so that a number of political, pragmatic objectives could be achieved. Once purified, the systems approach generated new forms of politics by articulating new problems and serving as a basis for new power networks. As I show, the choice of direction or configuration depended on specific contexts, but in any case the depoliticization of systems analysis was an expression of transnational pragmatism.

System-Cybernetic Governance: High-Modern or Nonmodern Technocracy?

In this section, I discuss whether the currently popular notion of high modernist governance or, more specifically, high modernist technocracy can be applied to system-cybernetic governmentality. In doing this, I want to reintroduce a somewhat forgotten debate on Soviet technocracy, a debate that, from the 1960s through the 1980s, provided explanations of how the Soviet system could change but which was to a large extent abandoned after 1990.[50] We need, I suggest, to re-engage with debates on Soviet and post-Soviet technocracy, for the debate on technocracy is not just a formal question as to who has the power to decide, unelected experts or elected politicians.[51] Space does not allow me to walk the reader through a full consideration of the century-long debate on technocracy; I will only touch on key moments in the debate on modern technocracy and its Soviet version, which should help the reader to appreciate the complexity of system-cybernetic expertise that does not map easily onto the traditional divide between democracy and technocracy.

According to the classic definition coined by the prominent French political philosopher Jean Meynaud, later used by Frank Fischer, technocracy is "a system of governance in which technically trained experts rule by virtue of their specialized knowledge and position in dominant political and economic institutions."[52] In his influential treatise on postwar technocracy, Fischer, however, argues that not all forms of scientific expertise-based governmental systems seek to replace political decision-making with technical decision-making. In line with Fischer, I stress that it is important to look at how the concrete, particular relations between technoscience, governance, and the political were negotiated in different contexts and times, for this would reveal the field of scientific expertise as a more complex phenomenon, which is not limited to political power grabbing.[53]

The history of technocracy as a term and as a phenomenon was embedded in East-West exchange from the very beginning. The very term "technocracy" emerged in the United States in the 1920s, with the pioneering work of Thorstein Veblen, who argued that engineers should participate in the management process because they were equipped with knowledge and know-how, enabling them to make what they thought were better, more rational economic decisions.

The idea that engineers should be involved in planning also surfaced in the Soviet Union at around the same time, when an expert consortium was appointed to govern the first national planning agency, the State Commission for the Electrification of Russia (GOELRO). While the political legitimacy of Western technocracy was fluctuating, especially after the war, its fate in the Soviet Union was truly torn between extremes. Historians showed that the relationship between technoscientific experts and the Communist Party of the Soviet Union oscillated violently between the Party's almost naïve belief in the ability of science to solve any issue, and paranoid control. In his study on the failed attempt to create a Soviet technocracy, Graham detailed how the Bolshevik Nikolai Bukharin rallied a like-minded circle of "manager-engineers," where the extraordinary engineer Peter Palchinskii played an important role. Called "an Industrial Party" by the secret police, this network was purged by Stalin in 1928.[54] Similarly, whereas Russian scientific management emerged as a vigorous intellectual movement following the Communist revolution, it was suppressed by Stalin only to be rehabilitated during de-Stalinization in the late 1950s in order to embrace the coming of system-cybernetic governance.[55]

But was there ever a late Soviet technocracy? After Stalin's death in 1953 the belief in scientific expertise for policy-making revived, but the institutional reform allowing the flow of scientific expertise into governance was slow.[56] One of the many efforts to institutionally reform the communist government by integrating scientific expertise came from Mikhail Lavrent'ev, who was a mathematician and vice president of the Soviet Academy of Sciences. In the 1960s Lavrent'ev suggested integrating expert panels into all planning areas in the Soviet Union.[57] The period of Brezhnev's stagnation was also seen as one of consolidation of Soviet technocracy. However, there was a strong organizational filter installed that prevented Soviet specialists from becoming technocrats, thus reserving the central decision-making power to the Party—a direct institutional link that would allow Soviet scientists to communicate their advice to the central organs was never established, thus all recommendations were filtered through appropriate sections at the branch ministries and the Central Committee.[58] Even under Gorbachev, when scientists were for the first time invited to the governmental roundtable for discussions on policy, they were questioned rather than asked to provide their own points of view. In turn, although many members of the Politburo had a technical education, they had almost no professional experience in their fields, having pursued an administrative and political career. Considering these aspects, I would tend to agree with Graham's suggestion that Soviet technocracy never really existed.[59]

In this context, should we not be tempted to write a history of Soviet system-cybernetic governance as yet another example of a failed technocracy? Tempting as it is, this plot, I suggest, would misdirect our attention from the productive and global impact of Soviet system-cybernetic governmentality. The struggle for Soviet governance was not a zero-sum game. For instance, in addition to the Politburo, which gathered the top commanders of Soviet ministries and the Party, and the Central Committee, and to which Soviet system-cybernetic governmentality was only loosely coupled, there were other spheres of spatial and institutional influence. From the mid-1960s one such space, particularly oriented to policy sciences, was established, patronized, and supervised by Prime Minister Aleksei Kosygin and his son-in-law, the vice chairman of the State Committee for Science and Technology (GKNT), Dzhermen Gvishiani. To be sure, the space for Soviet system-cybernetic governance was limited, but it was more diverse and productive than it has been thought so far.

Therefore, I seek to widen the debate on Soviet technocracy by re-embedding the Soviet case in the global history of policy and management sciences.[60] The intellectual and institutional process of the depoliticization of governance, or making "policy without politics," has its own history, predominantly within studies of transnational organizations, such as the European Union.[61] Research on Soviet technocracy, therefore, should focus on the links between the production of formal knowledge, informal social relations, and decision processes as a matter of elaborate discursive construction, where parallels that can be drawn between the Soviet bureaucracy and any large Western bureaucratic system are not metaphoric but real, resulting from intentional learning.[62] Through my cases of system-cybernetic scientific expertise I show that new types of knowledge may prompt institutional innovation, leading to erosion of the existing power structures. However, the outcomes tend to be context-specific and it is difficult to generalize.[63] Thus, in some cases, system-cybernetic ideas would reinforce centralist, top-down and/or deeply illiberal steering, whereas in other cases the same ideas could be mobilized to open up existing governmental institutions for greater transparency, data exchange, and horizontal governance underscoring self-regulation. This leads me to caution the reader not to read too much internal coherence into East-West system-cybernetic governance, as this was an internally heterogeneous and evolving phenomenon.

Considering this, I am skeptical about using the term "high modern" to describe system-cybernetic governmentality. High modernist ideology, which, according to James Scott, was a feature of Leninist-Stalinist rule, is characterized by

> the self-confidence about scientific and technological progress, the expansion of production, the growing satisfaction of human needs, the mastery of nature (including human nature), and, above all, the rational design of social order commensurate with the scientific understanding of natural laws.[64]

Adding that this belief is not a feature of scientific practice, but typical of what he called "bureaucratic intelligentsia, technicians, planners and engineers," Scott argues that it was in combination with authoritarian regimes that the high-modernist ideology led to fatal consequences in large-scale projects.[65] Scientific expertise, wrote Scott, made the world and society legible and thus amenable to control and social engineering; high modernist ideology underpinned the desire to control and the authoritarian state system provided the determination to act. In those cases where civil society was absent, there was nobody who could avert a high modernist Armageddon.[66] Scott draws heavily on secondary studies of prewar Soviet governance, particularly the ones of scientific management and the phenomenon of technocracy. He also refers to Richard Stite's notion of "administrative utopianism" as a feature of modern Russian governance.[67]

In contrast, I propose that the systems-cybernetic approach constituted a completely different resource for scientific governance, which was nonmodern in Bruno Latour's words rather than high modern. Although self-declared to be value free and universal, systems-cybernetic governmentality introduced an epistemology that underscored uncertainty, informality, and reflexivity, and forged new organizations and actorial identities, the outcomes of which were much more ambivalent than Scott's account of the authoritarian expert governance might lead us to think. First, the systems approach was coproduced by scholars from liberal and illiberal states. Second, the effects of Soviet system-cybernetic governmentality were ambiguous and could not be reduced to a colonizing project where scientific expertise is used to increase top-down control. Making economy, society, and nature legible required enormous resources, both financial and organizational, but also social and cultural. Although the desire which underpinned early Soviet interest in and support for the system-cybernetic sciences in the 1950s–1960s might have been a "high modernist," control-seeking one, the actual development of system-cybernetic governmentality significantly transformed the very understanding of control by introducing a new epistemology of risk and uncertainty. Furthermore, the outcomes of system-cybernetic governmentality were not limited to the implementation of centrally set policies in the Soviet Union. This becomes evident, I argue, when the system-cybernetic approach as a type of statecraft is understood not as a linear process, where inputs (desire and determination to act) lead to outputs (implementation of policies plus side effects), but as a *throughput*: a process in which new vocabularies, practices, networks, and organizations emerge. The thesis of high modernism, therefore, does not exhaust postwar system-cybernetic governmentality.

A Note on Method

This book draws on an extensive study of archival materials from the Archive of the Russian Academy of Sciences (ARAN), the Russian State Archive of the Economy (RGAE), and the IIASA archives. Part of my argument concerns informal practices and organizational culture, elements that were not always reflected in the archival documents. To capture them, I drew on memoir literature, but also on specially conducted, semistructured interviews with ex-Soviet and Western scientists, research politicians, and administrators who were involved in IIASA and East-West cooperation. In all, I interviewed thirty-five individuals, conducting the majority of interviews face to face, but a few interlocutors were reached by phone or Skype. The majority of the interviews were digitally recorded and transcribed, although in some cases, when I felt that my interlocutor might feel restricted by the record, I took notes by hand. Throughout the text my informants are anonymized, which may appear unusual in the context of contemporary history. However, I am convinced that historians, just like sociologists and anthropologists, need to consider the ethical implications of their interview materials, for an author is not in control of possible uses of the text. This is particularly pertinent with regard to the history of Soviet and Russian governance and science and technology: many of my interlocutors, who were active between the 1960s and 1980s, are still alive and professionally active, and some of those who have passed away have relatives who work in similar fields.

It has been habitual for historians of Soviet science to name their informants. Most likely the majority of these Western histories were disregarded by Soviet intelligence-gathering agencies; for instance, in his memoir Loren Graham recalled a Moscow meeting with Lysenko, a notorious Soviet scientist who banned genetics and whom Graham criticized in his books. Lysenko, to Graham's surprise, was not particularly upset by his treatment.[68] However, even in the Soviet era when Western literature was reserved to special collections, not available to wider audiences, some local actors were concerned about their representation in the West. For instance, I was told by an ex-Soviet scholar that he and his colleagues were seriously distraught by Richard Vidmer's article on Soviet management, where Vidmer praised those management theorists as Westernizers, naming them as his interlocutors.[69] These scholars indeed gave their views to Vidmer, but they did not expect to be named in his study, being apprehensive about the possible political consequences. In this particular case, nothing happened. Yet in the current context of the tightening of free speech in contemporary Russia and growing tension between Russia and liberal democracies it makes good sense to protect interviewees' identities. Furthermore, there are good reasons to conceal the identities of Western scholars, administrators, and research politicians whom I interviewed, because many of them are professionally active in fields with extremely high stakes, such as, for instance, energy or climate change. Although my study focuses on the historical period of the 1950s–1980s, it discusses some projects that are still relevant in the present, not least IIASA itself, which remains an important international think tank. Thus, my interpretations might reflect back on my interlocutors in ways that are beyond my control. For these reasons, I have chosen to completely anonymize my interlocutors.

The Organization of the Book

To argue that technoscience and politics intertwine is not to suggest that there is always a symmetry of power in this relationship, as the coproduction approach might suggest. It is particularly clear in the cases of institutional innovation that at some times political processes can prevail, while at other times scientists can steer the process according to their own interests. It is quite true that many scientific practices can have anticipated and unanticipated political effects, however, as I argue in this book, it is important not to overlook the role of individual actors in the process of the politicization and depoliticization of science. This is particularly evident in the case of the Soviet Union, where a personal change in the power structure was necessary to make way for system-cybernetic sciences.

In chapter 1, I outline the rearrangement of the Soviet power system after the death of Stalin in 1953 and, in particular, after the ousting of Nikita Khrushchev in 1964, when Aleksei Kosygin ascended to the top of the government as prime minister of the Soviet Union. This change of political and administrative elites coincided with the onset of a new discourse on the scientific-technical revolution, which was introduced in the Soviet Union in the mid-1950s and gained prominence in the 1960s, leading to the new notion of a postindustrial Soviet society. The theory of the scientific-technical revolution also posited a universal path of development, where the same technologies of governance—both hard, such as computer hardware, and soft, such as management and policy science—could be applied in communist and capitalist societies. Recent scholarship has revised the Brezhnev era as one that cannot be reduced to "stagnation"; in line with this, I show how Kosygin, bringing to power some of his close affiliates, began opening up the Soviet Union to Western trade and technology transfer and, in doing that, supported the transfer of US policy sciences. The talks on IIASA were initiated during the meeting of Lyndon Johnson and Kosygin at Glassboro in 1967, leading to the negotiations about the establishment of an international, East-West think tank. Chapter 2 traces the organizational process behind the establishment of IIASA, showing how otherwise quite different US and Soviet rationales were negotiated and combined. Johnson's administration sought to build a bridge to the East, this foreign policy orientation forming part of wider US efforts to influence Europe, both East and West, where the transfer of governmental techniques, such as management and policy sciences, played an important role in the 1960s. The Soviets sought to acquire advanced Western technology, particularly computer technology, and linked the systems approach and policy sciences strongly with the computer field.

In chapters 3 and 4 I detail the development of the transnational community of systems analysis. The Soviet government supported the adoption of the US approach to systems analysis in the hope of improving control over industrial and social planning and production. This governmental line was used as an opportunity for a particular set of scholars to forge a transnational network of systems science, the implementation of which drew on carefully devised techniques in building a particular organizational culture at IIASA. This transnational formation of the field of systems analysis was also performative and, in chapter 4, I detail the concrete managerial tactics that performed political neutrality in IIASA's everyday life.

In chapters 5, 6, and 7 I focus on specific case studies of systems analysis, global and regional computer-based modeling.[70] I argue that computer-based modeling was a particularly important area of application for systems analysis, because computer-based modeling involved the development of both hardware and software technologies and creative ideas for their application. Furthermore, computer-based modeling required the construction of a particular social setting. Finally, computer-based modeling was invested with political symbolism in both East and West. All these features made computer-based modeling a highly influential assemblage, which laid the foundations for a new, transnational governmentality. Some of the most innovative and, indeed, revolutionary ideas regarding governance were articulated in the application of the systems approach to the study of the environment, and unsurprisingly so, for as Loren Graham and Paul Josephson note, the Soviet government somewhat tolerated civil and professional movements in defense of the natural environment.[71] Yet the methodology of systems analysis posited the links between the environment, the economy, and society, opening up a new space for socioeconomic and, eventually, political criticism in the Soviet Union. In chapter 5, I outline the beginning of global modeling in the Soviet Union, which followed the pioneering report *The Limits to Growth* (1972), commissioned by the Club of Rome.

In chapter 6 I go on to analyze in depth the Soviet contribution to a prominent study on the environmental consequences of nuclear war, which led to the formulation of the hypothesis of nuclear winter. Carried out by US and Soviet scientists in 1983, this nuclear winter study not only had an impact on nuclear strategy and disarmament, but also powerfully introduced the focus on global problems to the Soviet government, which for the first time included global issues in its governmental program in the Party Congress in 1985. Moreover, the nuclear winter study underpinned some highly original ideas on the character of governance and the role of scientific expertise, espoused by the Russian mathematician and academician Nikita Moiseev, who drew on Vladimir Vernadskii's theory of the biosphere/noosphere to develop his own, distinct thinking, which had many parallels with the Gaia hypothesis of James Lovelock and Paul Crutzen's idea of the "Anthropocene."

Computer-based modeling was not only an experimental area of the application of the systems approach: the impact of computer-based modeling extended beyond its scientific results by providing an institutional framework for building horizontal alliances across the Iron Curtain. In chapter 7 I focus on the production of a regional, European model of transboundary pollution, which was produced at IIASA, 1983–1985, in order to illustrate the performative effect of this project. Just like the modeling efforts discussed in chapters 5 and 6, the acid rain model demonstrates the importance of informal practices in the production of an influential expertise. In this trio of chapters I argue that the performativity of computer modeling was transformative, because the scientific methodology required the Soviet Union to open up to the West, allowing ideas, data, technical equipment, and, most importantly, people, to move across the Iron Curtain. As a result of this, new governmental assemblages that involved new governmental objects, data, and expertise emerged. While meeting short-term political objectives, in the long term these assemblages contributed to making the East-West division redundant.

1
GRAY EMINENCES OF THE SCIENTIFIC-TECHNICAL REVOLUTION

The story of late Soviet technocracy can be compared to the gray side of the moon, the side that is neither visible nor invisible: debates about technocracy, once central to Soviet studies, are peripheral to scholarly interest today. And yet to ignore technocracy is to ignore a particularly significant and ambiguous part of the Soviet reality. Beginning in the mid-1950s the Soviet Union experienced a peculiar combination of continuing industrialization and preparation for postindustrial society. Automation of industrial processes promised to make manual labor redundant, whereas a rising number of white collar workers, managers, and scientific experts, a nascent Soviet technocratic class, led Sovietologists to speculate whether these changes might undermine the Party's monopoly on power. Operating with a simplified distinction between political and administrative actors, building on a notion of the power struggle as a zero-sum game, Western scholars pondered the question, if Soviet technocrats gained more power, would the power of the Communist Party decrease proportionately?[1] Approached from this angle, the ability of Soviet technocracy to challenge the monopoly of the Party was deemed a failure: the Party's ability to control managers and specialists appeared to remain unchallenged. Consequently, Brezhnev's period was labeled as "stagnation," and the collapse of the Soviet Union was attributed not to internal transformation through technocracy, but to nationalist secession. In the end, the arguments about converging industrial and technocratic systems were dismissed as unable to explain sociopolitical change, so that interest in Soviet technocracy faded away after 1991.[2]

In this chapter I argue that the role of Soviet technocracy has been unduly overlooked and that this neglect has important consequences for our understanding of the transformation of late Soviet governance and, indeed, its role in the shaping of global Cold War governmentality. This gray zone of Soviet governance was the realm of highly positioned political functionaries, scientists, and what I call "research administrators," individuals with an academic background, positioned in responsible posts in the state administration overlooking domestic research policy and international exchange, all of whom formed a new constellation of state power machinery. As such, this constellation was equally characteristic of both Soviet and liberal democratic regimes after the war: these actors, described by Frank Fischer as "a quiet and faceless power," redefined both the tools for governance and the world to be governed.[3] A belief that governance could and should be improved with the help of scientific methods and scientific expertise appealed equally to Marxist-Leninist ideology and American planners and policy makers, and we know now in detail just how damaging many of these universal governmental techniques were, with their emphasis on large-scale schemes of planning.[4] Furthermore, in political debates technocracy became conflated with the nonaccountable behavior of self-appointed scientific and political elites, misguided by their blind trust in numbers and their belief that man could control nature.[5]

However, Soviet technocracy also accommodated other, more sophisticated approaches to governance. Despite believing in their own omnipotence, technocrats could not exert full control; even when they did, their applications of what was presumed to be a neutral, universal science of governance had important unintended effects. Policy sciences were developed to grant more control to decision makers, but their application often did the reverse by revealing the uncertain consequences of their decisions. In the shadows of what has been described as high modernist visions expressed in large-scale projects in the irrigation of Kazakhstan, reversing Siberian rivers, the space program, and the nuclearization of the Soviet energy sector,[6] lurked a different understanding of scientific governance, which underscored the notions of complexity, contingency, and ultimately self-regulation, making no essentialist distinction between man and nature, but instead seeing people, machines, and living and nonliving matter as components of complex systems, only separated by different levels of organization. This was a new, in Latour's words, "nonmodern governmentality" emerging.[7]

The rise of a Soviet technocracy that increasingly relied on policy sciences began in the late 1950s. As its development does not fit neatly into the existing periodization of the Soviet regime into the thaw (1957–1964), stagnation (1964–1986), and perestroika (1986–1991), I suggest interpreting this new Soviet governmentality as a slow change that proceeded in direct connection with Western developments and in important ways was dependent on the administration of Aleksei Kosygin. In his capacity as chief administrator in charge of light industries, Kosygin contributed to the war effort by organizing supplies to the besieged Leningrad. From 1962 he was heavily involved in foreign trade and served as prime minister from 1964 to 1980. The rise of Kosygin, who was perceived by his contemporaries and historians alike as a dry bureaucrat, was not merely a peculiar moment in Soviet history, but also an indicator of a wider shift toward the rationalization of government. This has parallels with the situation in Western Europe: according to Louise Amoore, during World War II British professional accountants gained central roles in national policy and strategy making for the first time, because they produced food rationing quotas.[8] Accordingly, the managerialization of Soviet government was rooted in war planning, just as it was in the West, and Kosygin is a clear example of this larger process. Kosygin fostered a particular network of government officials who were able to bridge Party bureaucracies, the military-industrial complex, academia, and foreign relations. The central role in this circle was played by Kosygin's son-in-law, Dzhermen Gvishiani, a vice chairman of the State Committee for Science and Technology (GKNT), a governmental institution in charge of scientific and applied research policy and international transfer.[9]

This chapter thus introduces the little-known tandem of Kosygin and Gvishiani, who jointly sought to modernize Soviet governance by introducing new scientific approaches, building new institutions, and forging new, transnational networks of policy scientists. So far Kosygin and Gvishiani have been overlooked as mere bureaucrats by historians of Soviet science and technology. Although Kosygin played a role in foreign policy, he was never known for distinct political strategies, whereas Gvishiani was very active internationally, representing the Soviet Union at a number of international organizations, including the UN.[10] Indeed, Kosygin was the only member of the top nomenklatura who worked continuously under Stalin, Khrushchev, and Brezhnev, whereas Gvishiani was professionally active in the strategic departments in charge of technology transfer from 1955 to the end of the 1980s.[11] The Kosygin-Gvishiani tandem was a typical arrangement in the Soviet top nomenklatura: official and informal ties intertwined.[12]

It is important to focus on the tandem of Kosygin-Gvishiani in order to understand the Soviet role in the development and worldwide promotion of the new scientific governmentality, one that built on the systems approach. In part because of a technological imperative, in part because it was intellectually in vogue, Soviet technocrats directly borrowed the foremost Western policy sciences, such as OR, systems approach, and cybernetics. The leaders of the world's largest state socialist system dreamed of being able to organize and manage their country the way the Pentagon managed their departments, and jealously followed the stream of innovations flowing from the RAND Corporation. For instance, the State Planning Committee, Gosplan, argued that the methods developed at RAND saved 14 billion USD between 1962 and 1965, and Soviet technocrats wished to see think tanks established on the RAND model.[13] This chapter describes social networks in which such thinking emerged, tracing the ways in which the rise of Gvishiani and Kosygin intertwined with the development of a new intellectual paradigm of governance, the scientific-technical revolution.

Modernization Theory, the Scientific-Technical Revolution, and Postindustrial Communism

During the postwar era, liberal democratic and communist regimes shared a fundamental discourse on socioeconomic change, which emerged in a dialogue between the MIT economic historian Walt Whitman Rostow's modernization theory and the theory of scientific-technical revolution (STR). Cold War historians emphasized the central role of modernization theory in shaping US internal and foreign policies. Developed as a tool to limit the spread of communism by helping third-world countries embark on the US path of industrial development, modernization theory was also used by US Sovietologists to explain and predict Soviet society.[14] Modernization theory provided a powerful narrative of change, in its conceptual structure, as noted by Nils Gilman, agreeing with the Marxist-Leninist version of development, which set out clearly defined, universal historical stages of development.[15] As such, modernization theory can be understood as a story with a clear protagonist—the enlightened rulers, equipped with scientific expertise—and an antagonist, in the form of traditional society. An important point here is that the character of the political system had only a weak link to this trajectory of development: both liberal and illiberal systems were in principle able to embark on modernization process. Therefore, according to modernization theory, the Soviet state and society were understood as rather anomalous than antagonistic, even though Rostow did entitle his seminal work *The Stages of Economic Growth: A Non-Communist Manifesto* (1960). The Soviet system, wrote Rostow, was rather derailed by misguided communist ideologues, but the Soviet Union had a chance to get back on the track of development, with a goal of ultimately converging with the West. This is because Rostow saw only one form of modernity, communism and democratic-capitalism being merely different paths to the same end. Nevertheless, modernization theorists warned the US government that it was imperative to embark on modernization of the third world, if they were to prevent it from following the communist path of modernization.[16]

In this way, Rostow's modernization theory clearly appears as a strategy for Cold War competition. However, it was not the only influential approach explaining developmental trajectories at that time: its competitor was the theory of scientific-technical revolution, which differed from modernization theory in its even more universalist claims. The theory of scientific-technical revolution postulates that new technosciences, based on automatic control and digital technologies, lead to the restructuring of society by intellectualizing labor and thus reducing the working class, at the same time freeing up workers' time for leisure pursuits. Where did the idea of STR come from? Some suggest that STR is derived from the term "second industrial revolution," the first use of which has been attributed to the French sociologist Georges Friedmann, in his *La crise du progrès* (1936). While the notion of the industrial revolution emphasized the leading role of technology in socioeconomic development, the notion of STR placed the fundamental science along with technology as drivers of innovation, economic growth, and social change. It is widely agreed that this conceptual juncture was established by British scientist and political debater John Desmond Bernal, who employed a classical socialist argument that the progress in science and technology automated the production, in effect deskilling and socially disadvantaging manual workers, but he also called for the rationalization of administration, for administration, according to Bernal, had yet escaped the revolutionary impact of science.[17] Bernal postulated that science should become the "chief agent" of social change, acting in two ways: first by "paving the way" through technology to socioeconomic change, then, later as a motive, a conscious urge for further transformation.[18] Bernal argued, however, that progressive science, including the scientific-technical revolution, was by its nature "incompatible with capitalism."[19] According to this view, the scientific-technical revolution alone could not solve class antagonism and ameliorate the negative effects of private capital ownership, an idea that appealed to communist philosophers.[20] Beginning in 1957 Bernal engaged in the debates on the third industrial revolution, based on semiconductor electronics, which was also described as the informational revolution, to further advance his call for the social goals of STR.[21]

The idea of the ambivalent effects of STR gained wide influence through the work of a British scientist, Charles Percy Snow, who presented his thesis on two cultures and scientific revolution at Cambridge University in 1959.[22] But whereas Snow saw the industry as a dangerous system, encroaching to dominate society and destroy human values, others pointed out that the industry itself was changing, shifting to intellectual, creative, increasingly automated work. Such was the argument set out in Leonard Silk's *Scientific Revolution* (1960). An economist by training, Silk was an influential journalist at *The New York Times*, concerned with global issues and, as his *Scientific Revolution* shows, involved in the forging of a transnational discourse coalition, placing new technologies at the heart of future development, where the premium was placed on both speed and growth. To give academic weight to the volume, but also to link his agenda to the Soviet Union, Silk invited the Harvard-based econometrician, Wassily Leontief, to write an introduction. In the spirit of Cold War competition, Leontief dismissed the arguments that the Soviet Union would run out of breath in the competition of economic growth and stressed that the American advantage was "large-scale research," plugged into "rapidly expanding markets" for new products. Silk, in turn, argued that slow growth threatened the United States both internally and externally. Internally, slow economic growth would pose a risk of social conflict, whereas externally it would disadvantage the United States in its bid for world domination.[23] In contrast to the idea of an age of automation or cybernation, inspired by Norbert Wiener and promoted by such theorists as Donald Michael in his *Cybernation: The Silent Conquest* (1962) and Marshall McLuhan, Silk suggested a broader category of "research revolution" as a descriptor of the postwar condition in advanced societies. The most prominent extension of this line of thought belonged to Daniel Bell, who, albeit skeptical about many of the postulates about cybernation, developed a theory of a postindustrial society leading to the convergence of capitalist and communist regimes, as political ideology would be replaced with technical systems of control.[24] However, while the proponents of cybernatization, inspired by Wiener, saw cybernetization as a way to develop liberal order by making way for advanced self-regulation through multilevel goal-setting and feedback-based self-correction, Silk espoused a much more elitist view. In favor of large-scale research, Silk saw as fundamental having an "outstanding" leadership that would "set the goals that stir others to their best efforts."[25]

It was, indeed, a miraculous coincidence that the thaw or relaxation of ideological control in the Soviet Union from 1954 to the mid-1960s coincided with the onset of US modernization theory, as well as Western publications on the scientific-technical revolution. Thus at exactly the same time, in 1954, when the influential Chicago sociologist Edward Shils and the French philosopher Raymond Aron developed the theory of a unitary industrial society and first used the phrase "the end of ideology," claiming that political struggles would no longer be centered around the issue of the exploitation of the working class in the developed world, the Soviet Union was opening up its scientific institutes for new sciences, such as cybernetics, and declaring that the scientific-technical revolution would become the driver for the growth.[26] However, was STR becoming a new ideology? The Communist Party clearly understood the propaganda value of STR. From 1957 to 1961 the Soviet Union had many spectacular scientific achievements, such as Sputnik, the first man in space, the Soviet computer, and the bomb, capturing the public imagination as a rising red power. STR's career in the Soviet Union demonstrates the plasticity of views on the meanings of ideology, politics, and expediecy; the Soviet notions of STR emphasized its political and neutral aspects depending on the context.

Therefore, it is not surprising that the Soviets embraced Silk's and Bernal's version of STR, one of scientific research-driven economic growth, where research organization was directed and controlled by a strong leader and anchored in achieving social equality. Silk's volume was promptly translated and published in Russian in 1963, with a preface written by Dzhermen Gvishiani. However, this translation was distributed only within restricted organizations, intended for scholars and decision makers and not for the public, which suggests that although the rhetoric of the scientific technical revolution was part of the public political discourse in both East and West (British prime minister Wilson delivered his famous speech on "the white heat of the revolution of technology" in 1963), the oversight and control of the socioeconomic mechanism of this process was understood as belonging to governmental professionals. In parallel with these debates, a new research policy advocacy emerged in Britain and the United States, which called for a systematic and substantial governmental policy for scientific research. It is important that these policy networks included such key promoters of operations research as Patrick Blackett and Solly Zuckerman, who would later be involved in the creation of International Institute for Applied Systems Analysis (IIASA).[27] In the next section I show how all these factors contributed to the widening political and intellectual agenda for the Soviet version of STR, an agenda that reflected ongoing de-Stalinization in research policy, academic thought, and institutional reform, and, later, in the internationalization of the Soviet system.

While the Soviet discourse on scientific-technical revolution (STR) appears to have originated in policy debates about the material-technical basis of communism, the introduction of STR to Soviet policy and public debates took place in parallel with the Twentieth Congress and the ending of Stalin's cult.[28] In 1955 Nikolai Bulganin, the chairman of the Council of Ministers, announced that the Soviet Union was open to the transfer of science and technology from the West. The five-year plan approved in 1956 set a goal for Soviet industry to fully exploit the ongoing "scientific-technical revolution" in the furthering of the Soviet economy. After Bulganin's speech, the terms "STR" and "scientific-technical progress (STP)" were used interchangeably, the most prominent theoretician being Anatolii Zvorykin, a historian of science and technology who was also interested in economics and sociology and who authored programmatic articles on this subject between 1958 and 1960.[29] Parts of the writings of Bernal were translated into Russian and published as early as 1956.[30] Like Bernal, from the early 1950s on Zvorykin doubted the idea that science and technology belonged to the superstructure of Marxist society, eventually proposing that they should be understood as a direct productive force.[31]

While technoscientific advancement was regarded as a necessary condition of the development of the Soviet state, few Soviet scientists would have guessed at that time that STR would become a vehicle for the rejuvenation of Soviet social science. An important shift happened in the early 1960s, when Walt Rostow launched his modernization theory as an intellectual program to conceptualize development at home and abroad. It appears that Soviet scholars first encountered Rostow's ideas in the Fifth World Congress of Sociology in Washington, in September 1962, where eighteen sociologists, including such influential reformers of Soviet social science as Anatolii Zvorykin, Genadii V. Osipov, and Edvard Arab-Ogly, represented the Soviet Union. The influential research agenda-setting journal *The Issues of Philosophy* (in Russian, *Voprosy filosofii*), introduced at length Rostow's theory of stage-driven development from a traditional to modern society, at the same time criticizing modernization theory as a strategic instrument to expand US influence in the developing world.[32] The vigor of these debates indicates that Rostow's theory deeply unsettled Soviet intellectuals, who realized that the Marxist-Leninist models of development were at risk of being outcompeted.

It is probably not a coincidence that it was only after the Fifth Sociology Congress that *Voprosy filosofii* began to regularly publish articles on STR and scientific-technical progress (STP) as drivers of nor only Soviet economic development but also social change, including such themes as noncapitalist routes of development for the third world and the use of mathematical models and systems to plan such developmental programs.[33] The first of these articles, which thoroughly criticized Rostow, were published in the Soviet Union between 1963 and 1965. At the same time extensive criticism of the notion of a single industrial society and convergence theory appeared.[34] Major conferences to examine the history and the future of STR were organized in the GDR and the Soviet Union; for instance, one such meeting took place at the Institute of Natural Science and Knowledge in 1963, resulting in a compact but comprehensive volume that presented the approaches of Soviet historians and philosophers of science to STR.[35] Many books, booklets, and articles followed.[36] Similar treatises on STR were published in Eastern bloc countries, Czechoslovakia, and Romania.[37] In Eastern Europe the most prominent notion of scientific-technical revolution was formulated by a group of Czechoslovak scholars under the direction of the Marxist philosopher Radovan Richta.[38] Richta's volume *Civilization at the Crossroads: The Social and Human Implications of the Scientific-Technical Revolution* (1965) outlined the future development of Czechoslovak state socialist society pretty much along the same lines as Bernal's and Leonard Silk's, and was promptly translated into many languages, although not Russian (this delay might be explained by generally slow turnover of the Russian translation—the lag was usually three to five years—and by the "Prague spring" of 1968). Following the Soviet invasion of Czechoslovakia, Richta was not prosecuted, but he significantly revised his views, abolishing the idea of open paths of state socialist development. Richta's ideas were introduced to Soviet audiences only after 1973, under Gvishiani's patronage.[39]

Although the Czechoslovak revolt politically tainted Richta's writings in the eyes of Soviet ideologues, it is important to note that in Soviet academia there was considerable room for different opinions on the definition of STR. Scholars debated whether STR was revolutionary or evolutionary and whether STR effects were universal or varied depending on local circumstances. Some argued that STR had similar effects in communist and capitalist regimes, while others defended the uniqueness of Soviet STR.[40] For me it is important to note that these debates were harnessed to promote empirical social sciences, which would become the building blocks of the new Soviet scientific governmentality: beginning in 1966 the new, sociological research agenda of social consequences of STR was launched, with Zvorykin appointed as the head of the department dedicated to these problems at the newly established Institute for Concrete Social Research (IKSI). In the field of management science, Gvishiani's role was indispensable: in 1966 he declared the 1920s to be the golden age of Soviet but also Western scientific management, regretted what he described as an "absurd" disruption of this field under Stalin, and called for a speedy reinstating of scientific management as a field of theory and practice in the Soviet Union, building on local, Russian tradition and transferring the most advanced methods from the West.[41]

The intensity and institutional support that the STR debates and, from the mid-1960s, studies into socioeconomic effects of the STR had suggested that there was more to the STR than just an intellectual innovation. A discursive resolution was reached: it was agreed that both Western and Soviet societies had many shared features, both being industrial societies, but the convergence theory was inverted. The Soviet ideologues argued that it would be Western countries that would converge into socialism, while other Soviet scholars satisfied themselves with vague claims that the positive effect of scientific-technical revolution was limited to state socialism, STR being unable to resolve the "internal contradictions of capitalism."[42] Although compromise was awkward, it was also necessary, because it opened a discursive and institutional space for an East-West flow of innovative ideas, technologies, and practices, as both STR and modernization theories were highly political epistemologies.

Indeed, I propose that the Soviet government used the STR discourse as a highly strategic and political instrument. While the US government used modernization theory to expand US hegemony abroad, the Soviets embraced STR as a sub-theory of modernization, aiming to legitimize East-West cooperation but also their own interventions in the global South. The very fact that Gvishiani himself promoted STR theory in the Soviet Union is quite revealing here. Both sides were obviously guided by different rationales and invested different hopes in this process. Modernization theory postulated a universal path of development, driven by technoscience and industrialization, which would bring about a sociopolitical value change toward democracy, enabling US policy makers to meet the Soviets halfway. In turn, STR advocated the fundamental integration and co-transformation of social, economic, and technical systems. Just as the Americans used modernization theory to guide their foreign policy and development plans, the Soviets mobilized STR to legitimize their international activities, promoting socialist planning in developing countries, and as a bridge for technoscientific transfer from the West.[43]

Modernization theory can be understood as a strong story in which protagonists are moving toward the same future by somewhat different paths, the communist and liberal-democratic ones. According to Barbara Czarniawska, narratives are not just tales but important organizational devises, for narratives bind together distant, loosely coupled practices and imbue them with a coherent sense and, even more importantly, a purpose.[44] Accordingly, a story that enables a government and a scientific expert to identify and link observed changes into one chain of events is also a promise of control. Because the theories of modernization and the scientific-technical revolution offered a new narrative of global development, they should be understood not only as intellectual discourses, but also as ways of opening new vistas for governmental and scientific intervention.

Thus STR played a double role in relation to Soviet society: it was used by the Soviet regime as a heuristic tool to understand itself, but also as a discourse to legitimize international technology transfer. In turn, STR theory resonated well with modernization theory and was used by Western scholars to interpret Soviet society.[45] STR, in this way, was a powerful tool of sense-making that linked the two opposing regimes. In the next section I discuss the efforts of particular individuals to support and entrench the STR discourse in the Soviet government: the story of Soviet STR is not just an intellectual history, but also a story of military-industrial complex and East-West transfer, and, as such, it is a story of Kosygin and Gvishiani.

"He was never a revolutionary": Aleksei Kosygin

Kosygin's contribution to Soviet governance extended well beyond his widely described failed attempt to reform Soviet economic management from 1966 to 1969, but not enough is known about his influence inside the Soviet Union and abroad.⁴⁶ Although acknowledgment of Kosygin's importance surfaces occasionally in studies of separate branches of Soviet economy and technology, there is no systematic account about his governmental legacy. Several memoirs, published in Russian, provide at least some, if not entirely reliable, information about the personality of Kosygin.⁴⁷ The difficulty is that Kosygin, widely known for his extremely reserved, dry, and even sulky manner, never kept diaries and never wrote memoirs. In what follows, I discuss some of relevant moments in Kosygin's life story as it was connected to the development of scientific expertise around the State Committee for Science and Technology and the career of Dzhermen Gvishiani.

Aleksei Kosygin was born into the family of a qualified worker, Nikolai Kosygin, in Saint Petersburg in 1904. Originally a farmer hailing from the Kolomenskoe area near Moscow, Nikolai Kosygin moved to Saint Petersburg in pursuit of a better-paying job, in which he was rather successful and, according to his biographer, enjoyed for that time a reasonable standard of living. Nikolai's wife died when Aleksei was only four and the child, together with his two siblings, was brought up by their father, who took care to give his children an education. Indeed, the biography of the future prime minister of the Soviet Union was not limited to worker experience. Quite the opposite: a glimpse of Kosygin's early years reveals the development of an educated, ambitious, and successful entrepreneur and not someone who shot from a workshop floor to the Politburo. The young Aleksei Kosygin attended a Petrograd business school and embarked on a professional career as a manager of a gold-mining company, located in Kirensk, Siberia. In Kirensk Kosygin was in charge of management and trade relations, excelling in both. There he married Klavdia Krivosheina, of a well-to-do family of entrepreneurs, and had a daughter, Liudmila. The Kosygin family, as well as their nanny and Evenk housekeeper, lived in a comfortable house. In his grandson's memoir, the young Kosygin is described as an entrepreneurial "NEP-man," a phenomenon of the New Economic Policy that followed attempts at stabilization after the October Revolution, who was promoted from the mining company to work at the cooperative union in Novosibirsk.⁴⁸

Forewarned about the changing political climate and escaping the purges, Kosygin moved back to Leningrad in 1930, where he dissociated himself from the cooperative union and began to study engineering in the Kirov Textile Institute. Once again, Kosygin successfully climbed the career ladder. Just before the outbreak of World War II, Kosygin found himself promoted to people's commissar in textile and by 1940 served as a deputy chairman of a council in charge of mass-consumption goods. In December 1941 Kosygin was personally charged by Stalin to supervise the evacuation of factories from the European part of Russia to the east. In January 1942, now a representative of the State Defense Committee, Kosygin was flown by a military plane, accompanied by jetfighters, to besieged Leningrad, where he organized the evacuation of industrial plants and the arrangement of supplies to the starving city. In 1943, Kosygin devised and presented a recovery plan for the Soviet economy.

From these war experiences Kosygin made and retained close personal connections with several top military commanders, although, according to his contemporaries, he was never deeply involved in matters of the military-industrial complex.[49] One of the mysteries for his biographers is that, although part of Andrei Zhdanov's circle, Kosygin surprisingly survived the last purges, the so-called "Leningrad affair," in 1949.[50] From the late 1940s through the 1950s Kosygin gained, lost, and regained Politburo membership, in any case retaining his role as the chief administrator in the field of light industry. Historians attribute Kosygin's ability to survive to both his indispensable, practical understanding of the Soviet economy, and to his political cunning. According to his contemporaries, Kosygin had a severely dry manner and "only somewhat relaxed" during the thaw, some of which was probably consciously assumed behavior, a survival strategy learned under Stalin.[51]

Under Nikita Khrushchev, Kosygin was instrumental in making the Soviet Union catch up and overtake the West, although he deeply disapproved of Khrushchev's utopian statements, such as promises to reach communism in twenty years. His contemporaries noted Kosygin's dislike of Khrushchev's rushed schemes, but Kosygin cunningly tapped into Khrushchev's determination to modernize the Soviet economy to pursue his own projects. For instance, Kosygin not only personally supported the development of oil and gas fields in Siberia in the 1960s and 1970s, but was proactive in establishing the first high-level trade contacts with Italian businesses in 1962.[52] In 1959 Khrushchev even assigned Kosygin as the chairman of Gosplan, in which role Kosygin disciplined regional economic councils.[53] But Kosygin continued to have a complicated professional relation with Khrushchev and in the end he would participate in the coup against the unpredictable chairman of the Soviet state. Contemporaries' memoirs detail this ambivalent relationship: to celebrate Kosygin's birthday, Khrushchev threw a lavish party in his official summer house in Petrovo-Dalnee in February 1964, to which members of the Presidium, ministers of defense and foreign affairs, as well as families were invited. However, in the autumn of 1964 Kosygin called for Khrushchev's resignation in front of the Central Committee.[54] In contrast, Kosygin had a less formal relation with Brezhnev than he had had with Khrushchev: according to Kosygin's grandson, Aleksei Gvishiani, Kosygin and Brezhnev called each other by their first names.[55] Historians indicate a growing tension between Kosygin and Brezhnev at a later stage, but Kosygin's influence began to decline only in the late 1970s.[56]

Although Kosygin was not heavily involved in the military matters, these issues could not be completely alien to him. I have already mentioned Kosygin's role as a member of Defense Committee during World War II. He kept this affiliation after the war, and thus when Kosygin became the vice chairman of the Council of Ministers in 1960, he was also a member of the Defense Council. In 1964 Kosygin became prime minister of the Soviet Union and, in this role, assumed an active position in Soviet foreign policy as the chief spokesman in arms control matters.[57] Before his rise to the post of general secretary, Brezhnev was familiar with the development of military-industrial complex and espoused the avoidance of war at all costs; however, at the same time he was initially uninterested in foreign policy and delegated some tasks to Kosygin.[58] In this capacity, Kosygin also participated high-level international negotiations about foreign policy and defense, as, for example, in the important Glassboro meeting in June 1967, where the idea of mutually assured destruction was announced (and rejected by Kosygin), and later, in relation to the Soviet invasion in Afghanistan, to which Kosygin personally opposed.[59] In addition to this, Kosygin was involved in international trade; for instance, through the Dartmouth conferences he met David Rockefeller, first in 1971 and then in New York in 1973. Some rather daring ideas of East-West cooperation were voiced in those meetings: Rockefeller recalled that, during their meeting in 1974, Kosygin proposed Rockefeller to co-fund and co-own nuclear plants in the Soviet Union.[60]

In all, Kosygin's skills and position made him an ideal gatekeeper between civil and military-industrial sectors. Although his relations described Kosygin as being "never a revolutionary," Kosygin was a champion of the scientific-technical revolution, concentrating on solving practical issues in economic and research and development sectors while making sure that the solutions never directly challenged either existing political priorities or ideological discourses. As I show in the remaining part of this chapter, it was through Kosygin's circles that Soviet policy sciences were developed at home and, through international cooperation, spilled over into nonmilitary applications.

Enter Gvishiani

One would search in vain for Dzhermen Gvishiani in histories of the Soviet Union. Although this somewhat exotic name surfaces time and again in the context of technoscientific transfer or even espionage, little is known about the role that Gvishiani played in Cold War relations.[61] If in the scholarship Kosygin emerges as a rare if dry pragmatic, Gvishiani remains almost completely unknown.[62] However, this lacuna is hiding one of the most extraordinary actors of the late socialist era. A man with an inscrutable name, who held prominent posts, and had extraordinary connections around the world, including membership in the Club of Rome, Gvishiani mingled with global business and political leaders abroad, and promoted the theory of scientific-technical revolution, systems analysis, and computer modeling of global development at home. It is the task of future historians to trace Gvishiani's political networks: while his personal archival file is not available to researchers, there is some evidence that Gvishiani was no simple bureaucrat. For instance, when in the midst of the Cuban missile crisis in October 1964 Khrushchev invited the president of Westinghouse Electric, William Knox, for a talk aiming at sending threats to Kennedy, it was Gvishiani who was present alongside the head of the Soviet Union.[63] Promoted as an academician at the Soviet Academy of Sciences, Gvishiani was awarded honorary doctorates from several Western universities. A small planet was called after him by a Russian astronomer in 1976.

In many ways Dzhermen Gvishiani was a typical member of the Soviet nomenklatura: brought up in the provinces, he studied in the capital and had a strong link with the military.[64] Gvishiani was born in Akhaltsikhe, a town on a southern border of Georgia, in 1928, the same year as Kosygin's daughter Liudmila, Gvishiani's future wife. These two families could not be more different. Dzhermen Gvishiani's mother was Armenian, but his father, Mikhail Maksimovich Gvishiani, was Georgian. It was Mikhail who gave his son this unusual name as a tribute to the communist security organs ("Dzhermen" is a combination of "*Dzherzinskii*" and "*Menzhinskii*"). Mikhail Gvishiani (1905–1966) had only a primary education and made his career in the State Political Directorate (GPU) and then the People's Commissariat for Internal affairs (*Narodnyy Komissariat Vnutrennikh Del*, or NKVD), serving as the head of personal security for Lavrentii Beria, who rose to the post of the chief of NKVD in 1938.

The name of Mikhail Gvishiani surfaces in writings about the Soviet repression, as he directed a special unit in charge of surveillance and arrests. In 1939 Mikhail Gvishiani was listed as part of Beria's group and a candidate member of the Central Committee. In 1944 Mikhail Gvishiani supervised the resettlement of Chechens, which involved a mass execution.[65] It is not known, however, if Mikhail Gvishiani was in any way involved in the Beria's postwar projects of strengthening Soviet military-industrial complex with captured technology, transferred from East Central Europe to secret research towns in Russia.[66] After Beria's death in August 1953, Mikhail Gvishiani left NKVD as a reserve lieutenant-general, but lost his status in 1954. Thereafter he was put in charge of the Georgian Committee for Science and Technology.[67] There is speculation that Mikhail Gvishiani could have encountered Kosygin during the Leningrad affair, but I could not locate sources to support this hypothesis.[68]

This background of the Stalinist repression could hardly be guessed from memoirs that mention Dzhermen Gvishiani. In a way, the life trajectories of the father and son Gvishiani illustrate the shift that the Soviet power system underwent. Whereas brutality, as Paul Gregory notes, was a characteristic feature, indispensable for career advancement in Stalin's government, other, softer managerial values came to the fore by the late 1950s.[69] It is Dzhermen Gvishiani's polished manners and aptitude for diplomacy that come across in the recollections of his contemporaries. In an interview, a national security advisor under Johnson described Gvishiani as "very intelligent, not ideological man. Indispensible."[70] The British pioneer in the operations research P. M. S. Blackett wrote that Gvishiani was a "capable bloke."[71] In his memoir the president of the American National Academy of Science, Philip Handler, did not spare words in expressing his fascination with Gvishiani as "a sharply intelligent man," who had "a superb brain" and was "very civilised and urbane."[72] US presidential science advisor Jeremy Wiesner also recalled Gvishiani as a courteous diplomat who claimed to be in charge of Soviet research policy in the computer industry.[73] The active coordinator of many US-Soviet exchange programs Yale Richmond remembered Gvishiani as "a suave and sophisticated Georgian with a perfect command of English."[74] Others, such as the founder and director of the Kennedy Government School in Harvard, Howard Raiffa, recalled that Gvishiani commanded influence in the Soviet Union which far exceeded his posts (as a rule, Gvishiani served as a deputy director on many boards).[75] The accounts of Western scientists and policy makers mention suites in fancy hotels, such as the Four Seasons in Vienna and the George V in Paris, where Dzhermen Gvishiani would receive his guests. Impeccably and elegantly dressed, Gvishiani made such an impression on Alexander King of the Organization for Economic Co-operation and Development (OECD) as a representative of the world political elite, that King even wondered what Gvishiani was doing in the academic gathering.[76]

How did Gvishiani himself reconcile his international reputation as a professional and sophisticated diplomat and, furthermore, an adamant modernizer and world citizen, with his complex and difficult family history? It is hard to tell, but judging from biographical sources, it seems that this reconciliation was achieved mainly through denial: in his memoirs, Gvishiani never directly confronts this part of his family history. For instance, Gvishiani wrote about his pride in his father, who was military not only in his professional roles, but also in character: "a brave man, who was always very busy, concerned, subject to constant danger and also a great rider and gunman."[77] Never does Dzhermen Gvishiani expand on the Stalinist repression. Instead, he only hints that his family "knew almost nothing" about "tragic facts and events," quickly adding that if the scale of the repression had been more widely known, it would not have mattered anyway, because the Soviet victory in World War II more than redeemed this dark side of history.[78] This was not an unusual take on the difficult past. Here Gvishiani's position was not different from the one adopted by ex-Nazi engineers, many of whom obscured their relationship to the murderous regime by adopting different strategies, such as defining their loyalty first to technical projects of the state and thus distancing themselves from politics and violence. However, if Nazi engineers, as noted by Dolores Augustine, developed "elaborate strategies of self-justification," none such strategies were put in use by the Gvishianis and Kosygins.[79] They simply did not need to justify themselves. Instead, these families appeared to enjoy undisrupted legitimacy through the Soviet and post-Soviet eras.

And it really seemed that Dzhermen Gvishiani was brought up for a diplomatic career. As a child, he spoke Russian, Georgian, Armenian, and Turkish, and he would later become fluent in English, French, and Italian. Just like the Kosygins in the 1920s, Gvishiani's family had a housekeeper when residing in Vladivostok (Gvishiani's domestic help, however, was one of the Gulag inmates).[80] Dzhermen finished high school in Vladivostok, where the aid provided by the Allies fostered his interest in the West and where he began to learn English, in 1946. In the same year he enrolled in the Moscow Institute of International Relations (MGIMO).[81] Having completed his studies in 1951, Gvishiani did service in the marine fleet. In Moscow, Gvishiani excelled in networking. At MGIMO he met Liudmila Kosygina, a student of Soviet-American relations, whom he married in 1948.[82] This was definitely a step up the nomenklatura ladder: at that time Kosygin was in charge of light industries and was soon to become the minister of finance.

Higher education was indeed crucial for the formation of Soviet governmental elites that eventually came to occupy leading positions after World War II. For example, it was at the Industrial Academy in Moscow in 1929 that Nikita Khrushchev met Stalin's wife, then also a student, who brought him to the attention of the leader.[83] Later Dzhermen Gvishiani would help Khrushchev's grandson gain a position at the Institute of Systems Research. Furthermore, Dzhermen Gvishiani's sister married Evgenii Primakov, who would later become the director of the Institute of World Economics and International Relations (IMEMO) and, after the collapse of the Soviet Union, the head of the state security agency and prime minister under Boris El'tsin. Fluent in English and a specialist in Soviet-American relations, Gvishiani's wife, Liudmila Kosygina-Gvishiani assisted her father Aleksei Kosygin on several high-level business trips abroad, including a meeting with Queen Elizabeth II and, albeit not in an official role as a translator, President Lyndon Johnson in Glassboro. Liudmila rose to the position of first secretary and then counselor at the Ministry of Foreign Affairs, and later became the director of the Library for Foreign Literature in Moscow.[84]

In this way, the Gvishiani-Kosygin tandem could be understood as an important nodal point in East-West knowledge transfer, flowing through the central research policy-making organ (GKNT) and the leading academic institutes. Close family ties, but also spatial proximity characterized the networks of top Soviet elites. Initially the Gvishiani family lived in an apartment on Frunzenskaia embankment, but eventually moved into the apartment house where Kosygins lived, on Vorob'evskii Road, now Kosygin Street, in close proximity to the Moscow River.[85] Built in 1969, this building appeared to be an ordinary, functionalist apartment block. Indeed, several features, such as a nonstandard design, in particular wide balconies that were atypical for apartment blocks of that period and constructed of better than usual materials, revealed that this house was not built for common Soviet citizens. The small number of flats and only two entrances also suggest exclusivity. Most unusually for Moscow, the house was erected with a wide surrounding belt of greenery.[86] In the same building lived the presidents of the Soviet Academy of Sciences, Mstislav Keldysh and A. P. Aleksandrov; the area also included the homes of Brezhnev and several other high officials.[87] According to biographers, Kosygin's father never followed his son to Moscow and continued living in his communal apartment in Leningrad, where he also worked as a yard sweeper when retired.

The Soviet leaders of STR fostered their networks outside their working hours. As all members of the nomenklatura, the Kosygin-Gvishiani family spent vacations in summer houses. The families of the ex-NEP-man and ex-NKVD officer appeared to be close: many images document their vacations together. For example, an image dated 1948 shows the extended Kosygin family against a setting of palm trees and sunshine. Liudmila wears a modest pale pink dress with matching ribbons in her pleated hair; the athletic and handsome Dzhermen looks confidently straight into the camera. Another, later image documents the Kosygins and Gvishianis in, presumably, a governmental summer residence in Arkhangel'skoe. The spacious interior is decorated with tasteful oriental carpets, an obligatory landscape painting, and a grand piano (Gvishiani, indeed, was known for his love of the piano). Yet another picture shows a different summer house used by Gvishiani. Situated in Nikolina gora, where many Moscow-based artists and scientists, such as the prominent physicist Petr Kapitsa, had their summer houses (and where oligarchs such as Chernomyrdin and Khodorkovskii built their dachas in the 1990s), the image reveals a more down-to-earth interior, decorated with taxidermy and ethnic souvenirs.[88] It was probably to this summer house that—as Kosygin's grandson, Aleksei Gvishiani recalled—a military commander visited, arriving in an amphibian truck. The memoirs also allow a glimpse of the conspicuous consumption of the elite: Kosygin, reportedly, never drank vodka, but preferred champagne (brut). Gvishiani smoked only Pall-Mall cigarettes: a pack is displayed in Gvishiani's office, kept as a memorial museum at the All-Union Institute of Systems Research/Institute of Systems Analysis (VNIISI/ISA).

All these details of everyday life show that the activities of the extended Kosygin-Gvishiani family revolved around a gated community of Soviet nomenklatura, hardly ever exposed to the oppression of persistent shortages that marked the everyday life of the common Soviet citizen. Like all top nomenclature officials, Gvishiani received just under six hundred rubles as his salary at the GKNT, which, being only three times more than a decent salary in the Soviet academia, did not make him wealthy per se. However, as a top official Gvishiani qualified for a number of privileges, such as summer houses, and subsidized groceries, car, and housing. These perks, as well as salaries, were kept secret.[89] Furthermore, there was a fast track from such a gated community to the world outside the Iron Curtain, and the Gvishianis traveled a lot. For example, Aleksei Gvishiani, then sixteen years old, recalled accompanying Kosygin on his business trip to Italy in 1962, when they used this opportunity to visit Florence and Rome. A few years later Aleksei Gvishiani spent an afternoon in London pubs being entertained by the son of Prime Minister Harold Wilson.[90]

For people like Gvishiani, the Iron Curtain was not so much a problem as an asset. Given this exceptional arrangement for themselves and their families, it is not surprising that neither Kosygin nor Gvishiani were revolutionaries: they had little personal interest in changing the political organization of the Soviet system. But they believed that the survival of this system could only be achieved through modernization and the opening to the West. It is difficult to judge whether they anticipated any sociopolitical changes as a result of such West-oriented modernization. Yet, as I show in the following chapters, the Kosygin-Gvishiani tandem did play an important role in opening and sustaining channels for contacts, which resulted in many significant transformations inside the Soviet regime. The next section discusses the ways in which a set of special institutions was created, bridging policy and academic worlds to enable these East-West connections.

The Heart of the Gray Power: The GKNT

As I have mentioned earlier, Gvishiani's work affiliations were many. Having graduated from MGIMO he joined the navy and while serving pursued higher education part time, with a focus on industrial sociology. In the autumn of 1955 Gvishiani left the military as a reserve officer to take up a position at the State Committee for the Introduction of New Technologies (Gostekhnika, established in 1948) under the Council of Ministers, which was renamed as the State Committee for Science and Technology (GKNT) in 1965. In this instance, Gvishiani was appointed to the department in charge of foreign science and technology.[91] At the same time he chaired the Standing Commission on Co-ordination of Scientific and Technical Research of the Council of Mutual Economic Assistance (Comecon or CMEA, established in 1949). Gvishiani, in this way, was involved in East-East and East-West cooperation.

Both Gvishiani himself and historians emphasized that Kosygin preferred to rely on professionals or experts, in contrast to Brezhnev who preferred a politically loyal team. Yet this does not mean that Soviet specialists had more power to decide the key issues. According to Stephen Fortescue, although highly placed Soviet policy makers adopted scientists as their protégés, this personal proximity to power did not give scientists a mandate to formulate or otherwise impact policies. Rather, this was a social contract: in exchange for scientific evidence that was relevant to the politically set policy agenda, the protégé scientists received a mandate to access and redistribute resources in the academic sector.[92]

This model of patron and client applies well to the case of Kosygin and Gvishiani. Being in charge of the GKNT, Gvishiani was able to significantly influence national in research and development priorities. In turn, he was able to direct significant resources toward establishing new types of organizations involved in policy-relevant research, such as IIASA and VNIISI in the 1970s. However, the evidence shows that resources and influence flowed in only one direction: my interviews revealed that both IIASA and VNIISI scientists were highly frustrated about their inability to have an impact on Soviet governmental decisions.[93] In turn, I have not come across a single case in which any scientist succeeded channeling new policy ideas up through Gvishiani. The flow was, just as Fortescue suggested, top-down: Gvishiani ensured that resources flowed down to the academic sector to his trusted scientists, but it is very difficult to say to what extent scientific expertise found its way up.

Nevertheless, Gvishiani's career track illustrates well his determination to bridge policy and academic worlds by gaining credentials in both. Although most of his time was dedicated to managerial duties and, in the 1960s, high-level trade negotiations, Gvishiani sought to establish and consolidate his academic credentials. Thus he defended a candidate dissertation in philosophy and published his first book, *Sociology of Business*, in 1961. Contemporaries recalled this book having a significant impact, because it was one of first attempts to introduce Western management theories to Soviet audiences, which opened up a path for rehabilitation of some of the interwar Russian thinkers in scientific management.[94] It is important to note that Gvishiani's authority was sometimes challenged: his work received occasional attacks from his political opponents, mainly boiling down to accusations of promoting convergence theory. From 1962 to 1968 Gvishiani taught philosophy at Moscow State University and continued part-time research on US methods of management, which were the subject of his doctoral dissertation, defended at the Institute of Philosophy in 1968.[95] The dissertation was published as *Organization and Management* (in Russian, *Organizatsia i upravlenie*) in 1970; forty thousand copies of the second edition were printed and the book was reissued as late as 1998. Gvishiani also wrote prefaces to the Russian editions of books by leading Western scholars of management and forecasting, such as Jay Forrester and Erich Jantsch.

Yet I suggest that a genuine innovation, supported by Gvishiani, was an idea that management and control sciences should be integrated with a more ambitious and complex task of Soviet social science. The STR discourse postulated an ever-growing complexity of technoscientific systems, intertwined with complex social change. This complexity was understood as a challenge for both planning and running Soviet industries. Thus, although the STR discourse posited a technoscientific advance of communism, it also indicated the coming of new types of problems, many of which were social in character. It was to tackle these problems that the field of sociology was summoned: a discipline that was first banned as a bourgeois pseudo-science by Stalin was rehabilitated in the mid-1960s. Gvishiani was directly involved in this process, first as a member of the Soviet Association of Sociology and the director of a department for research on complex problems at the Institute for Concrete Social Research (IKSI) from 1969 to 1972, an institute that was founded with personal support of Aleksei Kosygin. At IKSI, Gvishiani patronized its research program on the social consequences of STR.[96] After IKSI was purged in the late 1960s and early 1970s, Gvishiani personally took care of several researchers, such as Nikolai Lapin, transferring them to the newly founded Institute for the Problems of Management and, later, to VNIISI, a multidisciplinary institute, which he founded and directed in 1976. I return later to discuss VNIISI at some length, as this institute was a Soviet attempt at establishing a think tank-style organization, after the example of IIASA, with the hope that it would become a Soviet response to RAND.[97] Before IKSI, Gvishiani also chaired a department at the Institute of Automatics and Telemechanics, and when IKSI was shaken up by political rifts, he moved to the newly established Nemchinov Institute for the National Economy, where he chaired a department of socioeconomic sciences from 1972 to 1974. In this way, Gvishiani moved like a whirlwind through the most vibrant research milieus that emerged in the 1960s. Gvishiani's name appeared as an author or editor on many publications in the new, strategically important fields of policy science and management, although his authorship has been questioned by some. Given his many obligations, it is very likely that Gvishiani was listed as a nominal author or patron of the relevant research fields.[98]

At the international level, Gvishiani's academic profile was anchored in the management discipline, which was at that time undergoing rapid professionalization:

he was a member of the American Academy of Management, the International Academy of Management, and the International Council of Management, as well as the Soviet-Finnish and Soviet-American commissions for management, the latter in cooperation with the Ford Foundation. But Gvishiani was more interested in the theories of management as an organizational activity, and especially in theories of leadership, and less so in the science of management, the area which was dominated by cybernetics in the Soviet Union at that time.[99] Indeed, Gvishiani wrote that his interest in systems analysis emerged out of practical concerns, related to decision-making in Soviet research policy.[100]

Gvishiani was no less active abroad than in Moscow. The very launch of Gvishiani's international career was enabled by the "new foreign policy," assumed by Khrushchev beginning in 1955. According to Zubok, a significant part of this new Soviet foreign policy involved a return to the 1920s' idea that the transfer of Western technologies would speed up Soviet development, but it also involved intense public diplomacy.[101] It was after the Twentieth Congress, which condemned the Stalinist regime, that Gvishiani embarked on his first trip abroad: by invitation from the British Trade Ministry, the Soviet delegation departed for London in 1956. The Soviet officials were hungry to see the world outside the Soviet Union: on the way, they stopped in Prague, the Czech spa town of Karlovy Vary, and Paris, using this opportunity to explore the hitherto inaccessible Western world.[102] From that time intense international networking followed. In 1958 Gvishiani spent a month in China and helped organize a German industrial fair in Moscow, which was then followed up with lengthy negotiations in Bonn.[103] Contacts with Italy were initiated. In 1955 the Italian industrialist Piero Savoretti began exploring opportunities to cooperate with the Soviets, which culminated with the Italian industry fair in Sokol'niki in 1962. But Gvishiani's first major international trade experience was associated with Kosygin's trip to Italy following the Sokol'niki fair.[104] During this trip, Kosygin pursued three priority areas for Italian-Soviet cooperation: oil and gas, the automotive industry, and personal computers. Gvishiani met with the heads of Fiat and Olivetti, including Aurelio Peccei, the future founder and president of the Club of Rome, and was also a member of the Soviet negotiating team, the work of which resulted a contract with Fiat to build its Togliatti factory. Worth USD 817 million, this deal was the largest East-West trade arrangement since the October Revolution.[105]

In addition to trade deals, Gvishiani represented the Soviet Union at a number of international organizations. The United Nations Advisory Committee on the Application of Science and Technology to Development (UNACASTD) in New York was established in 1963 to promote technology transfer to developing countries and to probe into social and other consequences of technoscientific progress (UNACASTD defined a set of policy problems, which later would be reflected in IIASA's agenda). Through UNACASTD, Gvishiani met Carroll Wilson, a prominent scholar and policy advisor of the MIT's Sloan School of Management. A frequent visitor in Moscow, Wilson would later invite Gvishiani to give a talk in Boston, Massachusetts.[106] Gvishiani was involved in the early stages of planning UN Institute for Training and Research (UNITAR) and was a member of the annual Soviet delegation to the UN Economic Commission for Europe, one of the key platforms for developing the methods of macro-economic statistics and exchange of data. In the United States, Gvishiani met and corresponded with Jerome Wiesner, science advisor to Kennedy and Johnson, and dined with Henry Ford and Thomas Watson of IBM.[107] Gvishiani also hosted the famous (and of dubious repute) businessman Robert Maxwell, a British media magnate of Czechoslovak origin.[108]

By the mid-1960s the Kosygin-Gvishiani tandem had reached the zenith of their power. New to the office of prime minister, Kosygin appointed Vladimir Kirillin as the chairman of the GKNT in September 1965. Kirillin, an established scientist, a specialist in thermophysics, and the previous occupant of such high posts as deputy minister of science and education, vice-chairman of the GKNT, vice-president of the Soviet Academy of Sciences, and member of the Central Committee department for science and higher education, was one of very few who were personally close to the overtly cautious Kosygin.[109] In their memoirs, contemporaries recall that Kirillin used to celebrate New Year's parties in Kosygin's dacha in Arkhangel'skoe, at which Keldysh, Kirillin's closest neighbor in Zhukovka, was also present. The friendship between Kirillin and Kosygin endured, regardless of political turbulence, and their mutual reliance was strong: indeed, when Kosygin left his post in 1980, Kirillin immediately resigned from the GKNT on his own initiative, a decision that was unprecedented for a Soviet official of such high standing.[110]

This triangle of Kosygin, Kirillin, and Gvishiani (note that Kirillin was also Kosygin and Gvishiani's neighbor in Moscow and his summer house was in front of Keldysh's dacha) would shape Soviet international cooperation in science and technology, the area which, according to Kosygin, was of fundamental importance for rejuvenating the Soviet economy. Kosygin viewed management reform as an indispensable component of economic reform, and, in turn, Gvishiani promoted empirical, applied branches of management science, something which was not an easy undertaking: empirical research was avoided by many Soviet scientists, because they found abstract theorization much safer than the minefield of empiricism and the deserts of data. Nevertheless, management was formally recognized as a legitimate scientific field in December 1965, and departments and institutes cropped up all over the Soviet academic system.[111]

East-West Transfer, the GKNT, and VNIISI

Soviet science policy was shaped by several interrelated organizations, most importantly the GKNT, the Presidium of the Soviet Academy of Sciences, and the Politburo, the central decision-making organ in the Central Committee of the Communist Party of the Soviet Union (CPSU). However, historians are not entirely sure about the actual role of the Central Committee in setting science policy; existing sources hint that the science department at the Central Committee served mainly as a postbox that processed received recommendations. Similarly, special councils at the Academy of Sciences fulfilled the function of information exchange points rather than policy-forming bodies. It seems, therefore, that the key organization that shaped actual directions of research was the GKNT,[112] which had a mandate to shape national priorities and intervene in the work of research and industrial organizations during any stage of implementation of the five-year plans, and, importantly, had a significant reserve fund at its disposal.[113] Located on Gorky Street (now Tverskaia Street), the offices of the GKNT were frequented by foreign diplomats and businessmen. The building buzzed and the institution was well provided with funds as with international contacts: in 1976 the GKNT's annual salary fund totaled 2,620,500 rubles and listed 1,034 employees.[114]

In all, the GKNT can be described as the key center that tied international contacts together, channeling them to the development of all branches of Soviet scientific research and industry. Although GKNT chairman Vladimir Kirillin was not a member of the Politburo, Kosygin was, so that through Gvishiani the GKNT had direct, informal access to the highest decision-making body in the Soviet Union. Also, Kirillin was an influential figure himself: born in 1913 in Moscow, into the family of a medical doctor, Kirillin specialized in thermo-engineering. He served as vice chairman of the GKNT and as the vice minister of education and science, as well as a member of the Pugwash committee in 1963–1964. Kirillin was also a deputy to Kosygin at the Council of Ministers; in turn, Gvishiani was Kirillin's deputy for international relations.[115] Kirillin chaired the GKNT for fifteen years until he stepped down from his position in 1980 to be replaced by Gurii Marchuk. Indeed, in 1980 Gvishiani was considered as a director of the GKNT, but Kosygin advised him not to take this position. In this way, the Soviet scientific-technical revolution was overseen by a triumvirate of power, Kosygin, Kirillin, and Gvishiani, in the 1960s and 1970s.

Although the GKNT was responsible for all areas of research and development, computerization of Soviet industry and academia was one of its foremost tasks. Indeed, it is difficult to overestimate the importance of computer technology in what I describe as a changing post-Stalinist technoscientific governmentality in the Soviet Union and the Kosygin-Kirillin-Gvishiani triumvirate played an important role in bringing about this change. A cluster of computer technology, systems analysis, and scientific management was purposively developed as a technical and intellectual resource for the Soviet government and managers that would enable them to detect and respond to the wider socioeconomic problems and challenges of the scientific-technical revolution. The dedication to this area of scientific expertise was reflected in the institutional structure of the GKNT, which established the Department of Computer Technology and Management Systems to coordinate a project of the all-union automated system (OGAS) and network of computer centers.[116] From 1971 on, the GKNT was involved in setting the framework for the national network of information centers for economy and management, facilitated with computer technology and plugged into one informational network, an ambitious project that failed to live up to its promise.[117] In relation to this, further institutions for new policy sciences were established, such as an all-union scientific research institute of organization and management[118] and a laboratory for economic mathematical methods and OR at the Institute of Management of the National Economy.[119] A special Institute of the Problems of Organization and Management (VNIIPOU) was founded at GKNT with direct support by Gvishiani in September 1971 (renamed as the Institute of Computer Technology and Informatization in 1986).[120] The system-cybernetic sciences were applied to govern different sectors, geophysical, industrial, and social, ranging from weather and water to libraries, health, and tourism. For example, there were plans to set up an automated hydro-meteorological agency, equipped with satellites by 1975; other examples include the automated system Weather (Pogoda), a photo-telegraph transmission system Pallada, automated systems for different consumer services, a system for emergency hospitalization in large cities, automated reader services in the Lenin library in Moscow, and a system for automatic process planning, accounting, and organization of tourism, including tracking foreign visitors in the Soviet Union.[121]

There were many bottlenecks that impeded the implementation of such automated systems, not the least being the pervasive informality that made the formalization and codification of organizational processes an especially daunting a task. One of key issues was the computer hardware itself, in particular input and output devices. The computerization of economic planning and organizational management entailed consistent attempts to fight and bypass the Coordinating Committee for Multilateral Export Controls (CoCom) embargo on the export to the Soviet Union of dual-use high-tech, including computers and other electronic and automated devices that could be used in both the military and civil sectors.[122] Archival documents show that the GKNT actively searched for ways to establish cooperation with the United States in the area of computer technology for business systems from at least as early as 1964. For instance, in 1965 a GKNT employee asked to visit leading American computer producers, such as RCA, IBM, Racecon, and Data Control Corporation, in turn offering American specialists visits to Soviet computer centers in Moscow, Minsk, Kazan', Kyiv, Erevan, and Vilnius.[123] In a true spirit of Cold War secrecy, the Soviets did not offer the Americans much in exchange: a list of the computers, suggested as suitable to be seen by foreigners, included Minsk-22 and -23, Razdan-2 and -3, M-220, BESM-6, and a perforator Vilnius, machines that were far from being cutting-edge examples of Soviet technology,[124] whereas the Soviets were particularly interested in the SDS-6600, SDS-6800, and IBM-360, believing that the application of these machines in Soviet industries would reduce the lag behind the West by five to seven years.[125] Yet the initiative did not come only from one side; US companies were keen to expand their markets and were considerably interested in selling their production and licenses to the Soviet Union. For example, beginning in 1967 representatives of Hewlett Packard paid regular visits to Moscow and Akademgorodok in Novosibirsk.[126]

According to historians, most of these efforts to get Western computer technology turned out to be futile, and from the 1970s on the Soviets relied on illegally obtained blueprints to produce their own versions of, for example, the IBM-360. However, I suggest that the Soviets' efforts to access Western computer technology should not be understood as a failure, but as an important process, in the course of which an new institutional and social basis emerged, opening a path for the development of a new language of international connectivity and new thinking about governance. In other words, the impact of this opening extended beyond the failed transfer of hardware. For instance, correspondence between the GKNT and American companies reveals a search for a neutral language to frame such cooperation: one GKNT official used the idiom "practical problems," such as constructions, transport, and management of production, which could be solved with the help of computers and which spoke to the "mutual interest" of the United States and the Soviet Union.[127] Furthermore, whereas hard technology could not travel easily across the Iron Curtain, soft technology, such as scientific approaches to management, in particular systems analysis, could, and so could people. Here a path for a more intensive exchange was opened by the US-Soviet agreement on cooperation in science and technology, signed in 1972, which included computer applications in management and systems analysis.[128] Cybernetics and the systems approach, in the eyes of the Soviet state, was part and parcel of the larger project of computerization.

That soft technologies of control were strategically linked to hard computer technology is quite evident if one follows Gvishiani's network and activities, in particular his support for cooperation with the United States in promoting management training in Western Europe. In 1968 scholars from the MIT Sloan School of Management visited the GKNT for the first time, and were received again by Gvishiani in 1969.[129] In October 1970, Richard Cyert and Richard Van Horn, both of whom would rise to the leadership of Carnegie Mellon University and embark on an ambitious computerization of the university, visited Moscow to negotiate the organization of an international management training school in Italy.[130] Cyert and Van Horn were accompanied by a representative of the Ford Foundation, which, according to Giuliana Gemelli, had a longstanding interest in developing management sciences in Europe. As I show in chapters 4 and 5, the establishment of this East-West institute, later called IIASA, grew from efforts in this field of cooperation.

In this chapter I have argued that a new, post-Stalinist governmentality emerged in the Soviet Union as a result of several postwar developments. Innovations in computer, information, and control technologies that emerged during the war informed a new developmental theory of the scientific-technical revolution that appealed to both East and West scientists and policy makers. The gospel of the STR, as well as the commitment of Soviet planning to new large infrastructure projects propelled computer technology and systems analysis into the avant-garde of Soviet governmental thought. If in postrevolutionary Russia the first attempts to develop methods for large-scale scientific management followed the GOELRO electrification plan of the 1920s, the post-Stalinist projects involved the extraction of Siberian oil and gas, building large transport systems, and managing growing metropolitan areas, all of which required computerization. Here the Gvishiani-Kosygin tandem played a hugely important role: Kosygin personally promoted the development of Siberian oil and gas while at the GKNT, Gvishiani mediated the deal with Germans to purchase of the pipes needed to build a pipeline to Europe. In 1972 gas production was launched in Siberia, and fifteen to twenty major oil fields were put into operation during the following decades. In 1973 Soviet gas began to flow to Western Europe and so did Soviet experts on large-scale planning and forecasting.[131] Gvishiani was not only the key Soviet negotiator in the large East-West trade and transfer agreements, but was also a patron of the emerging systems approach. As the vision of a scientific-technical revolution conveyed a picture of increasing socioeconomic complexity, the systems approach promised to provide the tools to cope with this complexity, including computer applications for management and policy-making. The state socialist regime would now engage with the issues of world energy, world trade, and world problems—and all of these in Laxenburg, a sleepy village on the outskirts of Vienna.

In retrospect, the Soviet strategic response to US modernization theory with STR served the interests of both sides. The Soviets did manage to gain access to some limited Western technologies. But in order to do so they constructed new discourses and organizations that facilitated a less tangible, but nonetheless important change in their understanding of the nature of the surrounding world and the role of governance and control within it. Although neither Kosygin nor Gvishiani appeared interested in political reform, they facilitated this birth of a new intellectual apparatus of governance.[132] The banner of scientific and technical revolution or STR was just that: a highly powerful discourse that legitimized an unprecedented, albeit controlled, opening of the Soviet system to the West, and the co-transformation of both. However, as I show in subsequent chapters, this legitimization was of central importance for the development of a new, system-cybernetic governmentality.

Did modernization and STR theories soften Cold War confrontation? On the one hand, although the Soviet Union was classified by Rostow as a country on a universal path of modernization, this did not replace the doctrine of containment. The continued effort to contain the communist bloc was expressed, for instance, in the export embargo on strategic goods like computer technologies from West to East. However, the US government keenly supported the transfer of soft technologies, hoping for a change in the Soviet mentality of governance, and, presumably, for a sociopolitical transformation. It also seems that the Soviets understood this strategy rather well and tried to use it to their own advantage. The Soviets recognized that in order to both strengthen their position in international trade and develop their inferior technical base at home they had to find a neutral way of interacting with the West. Here cooperation in policy sciences, or soft technologies, was clearly a window of opportunity for the Soviets to at least try to gain access to the hard, embargoed technologies. I therefore suggest that Soviet discourses on the STR and the US modernization theory enabled the opposing regimes to identify areas of common interest. In the following chapters I show how Gvishiani used his institutional authority to define certain research subjects as beyond censorship, politically neutral, and therefore eligible for East-West circulation and Cold War competition. In so doing Gvishiani opened up and managed those few points of passage across the Iron Curtain, be they institutions such as IIASA or less formal, personal links like the Club of Rome. Following Rigby, Stephen Fortescue suggests that a Soviet administrator's first duty was to fulfill tasks, which generated a degree of legitimacy for the Soviet system.[133] This observation can indeed be applied to explain the role and impact of Gvishiani, because it is quite certain that Gvishiani never intended to erode the Iron Curtain or undermine the Soviet regime. His goal was to make East-West transfer possible and controllable, but in this respect, as I will detail, the outcomes significantly exceeded the original expectations.

2

BRIDGING EAST AND WEST
The Birth of IIASA

> **Q. How to create even a semblance of trust when the hatred for each others' systems runs as deep as it does?**
> **A. Yes, therein lies the essence of this trouble.**
>
> —Willem Oltmans, "A Life of Science: Six Conversations with Dr. Philip Handler" (draft manuscript, IIASA Archives, Laxenburg, Austria)

When visited for the first time, Schloss Laxenburg, a royal hunting lodge just outside of Vienna, cannot help but impress the beholder. An ornate and elegant palace on the edge of the sleepy village of Laxenburg, the schloss is surrounded by acres of a beautifully tended park, embellished with Victorian medieval folly castles on artificial lakes and islands, and even an eighteenth-century horse racing track. Church bells ring on the hour and smoking is still permitted in the village *bierstuben*. It feels like stepping into Stephen Zweig's world of the historical and cultured Central Europe that withered away after 1914. It is also difficult to imagine that Laxenburg and the schloss lay in ruins after 1945. Thus when the International Institute of Applied Systems Analysis, an East-West think tank concerned with "global" and "universal" problems, moved into the by-then brilliantly restored palace in 1973, it was a strong statement of postwar reconstruction.[1]

The Old World met the Cold War world: computer cables were threaded through the baroque walls, scientists and their families arrived from East and West Germany, the United States, and the Soviet Union. Some of them brought their dogs, which ran free in the park while their masters hammered out programming codes to optimize control of a wide range of systems, be they capitalist, communist, or planetary. Indeed, there is still a note on the gate to the park saying that as it is natural for a dog to chase and bite a running person, hence joggers are welcome to enter at their own risk. How could this pastoral scenery be at all possible in a world torn by the arms race, political and industrial espionage, and vitriolic ideological attacks exchanged between communist and capitalist blocs?

This chapter revisits the establishment of IIASA in order to demonstrate the crucial role of East-West cooperation in shaping global governance, in particular those aspects that later became identified with neoliberalism: scientific, knowledge-based governance at a distance, capitalizing on scientific expertise and the idea of self-regulation. In the previous chapter I showed that it was precisely this mentality of governance, expressed in the notion of the scientific-technical revolution and the new policy sciences that bridged the opposing great powers. But how can cooperation and opposition be combined simultaneously? Here I find it useful to turn to the social psychologist Karl Weick, who observed that actors do not necessarily have to share values or hold a consensual worldview in order to engage in cooperation with each other. According to Weick, it is sufficient that the otherwise opposing actors pursue similar goals and, importantly, consider each other predictable.[2] I suggest that the establishment of IIASA can be interpreted as precisely such a forward-oriented arrangement to enable a certain form of cooperation between the opposing great powers: mutual predictability was enhanced by bringing together leading policy scientists from East and West, whereas shared goals were articulated through applied systems research.

The history of IIASA should therefore be understood as a coproduction of a new type of Cold War world, where interdependency was actively forged rather than merely discovered, although the logic of discovery, to be sure, had an important symbolic value. I add to Weick's model the contention that neither shared goals nor mutual predictability were a given, but continuously constructed, negotiated, and reasserted. The case of IIASA is an example of such intense work in shaping both shared goals and mutual predictability, which was carried out by a great many mediators.

Who were these mediators? IIASA as a diplomatic initiative was the result of actions by top governmental officials: Lyndon Johnson proposed creating an East-West think tank and Soviet prime minister Aleksei Kosygin accepted his proposal, both sides considering this step as part of cultural diplomacy or an exercise of "soft power" in the presumably less ideological areas of science and technology. Next, other actors, like policy-oriented scientists, translated this diplomatic project into a particular research agenda and institutional setting. As a result of this organizational translation, new practices, objects, and subjectivities were forged and, eventually, even new consensual norms of effective and appropriate governance, equally applicable to capitalist and communist systems. It is in this way, I suggest, that the birth of IIASA is also a story of how a new understanding of the world and of governance was developed that transcended the Cold War division.

Approached from this angle, IIASA should not be reduced to a mere instrument in the hands of the US and Soviet governments, cynically using naïve scholars to window-dress Cold War competition. The governments involved in the establishment of IIASA were genuinely interested in the prospect of the new, applied policy sciences. Accordingly, I argue that IIASA was a crucial node in Cold War networks where new epistemologies and geopolitics of nascent policy sciences were formulated. Whereas chapters 3 and 4 focus in a greater detail on the ways in which this new governmentality was forged through networks and performed in the everyday life of IIASA scholars, this chapter traces the origins of the institute, discussing the struggles to create and institutionalize IIASA as a transnational nodal point of policy expertise. I begin with an outline of the original diplomatic idea, which was translated into practice by several particular communities of scientists and policy practitioners. Then I proceed to detail the negotiations around IIASA's scientific goals, which were to construct new subjects of governance and new governmental techniques, that is, global problems and systems analysis.

The Origins of the Idea of an East-West Institute

The initial idea of IIASA was American, launched by Lyndon B. Johnson's administration. Initially called an "East-West Institute," the planned organization was to be part of a wider diplomatic attempt to ameliorate US-Soviet relations and signal a new US policy toward Europe.[3] On December 15, 1966 Johnson's advisers McGeorge Bundy, Francis M. Bator, and Walt W. Rostow announced the idea to establish a scientific institute which would bridge the East and West divide by exploring and solving "the shared problems of industrial nations."[4] Where did this idea come from? According to Schwartz, Johnson launched a bridge-building discourse in May 1964, seeking to improve US relations with the Soviet Union and Eastern Europe.[5] In this context, Johnson was persuaded by a group of scholars and policy advisors that an international scientific organization could serve as a tool to better communicate with both the Soviet Union and the Eastern Bloc.[6] During the 1960s the United States launched several schemes with the intention of strengthening its ties with European countries, but in the beginning, these schemes targeted NATO members and did not include East-West cooperation. For instance, there were attempts to develop a new field of future studies, through which US foundations financed Futuribles, a French organization dedicated to the new methods of future studies established by Bertrand de Jouvenel in the late 1950s.[7] Higher-profile efforts involved the foundation of CERN (1954) and the NATO Science Committee (1958), and the idea of establishing "an MIT for

Europe," a technical university close to Paris. The latter project did not materialize as it was shot down by de Gaulle in 1963.[8]

These and other efforts, according to John Krige, led to the formation of a strong network of "transnational elites," anchored in Western European and US research and political organizations, which emerged by the 1960s.[9] To this I add that the idea of an East-West Institute expanded this transnational network to include the state socialist bloc. According to Schwartz and Gemelli, it was a trio of presidential advisors, Francis Bator, George Christian, and the author of the modernization theory, Walt Rostow, who put the idea of the institute on the presidential agenda. A particularly important role was played by former presidential security advisor McGeorge Bundy, who was charged by Johnson with the task of seeing this idea to completion.[10] Indeed, several of my interlocutors involved in the early process of negotiations argue that the East-West institute became a pet idea of Bundy, which he supported in his capacity as leader of the negotiations during his presidency of the Ford Foundation. Also, even when Bundy was formally replaced in the negotiations about the establishment of IIASA by the president of the National Academy of Sciences (NAS), Philip Handler, Bundy continued to influence the negotiation process and, later, the actual work at IIASA.[11] In this way, Bundy provided political leverage to the institute, yet the concrete form and agenda of this cooperation was shaped by other actors.

Although the idea was to create a multilateral institute, one thus less vulnerable to the swings of bipolar Soviet-US relations, the driving force behind the establishment of the East-West Institute depended strongly on US-Soviet dynamics. The institute was formally proposed to the Soviet Union, represented by Aleksei Kosygin, during the Glassboro Summit in 1967. The Soviets clearly treated the East-West Institute as part of their cooperation with the United States: for example, the list of Eastern Bloc countries to be invited to join was drawn up in Moscow, and the Soviets did not reveal this list until the very last moment of the negotiations. That the institute was seen as a Soviet-US rather than a multilateral project is also suggested by the fact that the scarce documents pertaining to the negotiations were archived at the GKNT in the folders of Soviet-US cooperation and not in the multilateral section.[12]

As it is the case with many innovative initiatives, the roots of the East-West Institute were diffuse and different actors were involved at different stages. It is clear, though, that a very particular network was behind the idea: in the United States these were presidential advisors like Walt Rostow and Bundy, scientists with a background at RAND, and other leading figures in the fields of OR and systems analysis. Their Soviet counterparts included the close entourage of the *éminence grise*, introduced in the previous chapter: Dzhermen

Gvishiani of the GKNT, the central organ for research and technology policy, industry, and transfer in the Soviet Union, which was formally in charge of the negotiations about the East-West Institute.[13] Gvishiani, the Soviet counterpart of Bundy, conducted the negotiations on behalf of the Soviet Union and was appointed chairman of IIASA in 1972, remaining in this post until 1986.[14] Other leading figures of the Soviet Academy of Sciences, particularly Vice President Mikhail Millionshchikov, the head of the GKNT Department for International Economic and Technoscientific Organizations (OMENTO), K. V. Ananichev, and his deputy Genrik Shvedov and colleague Andrei Bykov were also involved.[15] A specialist in control science, Aleksandr Letov, participated actively in the negotiations and later become one of deputy directors of IIASA. Generally, the Gvishiani entourage included scientists with a background in OR and cybernetic applications to planning and management, most of whom were drawn from the GKNT.[16]

What kind of political agenda drove the US interest in the East-West institute? Historians have detailed that Lyndon B. Johnson strongly relied on science as an instrument of diplomacy, where the geophysical sciences played a particularly important role.[17] Similarly symbolic was the US focus on systems approach: the East-West Institute was a clear initiative to involve the Soviets in closer cooperation on the cutting-edge field of policy sciences. Yet why would the United States seek to transfer tools that could strengthen the industries of their political opponent, the Soviet Union? One possible reason is that these governmental techniques were not seen as politically neutral, despite public declarations to the contrary, but were understood instead as structurally designed to fit a liberal market economy based on individual rational choice, negotiation, and market regulation. The systems approach and decision sciences, in other words, were understood to be an extension of a Western, liberal system of government and therefore bearing the potential to transform the Soviet system from within. This was matched with keen Soviet interest, albeit for different reasons. In the 1960s the GKNT was intensely concerned about advancing Soviet research and development, seeking Soviet membership in various international organizations in this field. The Soviet leaders pretty much agreed that Soviet scientists, planners, and managers needed to learn, and urgently at that, from American systems analysis or "systems planning," which was described as a magical method that allowed the Pentagon to save billions and propelled American industries to the foremost ranks of innovation and efficiency.[18]

However, it was neither Bundy nor Gvishiani who came up with the actual format for the institute. One path that led to IIASA was the American attempt to establish a counterpart to RAND in Europe.[19] Another path was broken by an active East-West networker and pioneer of econometrics, Wassily Leontief (more on Leontief in chapter 5), who advocated the idea of an East-West institute dedicated to econometrics as early as August 1964. Leontief wrote that

> experience of recent years has amply demonstrated that countries with quite different social and political systems still face similar, if not identical fundamental technical problems of rational organization of productive processes, of efficient utilization of labor, capital and natural resources, of optimal spatial distribution of economic activities, etc. It is now also widely recognised that the same basic scientific approaches can be effectively applied to the solution of these problems both in highly industrialised and in economically less advanced countries.[20]

He continued, "Not unlike nuclear research, exploratory work in the new field of technical quantitative economics involves a combination of mathematical analysis with large-scale empirical inquiry; only in the latter instance the source of primary facts and figures are not accelerators but also very costly, large-scale information-gathering operations."[21] Indeed, it was during a Moscow meeting with Gvishiani that Leontief proposed creating an international institute modeled on the example of the International Atomic Energy Agency (IAEA) and situated in Vienna.[22] The subsequent implementation of IIASA was too close to Leontief's proposal to be a mere coincidence: before IIASA moved into Schloss Laxenburg outside Vienna, the institute was in fact temporarily housed by IAEA. Leontief, however, did not actively participate in the actual process of negotiations about the future East-West institute.

Another path-breaking initiative concerned activities revolving around the Club of Rome (established in 1968), an informal gathering of the world's leading industrialists and politicians, initiated by Italian businessman Aurelio Peccei.[23] Peccei began organizing the future Club of Rome at about the same time the idea of the East-West institute appeared on Johnson's agenda, that is, in 1966. Indeed, this coincidence led some contemporaries to think that IIASA was also Peccei's idea, something which greatly irritated some of IIASA's founders, including Philip Handler and Solly Zuckerman.

Yet there was a lot of overlap between the East-West Institute and the Club of Rome: Gvishiani and Alexander King of OECD were members of the Club of Rome, and Peccei played a role as a mediator in the negotiations about IIASA. For instance, several months before Bundy's press conference in 1966 Peccei lectured about future world challenges in Washington, DC and contacted Hubert Humphrey, then the US vice president, whom he tried to convince of the need to initiate a multinational project dedicated to "international problems."[24] The establishment of the Club of Rome in 1968 preceded the establishment of IIASA, but the Club's world-famous report *The Limits to Growth* was published in 1972, just a few months before the signing of IIASA's charter. The central message of this report, which presented a forecast of the future state of the world, was that the world economy would collapse if industrialization and consumption continued at the same rates. This study was based on a simulation using Jay Forrester's model of system dynamics, which was further developed by Donella and Dennis Meadows and their team at MIT. The report was published by the Club of Rome and widely disseminated, becoming a bestseller and leading to heated debates in both East and West (I return to this in chapter 5).

The Americans took great pains to ensure that IIASA would not be confused with these parallel efforts by Peccei, especially because Carl Kaysen, Bundy's advisor, and Handler regarded *The Limits to Growth* report quite negatively.[25] A prominent decision scientist, Herbert Simon was also strongly annoyed with the report: "Jay Forrester, seeking publicity for the report's findings, gained permission to present it at PSAC [the President's Science Advisory Committee] meeting. My reaction was one of annoyance at this brash engineer who thought he knew how to predict social phenomena. In the discussion, I pointed out a number of the naïve features of the Club of Rome model."[26] However, Gvishiani, as his memoir suggests, was much more relaxed about *The Limits of Growth*, later arguing in his memoir that at that time the idea of "global interdependence" was running into difficulties and that the most important Meadows's contribution was to demonstrate a need for and the inevitability of such interdependence.[27] Peccei, in fact, was informed about the progress of IIASA as a matter of courtesy, but not invited to the advanced stages of the negotiations (e.g., meetings in Moscow in 1969 and London in 1970), which "disappointed" him.[28]

The East-West Institute Moves beyond Diplomatic Initiative

On December 16, 1966 Bundy held a press conference in New York at which he announced he had been empowered by the president to pursue the establishment of an international center to study problems faced by advanced countries. Such problems, Bundy emphasized in his speech, were presented by the need for efficient governance of large sectors: large enterprises, cities, systems of underground and air communications, hospitals, and farms. No nation, he continued, had or could possibly have a monopoly on such methods of governance. The envisioned center, therefore, would unite "engineers, economists, managers, experts on industrial production and others" and would evolve into an educational organization.[29]

The press reacted promptly by baptizing the suggested institute an "East-West RAND" and "East-West think tank." Indeed, the parallels with RAND were not coincidental: in the 1960s the US government and scholars were both looking for new organizational forms to feed expertise to the governmental decision makers. It was at that time, as noted by Christina Garsten and Thomas Medvetz, when think tanks began to emerge, organizations which were highly heterogeneous, yet united by their aspiration to bridge academic knowledge and government.[30] Alongside this "think-tank-ization" of governmental expertise, a boom of international organizations took place.[31] The dual trend of establishing specialized organizations, first to produce policy-relevant research and second to engage in international cooperation, converged in the East-West Institute.

It is therefore not surprising that in early 1967 Bundy turned to Henry Rowen, the president of RAND, to commission a preliminary study by its influential OR scholars Roger Levien and S. G. Winter Jr.[32] The resulting report on "an International Research Center and International Studies Program for Systematic Analysis of the Common Problems of Advanced Societies" laid out all the keywords revealing a particular epistemology at work. This study underscored the importance of systems analysis, still a new and ill-defined interdisciplinary field that built on quantitative methods and suggested that systems analysis could form the core orientation of the institute. The focus on "problems" was derived from RAND's mission and the field of operations research, which aimed to produce concrete answers to managerial questions. Finally, the term "advanced societies" invoked an increasingly influential idea of the postindustrial society and served as a diplomatic gesture to the Soviet Union, hinting at a presumed high level of Soviet development and thus inviting the Soviets to join the organization on an equal footing with the West.[33]

The East-West Institute as a diplomatic idea was launched at the famous Glassboro Summit between Johnson and Kosygin, arranged to complement an extraordinary session of the UN General Assembly in New Jersey, June 1967. The Glassboro Summit was an important point in the history of the Cold War, because during this meeting the idea that mutual vulnerability could bring about stability was first voiced, and Johnson and McNamara attempted to persuade the Soviets to reduce their anti-ballistic missile arsenal (outraged, Kosygin almost stormed out of the meeting).[34] But it was also at Glassboro that Johnson formally suggested establishing the East-West Institute (Kosygin bought this idea). In his memoir Gvishiani writes that he first heard about the East-West Institute from Kosygin after the Glassboro meeting, at which Gvishiani's wife, Kosygin's daughter, was present but Dzhermen Gvishiani was not.[35] Having returned from what was his first trip to the United States, Kosygin expressed his enthusiasm about the East-West Institute to Gvishiani, promised to use his personal contact with Johnson if needed, and assured him that he "would not let this thing to get buried" by the Soviet bureaucracy. Following official procedure, a proposal was submitted to the Politburo; then, as Gvishiani recalled, the decision to appoint him as a Soviet negotiator was reached "unusually quickly."[36]

If actual negotiations about the East-West Institute were kept outside of the public eye, the activities behind the scenes were intense. For instance, Bundy wrote to Kissinger saying that "the Russians recognize and even applaud the bridge-building value, but they now seek to go ahead in ways which will avoid giving the venture a political tone or a high level of publicity. Having taken what is almost certainly a governmental decision, they wish to proceed in what they choose to call a 'nongovernmental' way." Thus Bundy asked Washington to proceed in "a quiet way," acknowledging, at the same time, the political significance: "Even a quiet 'nongovernmental' venture has political complexities, and these should be handled so that both the White House and the Department of State are protected from embarrassment." [37]

During the following six years up to 1972 American research administrators and researchers crossed the Atlantic many times, traveling to Western Europe and the Soviet Union in attempts to recruit support for the East-West institute. Indeed, the diplomatic warm-up stage began even before Glassboro, when in 1966, Bundy, accompanied by Carl Kaysen of Princeton University and Eugene Staples of the Ford Foundation, embarked on a long and intense trip to London, Paris, Bonn, Rome, and Moscow. On his trip Bundy was also accompanied by Francis Bator and Howard Raiffa; some spouses were also present. Bundy met Harold Wilson, then prime minister of Britain, and Chancellor Willy Brandt of West Germany, both of whom promised to support the institute.[38] In 1967 the political heavyweight Bundy was replaced as US negotiator by Raiffa and Handler, who, equipped with RAND's report, began painstaking discussions about a research agenda that would be plausible and acceptable to all sides and practical arrangements as to the location of the institute.

Progress was slow, with the Soviets frequently—typically for them—failing to show up at meetings, and disruptive political events intervening, such as the Prague Spring in 1968. However, the United States sustained interest and the talks were resumed surprisingly quickly after the events in Prague.[39] In October 1968, and therefore just after the Soviet invasion of Czechoslovakia, Gvishiani, Solly Zuckerman, and Peccei met in London to discuss the institute. Although no concrete agreement was reached at that time, in 1969 Bundy expressed confidence that the Soviets had decided to go ahead with the East-West Institute. In his memo to Kissinger, Bundy wrote that Gvishiani, whom he met in April 1969, exuded a "business-like" and "decisive" air, concerned himself with the next practical steps, and gave the impression that "the decision has been taken in Moscow."[40] The

Soviets were not so sure: as Gvishiani recalls in his memoir, in 1969 both he and Mstislav Keldysh, president of the Soviet Academy of Sciences, still doubted that this institute would ever come into being. In any case, the name IIASA was already in circulation by December 1969.[41]

The talks about the East-West institute were part of the intensifying institutionalization of East-West technoscientific cooperation. Although a formal treaty of cooperation between the Soviet Academy of Sciences and NAS was signed in 1958, it was only in 1969 that a president of NAS met a president of the Soviet Academy of Sciences. When Handler encountered Keldysh at the Royal Academy of Engineering in Stockholm, more than twenty years had passed since the beginning of the Cold War.[42] It was therefore a significant meeting, symbolizing a key shift to a new stage of transatlantic relations between the opposing systems.

The establishment of IIASA was part of a renewed US-Soviet agreement on technoscientific cooperation, signed by Handler in Moscow in May 1972. By that time, however, it seems that American organizers of the East-West Institute were cautious about the risk of politicization. For instance, before signing the cooperation agreement, Handler wrote to the president's Office for Science and Technology, saying that while they were welcome to make a statement of progress on IIASA at the Nixon-Brezhnev summit, "we do not feel strongly about this matter."[43] In the Soviet Union, IIASA was mentioned in the talks about the Soviet-US technoscientific cooperation along with other prominent examples, such as docking the two nations' space stations and joint projects in oceanology.[44] There were, however, some concerns that IIASA should not be reduced to a "mere ornament" in this larger context of East-West cooperation.[45]

Another significant development that reinforced Soviet interest in the East-West institute was a series of decisions made by the Soviet government with regard to the future development of the computer industry. In 1969 the Soviet government decided to abandon developing its own computer system and to clone the IBM systems instead. Accordingly, the Soviets actively sought to extract any innovative computer technology from West. It was not only their understanding that domestic research and development in computer technology would not be able to keep pace with US industry, but also their awareness of their internal organizational inefficiency that made Soviet research policy makers turn to international technological transfer. For instance, Gvishiani notes, in retrospect, that he found it easier to obtain new technologies from abroad than from the Soviets' own military complex because of secrecy and departmentalism.[46]

In this way, the curious title of the International Institute for Applied Systems Analysis was a technocratic cryptogram, containing keywords that helped place the institute high on the Soviet agenda of international cooperation. For the Soviets the category of "systems analysis" not only referred to an intellectual approach, but also served as shorthand for computer technologies. Gvishiani is quite candid about this, as he describes the hopes that the institute would help Soviet scholars "access the most contemporary methods of work and computer technology which was banned for export to the Soviet Union by CoCom."[47] Furthermore, the archival documents of the GKNT show that GKNT officials were openly requesting that Western businessmen bypass the computer embargo and tried to leverage negotiations about the East-West Institute to pressure the Americans into rescinding their embargo. For instance, during his visit to Moscow in May 1970, Handler was given a confidential paper containing a vague phrase which Handler tried to clarify, asking his hosts "whether explicitly this paragraph should be interpreted to mean that unless the United States regulations with respect to export of computers to the USSR are altered, the Soviets would not agree to participate in the Institute." Handler did not receive an explicit answer from the GKNT.[48] At a later stage Gvishiani, accompanied by Viktor Glushkov, the leading Soviet computer scientist in charge of the national computerization program (OGAS), insisted that the institute would acquire the best computers possible and was disappointed by the "cautious" approach of the Americans.[49]

Did the Soviets cynically hope to exploit the envisioned institute to meet the needs of their increasingly obsolete computer industry? On the one hand, this was certainly an important reason: for example, in 1972 the GKNT's official classification attributed operations research and systems analysis to a branch of "Control, Automation and Computer Technology."[50] The centrality of computer technology was also acknowledged in the US-Soviet cooperation agreement, which stated that, "with respect to computer sciences and technology, the Parties noted that both Academies are cooperating in the newly established International Institute for Applied Systems analysis and that they will also give appropriate support to the activities of the US-USSR Joint Commission regarding the application of computers to management, referred to above."[51]

On the other hand, there was definitely more to the Soviet interest than searching for a way to bypass the embargo on computer technology. According to Gavin and Lawrence, Johnson's diplomatic bridge building was a strategic move designed to shift the American mentality of governance to embrace global issues.[52] Although in a different shape, and albeit slowly, a similar shift was taking place in the Soviet Union. Beginning in the late 1950s Soviet economists searched for new techniques to revive Soviet planning, and they had a plentiful choice here: decision sciences, in particular those associated with the emerging systems analysis, but also predictive approaches emphasizing long-range and long-term processes were on the rise in the United States.[53] Moreover, as I showed in chapter 1, there was a new constellation of powerful networks emerging in the Soviet Union, which linked the fields of economic planning with science and technology policy, which were supported by the tandem of Kosygin-Gvishiani, and which built on the theory of scientific-technical revolution to legitimize East-West cooperation.

I argue, therefore, that the idea of the envisioned East-West institute should be interpreted in precisely this context of changing ideas about governance in both the United States and the Soviet Union. Soviet modernizers sought to learn from the United States: a good example of this orientation is the influential Gvishiani's volume on management theories, in which he described the history of Russian management only in relation to US developments. In such writings, as well as in the theory of the scientific-technical revolution, many fundamental elements of US modernization theory were received by the Soviets and translated to match their local context. As a result, a shared understanding of the drivers of economic and technoscientific progress, and also of the intellectual and material tools needed to implement this progress, emerged and made IIASA possible.

I do emphasize technoscientific development as the key rationale behind the East-West Institute. Nevertheless, foreign and defense policy mattered too, although these aspects could not be discussed explicitly in the negotiations. Enhancing mutual predictability was a key task of the American rationalization of nuclear strategy. This is supported by the fact that even when Johnson's idea of bridge building faded from the US foreign policy agenda, the project of the East-West Institute was retained. A possible reason for this could be what John Lewis Gaddis described as Nixon and Kissinger's notion of the world as structured by multifaceted powers, which could not be reduced to sovereign territory, the national economy, and weapons systems.[54] Accordingly, the containment strategy was modified to include mutual restraint, coexistence, and cooperation. In the world thus conceived there was a place for the future IIASA.

Cold War Policy Sciences: Constructing Neutrality

A single universal development trajectory, as posited by modernization theory, provided a solid platform from which to launch the idea of the East-West Institute. However, the actual design of the institute was a product of subtle negotiations about which sciences and research themes were appropriate for East-West cooperation, the key requirement being that the selected approaches should not conflict with either capitalist or communist values and governmental agendas. A mission impossible? Not quite. This institutional rapprochement was achieved through, first, organizational design, and, second, a choice of scientific disciplines, member organizations, and individual scientists. In this section I discuss the way in which certain notions of the political were censored from the agenda of the East-West institute, making way for a particular type of politics, which actually emerged as a result of its design.

As mentioned earlier, the East-West Institute was part of an intense and complex effort to create a new type of organization, able to link scientific research, traditionally undertaken by universities, and governmental policy-making. International organizations were deemed to be particularly suitable for such a purpose. The plans for the East-West Institute, indeed, demonstrate a wish to situate this initiative in a wider context of emerging organizations, including, for instance, the European Institute of Technology, the NATO European Computer Science Institute, the UN Economic Commission for Europe, even the Pugwash initiative for a World Science Center.[55] Consequently, as to the organizational design, there was no need for the founders of the East-West Institute to reinvent the wheel and they did not attempt to. Instead, several existing templates were used.[56]

The blueprint for the institute was prepared by RAND's scientists and, as mentioned earlier, the institute was described on several occasions as "an international RAND." It is quite curious that the fact that RAND was one of the key sites for US military research did not seem to bother the Soviets. Instead, the Soviets understood the RAND model to be a huge advantage. Many sources reveal the awe that RAND inspired in Soviet scholars and policy makers, which testifies to Audra Wolfe's observation about rather isomorphic values espoused by the American and Soviet military-industrial complexes.[57] And indeed, one of the meanings of "the political" referred to closed, military research. Following RAND's example, the East-West Institute allowed the possibility of performing industry-oriented research, but it was noted that research with direct military applications would not be pursued on the premises.

If RAND provided a model for combining fundamental and applied research and linking this research to governmental agendas, other, international organizations were used as templates for designing the form of Cold War cooperation. Here the most important sources of ideas were the European Organization for Nuclear Research (CERN) and the IAEA, established in 1954 and 1957, respectively. Other organizations were considered as strategic partners, such as the International Federation of the Institutes of Perspective Research, which focused on global rather than national issues. During the early stage of negotiations Gvishiani tried to establish a relationship between IIASA and the federation: "We, and first of all, Peccei, decided that it was necessary to consciously support both projects, considering that it was useful to have not one, but several new international organizations existing that engaged with global and universal problems." The Americans, however, did not support this idea of explicit cooperation. Another, similar, initiative formulated in 1966 was Nobel's Symposium, eventually organized by biochemist Arne Tiselius and Sam Nilsson in 1969.[58] Other organizations were deemed useful for further particulars; for instance, at a later stage, IIASA borrowed a summer school model from the Global Atmospheric Research Program (GARP).[59]

The institute was to be an international, nongovernmental organization or, according to Handler, a "quasigovernmental agency," which never received money directly from the government, with the exception of reimbursements for expenses. Nevertheless, if Western member organizations were academic societies and institutes located at arm's length from the government, the state socialist bloc was, of course, represented by the centrally commanded research institutes. The US member organization was the National Academy of Sciences, a venerable organization created by Congress in 1863. Through its National Research Council (NRC) NAS influenced the US government[60] and, according to Herbert Simon, actively engaged in creating the government's policy agenda.[61]

In turn, the physical location of the institute had to further reinforce the image of political neutrality. The RAND report recommended locating the East-West Institute in a country that did not belong to the NATO or the Warsaw pact, was not only "industrialized" so that it could ensure adequate standards, but also "attractive," that is, centrally located, politically stable, and open to scientists from all regimes. Acknowledging the difficulty of finding a country that would fit all these criteria, Sweden, Austria, and Switzerland were named as candidates, as well as France and Italy. Here it must be added that the number of possible locations, all of them in Europe, later grew to include obviously NATO and not-so-neutral countries such as Britain (the Oxford-Harwell area was proposed) and the Federal Republic of Germany (Munich). It was clear, though, that both the Americans and Soviets preferred Vienna to other proposals.[62] Practicalities were also thought through: such a center would employ a staff of a hundred and fifty to two hundred and cost three to five million USD a year to run, something that was described as a good value because the US contribution was calculated to amount to only a 0.5 percent increase in the annual NSF budget.[63]

Another meaning of "politically neutral" pertained to political ideology. This was a highly complicated issue, resolved, in fact, by employing a new idea that policy sciences were, by their own virtue, exempt from conflicting ideological values, whereas the humanities and social sciences based on qualitative methods were excluded from the envisioned cooperation. The NAS membership could have had some influence on setting IIASA's research agenda in order to exclude social sciences and humanities for the most part. Until the late 1960s NAS was dominated by physical and biological scientists; there were very few psychologists and anthropologists. The first non-natural scientist on the board of the National Research Council, Herbert Simon, claimed that "natural scientists simply were not sufficiently aware of the social science aspects of policy questions to respond appropriately to them."[64]

Thus it was system-cybernetic policy sciences that came to the fore. For instance, the 1967 RAND report states that there was no Eastern European or Western European operations research, just "operations research," a technique "relatively independent of social structures and national values." The same applied to "mathematical programming," "systems analysis," "program budgeting," and "cost-effectiveness analysis."[65] To get a clearer idea of where to start with the concrete agenda, Raiffa and Bower commissioned the Ford Foundation to survey the existing systems analysis methods from 1968 to 1969. A long list of different general and specific areas was produced.[66] A choice of equally "ideologically neutral" themes was also important, with industrial management, energy production, and distribution deemed suitably neutral, while public order, education, and health services were considered to be more ideologically charged and therefore less suitable for the East-West Institute. Recalling that data gathering had proven to be a reliable vehicle for international cooperation, RAND scientists suggested placing this task high on the institute's agenda.[67]

The choice of leaders cemented the founders' determination to make the East-West Institute an international bastion of policy sciences. When the organization of the East-West Institute was delegated to NAS, it appointed an advisory committee chaired by Kenneth Arrow. This committee included the presidential science advisor Joseph Bower, Carl Kaysen, Tjalling Koopmans, and Howard Raiffa.[68] Then, the guidelines for the search for a director indicated that a candidate must be able to combine the systems analysis imperative of problem solving with theoretical or methodological questions rather than addressing pure theory or methodology.[69] A list of potential candidates for director of the institute included not only the leading scholars in policy sciences, but also individuals associated with the research and development sector; for instance, one of the candidates was Ralph Gomory, the research director at IBM.[70] Thus were listed such luminaries of decision sciences as Richard Cyert, Kenneth Arrow, and Howard Raiffa ("the obvious candidate, but Harvard already has paid for 200% of his time").[71] Further candidates included some prominent representatives of state planning, such as the founding father of the French Commissariat of Plan, Pierre Masse ("too old"), the director of Johnson's the Great Society program Charles Schultze ("would be fantastic"), the pioneers in the mathematical methods of linear programming Tjalling Koopmans and Leontief's pupil Robert Solow ("another star"); both Koopmans and Solow were later awarded the Nobel Prize in economy (1975 and 1987, respectively). The other candidates included RAND scientists and federal budget planners like Charles Zwick, the Keynesian James Tobin, and the Belgian econometrician Jacques Dreze,[72] as well as the pioneer in public management

Arjay Miller of the Stanford Graduate School of Business. It was desired that the director not only have stellar academic credentials, but also sufficient energy to get the institute's administration going.[73] Although the documents predictably did not contain detailed political comments, it was noted that Herbert Simon, also considered a candidate for the director's post, would not be suitable because of his anticommunist views.[74] Later documents contained further names, such as RAND scientist Charles Hitch, and indicated that the search for a director should be extended to "mathematical engineering communities."[75]

In his memo to Henry Kissinger about his meeting with Gvishiani, Bundy described the future IIASA as "an institute of advanced methodological studies," which was concerned with "relatively abstract systems analysis of the sort that the theoretical types in our business schools do."[76] Consultations were arranged with leading American organization scholars, described as the finest minds available. A brainstorming meeting was arranged which included the pioneers of OR and dynamic programming and decision analysts Richard Bellman and C. West Churchman, George Dantzig, Thomas C. Schelling, Ronald Howard of Stanford, as well as Charles Schultze (then at the Brookings Institution), William Gorham (ex-RAND, ex-Great Society), Robert Dorfman, Frank Fisher, economist Roy Radner, and applied mathematician Herbert A. Scarf (ex-RAND), as well as Bundy, Bator, Bower, and Raiffa.[77] The British cybernetician Stafford Beer was listed among those interested in the project.[78] On the agenda of this meeting was the organizational structure and thematic directions of the center. A follow-up memo indicated that "even the Best Kinds" had difficulty in focusing on the question together.[79]

This search for a director of the East-West institute shows clearly that it was not to be a mere puppet in the hands of US and Soviet foreign policy makers, but an institution with an agenda of its own. These and other lineups of the finest minds in policy sciences (all male at that!) are also revealing for including many ex-RAND scientists, as well as the mathematics-oriented Keynesians. Although some of them were experienced Cold War warriors (Bundy, Kaysen), clearly an effort had been made not to include, or at least not at the advanced stages of the negotiations, either conservative neoliberals or Kremlinologists whose work described the Soviet Union as an enemy.[80] Furthermore, the search for a director of the East-West institute clearly also revealed a strong belief that the authority of scientific distinction was able to transcend political rifts. According to Handler, "To be effective you must be trusted. Our ability to hold that public trust derives from, first of all, the scientific distinction of the members of NAS: this is the sine qua non. Without that kind of membership all of the rest becomes useless."[81]

The East-West institute had to be a substantial addition to world science and not just another platform for diplomatic rituals, as many UN agencies notoriously were. This was a struggle, however, because Soviet intentions were often hard to read. For instance, the Soviet delegation did not show up at a meeting set up to agree on the key functions of the Institute, organized by the University of Sussex, June 16–21, 1968. In addition to political commitment, scholarly commitment was also lacking. Thus in Sussex Harvard economist Robert Dorfman indicated that it would be hard for this center to hire "the very best" because permanently working at IIASA meant emigration and abandoning a normal career path. For this reason visiting positions would work better, and the institute would not be a "great research center with a style and specialty of its own," but rather something resembling the Stanford Center for Advanced Study in the Behavioral Sciences (established in 1954 with the aim of promoting policy-relevant behavioral sciences): "an excellent and stimulating place to go for a couple of years to concentrate on your research in close proximity with other like-minded, first-class men from other places."[82]

In the end it was Howard Raiffa who was appointed director of the future IIASA. Raiffa's role in the professionalization of management studies and the decision sciences was comparable only to the one played by Simon. Born into a New York Jewish family, Raiffa had been contracted by Harvard University to establish the Kennedy School of Government; one of his roles was to make management, a discipline about which, as he wrote in his memoir, he had no clue, more scientific. Another important feature of Raiffa was his moderate political views. Retrospectively described as an arms control scholar, Raiffa was less interested in the laboratory models of game theory than the empirical investigation of observed "real life" decisions. In all, it seemed that under Raiffa's guidance the East-West Institute would find a way to begin sailing the rough waters of the Cold War.

All of these factors—the internal composition of NAS, the rise of decision sciences and systems analysis, as well as the Soviet belief in the political neutrality of mathematics-based approaches and cybernetics—contributed to narrowing down the disciplinary focus of the East-West Institute.[83] It must be added, however, that both sides showed some flexibility. For instance, the process of negotiations revealed that the Soviets could be less stubborn and unanimous than the Americans had anticipated. Describing his meeting with Gvishiani (who was considerably late) in June 1972, Raiffa recalled having "correctly anticipated" the Soviets' unwillingness to include projects on welfare, drugs, youth alienation, and police, but also nutrition and transplants in IIASA's agenda. However, Raiffa "was surprised" by the Soviets' positive response and even "enthusiasm" for research into fire protection, urban renewal, alcoholism, and genetics. In contrast, the Soviets pressured the Westerners to focus on large-scale engineering projects, like canals and airports—indeed, the subjects that were included in the RAND proposal of 1967, but later abandoned by the Americans in favor of smaller scale management programs.[84] Nevertheless, the French pushed urban planning projects, being quite candid (to Raiffa) that this was a way to introduce the social issues that were otherwise avoided by the Soviets.[85] Realizing that there was less internal consensus in the Soviet Union than previously thought, Raiffa chose to "be aware of sensitive areas" and "keep pushing and probing," so that the Soviets eventually agreed to include urban studies in the institute's research agenda.[86]

Meanwhile for the Soviets, it seems, the key issue was to ensure that the future IIASA would focus on the use of computers and mathematical modeling to solve the problems of management and control. The Soviet position was developed at the GKNT, outlining three large areas: "a) the problems of general theory and methodology of systems research as applied to the creation of structures and forms of organizational control systems for large industrial enterprises; b) the economic aspects of major technological projects; c) the problems of environmental pollution and optimal use of natural resources, d) the problems of health system organization and the application of systems analysis in medicine and biology."[87] This shows clearly that at this stage the Soviets were quite averse to including system-cybernetic governance of wider aspects of society in the envisioned IIASA, although by that time system-cybernetic governmental discourse was well-established in Soviet public discourse inside of the country.

Although the Soviets and Americans reached a consensus to include both nature and technology as sources of problems, not all problematic issues could be addressed. Such were any issues associated with the nuclear sector. Accordingly, the negotiators were particularly careful not to associate with disarmament activists (or any activists at all), especially the Pugwash movement. A good illustration of this position is the correspondence between Leontief and Bundy. In 1969 Leontief wrote to Bundy inquiring about whether the planned institute would include "technical economics." It appeared that Leontief was not included in the pre-IIASA talks, although, as I have mentioned earlier, he had fostered a similar idea since 1966. Bundy thus assured Leontief that this institute "would certainly include technical economics," but also warned about the politically sensitive character of this project, writing that

> we seem to be in a rather delicate period in the wider business of Soviet-American relations. And since I am dealing with fairly senior Soviet officials (albeit in a 'non-governmental' way), I think it might be just as well for you not to raise the question as a member of Pugwash group.[88]

In 1971 the charter of the East-West institute, now officially called IIASA, was drafted. The chosen location was Laxenburg, Vienna, because of a generous offer by the Austrian chancellor Bruno Kreisky and because the Soviets preferred Vienna. By June 1972 the French suggestion to house the institute at Fontainebleau, near INSEAD (Toulouse was also suggested), was dropped on the grounds

FIGURE 1. Signing the IIASA charter, London, UK, 1972. From left to right: Dr. Philip Handler, US National Academy of Sciences, Dr. Peter Warren, UK Cabinet Office, Lord Solly Zuckerman, UK Cabinet Office, Dr. Dzhermen Gvishiani, USSR State Committee for Science and Technology, Dr. Andrei Bykov, USSR State Committee for Science and Technology. Courtesy of IIASA.

that the French government could not ensure either full funding for the venue or a beneficial tax regime.[89] Up to the very last minute, working with the Soviets was not easy: Raiffa traveled to Moscow to discuss interim arrangements and the charter, only to find himself unable to get through the GKNT's secretary to see Gvishiani and to discover that neither Letov nor Bykov knew about his arrival or plans.[90] Nevertheless, when they finally met, Raiffa found Gvishiani "amicable and constructive" as always. In contrast, things went smoothly in Vienna thanks to the Austrian Ambassador to the Soviet Union, Walter Wodak, who mediated effectively between IIASA negotiators and Kreisky. "The Viennese," wrote Raiffa, were "gracious hosts" and "they really want IIASA."[91]

The IIASA charter was signed by the representatives of scholarly organizations from the United States, the Soviet Union, the United Kingdom, Canada, Czechoslovakia, France, the GDR and the FRG, Japan, Bulgaria, Italy, and Poland in London on October 4, 1972.[92] The United States and the Soviet Union fulfilled their commitment to support the institute with about one million USD each annually; the remaining members contributed the same amount together.[93] IIASA, in this way, was a truly exceptional case of Soviet international cooperation, because in no other major international organization, be it the UN, UNESCO, WHO, or

IAEA, did the Soviet Union match the United States financially (the Soviets usually paid about half of the US contribution).[94]

The newly born IIASA was both a symptom and a cause of the changing postwar governmentality. Following Gaddis, it does seem that the birth of IIASA was enabled by the US foreign policy of asymmetric containment, demilitarization of foreign policy, and desecuritization of ideology, propagated by Kennedy and Johnson. The idea of the institute also fitted well into the 1960s' concern with scientific expertise and policy sciences. Although some argued that the idea of IIASA was implemented because it became Bundy's pet project and "Bundy mattered,"[95] the institutional explanation should not be discarded. IIASA was an institutional response to the emerging new worldview of multifaceted power and multilateral relations. Furthermore, there was domestic interest, arguably both in the United States and the Soviet Union: in the following chapters I show that the negotiations around the establishment of IIASA served as a vehicle for consolidating the American policy and planning sciences as they were embedded in the ex-RAND, ex-Great Society community of scholars. For the Soviets, IIASA was part of the ongoing search for a way to advance the computer industry.

In the 1960s the governments in the East and West reformulated their national agendas to incorporate increasingly complex issues that could not be addressed within the boundaries of one state or by one government alone. As I have argued earlier, both intellectuals and policy makers argued that the scientific-technical revolution was launching new paths of development in "advanced industrial countries," so there was an acute understanding that new ways to foresee and control technoscientific, economic, and social change were needed. Furthermore, the Cold War agenda was part of this governmental concern as well: a struggle for world hegemony meant that national issues were fought on a global scale, but the world was also redefined as beset by such environmental and infrastructural challenges with which no single government could cope alone.[96] Both the scientific-technical revolution and the idea of the imminent coming of postindustrial society formed an intellectual base for Eastern and Western regimes to develop new contact areas, declaring them immune to ideological contestation. It is in these contact areas that shared, transnational goals and settings for building mutual predictability were conceived.

One outcome of this was a stark and even ruthless effort to depoliticize systems analysis. This is well demonstrated by some important omissions of both disciplinary fields and individual scholars. The absence of Leontief (a member of the Pugwash movement) and the anti-Soviet Herbert Simon—but also Stafford Beer—are telling here. From 1970 Beer was involved in applying the systems approach in practice to run the Chilean economy through the Project Cybersyn.⁹⁷ Although mentioned as a potentially interesting figure, Beer was not included in the negotiations. It has to be added that once diplomatic issues were resolved and IIASA was formally established, both Leontief and Beer cooperated with the institute. However, producing a politically neutral systems approach was an ongoing process, and different strategies of de-politicization were used at different organizational levels. The subsequent chapters detail how, through particular networks, organizational culture, and research projects, the systems approach redefined the Cold War world.

3

SHAPING A TRANSNATIONAL SYSTEMS COMMUNITY (1)

Networks and Institutions

> **Good systems analysis, like good politics, is the art of the possible.**
> —John Casti, *Linear Dynamical Systems*, 1987
>
> **Can anyone practice systems analysis without knowing it? The answer is a vehement yes.**
> —Stanford Optner, "Introduction," *Systems Analysis*, 1973

In 1979 McGeorge Bundy and Dzhermen Gvishiani wrote the foreword to *Organization for Forecasting and Planning: Experience in the Soviet Union and the United States*, a volume of essays by Soviet and American scholars at Moscow State University and New York University, and by managers and policy makers from the respective countries, who met at a series of seminars, held in Sochi, New York, Moscow, and Washington, DC, and funded by the Ford Foundation and the GKNT.[1] While the Soviet papers contained details about the bureaucratic structures of formal planning, US authors outlined the systems approach to management. Thus a portrayal of the Soviet State Planning Committee (Gosplan) was accompanied by Igor Ansoff's theory of management as a dynamic system, consisting of flows and regulated by a time dimension (such as the planning-programming-budgeting system, or PPBS). The influential editors of this volume made it clear that system-cybernetic governmentality was beyond the ideological struggle between communism and capitalism.

In this chapter I discuss the shifts in institutional and intellectual frameworks, policies, and social practices that enabled the Soviets to embrace an American science of governance—systems analysis. After Stalin's death, the communist ideological struggle with Western science did not cease, but a new space emerged, allowing for a universal understanding of exact sciences such as mathematics and physics. These sciences were understood to be simply beyond any ideological and, indeed, political concerns. But how could depoliticization be applied to systems analysis, a science of forging and controlling not only technical structures and processes, but also societies and ways of thinking? After all, systems analysis was a method to influence and thus to some extent control decision makers themselves. Mathematical methods, used to process large amounts of data and calculate efficiency, were a significant part of systems analysis, but so were fundamentally qualitative ways of defining the problems, shaping communication, and formulating criteria for choice. Should one interpret this East-West rapprochement of policy sciences as evidence of hypocrisy, because, as one could presume, the Soviets would certainly never embrace a liberal democratic technology of governance? Could this be a proof that system-cybernetic policy sciences constituted an illiberal governmentality, adopted by East-West technocrats? After all, back in the 1940s Patrick Blackett, the Nobel Prize winner and the founding father of operations research (OR), the predecessor of the systems approach, had defined OR as an aid for command and control *par excellence*. Also, the system-cybernetic notion of control promised vertical integration, that is, top-down command, within any complex system, a promise that certainly appealed to the Soviets.[2]

Questions like these bothered many historians of Cold War science. Indeed, the historiography of OR, to some extent including the systems approach, described the development of this field during the Cold War as a sprawling evil empire of technoscientific experts, who eventually morphed from being wizards of the Cold War military-industrial complex into prophets of neoliberalism. In their studies, Peter Galison, Paul Edwards, and S. M. Amadae highlighted the ways in which computerization, quantification, and automatic control led to military and nondemocratic applications.[3] The critics described a spillover of these approaches from the military to the civil sector, interpreting it as a colonization, in which a militarist and pseudorational logic captured previously political, participatory forms of governance in such areas as urban and social planning. Further, as early as the 1960s the dominance of quantitative methods in systems analysis, in particular cost-benefit calculus, was criticized from the sociological perspective, for instance by Ida Hoos.[4]

While these criticisms correctly identified parts of the emerging Cold War governmentality that were based on a paranoid vision of society or obsessed with an utopian idea of rationality, I suggest that these qualities alone do not explain the international appeal of systems analysis as a policy science, particularly its lasting legacy in policy analysis.[5] In their studies of scientific expertise in the authoritarian regimes, Paul Josephson and James Scott argue that large technological systems appealed to American and Soviet industrial planners alike, because they expressed a particular form of modernity, based on a belief in human mastery over nature and the capacity of human reason to control the future.[6] Similarly, and following Scott, Hunter Heyck proposed a classification of the US social science as high modernist in the 1950s–1970s, as it embraced concepts of system, modeling, and organization.[7] However, I doubt that the international appeal of the systems approach can be explained solely by presumed high modernist ambitions of control. One reason is that systems-based policy sciences were more heterogeneous than has been presented so far, with substantial internal tensions and disagreements involving such matters as the role of quantitative methods, and political process and participation.[8] Furthermore, criticism of utopian notions of controllability and rationality in policy science came not only from external actors, like environmental and civil rights activists, but also from the inside of the systems analysis field itself.[9]

Focusing on IIASA, the key site where the systems approach was forged as a transnational assemblage of new methods, disciplines, social networks, and institutions, I intend to show that there was an important side of the systems approach, which entailed a particularly new type of knowledge/power constellation, one which does not easily map to the instrumentalist, rationalist version of policy science. For one thing, system-cybernetic sciences were incredibly diverse internally. Ida Hoos wondered in 1972 how systems analysis was able to become so powerful despite being so ill-defined, with its methods lacking in precision and results so irreproducible. She also proposed that systems analysis was the central technology of governance in the twentieth century, because it not only provided solutions, but actively *constructed* policy problems.[10] Indeed, particularly from the early 1980s on, many proponents of systems research questioned many of the foundational principles concerning knowledge, rationality, and control typically associated with high modernism and large-scale technologies, pointing out the centrality of uncertainty in governmental projects. Most strikingly, this revision took place on both sides of the Iron Curtain.

In this context, the history of IIASA is of particular significance because it reveals the co-construction of a particular culture of scientific expertise as well as the world for which this expertise was intended. Although the idea of a system had circulated in philosophy and natural sciences at least since the seventeenth century, it was after World War II that systems analysis, systems theory, and the systems approach gained momentum. One of the tasks of IIASA was to create a scholarly consensus on systems analysis as a field, by enrolling relevant scholars and shaping their professional identity as systems analysts. As it turned out, this project was less about acquiring a clearly defined professional identity, and more about obtaining a set of skills, tools, and networks with which systems analysts could practice their policy-oriented science. Hoos critically described this set of skills and tools as "expertness," contrasting it with "a proper science."[11] However, I propose that it was precisely the focus on expertness, method, and social construction of knowledge that made the systems approach an innovative, postpositivist science.

In order to appreciate this, we need to look beyond the intellectual history, to the social and political history of the development of the systems approach. In this chapter, drawing on archival materials and specially conducted interviews with former IIASA resident scholars and administrators, I examine the academic, organizational, and political processes that shaped IIASA's agenda, paying particular attention to the strategies of politicizing and depoliticizing systems analysis as a platform of East-West cooperation. I reconstruct this process in order to demonstrate how the intertwining intellectual and social organization of the East-West community of systems scholars contributed to a formulation of a new governmentality of the world system.[12] My aim is to show how important and constitutive the social organization of systems approach was, in which horizontal networks cutting across national bureaucracies and state borders and organizational culture played a fundamentally important role.[13]

I argue that social and institutional contexts are particularly significant for understanding the ambiguous legacy of Cold War systems analysis. Whereas a growing number of institutes, departments, committees, and private companies had been dedicated to systems research in both East and West since the 1950s, informal organization of this scientific expertise was of utmost importance. Historians and sociologists theorized about informal processes in knowledge production with the help of such concepts as an association, a community, a network, a coalition, and even a tribe, where actors are bound through representations of intellectual kinship and rituals. Importantly, these notions of the organization of science were also articulated from inside of the systems analysis field.[14] The burgeoning academic debates over these concepts hint at the importance of this phenomenon of informal association in the context of formal bureaucratic structures and, in particular, international cooperation schemes, but they also show how difficult it is to find an appropriate conceptual apparatus to designate such informal practices. This difficulty is magnified by the fact that the character of a given association depends on a particular context. The same individuals may behave like a community bound by norms and rituals in one context, but appear as a loosely coupled network in another, or else form a tight, albeit short-lived coalition around a certain interest on yet another occasion.

In this chapter I intend to show the importance of such shifting forms of association in the development of East-West systems analysis. I distinguish several formations that played different roles at different times. The first was a strategic coalition, which gathered to forge a new transnational field of systems analysis. This strategic coalition was active mostly in the early stages of the organization of the East-West Institute, from 1966 to the early 1970s. The second formation was the internal informal organization within IIASA, which enabled the institute to perform its diplomatic role as a Cold War bridge from 1972 to 1990. A third formation was again a strategic coalition, activated at the moment of crisis in 1981 when the Reagan administration discontinued paying US membership fees, threatening IIASA's survival. All these informal associations were shaped with an aim to ease Cold War tension and socialize actors from the opposing regimes into a new fraternity of world system governance.

To illustrate this, I also describe in detail life inside IIASA, mostly as it was narrated by the scholars themselves. Their stories of encounters between Eastern and Western scientists and then working alongside each other reveal a great deal about mutual adaptation, possibilities, and the limitations of the allegedly neutral platform. Undeniably, the neutrality of IIASA was not confined to its charter, but had to be continuously reinvented and reaffirmed in everyday practices of scientific cooperation. Both operational definitions and everyday practices that aimed at maintaining the neutrality of IIASA acted powerfully and transformatively, affecting both the Eastern and Western sides in important ways.

Systems Analysis and the Systems Approach: Debates and Definitions

I begin with an overview of systems analysis and the systems approach, which is a necessary if daunting task. Indeed, I use both terms interchangeably as their meanings overlap: systems analysis is generally understood as being a more applied, quantitative method while the systems approach is understood as somewhat more general, including a high variety of qualitative and quantitative methods; I will return to discuss this distinction shortly. Major work has been done to trace the impact of the systems approach on such disciplines as electronic engineering, biology, the environmental science, linguistics, and economics and management science.[15] But the systems approach also played an important role in shaping of the late twentieth-century's governance. Existing internal histories of systems analysis, patchy and incomplete as they are, reveal the significance of new networks, joining academic, defense and private organizations, where RAND, the MITRE and IIASA were key actors.[16] Their legacy was significant and lasting: some early proponents of the systems approach in the 1960s and 1970s, such as Giandomenico Majone and Frank Fischer, became active participants in the normative elaboration of transnational governmental systems like as the European Union.[17] Also, prominent public policy theorists, who would later develop a more qualitative, discourse and social network analysis of public policy, such as Majone and Brian Wynne, had links with IIASA. This extraordinary link between theory and practice makes the East-West dimension of the history of systems approach an even more intriguing object of study. To probe the history of the systems approach is to conduct an archaeology of contemporary governance.

An overview of the origins and types of the systems approach is also complicated by the fact that systems studies were, and are, internally diverse and hybrid, and diversified into many subfields, such as systems theory, systems engineering, systems cybernetics, and systems analysis. These related approaches can be roughly divided into theoretical and applied areas, whereas theoretical or philosophical thinking about systems has a particularly long history in humanities and biology. This division is relevant for my argument, because IIASA would attempt to bridge the gap between applied and basic systems research. Also, both theoretical and applied approaches turned out to be suitable for East-West transfer and cooperation, this suitability being, as I will show, a product of special tactics.

As is the case with much of modern science, the development of systems theory in the twentieth century knew no national borders. The founding father of general systems theory, Ludwig von Bertalanffy (1901–1972), was born in Austria. He developed his ideas in the 1920s, but only gained prominence as a US émigré scientist in the 1940s.[18] Similarly, innovative thinking on systems emerged in prewar Russia in the works of Aleksander A. Bogdanov (born Malinovskii) and Vladimir Vernadskii in the 1920s and 1930s.[19] Bogdanov, a revolutionary and a philosopher, formulated his famous tectology (*Tektologiia*, 1912 and 1916), an organizational theory of a self-regulating industrial society, which relied not so much on trust in experts as on automatic technology. Vernadskii, inspired by the French philosopher Pierre Teilhard de Chardin, developed a theory of intertwined biological, material, and intellectual planetary systems, captured in the notions of biosphere and noosphere. A biosphere was, according to Vernadskii, a complex system of living and nonliving matter, whereas a noosphere was an intellectual system of a higher order, which interacts with a biosphere. Bogdanov outlined a theory of systemic organizational processes as a unitary foundation for all types of knowledge; Vernadskii postulated a multiplicity of systems that operated on different principles yet were interconnected and capable of influencing one another. These two thinkers were later invoked as original Soviet contributors to policy science (Bogdanov) and environmental science (Vernadskii); their significance was compared with that of Bertalanffy, whose thought was influential in the West.

Applied systems analysis was intellectually related, but institutionally different from these managerial, biological, and geophysical inquiries into general systems theory. The applied systems approach originated in the neighboring fields of electronic engineering, cybernetics, and operations research (OR), developed during World War II.[20] Calling these approaches "cyborg sciences" because they were united by an emphasis on information processing, computer simulation, and control applications, Mirowski claimed that OR was the ancestor of systems analysis, noting that the intellectual ambition of OR practitioners was relatively modest, limited to increasing the efficiency of given tasks, whereas system analysts espoused an ambition to become a universal theory of everything.[21] Other authors noted that the implications of systems analysis in different spheres of application differed widely: for instance, the principle of self-regulation leading to homeostasis applied to biological organisms, but not at all to economic systems.[22] Collier and Lakoff, for instance, suggest that the postwar systems analysis itself originated from the "science of flows" in the 1930s and 1940s, which evolved into a central component of what they describe as a government of emergency by ensuring the resilience of "vital systems."[23]

But what is a system? In the most general definition, a system is a whole which is more than the sum of its parts, and which has some kind of boundary from its environment.[24] Systems are orderly: a viable system—a system that is able to survive—is internally organized in a hierarchical way, where the interrelations among a system's components follow a certain set of rules. However, this order and these rules can be very complex: systems can encompass separate subsystems and be part of larger systems. The order is dynamic, changing, and the changes can be chaotic. The degree of systems' openness to their environment can vary.

A note on systems ontology is also due. Did systems thinkers mean that the world is a mesh of intertwining, really existing systems? Many of them did not; rather, they suggested that a system is not always a given object, unless it is an engineered, technical, man-made system—such as an electric grid or central heating—or an organism, such as a frog. A system can also be used as an intellectual technology, enabling a governor, in Foucault's words, to operate at a certain level of reality. In other words, a system can be understood as an epistemological frame. Thus conceived, the system approach is goal-oriented knowledge: it discerns complex situations, looking for a solution to a given problem. It is in this sense that one can speak about defense, transport, social, economic, and cultural systems.

At the very beginning, the forging of systems analysis as an intellectual technology was strongly associated with quantitative methodologies, devised for the use of governmental and industrial organizations, which tainted its reputation in the eyes of critics. Many opponents of systems analysis represented the Western conservative humanities and critics of modernity, such as, for instance, the US philosopher Lewis Mumford, who wrote about a particular authoritarian, system-centered "technics," by which he meant a translation of theoretical truths into "practical forms."[25] For Mumford, authoritarian technics were embodied in large-scale organizations and material infrastructures, regulated by state bureaucracies. Mumford contrasted such large, oppressive systems with idealized, small-scale, individual-centered assemblages, which he understood to embody democratic values. He criticized these new technologies of control, arguing that "through mechanization, automation, cybernetic direction, this authoritarian technics has at last successfully overcome its most serious weakness: its original dependence upon resistant, somewhat actively disobedient servo-mechanisms, still human enough to harbor purposes that do not always coincide with those of the system."[26]

Mumford was not alone in perceiving "system" as both a tainted word and a real-life phenomenon, a technology of power: the influential political theorist Jürgen Habermas juxtaposed the authentic zone of the world of everyday life with an inhuman "system" of governmental and corporate bureaucracies.[27] These critical debates, however, albeit influential in humanities, were based on a selective definition of "system," thus disregarding the high heterogeneity of system-cybernetic governmentality. There was more to the systems approach than instrumentalist OR studies, and not all systems analysis was harnessed to top-down government; some strands of this research sought radical innovation and social change. Some systems analysts were acutely aware of the pitfalls of the narrowly instrumentalist approach. As early as 1967 Yezhekel Dror argued for an "interdiscipline of policy science," emphasizing that if systems analysis were reduced to the tool of the PPBS, it would be useless for strategic planning and public policy. Instead, argued Dror, systems analysis should engage with complex and nonquantifiable issues.[28]

The history of the systems approach contains some quite astonishing applications indeed. Andrew Pickering described the radical psychiatry movement in Britain, in which doctors practiced communal cohabitation with mentally ill patients.[29] Similarly innovative and conceptually dependent on the systems approach was radical ecological thinking, in particular the Gaia theory launched by James Lovelock and Lynn Margulis in the early 1970s.[30] Also, symbolic interactionism in anthropology and even poststructuralist semiotics, which both claimed that meaning is dependent on relations and communication processes, drew their inspiration from system-cybernetic thinking.[31] Another example is the growing field of infrastructure studies in the field of science and technology studies (STS), which uses systems terminology.[32] If the analyses of weapon systems assumed the possibility of rational choice, something that was embodied in PPBS, the later analyses of complex systems emphasized the bounded and relational character of rationality.[33]

Systems analysis came to be understood not merely as an objective, neutral instrumental knowledge, but as a performative device, capable of bringing new realities into being. This aspect is largely overlooked in the histories of systems approach which aim to disclose systems theorists as wizards, seeking to perfect governmental control. However, I want to emphasize that some representatives of the systems approach understood it as a very different kind of epistemology, rooted in in a probabilistic, relational, and performative understanding of both reality that was to be explored and the very scientific instruments of knowledge.

Thus conceived, the systems approach deeply unsettled the traditional Newtonian understanding of control as a linear influence, applied through force on material objects with an aim to change them from one known state to another known state. Postulating that even a simple mechanical system could be seen as complex and on many levels indeterminate, the systems approach produced as much uncertainty as promise for control. Whereas some systems thinkers opted for a black box model and were concerned only with inputs and outputs, others—including the father of cybernetics Norbert Wiener—suggested a "white box model," in which some processes that take place inside the system should be studied in addition to inputs and outputs.[34]

My argument is that the systems approach was part of transforming postwar governance toward the growing importance of the institution of policy expertise, the introduction of new technologies (computers in particular), and toward the development of a new epistemology, expressed in postpositivist scientific approaches to governance and control. But most importantly—and this is what the next section is about—the transnational development of the systems approach gave rise to new constellations of power, new institutions, and new practices. Nowhere was this novelty more evident than in the joint effort of East-West scientists to develop this new, system-cybernetic governmentality.

The East-West Coalition for Systems Approach

The systems approach embraces many disciplines, but it was a rather particular group of scholars who were behind the creation of IIASA. I have already mentioned that there seems to be a general agreement on the fact that the many different approaches grouped under the operations research umbrella eventually morphed into systems analysis, and that in this field the word "system" was first used in relation to weapon systems.[35] There were, however, several subpaths in this development, based on different understandings of rationality, different epistemological foundations that evolved within different circles of scientists and policy makers. One such circle of US scholars gathered in a strategic coalition attempting to define the research agenda for the East-West Institute in the second half of the 1960s and the early 1970s. Some of the key actors in this process were members of the Cowles Commission and/or RAND, pioneers of the early development of OR, and men active in Lyndon Johnson's Great Society program. This strategic coalition advocated a particular type of systems approach, one that put a premium on policy-relevant science but also sought to advance the theories and instruments of governance, espousing a committed, global, transnational orientation.

The core of this strategic coalition consisted of US and émigré scientists, including the Dutch-born mathematician and economist Tjalling Koopmans; the great believer in economic rationality but also market socialism Kenneth Arrow, whose parents were Romanian Jews; and the US-born eminent mathematician George Dantzig, who hailed from an Irish-French family.[36] Koopmans, Arrow, and Dantzig were leading members of the Cowles Commission, an organization established in 1932 with the aim of promoting mathematical methods in economics, in particular macroeconomic modeling. Koopmans, Arrow, and Dantzig met at the commission in 1947, where Thomas Schelling was also staying at that time, and during the next decade the commission brought together many scholars who would later be involved in East-West cooperation.[37] In 1955, the prominent cybernetician Ross Ashby met with Raiffa at a seminar titled "The Formal Theory of Organization," organized by the former director of Cowles, Jacob Marschak.[38] Ashby's textbook on cybernetics was later translated into Russian and become very popular in the Soviet Union, while Raiffa became the first IIASA director. In 1949 Arrow moved to RAND; subsequently the US group for the organization of the East-West Institute would directly involve RAND, which produced the first blueprint for IIASA. In the 1960s the US committee for IIASA included regional, climate, and econometric experts, such as the prominent RAND analyst and expert on South Asia, Guy Pauker, atmosphere scientist Thomas Malone, and Arrow and Koopmans.[39] It is quite clear that the participation of former members of the Cowles group (Koopmans, Arrow, Dantzig, and Raiffa) in IIASA was not a coincidence but a strategic step on the road toward institutionalizing policy sciences: for instance, Koopmans dedicated a third of his Nobel Prize award to establishing a Dantzig fellowship at IIASA.[40]

This strategic coalition was extended to include some of the proponents of the theoretical approach to systems in shaping the new East-West think tank, though these general system theorists participated in the process less directly than the former Cowles members. These were the initiators of the Society for General Systems Theory (renamed the Society for General Systems Research in 1956), established in the United States in 1954: Kenneth Boulding, Ludwig von Bertalanffy, and Anatol Rapoport (all of whom either participated in IIASA events or were in close contacts with IIASA scholars). Russell Ackoff, the pioneering OR scientist and key promoter of systems thinking in management, was closely involved in the society, publishing regularly in its yearbooks.[41] Observing the fast multiplication of approaches in systems thinking, the society sought to unify and institutionalize this field by positing the systems approach as a transdisciplinary methodology, able to provide a new epistemological foundation for all sciences.[42]

At the international level, the spread of the systems approach was closely intertwined with US efforts to expand its political influence. In Western Europe, for instance, US techniques of OR and systems analysis developed at Vannevar Bush's Office of Scientific Research and Development (especially its Applied Mathematical Panel) were introduced as a scientific part of the new discipline of management, an effort that was vigorously pursued by the US government and foundations shortly before the idea of the East-West Institute was launched.[43] Here a link with the British OR community, with whom the Americans had a history of direct cooperation during the war, proved to be essential. For instance, Bundy brought the British physicist Patrick Blackett, the pioneer of the British OR, on his first mission regarding the East-West Institute to Moscow in 1967.[44] Bundy's advisor, the economist Carl Kaysen, worked hands-on in British air defense and produced the estimates of the damage caused by the Dresden bombing. On the British side, the lead negotiator on the East-West institute was the chief British governmental science advisor and former member of the NATO Science Committee Solly Zuckerman. Coincidentally, Zuckerman's colleague and the advocate of the large-scale governmental funding of science, J. D. Bernal, gained prominence in the Soviet Union as the author of a leftist definition of scientific-technical revolution.[45]

From the US point of view, France was deemed as a particularly useful platform for spreading US policy and management sciences in Europe, in part because France had its own deep tradition of policy expertise, continued by the engineers, the OR community, and, from the 1950s, increasing ranks of scholars associated with state planning.[46] French membership in the strategic coalition for IIASA involved no less than Louis Armand, the captain of French industrial planning, who presided over Euratom and was in charge of the national railway network. Another member was Pierre Massé, commissar of the state planning commission from 1959 to 1966 and theoretician of planning, who was also listed among candidates for IIASA director. Yet another was François Bloch-Lainé, the civil servant in charge of state finance.[47]

Pragmatic interest in the science of state planning was reinforced by a particular intellectual climate that was developing in France from the late 1940s. At that time economist Jacques Lesourne, industrialist and philosopher Gaston Berger, and controversial thinker Bertrand de Jouvenel developed a distinctly French take on policy science, *la prospective*. In contrast to US and British OR at that time, *la prospective* was not about finding a single best solution for a given problem, but provided managers and planners with a methodological framework for reasoning about the problem. This approach, developed to meet the needs of the French planning system, was based on bargaining about the plan targets among different groups.[48] Like the systems approach that emphasized the intertwining of natural, social, and technical structures, *la prospective* sought to bring together experts from diverse areas and facilitate their joint work across the boundaries of their professional domains. That the French *la prospective* was considered to be a policy science and intellectually close to the US systems approach speaks to the fact that de Jouvenel, but also the increasingly prominent sociologist of organizations, Michel Crozier, took part in the Sussex conference on the future East-West Institute in 1968.[49]

The strategic coalition for the East-West Institute also included actors from other European countries, such as Belgium, where a center for operations research and econometrics was established at the Université Catholique de Louvain in 1966. This center was also supported by the Ford Foundation and served as a link with RAND.[50] Its director, Jacques Drèze, was listed among possible directors of the East-West Institute. Italy was also a major partner, as it actively developed East-West trade; however, in contrast to Britain and France, the Italian member of the strategic coalition, Aurelio Peccei, came from the private sector, thus representing a new type of globally oriented actor that thrived on the links between corporate and governmental institutions.

There was also a strategic coalition of Soviet systems scholars and policy makers. In the following section I map some key features of the Soviet institutional and disciplinary landscape of the systems approach, which is necessary in order to understand Soviet involvement in the IIASA. If the Soviet adoption of cybernetics and computer technology has already been studied quite thoroughly by such scholars as Holloway and Gerovitch, much less is known about the history of Soviet OR and systems thinking. It is apparent that during the early stage, 1945–1956, OR and systems analysis were nearly completely absent from Soviet public domain, only to surface in the aftermath of de-Stalinization and the opening up to West.[51] Although first Soviet work on game theory was published during the 1950s,[52] it was only after the death of Stalin in 1953 and Khrushchev's rejection of Stalin's cult in 1956 that Soviet decision sciences would come into the daylight, with key scientists returning to the capital to found new laboratories and institutes. The turning point was the year 1955, when leading defense scientists and mathematicians Sergei Sobolev, Anatolii Kitov, and Aleksei Liapunov published an article defending cybernetics as a genuine science that had nothing to do with capitalist ideology.[53] The following decade saw the fast development of Soviet research into computer technology and cybernetics, which now was praised in the press and policy programs as a key resource to modernizing economic and social planning, management, and industrial production. Policy sciences were an integral part of this new, cybernetic future of communism.

In the early 1960s a wide array of scientific approaches, developed to aid management and policy-making, came to be publicly promoted and institutionalized in the Soviet Union. These approaches included cybernetic theory of control, linear and nonlinear planning, input-output modeling, OR, scientific forecasting, and what would become known as the systems approach. Sometimes these techniques were gathered under the umbrella of cybernetics, sometimes they were promoted as "mathematical methods" of governance. Beginning in 1957 the Soviet press presented computers as a new technology able to speed up decisions and, beginning in 1960, widely promoted the automation of management, describing the national economy as an informational system.[54] Although in reality Soviet firms were severely underequipped with computer technology, a strong expectation of the computerized future was in place in the Soviet discourses of the 1960s.

The first Soviet research unit dedicated to OR and game theory was founded in 1961 in the Leningrad branch of the Soviet Academy of Sciences, where Oscar Morgenstern, the founder of mathematical game theory, paid a visit in 1963.[55] Not long before, in 1960, Norbert Wiener had visited Moscow, giving a talk in an overcrowded auditorium (Ross Ashby would visit the Soviet Union in 1964).[56] Soviet mathematicians, like the influential Vadim Trapeznikov, the director of the prestigious Institute of Automatics and Telemechanics, traveled to the United States, returning deeply convinced about the need to apply OR and management science techniques in governance.[57] The establishment of a full-fledged network of OR institutes was initiated in 1964, alongside the first institutes dedicated to cybernetics. The founding fathers, defense intellectuals E. Popov and Germogen S. Pospelov, facilitated the establishment of OR as a research area in three major institutions: under the leadership of Nikita Moiseev at the Computer Center in Moscow, of Iurii Zhuravlev at the Mathematical Institute at Novosibirsk, and of Viktor Glushkov at the Institute of Cybernetics in Kiev, Ukraine.

Within the next few years OR was institutionalized in the republic branches of the Soviet Academy of Sciences, where it was usually placed in the computer science departments. Universities also introduced OR into their curricula. Soviet research institutes keenly followed Western progress in the field, as revealed by the speed with which the pioneering work *Methods of Operations Research* (1951) by Philip Morse and George Kimball was published. Morse and Kimball's book was based on declassified materials written originally for the US navy, and appeared in Russian translation in 1956.[58] From that time on, Soviet planners and managers expressed great interest in French and American methods. However, to introduce mathematical methods as a scientific tool of economic development in the dominant discourse of Marxism-Leninism and the institutional landscape where the central organs of the Communist Party had the supreme decision power was not a trivial task.

Arguably the first signal that high governmental officials were becoming open to the new science of governance was Wassily Leontief's visit to Moscow in the late 1950s. From then on, key Western texts pertaining to mathematical approaches to management were translated into Russian, usually within five years of their original publication in the West. For instance, as the Soviets particularly followed Lyndon Johnson's budgetary reforms, *The Economics of Defense in the Nuclear Age*, edited by Charles Hitch and Roland McKean (1960), was published in Russian in 1964. Popular brochures, such as Georgii L. Smolian's "Operations Research: an instrument of effective governance" (1967) were published and disseminated widely by the key agency for the popularization of science, Znanie (in English, Knowledge). As Smolian's text shows, in the Soviet Union OR was largely identified with the optimization of decisions with the help of quantitative methods, ideally using computer technology; these quantitative methods included game theory, which was institutionalized in parallel with OR and cybernetics. In November 1968 the first all-union conference in game theory was organized in Erevan, Armenia.[59] By the late 1960s OR was well-entrenched in the Soviet academic system, and during the next decade, the 1970s, systems analysis or the systems approach followed suit.

Many other applications of the Soviet systems approach emerged in addition to the ones that stemmed from mathematical OR. Due to the limitation of space, I cannot do full justice to the diversity of early Soviet systems research; I will therefore note just a few moments that are important for understanding Soviet participation in the East-West Institute.

Wiener's visit to Moscow in 1960 excited Soviet neurophysiologists such as the influential Petr Anokhin.[60] Philosophical engagement with the systems approach outside the engineering field dates at least the early 1950s, when the Moscow Methodological Circle was formed in 1952–1954; at these informal gatherings, young philosophy graduates discussed information theory and the systems approach.[61] The institutionalization of Soviet systems philosophy also began in 1960, when the admiral and chairman of the USSR Council on Cybernetics, Aksel Berg, published an article positing the need for study of the social impact of automation and emphasized that the systems approach provides a new perspective to management, from which production processes can be understood as "integrated systems of flow," regardless of their specific activity, be it extraction of natural resources or finishing a product.[62] It was also in 1960 that Russian philosophers Vladislav Lektorskii and Vadim Sadovskii published an article on von Bertalanffy's general systems theory (GST), arguing that GST could provide a framework for all sciences, because modern sciences are no longer interested in specific units, but rather in their interrelations.[63] In their article they carefully defend GST in relation to dialectical materialism, arguing that this theory is a mathematical description of concrete, empirical systems.[64] In 1962 an interdisciplinary seminar on structural and system analysis methods in science and technology was organized by philosophers Georgii Shchedrovitskii, Vadim Sadovskii, and Erik Iudin under the Scientific Council of Cybernetics.[65] Their key publications date from the late 1960s and an annual publication, *Systems Research* (*Sistemnye issledovaniia*) was launched in 1969.[66]

Examples of systems research in the Soviet Union include urban and cultural planning, such as the siting of cinemas and culture houses in relation to the density of the population.[67] The systems approach was introduced into organization and management theory, discussions of which emerged in the 1960s. For instance, in 1966 a seminar on organization theory as a separate scholarly field was organized at the department of Marxist-Leninist philosophy at the Leningrad Institute of Aviation (LIAP). Despite the title of the institution, the agenda of this nascent field clearly indicated openness to international intellectual influences beyond Marxism-Leninism: the report from this seminar on Soviet organization theory includes thinkers drawn from not only Russian tradition but also Eastern Europe and the West, such as Aleksandr Bogdanov, von Bertalanffy, the Russian economist and statistician Evgenii Slutskii, Fredrik Winslow Taylor, and the Polish philosopher Tadeusz Kotarbiński, who wrote *Praxiology: An Introduction to the Science of Efficient Action* (in Polish, 1955, translated into English in 1965). Elsewhere I detailed the importance of the emerging Russian thought on reflexive control as a semiotic system of projecting to the future, developed by Georgii Shchedrovitskii and Vladimir Lefevr.[68] The systems approach found its practical applications in the field of environmental governance, particularly forestry, where experiments were done on replanting forest with the aim of increasing biomass.[69]

These are just a few of many examples, which suggests that the landscape of post-Stalinist systems thinking was becoming heterogeneous, as it was in the West, involving the development of mathematical methods, a philosophy of science, and wide applications ranging from biomedicine and engineering to economics and linguistics. The professionalization of the discipline of OR was reflected in the Soviet research system, where new departments and units dedicated to OR emerged in the late 1950s through the 1960s. Thus some clarification of Russian terminology might be in order. First, the Russian concept of *"issledovaniia operatsii"* was a direct translation of the US "operations research" and not the British "operations analysis." The term was used to describe predominantly military weapons research, but also logistics; in time it was extended to civil sectors. Searching for their own, older tradition, Russian historians trace the beginning of civil Soviet OR back to the applications of mathematical methods to managerial problems of transportation as developed by Leonid Kantorovich and Mark Gavurin in 1939.

In a similar way, the Soviet vocabulary for systems approach was developed on the basis of Western definitions. Thus Soviet technical sciences adopted "systems engineering" (in Russian, *sistemotekhnika*) from Western literature, following in particular *System Engineering: An Introduction to the Design of Large-Scale Systems* by Harry Goode and Robert Machol (1957), published in Russian in 1962.

Five years later, in 1967, the term "systems analysis" (in Russian, *sistemnyi analiz*) first appeared in Soviet public discourses through the Russian translation of Stanford Optner's *Systems Analysis for Business and Industrial Problem Solving* (1965). Although the Soviet use of the phrase in public discourse occurred more than ten years later than it did in the United States, it should be remembered that in practice systems analysis was then still a minor field in both countries. The US government departments still struggled to furnish their offices with trained system analysts in 1965.[70] Furthermore, though in the 1960s the foremost Soviet institutes had access to the most recent publications in English, the delay could be explained by general cautiousness about introducing new concepts in the Soviet Union. Memoirs, for instance, detail attempts to organize a first conference on epistemological aspects of the systems approach in the mid-1960s, yet this effort was blocked by the Central Committee's Department for Science.[71]

Nevertheless, judging from the wave of translations and Soviet publications that arose in the late 1960s, Soviet interest in the systems approach was authentic and it was huge. When, in 1969, a compilation of texts by key systems theorists such as Ludwig von Bertalanffy, Mihajlo Mesarovic, Anatolii Rapoport, Ross Ashby, Oskar Lange, and Kenneth Boulding were published in Russian with an introduction by Vadim Nikolaevich Sadovskii and Erik Iudin, the iceberg of Soviet systems analysis had finally emerged.[72] The most prominent representatives were, apart from Sadovskii, Igor' Blauberg and philosopher Eduard Mirskii, who had been organizing seminars on systems analysis under the Scientific Council of Cybernetics of the Academy of Sciences since 1962.[73] These scholars represented the philosophical strand of systems analysis and they were based at the Institute of History of Natural Science and Technology. At the same time, an array of works on the systems approach became available in the Soviet Union. A prominent publication was a yearbook *Systems Research* (*Sistemnye issledovaniia*), published by the Institute of History of Natural Sciences and Technology from 1969 on, which had a circulation of six thousand. Initially this yearbook was limited to philosophical reflections, but it was broadened to include social and economic applications when it was taken over by VNIISI in 1976.[74] In 1976 systems approach was finally recognized as fully compatible with Marxism; accordingly, the symbolic rituals were duly observed: the Central Committee's Department for Science sponsored the publication of a volume on "systemic aspects" of Marx's thought.[75] Nevertheless, much Soviet systems thinking was as far removed from Marxist-Leninist epistemology as it could possibly be.

It is interesting that the Soviet strategic coalition for the East-West Institute included the representatives of systems philosophy, regardless of their often controversial status within Soviet academia. As I show in chapter 2, Soviet membership at IIASA was a matter of a high political priority, and it was tightly controlled and personally curated by Gvishiani.[76] Documents from the Russian archives show that it was mainly GKNT staff who conducted negotiations about the East-West institute, and that Gvishiani involved prominent mathematicians and economists, as well as historians and philosophers (such as Viktor Glushkov, Georgii Arbatov, Stanislas Emel'ianov, Iu. P. Vasil'ev, and Vadim Sadovskii), in later stages of negotiations about the establishment of IIASA.[77] The institute's strategic importance for the Soviets is also revealed by the fact that Aleksandr Letov, the key scientist in automatic control field who chaired the first all-union meeting in this field in 1953, later the president of the International Association for Automatic Control, was appointed as the first deputy director to Howard Raiffa in 1972. At a later stage Gvishiani also consistently engaged a certain type of scholar from several related fields, all of whom hailed from nonmilitary institutes, such as the Institute of Automation and Control, the Central Institute of Mathematical Economics (TsEMI), the Computer Center, the Institute of Management Problems at the GKNT, and the Institute of Natural Science and Technology (in Russian, *Institut estesvoznanie i tekhniki*).

If first Western associations for systems analysis emerged in the 1950s and 1960s, in the Soviet Union it was the establishment of IIASA that gave impetus to formal legitimization of Soviet systems research, which during these two decades was organized predominantly in informal clubs and seminars, with scientists scattered across various institutes or working under the umbrella of cybernetics.[78] To facilitate Soviet membership in IIASA, Gvishiani established the All-Union Committee for Systems Analysis under GKNT and the Academy of Sciences, and, in June 1976, the All-Union Scientific Institute of Systems Research (VNIISI), which was to become a counterpart to IIASA in the Soviet Union. Together with the Institute of Automation and Control (often translated into English as "Institute of Control Sciences"), VNIISI was the key Soviet partner of IIASA.[79]

It is worth pausing on the Soviet Institute of Systems Research, for it was an important addition to the empire of Soviet science and a sign of the institutionalization of a Soviet version of system-cybernetic governmentality. The significance of VNIISI is suggested by the fact that its archives are secret and not available to researchers, unlike other, similar institutes, such as the Institute of the Problems of Organization and Management VNIIPOU. Established as a Soviet counterpart of IIASA, VNIISI was also modeled after RAND and intended to be a multidisciplinary think tank that generated policy-relevant knowledge. The Soviet section of the GKNT's international team of scholars in management of organizations, cybernetics, and OR (originally established in 1970) was transferred to VNIISI.[80] The mission of this new Soviet center for systems analysis involved the development of the theory and method of systems analysis, to be applied to complex, large-scale, and long-term problems of the national economy, in particular those deemed to be the most urgent in the context of the scientific-technical revolution. One such task was the methodology of modeling the long-term development of both national and world economies, exploring the interaction between economic, social, technoscientific, and ecological factors.[81] In addition, VNIISI did research on innovation: a Sisyphean task given that the growth of the Soviet economy increasingly stalled, starting in the 1960s.[82]

Nevertheless, there was hope of and a commitment to a system-cybernetic rejuvenation of Soviet scientific governance. Funds flowed into the Gvishiani institute. A special building for the institute was erected on the Sixtieth Anniversary of October Revolution Street, where many important research and policy organizations were situated. The exclusivity of the conditions enjoyed by VNIISI staff is apparent when compared with staff at other new research institutes, which were established with a similar rationale in mind, to respond to the ongoing scientific-technical revolution, such as the Institute for Concrete Social Research (IKSI) in Moscow. VNIISI was allocated forty-three apartments for its staff, while a document pertaining to the establishment of IKSI mentioned only 400m^2 for housing, which amounts to about six decent apartments. When it was established, IKSI's annual salary fund was 17,000 rubles, whereas the VNIISI salary fund was 133,000 rubles. Even "a special buffet," a famous perk that offered better-quality food to Soviet elites, was introduced at the new VNIISI,[83] to nourish its staff, which grew from 154 employees in 1977 to 685 by 1980.[84] The functionalist architecture spoke of modernity, and further facilities to cater to the staff were constructed around the main building.

Food was certainly important, but even more so was technical equipment. VNIISI staff used Western computers and had a rather up-to-date conference room equipped with computer projectors. Much of the staff came from the institutes that Gvishiani had previously supported, such as IKSI (Oleg Lapin) and the Institute of Control Sciences (Sergei Dubovskii, Stanislav Emel'ianov) and the Institute for the USA and Canada Studies (Boris Mil'ner). Through IIASA, but also directly, VNIISI maintained close relations with leading Western scientists in the fields of systems analysis, decision sciences, and computer modeling: the leading Soviet systems theorist, Vadim Sadovskii, corresponded directly with Bertalanffy and Anatolii Rapoport, while Viktor Gelovani cultivated a close personal relationship with Dennis Meadows.[85] Indeed, the modeling of global development was one of VNIISI's priorities from 1976 on.[86] Although Western scientists frequently visited VNIISI and VNIISI staff regularly stayed at IIASA, the leading representatives of VNIISI first visited the United States only in the late 1980s.[87]

In this way, I suggest that IIASA was an important, indeed central gateway enabling key Soviet systems scholars to access their Western colleagues, while it legitimized and institutionalized the systems approach in Soviet academia. The list of first Soviet IIASA fellows includes leading cybernetics and computer scientists, such as Glushkov and Marchuk, as well as economists, such as Abel' Aganbegian and Leonid Kantorovich, all of whom visited Laxenburg in the 1970s.[88] The first research planning conferences in 1973 discussed energy, municipal and regional, biological and medical, and ecological systems and sought to attract some of the leading scientific authorities in these interdisciplinary fields. Thus the seminar listing of 1973–1974 includes the names of James Grier Miller, author of the living systems theory, and Nikita Moiseev, research director of the Computer Center of the Soviet Academy of Science and the initiator of Soviet participation at the global biosphere program. In addition to Howard Raiffa, Dantzig, and Koopmans, other names include prominent global modelers like Dennis Meadows, Lawrence Klein, and William Nordhaus.[89] Stafford Beer, who held a fellowship at IIASA's project on the management of large organizations in 1974–1975, presented his model of the cybernetization of the Chilean economy, thus speaking *after* the CIA overthrew Allende's regime in 1973.[90] As such, if there was a transnational society of systems thinkers emerging, it gravitated around IIASA.

Yet was not the world divided by a struggle between the two opposing systems, communism and capitalism? How could systems analysis bridge, rather than reinforce, this ideological divide? As I have mention in the introduction, the cryptic name of the institute itself was a response to this tension. As the second IIASA director Roger Levien recalled, several other names, such as "Institute of Cybernetics" and "Institute of Systems Management"—the Soviets were particularly keen on using "cybernetics" in the title—were proposed. The choice fell to "applied systems analysis," Levien tells us, because

> 'systems analysis' had several virtues, not the least of which was its ambiguity; no one was quite sure what it included or what it excluded, but it conveyed well the sense of modern analytic tools applied to the study of complex systems, such as those that are at the locus of all major societal problems.... Precisely because it [systems analysis] did not denote a commonly accepted discipline with a well established international community of practitioners, this birthright left IIASA the task of creating its own discipline and community.[91]

Many persons, including those I interviewed, agree with this description. According to a long-term IIASA employee, "ambiguity was a resource. What is systems analysis? This is what IIASA does. What does IIASA do? Applied systems analysis."[92] The magic task of the new institute was to imbue this circular definition of "applied systems analysis" with concrete meaning, which was done through social networks, research projects, and decision aids. Even here pragmatism ruled:

as Levien noted, "the result was generally successful, although not always systems analysis," as IIASA hosted many different projects.[93]

Systems analysis, as I mentioned earlier, could be used to establish the vertical integration and control of different functions in a given system. Yet it proved to be quite difficult to come anywhere near a vertical integration of the field of systems analysis itself. Even the approaches originating from RAND were open to interpretation when applied locally. Still, an attempt at such integration was one of IIASA's declared missions. This idea was initiated by a former RAND scholar, Roger Levien, in cooperation with Vil' Rakhmankulov of Moscow's Institute of Automation and Control. In 1973, Levien divided systems analysis into three blocs: the first was comprised of foundational theories developed by control, information, and economic sciences; the second consisted of the art of practicing systems analysis, which involved practical issues of problem definition, communication with decision makers, and implementation. As a third bloc Levien nominated methodology, or a description of systems through computer simulation, flowcharting, or budgeting.[94] Drawing on this classification, Levien began preparing a handbook on applied systems analysis in the mid-1970s, but at a later stage this project was handed over to a pioneer in US OR research, Hugh Miser, and the retired ex-RAND researcher Edward S. Quade.[95]

The involvement of Quade illustrates the wish to legitimize the new, transnational approach by positing its link with the US ex-OR research community. Quade gained a reputation as a military systems analyst at RAND and authored some of the first reflections on the soft issues of governmental applications of policy sciences. His own approach to systems analysis emphasized the openness of the field, putting a premium on the interaction between the analyst and the client. According to Quade, systems analysis was not rigid scientific theory or method, but rather "a research strategy," even "a practical philosophy of how best to aid a decision maker with complex problems of choice under uncertainty."[96] Big hopes were placed in this volume, which was expected to become a flagship of IIASA's intellectual rationale. Thus when the promotion materials for this handbook, eventually published in 1985, did not acknowledge IIASA's role in its production, this caused a great stir at the IIASA Council.[97] This handbook was, after all, integral to the institute's external image and self-presentation as an East-West strategic coalition, mobilized to promote systems research as a distinct field of policy science.

From the 1950s on, the use of systems analysis to aid in decision-making was a matter of prestige in both government and industry. However, the scientification of governance should not be reduced to mere political symbolism. If, as I argue, the development of the systems approach had a strong international orientation from an early stage, it is not surprising that it was the policy scientists who turned out to be best equipped to use the window of opportunity offered by Johnson's bridge-building to develop and promote their approach. The strategic coalition for IIASA involved a very particular group of prominent US scientists, who overlapped with other international networks, mobilized to both develop new disciplines (econometrics, optimal planning) and gather new data. Unlike their US counterparts, the Soviet members of this strategic coalition operated under a narrowly defined political priority of broadening East-West technology transfer, in which Gvishiani played the key role. Moreover, the Soviet coalition also included several philosophers, whereas there were no representatives of philosophy in the US group. In this way, the basis for the future branching out and diversification of IIASA's scholarly agenda was established at an early stage. How was this "interdisciplinary" policy science actually conceptualized, organized, and enacted? The next chapter focuses on the everyday life of resident scholars inside the institute.

4

SHAPING A TRANSNATIONAL SYSTEMS COMMUNITY (2)

Family versus War Room

There is a particular iconography associated with Cold War governmental imagination, of which perhaps the best-known image is the war room from Stanley Kubrick's film satire *Dr. Strangelove, or How I Learned to Stop Worrying and Love the Bomb* (1964). A war room is presented in this film as a safe, enclosed space, a control center, where the US government interacts with the outside—both its own people and the Soviet Union—mainly through technologies of communication. This fictional center of command turned out to be so convincing that it not only led the newly elected Ronald Reagan to ask to see the war room at the White House, but it also inspired historians like Paul Edwards to extend this metaphor to the Cold War itself as a "closed world." Insulated in this war room, wrote Edwards, military and governmental commanders relied on technologically mediated representations of "reality," the effect of this technological mediation being an emotional distancing. For Edwards, a war room was thus a metaphor for cybernetic, computerized governance where, paradoxically, the rationalization of control through technologies enabling government action from a distance could potentially provoke risky, irrational behavior.[1]

The image of the control room as a central power site in the bipolar Cold War world, driven to madness by rationalization and technologization, recurred in the burgeoning popular and academic studies of the strategic centers of calculation and control. The most widely analyzed such center was the RAND Corporation, described as an organization inhabited by scientists cultivating a particular macho and paranoid culture, detached from "the real world."[2]

The centrality of RAND to Cold War governance was projected back from the opposing system, as the Soviets continuously sought to gain as much firsthand information on RAND as possible, with some success.[3] In this context IIASA emerges as a strange, nearly incomprehensible animal, for what possible function could "an international RAND" perform in the closed world of the Cold War? It is not surprising that IIASA turns up now and again in some marginal literature on Cold War conspiracies. But in this and following chapters I show that the Cold War world was not as closed as one might think, and IIASA is a proof of this. Whereas Nils Gilman suggests that the development of the scientific governmentality of the Cold War was an expression of "American life," I claim that this scientific governmentality was not limited to the United States or to liberal democratic countries, but, instead, featured in the authoritarian regime of the Soviet Union.[4]

In what follows, I examine the use of informal practices and new metaphoric language, created to counteract precisely this "war room" mentality, thus helping to form East-West scientific and policy communities, a phenomenon that questions the thesis of the closed, Cold War world.

This chapter is divided into two parts. First, I detail the role of sense-making and informal practices in performing IIASA's work during the founding stage. Then I discuss the evolution of IIASA, an organization which was first developed as a platform for the construction of systems community as a nonpolitical entity. But IIASA turned out to be not only a platform, but an actor on its own, something that became evident during the reversal of US policy toward IIASA and East-West relations following Reagan's ascension to power. Thus I conclude this chapter by discussing the mobilization of a systems community to defend the East-West co-production of policy sciences in 1983–1985.

Family versus War Room

A symbol of the diplomacy underscoring links rather than confrontation between East and West, IIASA could not be simply reduced to a control center, closed and isolated from the external world. It was meant to be a new type of organization, an international East-West think tank—but what could this mean in practice? What kind of meanings could be mobilized to make sense of this new animal that did not fit into the Cold War rhetoric of hostility and competition? During my fieldwork I was struck by the efforts of the initiators of IIASA to find an appropriate terminology to describe this organization, both externally and internally. The external representation of IIASA drew heavily on the existing universalist vocabulary widely used to describe the new population of international organizations. This vocabulary emphasized IIASA's role in establishing links across national borders and as a politically neutral space for the advancement of universal, scientific knowledge. But the internal representation of IIASA was more peculiar and was carried mainly by oral discourse, the narratives circulated inside the institute.

In my interviews with different actors involved in the creation and running of IIASA, I encountered a strongly established internal idiom, "the IIASA family," a phrase that recurred in virtually every interview, when the interviewees tried to explain the character of this organization. It is quite clear that the metaphor of a family connotes a rather different range of meanings than the metaphor of a war room, although some families may have strong militant and mobilizing role, for instance, in tribes and the organized mafia clans. The important difference here is that family and war room suggest different modes and locations of action, but also different mechanisms of discipline. If a metaphor of a war room refers to a space for sovereign governance, where the chain of command is clearly defined, family, too, connotes hierarchy, but also a particular mode of interdependency in which family members share their origin and obligations to each other. Both bureaucracies and families are fundamental disciplinary mechanisms in modern societies, but the key difference between the two is the link between the organizational role and personality: if bureaucracies rely on depersonalized rules, families are all about personalization. My interlocutors referred to the "IIASA family," emphasizing that the institute enabled close, informal ties among its fellows. In this chapter I suggest that the use of the metaphor of family to make sense of IIASA as an organization was part of both internal and external management, aspiring not only to integrate the ever-changing staff, but also to consolidate policy coalitions, mobilized to protect the interests of IIASA as an autonomous actor in the context of shifting foreign policy priorities.

It is difficult to overrate the importance of the internal legitimizing discourse in the everyday life of IIASA. The construction of an East-West meeting platform was not only a question of finding an appropriate organizational structure, but also a matter of creating conditions for communication and cohabitation, enabling the many differences between participating members to be bridged, IIASA was a medium-sized organization that grew from a staff of fifty in 1974 to a hundred in 1980; it also hosted a great many scholars from more than twenty countries passing through on short-term contracts.[5] The archive of the institute speaks volumes about its efforts to document administrative and research activities; in fact, I was told by the administrators that meticulous documentation was intentionally pursued, because this was understood as a vital strategy to manage risk in the volatile geopolitical context. Anticipating disagreements and even a falling out among members, in the 1970s–1980s IIASA was continuously preparing to defend the rationale of its existence. To ensure this, not only detailed plans and reports were produced, but regular external audits were commissioned from independent firms. But all this formal monitoring was not the only and, perhaps, not the main resource that assured the life of IIASA: I was told that informal solutions which did not directly challenge the formal rules of participation were widely employed. Informality was used by the leaders of the institute and individual projects to get things done where the formal rules did not work. Albeit practical, this presence of nonbureaucratic informality also had to be justified; thus enters the metaphor of family, a way of making sense and legitimizing nonbureaucratic practices in the East-West Institute.

But one also needs to consider that modes of organizing and internal narratives of organizations do not emerge out of thin air. Indeed, the idea of organizing as an explicitly meaning-making activity was a relatively new phenomenon, contemporaneous with the establishment of IIASA. From the 1970s on, the idea of corporate or organizational culture gained currency in Western societies as a result of both a shift from industrial to intellectual labor, and the accumulation of findings from the new discipline of the era, management studies. Managers began to increasingly rely on an idea that organizational culture could be manipulated in order to benefit a company's performance.[6] Organization theorists claimed that a deeper, normative integration of workers with their company was typical of new, postindustrial organizations. In many organizations "family" became a popular figure of speech to designate precisely such a normative integration.[7] Although as it is often the case with colloquial expressions, it is difficult to establish with certainty when and for what reasons the family metaphor was introduced in IIASA's internal self-narrative, one can speculate that the first director, Howard Raiffa, an expert in policy science, was suitably positioned to encounter and translate recent organizational theories into reality, intentionally and carefully crafting a particular organizational culture, which led to the formation of a transnational community of systems analysts.

The founding stage in the making of IIASA's "systems family" took place during Howard Raiffa's directorship, 1972–1975. Archival documents reveal internal debates on the issue of academic quality, which was understood as being of the utmost importance, because IIASA sought to gain recognition as a real think tank; its creators wanted to avoid by any means the image of being just another decorative component of Cold War diplomacy. However, there were a number of issues pertaining to the everyday life, such as interpersonal and agenda disagreements in relation to Cold War polarization, and the very real risk of espionage that threatened to compromise the scientific reputation of the newly established institute. To counteract these risks, Raiffa introduced a set of measures intended to establish a highly informal and open culture. This was achieved, in the first place, by removing all physical obstacles to any search for information by Soviet intelligence services. For instance, the director famously never locked his desk drawers and even chose individuals with known KGB credentials as his assistants, thus making it clear that he had nothing to hide.[8] Secret intelligence was not very secret either: several of my interlocutors recalled that many Russian secretaries were "very nice people, but also very obviously KGB," noting that regardless of their evident presence, the atmosphere in the institute was never tense.[9] The themes of research were also carefully adjusted. True, systems analysis, as I mentioned earlier, was in many ways linked with highly strategic technologies, which were embargoed by CoCom countries and which the Soviet Union desperately attempted to acquire. But in this case the threat of espionage was seen by the interviewed scientists as simply irrelevant, because the studies pursued at IIASA used only open data. This strategy of using open data was both an asset and an obstacle, because it did complicate cooperation with the Soviet Union, which tried to keep as much data as possible outside the public domain.

If openness was used to deter espionage, informality turned out to be an irreplaceable instrument in navigating geopolitical waters. Dealing with the risk of espionage was an unavoidable part of a Cold War international organization, but it in the case of an East-West institute, it appears that it was not so much espionage as external, geopolitical tensions that required the most attention. The risk was that IIASA could become yet another dysfunctional international organization, torn by national or bloc interests. This was particularly evident in personnel recruitment from the Soviet Union, where multiple political logics intertwined, some internal to Soviet academia, and some rooted in geopolitical clashes. As I will show, the geopolitical dimension was always present on the leadership agenda and was carefully managed.

Informal culture was, however, coupled with, and probably made possible by, the fact that IIASA's directors enjoyed rather strong personal autonomy in matters of decisions over the staff. Archival documents reveal that the coupling of informality and strong directorship was consciously and strategically achieved at a very early stage in the life of the institute. The top staff were hired proactively (unlike in UN organizations, where member countries nominated their candidates) and often quite informally. Thus in 1973–1974 Raiffa looked for ways to concentrate academic excellence at IIASA, relying on insider knowledge of some of the finest minds in the field of decision theory. He was aware of the importance that the scientists invited should be genuinely willing to work together. High salaries and the location of the institute were important assets, but the mutual esteem of the scholars was equally vital. According to Raiffa, "Tjalling Koopmans accepted to come because George Dantzig promised to come, who was eager to work with Alan Manne, who would come if Koopmans was there, but also Manne wanted to ski in Austrian Alps."[10] All three, Koopmans, Dantzig and Manne, experts in energy economics, joined intellectual forces to engage in a completely new area for them, namely Buzz Holling's ecology project, the aim of which was to create an innovative computer model of the spread of budworm pest in Canadian forests. This was one of the first successful IIASA projects, and one which revealed the possibilities of mathematically forecasting complex, interrelated systems.

Yet informality does not automatically result from merely disregarding formal rules or bureaucratic regulations. Informality is always a context-bound condition that revolves around an organization's specific rules and draws on the organization's knowledge. This became evident in the mediation of the differences between Eastern and Western organizational cultures: a particular version of informality had to be developed that would enable IIASA to serve as a bridge between East and West. Whereas Raiffa's in-depth knowledge of social relations and individual cultural habits was instrumental in bringing top US scholars to IIASA, neither he nor anyone else at that time had any detailed knowledge, or even intuition, about many of incoming Soviet scholars. Could an internal mechanism of evaluation be enforced to sort out productive scientists from less productive ones? This was not considered to be a solution. Retrospectively, Raiffa explained his staffing strategy, saying that the formal evaluation of scholarly output was irrelevant, because scholars were primarily self-motivated and competing against other scholars:

> There is little to gain and a lot, possibly, to lose in morale if we attempt to control the output of our scientists. Our most effective means of controlling the quantity, quality and suitability of our output is to select wisely the people who are supposed to produce this output.[11]

But was not this approach severely limited, given that the control over the inflow of Soviet scientists was so limited? Whereas Western scholars could be approached individually, contacts with Soviet scholars were funneled through the GKNT and the Academy of Sciences.[12] All official invitations to Soviet scientists had to trickle down through the complex bureaucratic system, a slow and painstaking process during which the lists of invitees were modified to accommodate competing interests within the Soviet research institutes and the GKNT. Archival documents disclose constant grievances from IIASA's directorate and project leaders about the Soviet Union sending poorly qualified scholars during first years of the institute's existence. Even in the early 1980s, IIASA's leadership complained that too many Soviet scientists were narrowly trained specialists, lacking the skills needed to fully participate in interdisciplinary projects, and many were not sufficiently fluent in English.[13]

What was to be done? Raiffa recalled that the best, in fact, the only way to ensure that IIASA would receive relevant Soviet scientists, was to use a personal, informal strategy of dropping their names to Gvishiani in conversation, for instance, during walks in the woods. According to Raiffa, Gvishiani would never personally either confirm or disapprove any of his suggestions, but eventually some of the mentioned scholars would appear on the official lists of invitees proposed by the Soviet Academy of Sciences.[14]

Similarly, Raiffa recalled that it was virtually impossible to reach any agreement on the research agenda in the official IIASA council meetings. Such issues were also resolved informally: the members of IIASA's council discussed all key points off the record beforehand. This practice itself was something of a public secret: the institute's administration was fully aware of the importance of the informal preliminary talks and did their best to facilitate this practice by inserting long breaks in the schedule of the council's meetings.[15] Informality, in this way, was enabled by the means of formal organization.

In a similar way, informal practices, discipline, and formal organizing were intertwined in the internal life of IIASA. All three qualities were encapsulated in the metaphor of family. The elitist culture of informal hiring was part and parcel of a rather stringent paternalist supervision of cultural habits of systems scholars. And indeed some of these scholars were rather unorthodox, especially those Americans who came from wealthy and privileged backgrounds. For instance, in his memoir Raiffa described—with some admiration at that—a doctoral student who not only drove a Porsche, but also rejected a lectureship at MIT because the position interfered with his vacation plans. It soon transpired that the nonbureaucratic, informal culture of IIASA's family, developed by Raiffa, was rather rigid as compared to the hippy lifestyles of younger Western scholars. That the culture of IIASA's family was clearly a disciplining device is evident in Raiffa story, where he recalled his efforts to make the casually attired US staff more acceptable to the presumably more formal Soviet scientists, insisting that his Porsche-driving doctoral student acquire a sports jacket and that his assistant, Alan McDonald, cut off his ponytail. A woman administrator was asked to wear less "sexy" clothes.[16]

These efforts to make the Americans look presentable suggest that the declared openness and informality was a product of a carefully controlled, everyday performance. The West performed for the East, but in a way that would not challenge the Eastern perception of an appropriate behavior. Indeed, the interviewed IIASA staff told me that the success of IIASA was largely due to its organizational culture, and this organizational culture was defined as Western. But there was more to the disciplinary mechanism than a superficial adjustment to dress codes: many other adjustments were made to accommodate the Soviet membership in this transnational community of systems analysis. The mobility of scholars was one such sensitive question. Raiffa, for example, recalled teaching the Soviets by example that good science could be produced only by granting young scholars the opportunity to travel freely across national borders. However, Raiffa also admitted to being particularly careful not to let Soviet scientists overstay their term, seeing this as a necessary measure in preventing them from defecting to the West.[17]

In addition to these social and political concerns there was another, no less important factor that influenced the development of the informal culture of the IIASA family: the technical and spatial infrastructure. I mentioned earlier that the Soviets supported the East-West institute, hoping to use it as a channel to bypass the Co-Com embargo on computer technology. Indeed, the role of computer technology was crucial not only during the formative stage of IIASA, but remained relevant over the next two decades of the Institute's existence, although not exactly in the way that was anticipated by the Soviets. First of all, IIASA was never equipped with state-of-the-art computer technology and this was a conscious decision by IIASA's council, part of its strategy to discourage Soviet espionage.[18] Older computers meant slower computers, and slow machines turned out to play a particularly important role in providing East-West scientists with a unique, almost private space for uninterrupted communication. As my interlocutor recalled, "we used to spend entire nights in the central computing facility. We used to wait for results to come from the computer with our six packs of beer as dawn was breaking. The slow technology had a very positive impact on personal interaction at that time."[19] Computer technology, in this way, provided IIASA's scientists with a special space and time for interaction that could be compared with the canonical image of a Central European café as a cosmopolitan meeting space, except that there was beer and not coffee to be consumed and a humming computer instead of live piano music. In addition to computer labs, sport provided yet another area where East-West scholars could interact informally. For example, scientists played a modified form of softball in the Laxenburg park every Friday in the 1980s; these sessions were continued in the *bierstube*.[20]

But the "IIASA family" was not merely a metaphor. There were actual families at IIASA: top scholars were attracted in part by a generous policy enabling them to bring their wives and children (and yes, the majority of IIASA scientists were male, Donella Meadows being a prominent exception). To provide for a good quality of life outside working hours, leisure facilities were built through a grant from the Ford Foundation, which funded construction of a special restaurant for the staff, tennis courts, and even an annex for the American International School to accommodate the children of IIASA fellows. Raiffa reported to Bundy that this grant was used to enhance the cultural life of the IIASA staff by bringing in lecturers, organizing concerts, buying outdoor furniture, and even hiring tax advisors.[21] Scholars' family activities led to further integration, especially

FIGURE 2. Schloss Laxenburg, 1962. Courtesy of IIASA.

through the Women's Club, a network that was sustained by many women even after their partners left IIASA. Furthermore, the role of the fellows' wives was central in forging personal links across the Iron Curtain, as they were often the ones providing for the "real" home environment. For instance, Raiffa personally endeavored to bring the staff together, as he and his wife often hosted administrative staff for dinner in their apartment on Operngasse in Vienna.[22] It may well be that the metaphor of "IIASA family" remained viable after the 1970s, thanks to these carefully crafted practices, linking professional membership in the institute and personal lives.

Integrating Soviets into the IIASA Family

If some US scholars were nudged to modify their hippy lifestyles to fit into this East-West family, how did Soviet scientists experience their stay at IIASA? Published sources and interviews reveal varying impressions. For example, a Russian

FIGURE 3. Schloss Laxenburg after reconstruction, 1978. Courtesy of IIASA.

mathematician I interviewed joined IIASA in the early 1980s to find, in his words, a social milieu very similar to the one at home, the prestigious Steklov Mathematical Institute in Moscow. According to this scholar, the elite Soviet mathematical communities espoused rather democratic principles and informal relationships between professors and junior scientists, in this respect being completely different from other, more hierarchical scholarly environments, such as those of economists.[23] Some other scholars from East Europe voiced similar opinions: a Polish scholar even recalled that the atmosphere was much friendlier during the Cold War than it was at the time I interviewed him, because earlier directors made a particular effort to make sure that everyone felt welcome.[24] Also, some Soviet scientists came from elite academic institutes, which were, as David Holloway notes, rare islands of freedom in Soviet society.[25] These scholars told me that they did not encounter a big cultural difference; for them the key benefit of IIASA was the opportunity to freely access its increasingly rich library and, importantly, unlimited use of its photocopier. According to one member of administration staff, one could always be certain to find a visiting Soviet scholar at the copying machine.[26]

Yet I was told different stories by other ex-Soviet IIASA fellows. A scientist from Akademgorodok, a purpose-built Soviet science town in Siberia, which was known for its substantial intellectual but also social autonomy, painted a less glossy picture of his experience at IIASA in the 1980s, the period when, according to my other interlocutors, Soviet control was already more relaxed than in the 1970s. This Russian scholar, who embarked on a highly successful career after 1991, was exceptionally frank about how his experience at IIASA in the 1980s was weighed down by surveillance and financial constriction. He recalled often being followed when visiting his colleagues' homes in Vienna, and detailed his feeling of humiliation when he had to give about half his salary to the Soviet embassy every month, and in consequence struggled to keep up with the lifestyle of Western scholars. Another ex-Soviet scientist recalled receiving a salary of about USD 5,000 and giving about 70 percent to the Soviet embassy in the 1980s.[27] These stories were corroborated by my Western interlocutors, who recalled that Soviet scholars almost never joined them on skiing trips or outings to restaurants.[28] The obligation to return large part of their salary (the Polish Academy of Sciences also made their IIASA fellows return as much as 70 percent[29]) was an informal way of ameliorating the financial damage to the Soviet apparatus caused by the fact that IIASA was one of few international organizations where the Soviet Union fully matched the US financial contribution.

There might also have been some concerns about security that limited the integration of Soviet scientists into the IIASA family. One ex-Soviet scientist recalled feeling quite free to invite his foreign colleagues for dinner at his privately rented apartment in the prestigious Schönbrunn area of Vienna, but he became aware of possible eavesdropping when he moved to the specially built compound for Soviet citizens in 1985. Believing that his spacious apartment was bugged, this scholar resorted to the classic methods of using background noise to obscure his conversation with guests, by turning up the volume of the radio.[30] In this way, for many Soviet scholars taking part in the IIASA family meant overcoming a number of daily inconveniences pertaining to economic inequality and security control, something that clearly overshadowed the informal and liberal spirit of the institute.

Nevertheless, the interviews and memoirs reveal that financial and security issues were perceived as a minor inconvenience by the Soviet scientists, who regarded the fellowship as an opportunity to spend a longer period in Western Europe and to embark on more ambitious scholarly projects: an IIASA fellowship was considered to be a highly prestigious, selective appointment. Indeed, knowledge about IIASA inside the Soviet Union was limited to a narrow circle of select, elite scientific institutes, and the choice of fellows was equally obscure both for Raiffa and the Soviet scientists themselves. One ex-Soviet scientist told me that although he knew about IIASA's existence in the 1970s through its publications and conferences, he had never considered applying for a fellowship; instead, he was "summoned" by the GKNT to participate in IIASA's research program on the environment.[31] Centralized cooptation of IIASA fellows was not limited to the Soviet Union: the participation of Dutch scholars was organized through centralized calls for particular experts in relevant areas, issued by the secretary of the Dutch member organization and disseminated among the institutes that were deemed to work at a suitable level.[32] The process in the Soviet Union, however, was much more opaque and much less predictable.

The Soviet fellows at IIASA ranged from well-established to young and promising scientists; they were also of unequal standing in the political hierarchy of the Soviet academia. For all of them IIASA served as a bridge to West, yet their individual abilities to use this bridge differed. There was a big difference between the top scientists and research administrators and ordinary, if highly esteemed scholars. Some Soviets traveled much more than others and did so in a very different style. Gvishiani visited the United States as early as the 1960s, whereas it was only in 1972 that the president of the Academy of Sciences, Mstislav Keldysh, crossed the Atlantic. Gvishiani and directors of Soviet institutes clearly had much more latitude for movement when in the West, not least financially, but all these visits stimulated comparisons of communist and capitalist standards of life. A verbatim account of Keldysh's report about his trip to the United States, presented at a meeting of the Council of the Academy of Sciences, included a transcript of the discussion that followed. The first question was posed to Keldysh by Petr Kapitsa, a prominent physicist, who cheekily inquired about the salaries of American professors and the cost of a good suit in the United States,[33] hinting that as long as a Soviet professor could not afford to buy a good suit, it made no sense to speak about catching up with American science. At IIASA the economic disparity was the elephant in the room that loomed over East-West cooperation. This, in combination with the earlier-mentioned obligation to hand over part of one's IIASA salary to the embassy, was a mundane aspect of everyday life, which undoubtedly dispirited Soviet scholars.

In this context, the elite Soviet scientists and research administrators enjoyed strikingly different lifestyles and freedom of movement. Upon their visit to Paris, Gvishiani and Kirillin stayed in the plush George V hotel, an experience which was surpassed by the hospitality of the president of France, who spontaneously offered the Soviet *éminences grises* a weekend trip to Corsica. The presidential private Caravelle jet whisked Gvishiani and Kirillin away for an overnight excursion to this Mediterranean island.[34] Other leading Soviet scientists also amused themselves with spontaneous trips when in the West. When visiting IIASA, Nikita Moiseev, the research director of the Soviet Academy of Sciences' Computer Center in Moscow, drove to Lichtenstein during the Christmas holidays. He crossed the Austrian Alps only to discover at the border that he did not have the necessary visa. The kindly border guards, however, allowed Moiseev to turn his car around on Lichtenstein's territory, thus enabling him claim a visit to this state.[35] Although this story might strike the reader as a somewhat trivial misunderstanding, one should not underestimate the significance of such adventures for Soviet scholars. Used to passing through innumerable bureaucratic hurdles and formalities, they experienced these free, spontaneous travels not only as a gust of personal freedom, but also as confirmation of their special status within the tightly controlled system. It is also quite probable that these experiences reinforced their loyalty to the Soviet government, a stay in IIASA being a reward for loyal service at home.

As a bridge, IIASA did not merely enable one way, East-West traffic, but also facilitated the trips of Western scholars to the Soviet bloc. High-level conferences, such as, for instance, the UN meeting dedicated to the debate on global problems took place in Tallinn, Estonia, in 1979.[36] But no less important were many workshops and project planning meetings organized in the Soviet Union—predominantly in Moscow, but also in other Russian cities like Leningrad and Akademgorodok, where the leader of the IIASA energy study, Wolf Häfele, developed cooperation programs in the field of nuclear energy, and non-Russian republics, such as the Baltic states and Caucasus. The scientific utility of those workshops was often limited: one scientist who participated in such a jointly organized event in the Soviet Union recalled having to endure endless abstract presentations, containing no empirical or statistical data and badly delivered at that.[37] Nevertheless, according to other interviewed scientists, some of these visits strongly contributed to building trust among some individuals. Typically these were social components of trips to the Soviet Union that Western scientists recalled with a great deal of pleasure. For instance, a workshop organized by academician Vladimir Mikhalevich at the Institute of Cybernetics of the Ukrainian Academy of Sciences in Kyiv, began with a cognac session at 10 a.m. The drinks continued to flow as someone carelessly mentioned that it was Saint Patrick's Day in Ireland. As a result, some of Western participants had to be literally carried to the plane that was to take the East-West scientists to Leningrad, where another workshop was awaiting them.[38]

Both the organizational culture and social life at IIASA animated this unprecedented institute. But a well-running organizational machine was not a mere medium for the production of a new type of policy science, systems analysis. In the remaining part of this chapter I discuss the ways in which IIASA turned out to be instrumental in forging links between scientific knowledge, governance, and politics across the East-West divide, eventually assuming an increasingly strong identity as an actor in its own right and not just a bridge between the competing great powers. Inquiring into this process, I point to the emergence of a particular assemblage of theories, institutions, and practices that question the bipolar image of the Cold War world.

Systems Approach: From Depoliticization to Aesopian Language

The link between politics and systems analysis was multifaceted and complicated: systems analysis, a science deemed to be most appropriate for apolitical cooperation across the Iron Curtain, found its first governmental applications in the United States in the area of weapon systems design and the development of what was supposed to be a rational foundation for US foreign policy of containing communism. This application of systems analysis, according to Beryl Radin, led to the emergence of what was called "policy analysis" in the State Department, where George Kennan was charged with the task of planning a long-term policy toward the Soviet Union in 1947. Kennan's task was later continued under the leadership of Walt Rostow during Johnson's presidency.[39]

Although this trajectory of the development of systems analysis was embedded in military applications, according to Radin, there was also a parallel development of civilian applications of systems analysis, where systems analysis was introduced into different US government departments through the method of program-planning-budgeting-system (PPBS), a method which originated in military OR. PPBS was spread through the Systems Analysis Unit, established by Robert McNamara at the Department of Defense in 1961. The very idea of PPBS was to bypass the bureaucratic circulation of information and decisions along the formal chain of command. This was achieved by establishing additional policy-analysis units that had direct access to all information and top decision makers.[40] In this way the introduction of civilian applications of systems analysis involved both intellectual and institutional reform, inserting new actors and practices into governmental process. Like in the United States, in the Soviet Union the link between military uses of systems analysis and its civilian applications eventually grew weaker. Moreover, like in the United States, in the Soviet Union the introduction of policy science also involved an institutional reform.

The development of systems analysis as a nonpolitical technology of governance, therefore, was bound to the contexts of its use. In this section I detail how the pioneers of the systems approach not only adjusted this technology to the institutional context, but also used the systems approach to redefine this very context. As I showed in chapters 2 and 3, in the 1960s systems analysis was posited to be a neutral instrument of governance, suitable to fulfilling Johnson's diplomatic program of bridge building, but also echoing the Soviet interest in high-technology transfer. But both the epistemology of systems analysis and its practice in organizations required deeper institutional transformation in both liberal democratic and authoritarian systems. Historians, such as Michael Latham, suggest that the ideas guiding Johnson's Great Society program, particularly the belief that scientific expertise could resolve social and economic issues within US society, spilled over into US international relations.[41] Drawing on the Vietnam example, Patrick Cohrs suggests that by disseminating the US model of expert governance in developing countries, Johnson's administration hoped to combat more radical forms of politics by promoting moderate views.[42]

Cohr's observation may also apply to the East-West institute, but in this I would like to add that the modernization theory-driven cooperation clearly was expected to have a more substantial, subversive effect by at least pluralizing the sources and types of power in the communist regime. The case of IIASA is quite remarkable, because this is where the competing development theories—the US modernization theory and the Soviet theory of scientific-technical revolution—converged to legitimize an institutional innovation. It is this broader intellectual context, I argue, that made possible the construction of systems approach as an apparently apolitical, yet subversive technology of governance. Here depoliticization stemmed not only from US activities, but also from the formative context of East-West cooperation, particularly at IIASA. That East-West transfer of systems analysis drew on mutual efforts to depoliticize this governmental technique is particularly evident in the strategies pursued at IIASA, where different notions of the political were identified and neutralized by designing organizational structures and employing specific discourses. I want to emphasize that depoliticization is not a negative strategy, but a productive process, in which different meanings of "the political" are defined and used selectively in relation to the context. Let us look more closely at these pragmatic strategies of depoliticization.

Perhaps the most divisive notion of the political is captured by the controversial German philosopher Carl Schmitt, who reserved the meaning of the concept of the political to a friend-foe divide, leading to a military conflict.[43] It was precisely this notion of the political that Johnson's bridge-building policy sought to transcend. In practice, the friend-foe tension was neutralized by carefully selecting those scientific approaches, research objects, and applications of research findings that had the weakest possible links to the military, IIASA's research agenda explicitly excluded any areas of direct military application or closed research.

However, what constituted military research was not always evident and sometimes subject to negotiation. For instance, in 1975 Thomas Brown of Pan Heuristics, a subsidiary of the US defense company Science Applications Incorporated, approached IIASA's director with a proposal to establish a working group modeling Soviet-American strategic interaction. The rationale of this project was to advance econometric and military modeling by bringing insight into how experts from each side think. On this basis an "accurate forecasting tool," grounded in empirical and psychological reality, would be developed and equip each side with an instrument for mutual prediction.[44] In its intention to develop mutual predictability, this proposal was completely in line with the tasks set out by Walt Rostow's unit for policy analysis, which I mentioned earlier. However, IIASA quickly signaled that its agenda differed from this systems research community: James Bigelow responded to the proposal by writing that this was "precisely the kind of idea, that regardless of its technical feasibility, IIASA would utterly refuse to work on."[45]

Another notion of the political refers to membership in a political party and adherence to certain ideological principles. Thus conceived, the political was neutralized at IIASA by positing a particular actorial identity of the systems analyst. Drawing on the long German tradition of the apolitical engineer, expert, and technician, a systems analyst was construed as an independent professional, loyal to the state, but free from party politics.[46] Obviously, this was still a problematic definition, because the idea of an apolitical expert disagreed with the communist definition of the engineer and manager as a committed builder of socialism.[47]

The situation was further complicated by the ongoing debates in the West, where, since the mid-1950s, the tension between political and scientific governance had been exacerbated by heated debates on the death of ideology, pursued by the theorists of the postindustrial society, such as Daniel Bell, Raymond Aron, and Edward Shils. In 1960 Bell published *The End of Ideology*, arguing that, in an affluent society, workers saw their condition hugely improved and consequently lost interest in political struggle mediated by ideology.[48]

The Soviets embraced the idea of a postindustrial society, but fiercely rejected the suggestion that ideological class struggle would wither away. But the depoliticization of governance in the post-Stalinist Soviet Union was already taking place, albeit incrementally. In the early 1960s institutional reform began with the systematic introduction of scientific experts into the governmental apparatus in response to the urgent need for efficiency and solutions for increasingly complex technical systems. The Soviets borrowed Bell's ideas selectively, welcoming the intellectualization of labor through the shift to automation of industrial production, but removing any hints about possible implications of this process for the power structure, such as a diminishing role for the Communist Party in policy making. In this context it turned out to be much easier to depoliticize the kind of expertise concerned with matters that transcended national political agendas.

Bell noted the shift in the US political discourse, locating the key concern not in the clash of ideologies, but in the achievement of common goals, both domestic and, later, international, attributing the origins of the discourse on common goals to John F. Kennedy's commencement address at Yale University in 1962.[49] From the mid-1960s this discourse of common goals, which could be achieved through the means of teleological governance, powered by systems analysis, was adopted in some Soviet policy circles, thus opening up a space for apolitical expertise that was not torn by the issues of loyalty to national interest.

In order to make this discourse of common goals work, a particular organizational structure had to be designed to soften the tensions arising from diverging national agendas. This was the foremost task at IIASA. First, academic organizations, and not governments, were nominated as member organizations of IIASA. This model of the neutralization of the political was widely used by many international organizations, including CERN, where independence from sovereign politics was expressed in the principle that any individual scientist could participate at CERN regardless of nationality, thus, as Dominique Pestre has put it, "escaping the burdens of the nationalism."[50] In the case of IIASA, to be sure, this neutralization was partial with regard to East European countries, where academic organizations were closely controlled by governments. Also, CERN's principle of universal, world science was applied by IIASA to only a limited extent, because participation in IIASA was restricted to scientists from its member countries.[51]

At IIASA, but also at CERN, the institutional reconciliation between the two, national and international dimensions, was normally addressed at the top level, the council meetings: several interviewees admitted that they had been aware of political rationales, that is, national interests, lurking behind research projects at IIASA. For instance, the choice of Canadian or Siberian forests as a research object was acknowledged, albeit silently, as a political concession to the respective national interests. The shaping of a research agenda beyond particular national interests was easier to achieve at CERN than at IIASA, because CERN was able to refer to the physical construction of a laboratory as powerful support for its universal orientation, while IIASA lacked a similar reference to a material tool, dealing instead with soft technologies of aiding in decision making.[52] But if CERN's mission was to put European science at the same level as US science, IIASA aimed even higher, aiming to forge a new type of global governance. And whereas there was a trend to form nationally homogeneous departments at CERN, as noted by Pestre, IIASA scholars genuinely mixed across research programs. Finally, while both CERN and IIASA hosted scholarly communities that shaped and advanced their own professional interests, which did not always agree with the interests of national member organizations, what was even more important was that these international platforms provided a new type of context where *new interests* emerged.

Anchoring common goals in a concrete research agenda was another difficulty that IIASA's leaders tried to overcome. At all costs what was regarded as a futile ideological debate had to be avoided; thus the application of systems analysis to social issues was deemed unworkable. However, what exactly constituted social issues was a particularly murky zone, where consensus of East-West systems analysts had to be negotiated on a case-by-case basis. For instance, the subject of public health (which obviously involved multiple social issues), was approved and included in IIASA's demographic and urban planning projects. However, although IIASA launched a project on international negotiations with an emphasis on complexity, multilateral participation, and the impacts of technology in 1986, it was not until 1989 that scholars began to call for widening IIASA's agenda to social science-based policy analysis. Up to that time there had been a general preference for what was seen as technical and natural scientific areas and "harder," quantitative approaches; according to Raiffa, "the languages of the Institute [were] English, Mathematics and Fortran."[53]

Yet speaking a common language and working toward articulating common goals was an important strategic orientation. Presenting a long-range strategy, Raiffa noted that the institute could not be too careful in considering and even hosting external events related to "highly political" subjects, such as world trade, catastrophe intervention, and the ongoing UN conference on the Law of the Sea.[54] The solution was found in a focus on what were defined as universal and global problems:

> Universal are those problems such as organizing the pick-up of solid waste refuse in all our cities. Every single city has the same problem—it's universal. By making a detailed study of what happens in New York City, or Leningrad, or Tokyo, we do not have in mind solving those problems for those cities—it would be nice if this were a by-product—but we want to understand the problem itself, because the methodology and philosophy of approach might be transferable on a universal basis.... Global problems are the problems which require a concerted effort by many nations to provide a solution. The Law of the Sea is an example of one. What we do about man's effect on climate, what we do in terms of international computer networks, or international river systems are examples of more global problems.[55]

Accordingly, during the first years of its existence IIASA focused its research agenda on universal problems, which, as is evident from the above quote, were understood to be suitable objects for international transfer. From late 1970s on, the interest was widened to embrace global problems and more active and direct involvement in globally concerted policy action.[56] It should not be forgotten that back then, as at the moment of writing in 2015, neutral platforms for studying transnational issues were in huge demand. Scientists and policy makers from industrialized countries looked for places where they could gather to conduct preparatory discussions for international legislation. As one interviewee recalled, US government officials supported IIASA because they thought it would provide for "a place in Europe where we can talk about common problems, such as insects in forests, perhaps, dirty water."[57] But this observation refers to a particular, in fact, quite advanced stage of policy negotiation. In order to become common, problems had to be framed proactively and carefully so that they could become acceptable for different governments. This required active management of the context, making way for the introduction of what could be understood as controversial issues. My British interlocutor related to me his experience of introducing research on risk to the East-West agenda as he was advised by his Russian colleague at IIASA:

> [You should not] go to Moscow and start talking sociology of science, because they will throw you in the Moscow river. Instead, you should talk technocratically, to find a way to socialize technocracy. That was an interesting challenge, one I recognize in East European colleagues. You can talk about siting issues. Siting can be a technocratic problem of optimized localization, rather than a problem recognizing that there might be deeper influences of political and normative and ontological kind if we need that stuff anyway.[58]

Here this Russian scientist told my interlocutor that there was a way to debate issues associated with controversial subjects, such as hazardous waste in the Soviet Union, by using a proxy of an entirely technocratic discourse, consisting of both the language and institutional setting of expertise, associated with siting and optimal planning. This and other examples show that some Soviet technocratic discourses could be compared with the Soviet cultural discourses in that they carried hidden, what was called Aesopian, meanings.[59]

In this context of mutual adjustment through defining methods, selecting research objects, and choosing a particular language, a question arises as to whether and how the depoliticization of IIASA's organizational structure and research agenda related to the views of individual researchers. Perhaps this discursive maneuvering, quite necessary from the diplomatic point of view, was perceived as political censorship by researchers. The threat of censorship was explicitly recognized by the directorate, and close control of the work of individual researchers at IIASA was deemed to be inappropriate in principle. Again, it was Raiffa who suggested that resident scientists should be free to publish whatever they saw fit for their own scientific purpose under their own names, in whichever outlets they found suitable for their own individual goals. Institutional monitoring, in turn, would apply only to those materials that were published and promoted as IIASA studies. Even in this case, it was decided that the council would not act as a review board, thus ensuring that political diplomacy would not directly control scientific production.[60]

An overarching strategy of separating individual research and broad institutional agenda is one thing, but the actual behavior of individual scientists as political subjects must also be considered. Some of IIASA's scientists may have used technocratic language to subvert Soviet censorship, but what about the scientists' own attitudes to political events on both sides of the Iron Curtain? My interviews with IIASA scholars revealed rather reflexive and strategic self-censorship in their everyday interactions. This particularly applies to East European scholars, who acutely felt that political discussion was risky. A Polish scientist recalled that he avoided discussing the introduction of martial law in Poland in 1981–1983 with his colleagues at IIASA; his Russian colleagues even explicitly advised him against ever speaking out on this particular situation.[61]

But not only East Europeans fostered their internal censor. Even when heavy drinking was taking place at Russian scientists' homes, some Westerners feared that they might put their hosts in politically inconvenient situations and, accordingly, picked their conversation topics cautiously.[62] I have not, however, come across any single case of a Soviet scientist being reprimanded by Soviet authorities for taking too much liberty with his social life or views in Vienna. The only casualties, it seems, were Western scientists suffering from heavy hangovers after partying with their Soviet colleagues. The institute, in this way, appeared to be a privileged island of (carefully managed) freedom for the producers of scientific governance in the volatile Cold War world.

Finally, an important part of Cold War politics needs be considered, namely cultural diplomacy. Even those Western scientists who fostered a purely pragmatic interest in IIASA as a way to advance their individual scientific projects or gain access to literature, found themselves involved in the rituals of Cold War cultural diplomacy. An Austrian scientist who worked on the food program of 1976 recalled regarding his stay at IIASA as an exceptional opportunity to access data on world populations and food for the purposes of global modeling. Yet he could not help but become aware of the political aspect of the institute as his first day at work coincided with celebration of the October Revolution.[63] Not only Soviet, but also Western rituals were staged at IIASA: Canadian pancake breakfasts were organized regularly, and one of the greatest annual festivities was the July 4 celebration. During one such event a live elephant was brought to the gardens of the schloss as a symbol of the Republican Party. In this way IIASA combined the requirements of cultural diplomatic representation of the member nations with attempts to foster a research environment that transcended national and political boundaries.

I need to add, however, that there was more politics at IIASA than just the clash between communist and capitalist ideologies, complications related to military competition, or cultural symbolism. In spite of IIASA's declared interest in global and universal problems, there were telling lacunas in its research agenda, testifying to politically motivated selection. One such lacuna was nuclear security, a subject

FIGURE 4. Celebration at IIASA. Mr. Lukas, resident in Laxenburg, had bought the 2 old elephants from a circus and the animals were living in a shed in Laxenburg but were also often seen in the park and around the village. Courtesy of IIASA.

FIGURE 5. Elephants as symbols of the Republicans in the backyard of the Leopold Schloss's restaurant, the 4th of July celebration, Laxenburg, Austria. Courtesy of IIASA.

that was not addressed at IIASA until the Chernobyl catastrophe in 1986, although the Institute developed a pioneering study of world energy systems in close cooperation with the International Atomic Energy Agency (IAEA). Only after Chernobyl was a new research program dedicated to technological risk launched.

Furthermore, one should not jump to a conclusion that politics at this East-West platform was merely a phenomenon to be purged and controlled. On the contrary, there were also other, activist politics emerging through IIASA's activities, which effectively undermined the ideological East-West divide. As I show in the subsequent chapters, IIASA was home to some of the most progressive and radical thinkers on environmental governance. Although IIASA visitors' lists always contained the names of leading economists who promoted rational choice theory, criticized as nondemocratic technocrats by civil movements and historians of governance alike, the institute also hosted pioneering climate scientists and advanced a global environmental agenda. In line with this, I suggest conceptualizing IIASA as a heterogeneous laboratory, where the Cold War world of the 1950s morphed into a new way of being and where the systems approach generated new forms of politics.

FIGURE 6. IIASA scientists' soccer game "USSR" versus "The rest of the world" refereed by Peter de Janosi, IIASA director (1990–1996) (fifth from left, standing), Laxenburg, 1978. Courtesy of IIASA.

FIGURE 7. IIASA scientists at work, probably the 1970s. Courtesy of IIASA.

Coproducing the World System beyond East-West

Given the significance of the geopolitical tensions described above, a striking feature of IIASA was that the institute served to produce a unique, albeit loose, transnational association of systems scholars, an association that forged a new way of thinking about governance in East and West alike, as I describe in the chapters that follow. In this section I discuss several cases of East-West cooperation that demonstrate IIASA was not just a place for performing rituals of Cold War diplomacy, but a platform where significant innovative contributions to policy science were developed through a genuine symbiosis of East-West expertise.

To begin with, IIASA enabled contacts among scholars who would otherwise struggle to meet. For instance, Herbert Simon espoused strongly anti-Soviet views and refused to visit the Soviet Union, although his work was available in Russian (e.g., *Administrative Behavior* was translated in 1974). Yet Soviet scholars could meet Simon at IIASA, where he gave talks on procedural rationality and ill-structured systems in April 1979.[64]

Perhaps the most salient example of such East-West symbiosis in advancing policy science was the combination of Western intellectual entrepreneurialism and the modeling skills of Russian mathematicians. One example is the influential theory of increasing returns and path dependence, developed by the American economist Brian Arthur during his fellowship at IIASA (1977–1982).[65] Arthur derived his idea in part from his observation that IIASA's staff tended to buy either VW or Fiat cars. Arthur formulated a hypothesis that personal imitation on a small scale might lead, practically by chance, to VW's domination of the car market. He questioned the neoclassical economists' idea of equilibrium, using the example of the standard typewriter keyboard to show that economies contain many apparently insignificant events that can have massive consequences in the future. In particular, Arthur focused on proving that competing technologies may lead to a lock-in effect. For example, the QWERTY keyboard, invented in 1873 and widely used in countries with the Roman alphabet, remained in use despite the invention of much more convenient, faster keyboard systems, such Dvorak and Maltron.[66] These examples led Arthur to formulate the insight that the fittest technologies do not always survive and that "small events" get amplified into trends through positive feedback. However, according to Arthur himself, none of his US colleagues could help him calculate the stochastic processes of the impact of micro decisions on further industrial development (he approached Joel Cohen and Samuel Karlin). The mathematical apparatus for proving Arthur's path dependency theory was developed by his officemates, Ukrainian mathematicians Iurii Ermolev and Iurii Kaniovskii, who used the so-called Kiyv methods of stochastic gradient theory.[67] Arthur's case not only illustrates East-West transfer, but also shows that in some cases Soviet ideological determination to prove the inefficiency of the market system did not contradict, but in fact reinforced the advancement of a postpositivist, more complex understanding of economic dynamics.[68]

Furthermore, IIASA facilitated the dissemination of some lesser-known Russian economic theories in the West. One example was the case of Nikolai Kondrat'ev's theory of long-wave development cycles, originally developed in the 1920s and 1930s. According to Kondrat'ev, the development of the economy was not linear but cyclical, with overlapping cycles of different lengths: for instance, in addition to the widely recognized seven to eleven year business cycle he distinguished long term economic cycles of growth and decline measuring 50 years and more.[69] Using statistical time series analysis covering about 140 years, Kondrat'ev detected such long cycles in many areas, including the wholesale price level, the interest rate, foreign trade and workers' wages.[70] During the 1980s IIASA sponsored many research initiatives which probed the applicability of long-term cycles theory to different areas. While this type of research into long-term processes deserves a study of its own, I would like to point to just one prominent example where Kondrat'ev's ideas were used to construct a decision aid, illustrating the East-West travel of ideas, technologies and people.

During their stay at IIASA (1983–1984), the US pioneers in global modeling Dennis and Donella Meadows developed a resource simulation game, which drew on WORLD3 at IIASA. The WORLD3 model was produced to simulate global interaction among production, consumption, environment, and pollution, with a time horizon of 200 years, from 1900 to 2100, and its findings were presented in *The Limits to Growth*. At IIASA this model was simplified: the time horizon was shortened to represent ten cycles of decision making, each five years long, and the scale was adjusted to a national economy.[71] This game was commissioned by US-AID, originally intended to be used by US government officials, but it later became a tool for training energy and environment managers in Latin America to give insight into sustainable development. It involved a thirty-year planning horizon, and officials of UNIDO's Vienna office were consulted in its development. Further assistance in developing the game came from MIT engineer John Sterman and a group of IIASA scientists; Dick Duke of Michigan University also consulted with Meadows, as he was visiting IIASA at that time.[72] Building on this experience, the Meadows created STRATEGEM-2 (Strategic Games for Educating Managers), a game that communicated Kondrat'ev's long-wave theory to managers.

Funded by a 500,000 USD grant from the Canadian government, STRATEGEM-2 was used by companies in the West, but also spread in the Soviet bloc,[73] where business games were becoming hugely popular in the 1980s, as managers sought alternatives to fix the inefficient system. The transfer of business games, particularly those assisted with computer simulation, was anchored through the International Federation for Automatic Control (IFAC) and the Simulation and Gaming Association (ISAGA). ISAGA, in cooperation with the Institute of Control Sciences in Moscow, even organized an international workshop on simulation and gaming in Almaty, Kazakhstan, in June 1985, where Meadows presented his game.[74]

The goal of STRATEGEM-2 was to demonstrate how investment and production policies that were rational from individual companies' point of view interacted in the economy as a system, producing the long waves of under- and overexpansion of national economies.[75] The game simulated processes over fifty years; while playing it, managers would experience the overshoot and collapse of their industrial sector. More importantly, Meadows emphasized that his game had a moral message. By revealing the systemic outcomes of individual actions, STRATEGEM was meant to communicate to the players that "they were the only source of change," being "fully responsible for the behavior."[76] According to its authors, this game was a tool for awakening responsibility in the players, by showing that the long wave and collapse emerged not from random factors or incomplete information, but as "a consequence of bounded rationality." In turn, the long-term simulation compensated for the otherwise common loss of institutional memory of overshoot and collapse in investment, because in natural life many managers who experienced a downturn would not live to see the next long wave.[77]

In addition to the scientific tools and theories produced at IIASA as the synergetic effect of this East-West cooperation, a sociotechnical link between East and West was forged literally, IIASA provided the first computer link across the Iron Curtain. The institute was connected via a cable to Vienna Technical University's CYBER 74, and as early as 1973 had an input-output unit that gave scientists remote access to the CDC 6600 supercomputer located in Frankfurt.[78] Experimental connections with Moscow were also established in 1974, when IIASA established a data link to the Moscow Institute of Control Sciences. Moreover, this Soviet institute boasted a British machine, ICL 4/70, which made its way to the Soviet Union despite the embargo, thanks to British lobbying.[79]

It was also no accident that mathematical modelers at IIASA, VNIISI in Moscow, and the UN world economic agencies used the same type of computer, PDP-11, IIASA's machine, a 16-bit PDP-11/70, was not a powerful one, but the institute had time-sharing arrangements allowing it to use several large computers in other European countries. Most of the other computer equipment for IIASA was obtained from Control Data Corporation, a key partner of the institute and the operator of what was at that time the world's largest international time-sharing network, CYBERNET.[80]

All of these connections were a part of larger computer revolution that began in the second half of the 1960s. Construction of data networks started by linking national and branch organizations, which was followed, from the 1970s on, by international links. Whereas in the Soviet Union this computer network project was incorporated into OGAS, a gargantuan and unimplemented program led by Victor Glushkov (who was also active at IIASA), the Soviet Academy of Sciences created its own data network, Akademset', which was used exclusively for research purposes by 1981.[81]

Technical infrastructure was seen as crucial for integrating national efforts in order to conduct global studies, IIASA served as a computer data link, connecting, first, the national member organizations in Moscow, Bratislava, Budapest, and Pisa in 1974, and then actively exploring joining the European information network.[82] This led to the development of IIASANET: data links were established with INION and the Institute for Scientific and Technical Information (VINITI) in Moscow. Gvishiani's VNIISI was also linked with Sofia, Prague, and IIASA.[83]

Data links contributed strongly to the material coproduction of the world system beyond the East-West divide, but this process was not smooth. There were many conflicts, often rooted in scientists' differing understanding of the governmental system and the role of scientific expertise, which influenced the conceptual design of the models they intended to serve as aids in policy decisions. In an interview, a West German scholar recalled arguing with a Russian mathematician over optimal planning models. According to him, this Russian scientist had designed an overtly centralized model intended to serve one decision maker. The German scientist criticized it, arguing that in real life there were many different actors involved in a democratic system. "He looked at me and said that rational agents would choose this model anyway. I told him that research shows that people often are irrational, to which he responded that he did not model for fools."[84] What such anecdotal stories capture is that the development of even presumably technocratic models could lead to explication and clashes over underlying social assumptions.

Building computer infrastructure enabling data links across the East-West divide was an astonishing achievement for the early 1980s. However, this infrastructure did not solve the problem of secrecy, which was particularly pressing as far as Soviet data were concerned. The lack of Soviet statistical and other data was strongly felt in the IIASA study on world energy, led by Wolf Häfele. This project included the Soviet bloc through cooperation with the Siberian Power Institute of Irkutsk. The energy program was IIASA's flagship project, generously funded and ambitious in scope, and the first case in which Eastern data were used alongside Western data in a single model.[85] As remembered by a scientist involved in this study, a good deal of creativity was employed in the making of this study:

> In those days the Soviet Union was still not giving the data away, but although the data was secret, it was still possible to work together. One of our colleagues from East Germany and another one from Prague ... would go to Russia to present their estimates, although we did these estimates with our colleagues from Russia. And they go to Moscow, the Soviet Academy of Sciences, the Energy ministry, and if the local experts say that our estimates are unrealistic, then we go back and rewrite the data until we get a better response. In this way the Soviets gave us not the data, but feedback.... After all we had some data on how much gas Russia had, Soviet plans for nuclear energy, coal reserves, all these were better known. It was not easy to work, but the biggest problem was not [the] East-West divide, but disciplinary barriers, IIASA was one of the first interdisciplinary institutes, yet these barriers were more difficult to overcome than political ones.[86]

This account clearly shows the importance of organizational and discursive staging scientific impartiality: although the estimates were coproduced with Russian colleagues, scholars from Western and Eastern Europe had to pretend they were "uninformed foreigners" in Moscow, thus creating a social space for informal, unsanctioned feedback. It also demonstrates that there was considerable room for maneuver in attempting to overcome politically motivated censorship. As my interlocutor claimed, IIASA drew on its international status (by sending non-Soviet scientists to the Soviet Union) to verify the data. Committed to international cooperation, Soviet institutes could not easily dismiss IIASA's scientists. But because IIASA scholars could not receive raw Soviet data, they relied instead on Soviet economists' informal loyalty to the universal mission of advancing science, using this loyalty to extract approximations of the data for the first study of the world energy system. In other cases the Soviets were more forthcoming in sharing their data, as in the study of large organizational systems comparing the Bratsk-Ilimsk Territorial Production Complex in the Soviet Union, the Shinkansen project in Japan, and the Tennessee Valley Authority in the United States.[87] Bridging the East-West divide was clearly an easier task when the goal of a study was a retrospective overview.

IIASA Repoliticized

When détente collapsed in the early 1980s, IIASA encountered a serious crisis. At the end of 1981, the US National Academy of Sciences (NAS) informed the IIASA council that it would discontinue payment of its membership dues starting in

1983. This was motivated by severe cuts in funding from the National Science Foundation (US membership cost 2.3 million USD per year and IIASA's annual operating budget was around 10 million USD). For IIASA's council, however, it was clear that this unexpected announcement was not merely about financial hardship. The withdrawal of NAS was part of the hardening of US foreign policy toward the Soviet Union, and IIASA, despite its carefully construed nonpolitical and nongovernmental status, found itself in the eye of the geopolitical storm. Security concerns about IIASA's reputation were voiced in the media: in 1981 a Soviet member of IIASA staff was caught trying to obtain confidential data about North Sea Gas in Norway. The spy was immediately sent home, but this incident gave the United States an excuse to reconsider its membership.[88] Other countries followed suit: in 1982, the British member organization, the Royal Society, declared it was withdrawing its membership on the grounds of complications regarding US membership, but also stating that the Department of Environment, the UK funder of IIASA, was disappointed with the institute's scientific outcomes. In turn, from the very beginning of its membership, the Royal Society considered IIASA's agenda too oriented toward social science.[89]

This changing geopolitical climate led to a rapid formation of a strategic coalition to defend IIASA, involving both former and present IIASA leaders and associates, such as Bundy and McNamara. The representatives of the national member organizations and Austrian chancellor Bruno Kreisky wrote letters to Reagan, stating their support to IIASA.[90] Having just recovered from pneumonia, Gvishiani rushed to the council's meeting in the Vienna Woods to assure IIASA's director that the Soviet Union would continue paying its dues and to confirm that the Soviets would be open to funding IIASA from private sources.[91] Understanding that Reagan's position was motivated by the Soviet Union's military involvement in Afghanistan and intervention in Poland, the strategic coalition sought to remind the US government that IIASA was, after all, not a bilateral but a multilateral organization, and that it provided one of few platforms for "informal, off-the-record" discussions about such sensitive issues as East-West transfer and arms control. They invoked the importance of East-West transfer time and again, arguing that the data on Soviet energy resources was available almost exclusively through IIASA's energy program.[92]

In addition to Gvishiani, Raiffa, and Bundy, who had more than fifteen years' experience of direct and indirect participation in the steering of IIASA, the strategic coalition for saving IIASA gathered representatives of a particular school of policy sciences, such as McNamara; it also included scientists and policy makers previously involved in Johnson's Great Society program, as well as liberal democratic American scientists and policy activists. A prominent role was played by former diplomat Chester Cooper, then a consultant at Resources for the Future, which ensured that the American Association for Advancement of Science (AAAS) would take over the role of the member organization NAS. Raiffa joined as the representative of AAAS and began to rally supporters and potential funders, as AAAS could not pay the membership bill. This lobbying effort was successful: US membership was maintained, with money coming from various government and private sources, although the US financial contribution to IIASA was significantly reduced.

In Britain the situation was much more complicated due to the greater centralization of government science funding. When the Department of the Environment discontinued funding for the Royal Society's membership at IIASA in 1982, the UK Fellowship of Engineering expressed the wish to become a British member organization replacing the Royal Society, but struggled to foot the hefty bill for membership.[93] To raise funds, some rather unorthodox solutions were attempted: in 1983 a UK Committee for IIASA was established and funded by Hermann Bondi, an influential British science administrator who had earlier headed the European Space Research Organization and helped to develop the European Space Agency, and Robert Maxwell, the media magnate. However, having failed to raise the required funding, this committee disbanded in November 1984.[94] Uncertainty over the future continued to shake IIASA during the 1980s: Italy declared it would withdraw its membership "mainly for budgetary reasons" in 1986 and France left in 1988.[95]

In this precarious situation IIASA's leadership was forced to employ all its entrepreneurial skills and look beyond governmental sources for income. In 1984–1985 Raiffa developed the brave idea of establishing what he called "regional IIASAs," extending to third world countries, and even obtained the support of the prominent French OR scientist and one of the forefathers of *la prospective* studies, Jacques Lesourne. The old networks were mobilized, such as the International Federation of Operational Research Society. However, the idea of regional IIASAs did not come to fruition.[96]

In 1985 IIASA turned to the corporate sector, although it realized that private funding posed a significant risk of reducing IIASA's credibility as a scientifically impartial organization. Just as in the case of the depoliticization of systems analysis, described earlier in this and the previous chapter, establishing links with the corporate sector involved careful boundary management. After all, IIASA was already doing some research on corporate governance. This orientation was in fact strongly encouraged by the Soviets, who had a longstanding interest in corporate management. For instance, in 1978 Gvishiani and Boris Mil'ner, the prominent economist and organization scholar and vice-director of VNIISI, participated in a workshop on corporate planning, which was chaired by Giscard d'Estaing and arranged in partnership with the European Institute of Business Administration

(INSEAD) in Fontainebleau, France. Speakers included the US management theorist Igor Ansoff, top managers from the Soviet Elektrosila (at that time one of the world's largest electric motor enterprises), Metalexport of Poland, the Latvian Gosplan, General Electric, the French Commissariat du Plan, Hewlett-Packard Europe, Shell, FIAT, Daimler-Benz, and the vice president of Coca-Cola, who all agreed that despite advances in policy sciences, concrete applications of management science, particularly the systems approach, were insufficiently used in their organizations. However, this should not diminish the significance of the fact that application of the same methods at L. M. Eriksson, Électricité de France, and the system of state socialist planning were discussed in this workshop. This suggests that a parallel between late Soviet and corporate governance was not just a metaphor, but a consistently pursued activity.[97]

The intertwining of systems analysis with state and corporate governance in both blocs was also evident at IIASA, where, for instance, a project to gather several hundred corporate executives in a series of "Global Future" conferences was presented to the IIASA council in 1985. This envisioned network of experts and executives was to involve a consulting company, Business International, and elite business schools, such as INSEAD, Harvard Business School, and the MIT Sloan School of Management. The idea of IIASA corporate associates was proposed by Chester Cooper, then special advisor to the director, and Robert Schneider of Xerox Corporation,[98] while the idea of the business school network was proposed by the Soviets, clearly in hope of opening a path for more transfer of know-how to aid the failing Soviet economy.[99]

Another example of the efforts to link Soviet management and policy elites with Western corporate circles was the first joint workshop on systems analysis organized by MIT and VNIISI in Boston, Massachusetts, in 1985.[100] In addition to high ministry officials, the workshop's program involved the research institutes hosting *perestroika* economists such as TsEMI, its spinoff, the Institute of Technical and Economic Forecasting, VNIISI, VNIIPU, the GKNT, and IMEMO. Finally, the culmination of this exchange was the launch of joint East-West ventures, which drew on IIASA's networks at the end of the 1980s. The first such East-West joint venture, Baltic Amadeus, was established in Vilnius, then Soviet Lithuania, to import Western office equipment and computers.

In all, it seems that the turbulence following the withdrawal of the NAS from membership and the loss of a steady flow of funding from the US government not only led to a search for new strategies to ensure the survival of IIASA—now both a bridge between East and West, but also a home of the systems approach community—but also to the strengthening of the links among leading systems analysts, politicians, and corporations. Both impacted on the internal organization culture of IIASA: while the metaphor of family was still in use, the actual practices acquired an increasingly disciplinary character. There was a parallel between the end of détente and the transformation of Raiffa's carefully assembled internal culture of informality. The decrease in informality was also a sign of its time: by the mid-1980s, according to Gideon Kunda, the norm of a highly intensive, strong culture in a high-tech corporation was firmly established, and many managers sought to implement it in their organizations.[101]

The crisis directorship of IIASA was drawn from one of the largest US corporations, General Electric, Thomas Lee (1984–1987) and Robert Pry (1987–1990). Lee, a former head of strategy for General Electric and professor at MIT's Sloan School of Management, replaced the prominent environmental scientist Buzz Holling. Pry came from a similar background, with combined experience at General Electric and MIT. The new ways of running the family of systems analysts shocked and terrified some of the IIASA staff. Lee, for example, banned the use of alcoholic drinks on the premises, especially during working hours. He stood at the entrance gate to the institute, telling off staff members who came in late. The much-appreciated overnight sessions with six packs at the computer center were prohibited, for, according to Lee, overtime work was a sign of incompetence and lousy management, to the massive dismay of the computer scientists. In particular Russian scientists lamented not being able to offer their colleagues shots of vodka in their offices. The frustration of the staff can be seen in the defensive tone of letters sent to Lee, like one asking for permission to serve wine at a farewell party. The next director, Pry, was even more control-oriented, particularly with regards to finance. To enlighten his administration staff, Pry supplied them with hefty management handbooks. During my fieldwork I noticed one such massive copy, balanced on the top of a desktop computer. The book was very useful, I was told, for it stopped the PC box from vibrating.[102]

In the 1980s IIASA turned to the corporate sector for funding, and even began offering applications of systems expertise to private companies. Did this shift signal an emerging link between the systems analysis community and the emerging neoliberals? More research is needed before we can draw any conclusions. If anything, IIASA's transnational systems community was for more, not less, governance. They were ex-RAND, ex-Cowles Commission, and pro-OR, but also much more conscious of the limits of narrow rationalistic and economic methods than some of their contemporaries. Indeed, as I show in the subsequent chapters, this particular systems community championed a postpositivist, reflexive approach to policy sciences emphasizing the performative power of the scientific method.[103] The systems approach evolved from being a reductionist technique, applicable only to simple systems, to a more complex, critical venture that emphasized meaning-making frameworks for the development of decision aids.[104] Narrow scientism was criticized by systems theorists themselves, as in Russell Ackoff's paper on the heart and science of systems analysis. By the mid-1980s the turn away from hard, laboratory-based studies predicting the future toward postpositivist, reflexive expertise plugged into policy making, was clear. Biosphere studies, carried out by such prominent scholars as William Clark, led the shift in approaches to scientific expertise, as did the work of Giandomenico Majone in cooperation with Mary Douglas, Jerome Ravetz, and, later, Brian Wynne.[105] IIASA managed to recruit some of the world's top scholars, motivated to search for solutions to global problems. At the nadir of IIASA's existence, when the institute faced huge financial uncertainty due to the withdrawal of the United States and Britain, the prominent demographer Nathan Keyfitz chose IIASA over Berkeley, even though this decision entailed a significant cut in pay.[106]

We also need to ask whether this East-West allegiance in the search for better governmental techniques is proof that the systems approach contributed to legitimization of an rather illiberal, antidemocratic project of elite technocrats. Did not the issue of human rights fall victim to the depoliticization of the systems approach? Similar arguments are often voiced in criticism of technocracy, of which the systems approach is habitually seen to be a part. And indeed, as I showed in this chapter, the transnational practice of systems analysis relied on a careful management, which excised potentially controversial areas from IIASA's agenda. Nevertheless, I also argued for the need of a more nuanced view, which takes into consideration the variety of ideas espoused by systems analysts and their role in the context of the Cold War. Certainly, East-West rapprochement with an aim to develop a universal science of governance was a result of an intense depoliticization of the systems approach. For East-West diplomacy, this so-called technocratic approach was to a large extent instrumental: the promise of optimization through linear planning, and of making command and control processes more effective, appealed to the Soviets, whereas US governmental elites hoped these techniques would have a subversive effect. But perhaps Mirowski was not entirely correct in claiming that the politics of decision sciences was all "centralized, hierarchical, and deeply fearful of loss of top-down control."[107] According to Mirowski, this desire for top-down control was illustrated by Arrow's impossibility theorem, which cast the system of democratic majority voting as a tool, inferior to the computer and unsuitable for making collective, rational decisions.[108] Arrow was then critically described as the main proponent of a technocratic system, one that is guided by a laboratory notion of rationality and that completely excludes public participation.[109] And yes, this is exactly what the Soviets hoped for, at least in the early 1970s.

But then, as most technical systems do, systems governmentality had unexpected effects. The systems approach offered new cognitive and digital tools of control, and the production and use of these tools required a sophisticated infrastructure, which served as a platform for innovative ideas that eventually deeply challenged Soviet authoritarianism. In the end, system governmentality led to the emergence of a new, different politics. Even if Arrow could be accused of a lack of political sophistication, there was more politics to systems analysis than the critics of rational choice had cared to notice. The systems approach led to a postpositivist, constructionist, and relational understanding of objects and subjects of governance. In its later, more sophisticated version, systems analysis also posited the importance of such principles as self-regulation, the free circulation of data, and openness. To ensure these, new algorithms had to be created, as well as new institutions, practices, and a culture enabling the production of such expertise.

The birth of IIASA was driven by diplomatic initiative. Yet IIASA researchers were not mere emissaries of their respective home organizations and/or governments. In the remaining part of this book, I argue that IIASA scholars, involved in forging the systems approach, were conscious makers of a new world, a world that cut across national boundaries. In so doing, however, they drew keenly on national authorities for legitimacy, power, and money, and in this way contributed to the perpetuation of these national structures. While East-West scholars used the emissary rhetoric at home to argue for the national importance of IIASA, inside IIASA they pursued a different strategy. At the level of everyday life at Laxenburg, the tension of being a governmentally funded nongovernmental organization was resolved by adopting an orientation to informal practices, internally legitimizing them through the idiom of the "IIASA family," coined to distinguish IIASA from national bureaucracies for academic research, and, at the same time, externally projecting the image of a modern, global organization, seeking to redefine governmental interests such that they would embrace the entire world.

The term "IIASA family" in practice served as a social glue for an emergent transnational community of systems analysts based in Laxenburg. Several of my interlocutors, who came from the United States and Western Europe and worked at IIASA from its beginning in 1972, emphasized that their key impression was that the people from the Soviet bloc were "just normal." In turn, systems analysis was also normalized through IIASA: it evolved from being a clandestine undertaking developed at the semisecret institutes of the military-industrial complex, into a basic decision science aiming to provide a knowledge platform for policy decisions in the civilian sector.

This was a complex process in which the professionalization of systems analysis went hand in hand with the socialization of Eastern and Western scientists, as they mutually negotiated the fundamental features of this new policy science. In the IIASA family project, the US-Soviet competition was effectively replaced with IIASA's own project, namely, its organizational survival in a highly uncertain, politicized environment. This survival could only be guaranteed by fostering a particular science—systems analysis and social practices such as horizontal networks and informal relations. In the chapters that follow I will describe in more detail the development of a new mentality of scientific governance.

5

THE EAST-WEST POLITICS OF GLOBAL MODELING

In this chapter I focus on computer-based global modeling, a new technology of knowledge production that emerged in the early 1970s and played an important, transformative role in Soviet governance by opening it up to East-West cooperation. Global modelers conceptualized the planet as a complex, interconnected system, the understanding of which required transnational scientific cooperation, enabling both scientists and data to cross national boundaries and Cold War divides.[1] Furthermore, Soviet scientists forged and used models of possible long-term futures of the world to reveal and criticize problems being experienced, but not always acknowledged, in the Soviet Union. A history of computer-based global modeling is, therefore, a history of East-West transfer, the transformation of the late state socialism and globalization.

The first computer-based global models of social and economic development were produced under the auspices of international organizations, which brought together individuals from the Eastern and Western blocs: the Club of Rome, the United Nations agencies, and, most importantly, IIASA.[2] Although historians habitually refer to these international organizations as examples of the emergence of global governance, we still lack evidence about concrete projects that were pursued within the framework of these organizations and their outcomes, particularly less tangible ones such as professional and social networks.[3] This chapter fills this gap in knowledge by examining several cases of East-West cooperation in computer-based global modeling carried out by the UN and IIASA.

But what is global modeling? Indeed, "global modeling" refers to a great many different concepts and techniques, which could be digital or analog, purely conceptual or calibrated to run on particular computers. Computer-based global modeling so far has been overlooked in histories of computing, although the impact of computer-based global modeling on modern governmentality cannot be overestimated.[4] Thus the first historical studies of global modeling originated in the field of environmental history and the history of Earth's systems, suggesting that global modeling had important epistemological implications for governmental practices.[5] First, global models encouraged policy makers to look at complex relationships that stretched beyond national borders. Second, global models posited a possibility and therefore a need to look further ahead, to operate with longer time horizons, and to evaluate present-day policies in light of their long-term consequences. Even when the computer power to process large volumes of data was still limited, the idea of computer-assisted long-term planning fascinated both scientists and policy makers: even before adequate technology and data emerged, in 1961 the United Nations adopted the resolution *Planning for Economic Development*, calling for long-term projection and planning of the world economy.[6] Third, to be able to plan for the long term became synonymous with being an advanced, postindustrial state, and the foremost tool for this kind of planning was the computer. In line with Peter Galison and Bruce Hevly, I suggest that being an expensive undertaking, requiring huge investments in computer technologies and transnational cooperation in collecting and sharing data, global modeling was part of "Big Science" and, as such, a symbol of state power.[7]

Another important aspect of global modeling is that it was based in a very particular social setting. Global computer models were traditionally associated with the small, closely knit teams that created them. As a result, this technology was tied to its producers: the majority of global computer models could not be easily reproduced or circulated through anonymous channels. Unlike computer hardware, the blueprints of which could be stolen through espionage, transferred internationally, and reproduced in another context, computer software for global modeling often had to be *coproduced* through *face-to-face* collaboration in order to be transferred. This is because the ability to run global models depended on almost tacit knowledge of particular systems, a feel of certain conditions under which the given machine would become unstable or tend to err in a certain direction. As a result, computer modeling platforms were disseminated through personal connections among the modelers.[8] Hence, the history of global modeling is also a story of the emergence and spread of particular informal groups of both scientists and policy makers. These informal groups of global modelers were probably too loose and ad hoc to be described as transnational communities, but, following Fleck, they certainly could be understood as distinct thought collectives, mobilized by their aim to produce a new type of science, global modeling.[9]

This chapter discusses several such thought collectives, which were both influential in the Soviet Union and active at the international level: these are the scientists based at the Computer Center and the Institute for Systems Research (VNIISI) of the All-Union Soviet Academy of Sciences in Moscow. Both the Computer Center and VNIISI were strongly anchored in international networks through the United Nations and IIASA. In what follows, I briefly review the origins of global modeling in the Soviet Union and the West. Then I proceed to describe the development of several international nodes, by which I mean ad hoc, temporary constellations of technology, scientists, and political rationales, which led to the East-West coproduction of the model of a new, long-term, and global future.

How to Join Capitalist and Communist Futures

How could it be possible to accommodate capitalist and communist futures in one world model? Did the communist future not exclude a capitalist economy and society by default? In previous chapters I have outlined several strategies of depoliticizing the systems approach as an instrument of scientific governance. Here I propose a particular case of global modeling as an example of how a technology, which had been depoliticized, could continue having deeply political implications, undermining some of the foundations of the existing ideological systems. Global modeling belonged to a branch of exact science, based on mathematical methods and computer technology. It also built on universalism and global thinking, both of which have a long cultural and political history. But global modeling gave a particularly powerful form to the idea of global interconnectivity in the last three decades of the twentieth century. Although always highly specialized by being geared to particular sectors, global modeling relied on systems thinking, probing into deeper, unexpected changes resulting from the intertwining of industry, society, and the economy.

Earlier I discussed the role of scientific-technical revolution as a developmental discourse, recognized on both sides of the Iron Curtain as a driver of universal change that produced the new idea that the future could not be divided strictly into capitalist and communist camps.[10] Yet what brought the communist and capitalist regimes together was not even the shared understanding of the importance of the scientific-technical revolution per se, but the insight that economic growth, driven by the scientific-technical revolution, had complex global consequences. This became quite apparent in the changing Soviet discourses. In a somewhat roundabout way the idea of a worldwide scientific-technical revolution significantly changed the meaning of "global" in Soviet scientific and policy thinking. If, as archival documents reveal, Soviet economists used the term "global models" to refer to models of the national economy in the 1960s, a decade later, in the 1970s, they used the term to refer to the world economy.[11] At the same time, Soviet international relations theorists used the word "globalism" to refer to US ambitions for world hegemony. Accordingly, the latter definition of "global" was charged with negative undertones in this context.[12] A completely different use of "global" emerged in Soviet geophysical sciences, where scholars used it to describe planetary processes as early as the 1950s. I suggest that it was through computer modeling that this geophysical notion of "global" eventually migrated into Soviet economic and, at a later stage, political discourses. The culmination of Soviet global thinking was reached in 1985 when the notion of "global problems" was used for the first time to describe world issues in the official documents of the Congress of the Communist Party.[13]

The emerging understanding of the global system as a phenomenon that was simultaneously natural-geophysical and man-made, a phenomenon that was undergoing a deep transformation following the scientific-technical revolution, was articulated and actively promoted by a new type of actor on the stage of world politics: international organizations. The first impetus to computerize planetary processes involving nature, economics, and population came from the Club of Rome, an organization established by Aurelio Peccei that joined members of state governments, industries, and academia hailing from both East and West.[14] In the early 1970s the Club of Rome commissioned the creation of a world model from American engineer Jay Forrester and a group of researchers directed by the young Dennis Meadows at the Massachusetts Institute of Technology.[15] Consisting of five interacting blocks of agriculture, natural resources, pollution, population, and capital, this model was used to demonstrate the strength of relations between these different sectors. The key goal was heuristic: to demonstrate that such relations existed and were strong, rather than to produce a reliable, detailed forecast of the future state of these sectors. In fact, the ambition to forecast world trends accurately was futile, not the least because of a lack of robust and detailed empirical data pertaining to all countries.[16] It is important to note that in Meadows's model the long-term dimension emerged as an unintended side effect: this model extrapolated the possible development of world economic growth until it obtained an interesting result, namely, a dramatic decline of the world economy, population, and living standards in 2050. Thus, it was not the desire to know the future lying many decades afar that drove the modelers, but rather the long-term future emerged as a side effect of this heuristic experiment. The results, published in the report *The Limits to Growth* (1972), were used by the authors to argue that the long-term effects of current economic growth had to be considered in order to avoid a future disaster: the collapse of the world economy because of rising population and pollution. If humanity wished to maintain its living standards in the future, the report suggested, the leading Western nations had to revise their consumption habits and accept the idea of no growth.[17]

How did the Soviet Union, struggling to "catch up with and overtake" the West, react to *The Limits to Growth*? First of all, this report did not take the Soviets by surprise, because through Gvishiani the Soviet government had a direct link with the academic and policy circles in which this study originated. Gvishiani first met Aurelio Peccei, then the head of Olivetti, during his business trip to Moscow in the early 1960s, and since then Gvishiani had interacted regularly with Peccei and Alexander King of the OECD to become a member of the Club of Rome.[18] This network was used to bring innovative ideas to the Soviet Union before they were made public in the West: Gvishiani, for instance, invited Forrester and Meadows to Moscow to present their world model to a group of leading Soviet scholars in computer science and modeling in the winter of 1970. East-West scholars also met to discuss the thesis and methodology that would be used in the report *The Limits to Growth* in a seminar organized in Italy, in 1971.[19]

The very organization of the visit of Forrester's team to Moscow testified to the fact that the top Soviet research administrators were not only seriously interested in global modeling, but also willing to convey the importance of this approach to the Party elite: the American scientists were whizzed straight to the villa of the mayor of Moscow, where in an informal environment they briefed high Soviet officials, including Gvishiani and his protégé, the future head of global modeling at VNIISI, Viktor Gelovani.[20] Later events that followed the publication of *The Limits to Growth* and the subsequent controversy over its thesis of the risk of overpopulation, made it clear that the Soviets were able to differentiate between the fiercely Malthusian implication of *The Limits to Growth* and global modeling as a new type of technique for generating policy-relevant knowledge.

This dual approach was evident in the Russian translation of the report: the thesis of no growth was censored out of the Russian translation, whereas the author, Dennis Meadows, was warmly welcomed in the Soviet Union, which he visited more than twenty times to lecture on computer-based modeling in Moscow and a dozen other cities. Before the publication of *Limits*, Gvishiani initiated the translation of Forrester's *Industrial Dynamics* (1961), which was published in Russian under the title *The Foundations of the Cybernetics of Firms* in 1971.[21] Gvishiani also supported the translation of *The Limits to Growth*, which was done at the Institute for Information on Social Sciences (INION). However, the Russian translation of *Limits* was distributed only in limited circles within the

Soviet Academy of Sciences and held in the tightly restricted special collections at the Lenin Library in Moscow.[22] Although some entrepreneurial individuals secretly copied the INION's translation of *The Limits to Growth* and sold these copies for 300 USD on the black market, the wider Soviet public had access only to the ideological commentaries on this report.[23]

In all, in the Soviet Union, just like in the West, *The Limits to Growth* was received with both fascination and skepticism. Although it has been described as the most criticized model ever, *The Limits to Growth* played an important role in opening up Soviet interest to a fundamentally new understanding of the parameters required for scientific governance. Both my respondents and published sources reveal the strong interest of Soviet scientists in developing the technique of global modeling and applying it to different policy areas, and inviting Western scholars to the Soviet bloc to raise the profile of this new, cutting-edge field. For instance, Mihajlo Mesarovic, a prominent American systems theorist and computer scientist of Serbian origin, the author of another global model also sponsored by the Club of Rome, presented his work at the House of Friendship in Moscow, the public forum from which many prominent Western scientists addressed Soviet audiences.[24] But the popularization of science was just one area; what interests me here are the developments which took place in less public institutional settings, equipped for hosting long-term collaborations between East and West scientists. In the next section I show how global modeling was developed at two international platforms of East-West interactions: IIASA and UN. Then I return to the developments inside the Soviet Union to discuss the consequences of these international interactions for the authoritarian, centralist governance.

Global Modeling at IIASA

IIASA played a fundamental role in the development of global modeling thanks to its unique institutional design and scientific agenda for developing cutting-edge policy sciences. As I mentioned earlier, during the process of establishing IIASA, the trajectories of the future members of the Club of Rome and the US-Soviet negotiators often intersected: for instance, Peccei facilitated the meeting of Gvishiani, Bundy, and Zuckerman in 1968 and was involved, although not always directly, in the negotiations.[25] It is interesting, however, that this intertwining of the networks of the Club of Rome and the East-West institute turned out to be both an asset and a problem. Purely coincidentally, IIASA's charter was signed just a few months after the publication of *The Limits to Growth* in 1972. As the report's no-growth message was traveling around the globe causing controversy, some of the signatories grew extremely anxious that the public might confuse IIASA and the Club of Rome, which would taint the reputation of the newly established institute. Indeed, some of IIASA's founding members were fiercely critical of the Forrester/Meadows model.[26] Zuckerman, for instance, argued that global problems should be faced "in a hopeful and scientific spirit and not in one of hysterical computerized gloom" in his address to the UN conference on the Human Environment in Stockholm in 1972.[27] MIT scholar Carl Kaysen, who was McBundy's right-hand man in the negotiations over IIASA, was similarly skeptical about Meadows's model, not least because it placed the crisis in the long-term horizon, whereas according to Kaysen focusing on the contemporary crisis would make more sense.[28] Even Gvishiani initially criticized *The Limits to Growth* at IIASA's council meetings.[29]

It is quite clear that in this context of ongoing controversy around the findings of the first global model, it was far from self-evident that IIASA should include global modeling in its research agenda. Some insisted that the newly born IIASA had to carefully build its scientific reputation and, consequently, avoid controversial projects. But many also realized that global modeling was a genuine innovation and therefore offered an opportunity to situate the institute at the forefront of science. The dilemma of whether to embrace global modeling at IIASA was finally resolved by Howard Raiffa. Following a suggestion by Tjalling Koopmans that IIASA could organize conferences on "global simulation," Raiffa proposed that instead of developing original global models, IIASA should become a clearing house for global modeling experiments undertaken in different countries.[30] Accordingly, methodological studies of "long-run global simulation" and a series of conferences on this topic were included in IIASA's research strategy for 1973.[31] Beginning in 1974 IIASA hosted six symposia on global modeling and, indeed, successfully profiled itself as the first platform for sustained international exchange in the area of global modeling.[32]

I suggest that IIASA's global modeling conferences played an important role in socializing scientists from East and West into a shared understanding of the possibilities, but also, importantly, the limitations of global modeling. First of all, global modeling was institutionalized as a "normal," albeit postpositivist science. In their internal discussions and published papers, scientists acknowledged that many of the projections generated by global models could not be verified by empirical experiments. Furthermore, the modelers recognized that modeling results were often messy and inconclusive, and many modelers, although not all, never attempted to hide the inconclusive character of their studies. Scientists, for example, agreed that precision was at best something to be aspired to, but could hardly ever be achieved. Although for a lay observer mathematical methods appeared to be precise, the complex calculations involved defied the notion of order, precision, and control: big numbers behaved chaotically and the data produced by computer models were subject to random errors generated by the computer. Another peculiar feature of global modeling was the discrepancy between shortage of input data, which were often severely limited and imperfect, and overflow of output data. Indeed, computers would churn out such volumes of alternative calculations that further software filters had to be designed to figure out which results made sense and which did not.[33] As such, global modeling provided neither accuracy nor proof, but uncertainty.[34]

In this context, it turned out that particular social skills were necessary to be able to navigate this complex world of global modeling. For instance my interlocutor, a Russian mathematician, emphasized that a particularly high degree of "mathematical culture" was prerequisite to being able use a global computer model properly. According to this scientist, such a mathematical culture could not be learned from books, but could only be acquired from close and lengthy interaction in modeling teams.[35] It is doubtful that IIASA, where most scientists were visiting and the directors were appointed on temporary contracts, could ever become such a highbrow milieu of mathematical modeling, where sustained face-to-face contacts were paramount. However, IIASA could and did provide mathematicians from East and West with a unique place for encounters that led on to the development of cooperation outside IIASA (I return to this in subsequent chapters).

Discretion was another important quality that IIASA conferences could offer the emerging world community of computer modelers. Being an international, nongovernmental organization, IIASA could more easily position itself as immune to bias toward particular national or industrial interests. Printed sources and interviews alike underscore the importance of IIASA's organizational culture of discretion, which enabled computer modelers from East and West to discuss quite politically unorthodox versions of the future development of economic, social, and even political systems. For example, in 1980 IIASA's conference on global econometric modeling discussed possible implications of the Peoples' Republics of Poland and Hungary joining the European Economic Community: a rather extraordinary example of an economic forecast that appeared to defy geopolitical dogmas and to question the notions of stagnant late state socialist governmental imagination.[36]

But discretion was highly important, not only for political, but also for commercial reasons. Scientists were anxious about the risk that their models in progress could be secretly copied, threatening their potential future income from commissions. However, complete discretion also posed a serious problem: without access to a model's architecture, no outsider could tell whether a particular model really worked, that is, if a model had an internal dynamic in which inputs did not straightforwardly determine outputs. Indeed, the history of modeling shows that the refusal to disclose the internal architecture of computer models ultimately jeopardized their authority.[37] As I show in this and subsequent chapters, the success of computer-based modeling as a policy tool depended on carefully managed transparency, a condition that had deep implications for the Cold War divide.

Global Modeling at the UN

Whereas IIASA offered a place for scientists to discuss their global models in a discrete environment, where the informal exchange of ideas and mutual scrutiny behind closed doors was made possible, UN agencies operated on rather different principles. Based on governmental membership, UN agencies could not offer the same level of discretion and informality (since IIASA's members were not governments, but academic organizations). Nevertheless, the global modeling pursued at UN agencies was significant, because the UN had a particularly important mandate to collect and share data from all countries. Even in this large organization, the importance of personal contacts and, to a more limited extent, face-to-face cooperation, was paramount. This is exemplified in the efforts to develop computer models of the world economy under the aegis of the UN.

Of course, the UN was not the first to take an interest in the world economic system. It has to be recalled that the institutionalization of mathematical modeling in economics dates back to 1930, when the Econometric Society was established by Ragnar Frisch in the United States. However, these early models were mainly theoretical exercises, and econometricians began to fill their models with data only after World War II. As mentioned earlier, in 1961 the UN began promoting long-term economic planning based on new computer technologies. In 1965 the UN acquired its first mainframe computer and from about that time began organizing a series of econometric conferences. To meet its needs for international data calculation, the UN established its International Computing Center in 1971.[38]

Initially the United Nations supported econometric research as part of their worldwide development program, the rationale for which was initially shaped in line with modernization theory. According to this view, third-world countries should imitate Western standards and implement Western economic structures. At a later stage the UN's developmental agenda was widened to include environmental issues, because they were proved to have a strong link with economic growth in *The Limits to Growth*. Thus, following the ground-breaking publication of *Limits*, in 1973 the UN initiated a study of the interrelationships between growth, resources, pollution, and abatement policies.[39] For my argument it is important that it was this coupling of the economy and the environment that justified the inclusion of communist and capitalist regimes into a single modeling system: the geophysics of the Earth did not observe national boundaries or ideological divides, and computer modelers had little choice but to respect this, if they wished their models to make sense.

In this context the key Soviet organization to liaise with the UN's program for the planning of world development was the Central Institute for Mathematical Economics (TsEMI) at the Soviet Academy of Sciences in Moscow. Established in 1963 and directed by Nikolai Fedorenko (also a member of the Club of Rome), TsEMI enjoyed limited scientific autonomy in the Soviet empire of science and actively sought to link to the most prominent research milieus in West.[40] Hence in 1965 Fedorenko attended the first econometrics congress in Rome at the invitation of Wassily Leontief;[41] TsEMI was also involved in the Copenhagen conference on long-term economic planning, organized by the UN Economic Commission for Europe in 1966.[42] Archival materials show that TsEMI regularly corresponded and exchanged publications with such pioneering modelers of long-term scenarios as Ragnar Frisch, Jan Tinbergen, and Richard Stone during the 1960s.[43]

Here the key actor was Wassily Leontief, who could be fairly described as a tireless mediator between the emerging communities of Western and Soviet econometricians, although, as the reader may remember, Leontief was asked to refrain from assuming an active role in the negotiations around the East-West institute in the late 1960s. A recipient of the Nobel Prize for his method of calculating interbranch balance in 1973, Leontief was born into a well-off family of Russian industrialists and academics in 1909 and grew up in Saint Petersburg, where he witnessed the October Revolution unfold literally before his eyes.[44] Leontief left Russia in 1925 to return for the first time in 1959. At the beginning of his exile he worked at the University of Kiel in Germany, one of the first institutions in Europe to study the world economy. In the 1930s Leontief was invited to advise the Chinese government on developing its railway infrastructure. It was during his long trip to China and back that he first encountered the third world. In 1931 he was invited to join the US National Bureau of Economic Research and soon thereafter became a professor at Harvard. Leontief first presented his theory of systems dynamics to the military in Washington; in 1948–1949 his empirical input-output studies were funded by the Rockefeller and the Ford foundations under the Harvard Economic Research Project.[45] Leontief's mathematical skills, his life experience, and his proximity to government agencies made him a rather unusual nonacademic economist, who was keenly interested in the development of large-scale and long-term models.

It was during de-Stalinizaton that Leontief's work entered the Soviet space to later become a standard reference in Soviet global thinking.[46] First banned by

Stalin, mathematical methods in economics were rehabilitated thanks to the efforts of the mathematician Vasilii Nemchinov in the mid-1950s. Although input-output methods were developed by Leonid Kantorovich as early as in the 1930s, historians suggest that it was Leontief's pupil, the Polish economist Oskar Lange, who also disagreed with Hayek, claiming that it was possible to apply a neoclassical economic model to a centrally commanded economy, and thus inspired the Soviets to introduce input-output methods to calculate their economic plans.[47] In turn, in 1959 Leontief was officially invited to Moscow, a visit which he described in his memoir as unsatisfactory, his impression being that the Soviet economists whom he met were not mathematically competent: reportedly, Soviet economists presented to Leontief examples of the application of his own methods which unfortunately contained many mistakes. However, following this visit Leontief began vigorously building East-West links: he established and chaired the US-Soviet Statistics Bureau in Cambridge, Massachusetts, where many young Soviet administrators were subsequently trained.[48] In this context, it is not surprising that it was Leontief, so well personally integrated in East-West networks, who was commissioned to direct the first study of the world economy for the UN.

At the request of the UN Center for Development Planning, Forecasting and Policies, Leontief created the first world trade balance model, the results of which were reported in *The Future of the World Economy* (1976). One of his coauthors was Stanislav Men'shikov, a Russian economist who would later feed the data gathered for Leontief's report to the information-starved economists in Moscow. The data, typically, did not flow easily in the opposite direction: Leontief's report did not list any Soviet sources.

Outlining scenarios for world development for the next twenty-five years, *The Future of the World Economy* tread carefully on the terrain of Cold War political divisions. First, the rationale for making such a model was motivated by environmental concerns, deemed to be globally relevant and universal to all countries irrespective of their political ideologies. The structure of the model was primarily economic, as it built on investment and trade flows, but it was precisely because of the environmental effects of economic growth, argued Leontief, that the introduction of a long-term perspective into the study of economic development was necessary.[49] Second, the political implications of Leontief's analysis were carefully managed. For instance, the finding was that the developing countries could not narrow down the income gap between them and developing countries by the year 2000 without additional and significant foreign investment. As such a statement would have placed direct responsibility on Western governments, it was therefore regarded as politically controversial by the UN; in the end this finding was only left implicit in the report.[50] Third, Leontief employed several ways to depoliticize the very conceptual structure of his model of the world economy.

For instance, the model elaborated on possible changes in internal economic structures in developing countries, but no change at all was modeled for the communist regions. Then world regions were defined according to their economic-administrative system and geographical features. Hence the Soviet Union and Eastern Europe were called "developed centrally planned regions"; meanwhile Western Europe was split into high- and medium-income regions.[51] As a result, Leontief's model, on the one hand, erased the communist and capitalist divide from the future of the world economy and, on the other hand, conserved the political status quo by refusing to model any possible changes within the communist system.

Modeling Soviet Decline

Both Meadows's and Leontief's models grew out of attempts to clarify the possibilities of economic development and its consequences for the environment from a long-term perspective. Although these models used new computer technologies, the concern with the environment obviously was not a novelty in itself. In Soviet Russia an important role was played by the Russian intellectual tradition, which was particularly conducive to the emerging global environmentalist thinking. Indeed, the Soviet intellectual interest in modeling global processes predated both Meadows's and Leontief's studies, because it stemmed from prewar thinking, in particular from Vladimir Vernadskii's theory of the biosphere/noosphere, formulated in the 1930s.[52] Beginning in the 1960s Vernadskii's thought was promoted by the prominent Soviet biologist Nikolai Timofeev-Resovskii and the equally prominent mathematician and research director of the Soviet Academy of Sciences' Computer Center in Moscow, Nikita Moiseev.[53]

As in Western scholarship, Soviet efforts at global modeling oscillated between the poles of economy and geophysics. Under Moiseev the Moscow Computer Center became the center of geophysical modeling, with a particular focus on climate and ecological systems. The center also focused on interaction between the economy and the environment, with a particular interest in systemic breakdown, which was directly inspired by *The Limits to Growth*, as it was discussed at Moiseev's seminars.[54] Moiseev himself was first introduced to the *global problematique* of the Club of Rome by the prominent Canadian economist of Russian origin Paul Medow, who lectured on Forrester's model at the center in the early 1970s. Medow, in turn, invited Moiseev to take part in a meeting organized by the Club of Rome and RAND.[55] In all, global modeling at the Moscow Computer Center evolved at the interstices of cutting-edge scholarship, where disciplinary boundaries were negotiated in relation to both intellectual and pragmatic rationales, all of which, as I show later, underpinned intense forging of transnational networks.

Just like his Western colleagues, Moiseev found Forrester's and Meadows's world models mathematically imperfect and limited in their conceptual structure. According to Moiseev, the world models were not useful at all as tools for policy decision making, because they dealt with highly aggregated numbers. In addition, Moiseev was generally skeptical about the use of modeling in economic planning. This skepticism was rooted in his hands-on experience with the development of statistical variables for social and economic indicators at Gosplan, where Moiseev became convinced that socioeconomic processes are simply too complex to be translated into statistical language, not the least because different governmental agencies attributed different meaning to the same phenomena. The internal departmental infighting that he witnessed at Gosplan also put off Moiseev from economic modeling.[56] However, understanding that economic utility was a strong argument that could be used to obtain governmental funding for global modeling, Moiseev did compromise, contending that global economic models could be created in principle, but only on the basis of "proper" geophysical modeling. In any case, Moiseev's position remained firm, arguing that if natural processes were not properly understood and represented, it was pointless to model the economy, as it was dependent on natural resources.[57]

A rather different approach to global modeling emerged at the Institute for Systems Research (VNIISI), which listed global modeling as one of its research priorities. VNIISI's global modeling program was directed by another Georgian, Viktor Gelovani, who established a close personal link with Dennis Meadows. If the Moscow Computer Center made a major contribution to the field of geophysical modeling, VNIISI innovated global economic modeling in the Soviet context.[58] Both the Moscow Computer Center and VNIISI cooperated closely with IIASA and the UN, where both Gvishiani and Moiseev played important personal roles.[59] Whereas Gvishiani was the director of VNIISI from 1976 to 1992 and vice director of IIASA from 1972 to 1987, Moiseev was involved in launching the water project at IIASA and organizing the center's participation in the major UNESCO program "Man and Biosphere," which launched an ambitious international study of the intertwining man-made and natural systems on the planetary level. In consequence, Gvishiani's and Moiseev's networks intertwined: for example, Moiseev's group presented a paper on computer-based modeling and the idea of the noosphere at the ninth IIASA conference on global modeling in 1981;[60] also the Balaton Group at IIASA was established jointly by Meadows and Gelovani in 1982 and included junior scientists from the Moscow Computer Center.[61]

Internal Soviet institutional competition apart, an important feature of the East-West exchange in global modeling was building horizontal, transnational relations between strong scientific milieus. Here, interestingly, global modelers were not on a quest for originality. The development of Soviet world models could be compared to a creative bricolage rather than to creation *ex nihilo*. For example, in an interview, a Russian mathematician involved in the development of one of the first global models stressed that his team did not strive to compete for originality; on the contrary, they found it perfectly acceptable and purely expedient to borrow existing models created by Western scientists. Remember, the first computer-based world model simulating the interaction between the ocean and atmosphere was developed by American scientists Syukuro Manabe and Kirk Bryan in 1972. Somewhat later the Soviets began developing their own geophysical global models, adjusting Western models to local research goals and computer equipment, namely, the center's BESM-6.[62]

In 1977 the Moscow Computer Center launched a research program to build a world ocean-atmosphere model suitable for environmental analysis; this model was completed in 1982.[63] The center borrowed a global circulation model created by Yale Mintz and Akio Arakawa at the University of California Los Angeles, later improved by Lawrence Gates, first at RAND (1971) and later at the University of Oregon (1978).[64] Well anchored in Soviet networks, Gates did not mind giving his model to the Soviets and even proposed sending two American scientists to Moscow to help adjust the model to the BESM-6.[65] Indeed, not only models, but also data were shared: the Moscow Computer Center received atmospheric data from the Norwegian Meteorological Center.[66]

The conceptual rationale of Soviet global models echoed the concerns of *The Limits to Growth*, but extended them further with an aim to reconceptualize the role of humanity on Earth. Thus, Moiseev envisioned an integrated model of the biosphere, coding the natural, socioeconomic, and cognitive environments into one modeling system, which would ideally allow the study of "large scale effects of anthropogenic activities."[67] This model simulated interconnections among global climate, the ecology, and economic systems, aiming to identify the conditions under which environmental change would set boundaries for economic development.[68] As mentioned above, the economy was of secondary interest for Moiseev's group: this model, involving land, ocean, and atmosphere blocks, was first used to simulate CO_2 emissions and climate change in the early 1980s. Another aspect illustrating the difference and possibly some rift between Moiseev's and Gelovani's teams is that the Moscow Computer Center's global model was created independently of IIASA: the center's scientists did not participate in IIASA's global modeling conferences, instead fostering their own, direct links with the leading American atmosphere modelers.[69] The center's cooperation with IIASA would intensify only in the 1980s, when it became clear that even geophysical global models could lead to the formulation of innovative political and policy ideas.⁷⁰ Here the most prominent study was the examination of the environmental effects of a nuclear war, leading to the hypothesis of global nuclear winter, discussed in detail in chapter 6.

The effect of global modeling efforts at VNIISI was quite different but no less significant. If global modelers at the Moscow Computer Center first and foremost developed their models as heuristic tools for gaining new scientific knowledge about geophysical systems, VNIISI sought to generate policy-relevant knowledge. Global modeling was a prominent part of VNIISI's research agenda from its establishment in June 1976: the first report of annual activities included the development of a conceptual framework for global modeling.⁷¹ VNIISI was exceptionally well positioned to tap into international science, because it was created to be the Soviet counterpart of IIASA and as such was effectively in charge of many administrative duties in relation to the Soviet membership. Claiming that the Eastern Bloc lagged behind the West in global modeling, the institute's purpose was to catch up with the West by developing interdisciplinary research on large-scale, complex, and global problems. It should be added that the modeling of global development at VNIISI was also based on Marxist-Leninist principles.⁷²

Patronized by Gvishiani, VNIISI was safeguarded from political volatility and had a direct link to the very heart of Soviet power. For instance, in 1977 a high-level meeting of global modelers, including members of the Club of Rome, was organized in Moscow, which five members of the Politburo, the de facto highest decision-making body in the Soviet government, attended.⁷³ The global modeling program at VNIISI was cochaired by Gvishiani himself and applied mathematician Viktor Gelovani.⁷⁴ This global modeling group stemmed from a GKNT team for operations research, involved in creating complex models of world development.⁷⁵ This team also included a prominent scientist, Sergei Dubovskii, with modeling experience from the highly esteemed Institute for Control Sciences. These and other scholars who later shaped the core of VNIISI were closely involved in the formation of IIASA's research agenda from 1972 on.⁷⁶ In the context of Soviet academia, VNIISI was an important, large, and well-funded organization. Unlike IIASA, which never hosted more than a hundred scholars at a time, and in the true spirit of a Soviet organization, VNIISI employed more than three hundred staff and grew to almost seven hundred by the late 1980s.⁷⁷ The institute was well provided with a large building and its technical equipment was more than adequate: VNIISI modelers used PDP-11/70, an American computer.⁷⁸

The principal task of VNIISI was to forecast the development of countries and regions over a twenty- to thirty-year period.⁷⁹ The idea of forecasting social and economic development up to the year 2000 stemmed from the work of the US Commission for the Year 2000.⁸⁰ Such forecasts were made in the Soviet Union in the 1960s, although most of them were kept secret. A glimpse at the archives and memoirs reveals a much more complex and diverse landscape of Soviet scientific expertise than previously thought: at VNIISI, scientists looked further ahead to test the impact of globally significant changes on the Soviet Union. For instance, the first global dynamics model developed at VNIISI forecasted the impact of the arms race on the Chinese economy. The model showed that increased investment in defense would devastate the Chinese economy; accordingly, the scientists concluded that China was not likely to embark on military expansion, suggesting that the Soviet government did not have to invest to counteract Chinese military growth. Ironically, this model used the existing intelligence data on China, but could not model any nuanced impact on the Soviet Union, because Gosplan refused access to the Soviet data.[81]

Nevertheless, other studies attempted to explore the development of the Soviet economy as part of global dynamics. In 1981 VNIISI had a model that consisted of three blocks representing the United States, Japan, and China; in 1983 this model was expanded to include the communist bloc. Unlike Leontief's model for the UN, which did not divide the world according to nations or political regimes, VNIISI's model divided the world along political allegiances into nine blocks: the Soviet Union, the Eastern European bloc, the European community, the United States, China (which was of growing concern to the communist leaders), Japan, "other capitalist countries," then OPEC countries and developing countries. The sectors this model included were demography, trade, energy resources, the environment, and climate.

However, just as before, Gosplan was not forthcoming with Soviet economic data; only highly aggregated statistics were available, which were not suitable for the forecast. What did VNIISI modelers do? They turned to their personal, transnational contacts to solve this data gap. The key was Leontief's above-mentioned colleague, Russian economist Stanislav Men'shikov, the vice director and then director of the UN Department of Prognosis, Planning and Development, 1974–1980.[82] This cooperation built on strikingly intertwined sociotechnical networks, which joined machines, organizations, and individuals: Men'shikov worked with Leontief on the UN's world economy model. Furthermore, Leontief's world economy model was computed at the Feldberg Computer Center on a PDP-10, the same type of machine used by VNIISI.[83] Then, IIASA provided the data about global markets to VNIISI scientists.[84] Indeed, the Russian scholars interviewed recalled that they could easily obtain CIA reports on the Soviet economy, industry, and society, but not the data from Goskomstat, the Russian state statistics service.[85] This work resulted in a gargantuan modeling system joining 47 models of subsystems, 4,700 averaged points, and 5,000 variables, and based on the quantification of 370,000 empirical observations. On this basis the world system and Soviet development was projected for the next twenty years.[86]

It should be clear by now that for Soviet scientists to model such long-term projections they needed to be able to leave the isolation of a computer laboratory and engage in highly heterogeneous practices, such as communication across different disciplines, forging social and political alliances, continuously probing the limits of mathematical methods. These efforts, however, were not limited to satisfying pure scientific curiosity, but were, instead, mobilized to criticize the status quo of the Soviet society: Soviet scientists used long-term projections to reveal current problems that the Soviet Union faced, but which could not be easily introduced into public debate, as they undermined the official ideology of victorious communism. Long-term projections into the future, meanwhile, constituted an important rhetorical resource to articulate the present problems, the authorship of criticism belonging as much to the machine as to scientists.

Thus VNIISI scientists reported to Prime Minister Kosygin and, later, Nikolai Tikhonov, in 1979, 1982, and 1984, each time demonstrating that the growth of the Soviet economy would sharply decline in the future unless the Soviet government greatly upped investment in research and development.[87] This was not a trivial warning. Indeed, very few communist scientists dared to model the deceleration or, worse, stagnation of the Soviet economy. For instance, TsEMI's director retrospectively wrote that he "just could not accept" even as a hypothesis the zero-growth option proposed by Meadows's report.[88] In turn, the hypothesis of zero growth was censored out of the Russian translation of *The Limits to Growth*.[89] Yet there was some, albeit limited, space for Soviet scientists to offer negative feedback to the government. A well-known example is that of the Russian economist Gregory Khanin, who repeatedly wrote letters to the Central Committee reporting his own estimates of the future Soviet economy, which were much lower than the official figures.[90]

Whereas Khanin was tolerated and, probably, ignored, other scientists were less fortunate: for instance, the East German scientist Wolfgang Harich calculated a version of nongrowth communism, for which he faced serious repercussions.[91] Another example of a reaction to economic forecasts showing the decline of Soviet economic power involves IIASA's project on modeling economic growth, directed by the West German economist Wilhelm Krelle. Dissatisfied with Krelle's results, several Russian scholars complained that it was "a big mistake" to show that the impact of the Soviet Union on world economic development was minor. Had Krelle used the official Soviet forecast for the year 2000, wrote the disappointed scholars, the global role of Soviet trade would have appeared to be much more significant.[92] This was still a mild criticism; Soviet modelers knew that they were walking a fine line of permissibility: according to my interlocutors, VNIISI scientists did fear repression and this is why the scenario of the collapse of the Soviet Union was not tested at all.[93]

Furthermore, the process of developing the VNIISI model of the future Soviet economy revealed a deep internal split among the scientists involved, who disagreed about the actual purpose of long-term analysis. One scientist involved in this project told me that several VNIISI economists involved in the development of this model simply refused to believe that the modelers seriously expected to produce unanticipated results. Well-drilled in the communist planning system, these economists assumed that the modeling exercise was merely a ritual, an attempt to create "a mechanical proof" for plan targets specified in the Party directives. Others were anxious that their results might be understood as a criticism of the standard of Soviet life, so demographers simply refused to take into account the influence of the quality of life on birth rates.[94] The final report was also autocensored: it is very likely that the curve pointing out the decline of Soviet growth from 4.5 percent in 1980 to 2.1 percent in 2000 was also a cautiously selected one. Indeed, this curve was diplomatically accompanied by another curve, which showed that US growth would slow down even more.

Nevertheless, it is clear that some Soviet modelers regarded their task as a serious and genuine contribution to policy making by "speaking truth to power," to quote Aaron Wildavsky, and not just a mere ritual. They also sought to make their study public. In 1984 this VNIISI modeling exercise was described in a report titled *On the Threshold of the Millennium: The Global Problems and Development Processes in the USSR*; the following year some of the results were published in VNIISI proceedings. However, General Directorate for the Protection of State Secrets in the Press (Glavlit) requested that most of the information concerning the Soviet Union be removed in order to make the results suitable for a wide audience.[95] Whereas Soviet censorship found it acceptable to publish studies on the complete extinction of Soviet citizens during a nuclear winter (discussed in the next chapter), it refused to release a forecast of the slowing down of Soviet economic growth from an optimistic 5 percent to what was considered a meager 2 percent.

On the basis of these examples I argue that although there were pretty clear boundaries to the criticism of the Soviet regime, some Soviet global modelers persistently tried to push them. Soviet scientists used a sophisticated tool, computer-based global modeling, as a vehicle to criticize the existing Soviet economic policy by showing its imminent failure to the Politburo. In this way, the long-term projections, I suggest, enabled new kinds of criticism before the new policy of openness or *glasnost'* launched by Mikhail Gorbachev in 1987.

For the Soviets, the struggle for the long term was inevitably a struggle for access to models, data, and computers. It is difficult to overestimate the role that the scientific methodology of global modeling played in international cooperation. No global model could run without empirical data. No national model of natural or economic systems could be realistic if it was decoupled from global processes. Nothing clashed harder with the Soviet bureaucracy, pervaded with secrecy and compartmentalization, than the idea of the unrestricted international circulation of data. Here the modeling of geophysical processes and studies of the environment offered Soviet scientists some room to maneuver and formulate different versions of the Soviet future. If in the decades from 1960 through the 1980s hardly any Soviet demographic statistics were available, as Gosplan would not disclose the population mortality rates from the 1930s to the 1940s,[96] the data on the atmosphere and the ocean could be circulated more easily, which explains the Moscow Computer Center's focus on geophysical global models. But then models and data were coproduced: for instance, global models required new kinds of data drawn from specially conducted experiments, because, for example, nitrogen reactions were different in Siberia and Latin America. The modeling itself was not easy to replicate: without direct, face-to-face communication, wrote Moiseev, sophisticated mathematical models could never become "real."[97]

It is clear that global modeling was both an instrument of knowledge and a symbol of power: for the Soviet government global modeling was part of the struggle for superpower status. Soviet scientists aspired to use big computers to project large sets of data over a long-term and long-range world future and to do this just as well as US scientists. Brimming with political prestige, global modeling served as an important source of authority for Soviet scientists, who wished to innovate not only in science, but also in policy making. And they were innovative: global modeling posed deep challenges to the secrecy and compartmentalization of Soviet scientific expertise. In this chapter I showed that the development of global modeling required international, face-to-face cooperation to coproduce both the models and data. Responding to this, the Soviet government eventually began to release control over small communities of modelers, which remained at arm's length from central power. This was the case when a new scientific epistemology and technical infrastructure led to a major sociopolitical change, albeit limited to highly professional groups and, in the Soviet Union, rather narrow institutional contexts, yet vitally important for the incremental transformation of Soviet governmentality. Second, global models made visible—through graphs, maps, and statistical curves—different, unexpected, and negative consequences of long-term developments. In some areas, such as environmental or global economic trends, this long-term, global future was actively portrayed as politically neutral, because it affected all countries included in the model. It is highly significant that Soviet scientists used references to such a politically neutralized global future to criticize contemporary Soviet realities.

I want to stress that global modeling drove a deep, epistemological transformation of the notions of knowledge, certainty, and control in the computer-based Soviet governmentality. I have already suggested that the impact of the epistemology of computer modeling on government was not limited to what Donald MacKenzie calls the mechanization of proof, where computers are used to verify software and generate trust. Rather, Soviet discussions about the methodology of global computer-based modeling articulated and disseminated a nondeterminist worldview, in which a great many areas of nature and human activity were understood as probabilistic or even purely uncertain.[98] Computer models, in other words, were used as a safe medium in which to challenge the Soviet government's belief in control. In turn, a long-term perspective was used to challenge present decisions and trends. In this way, instead of producing certainty, global computer models time and again reminded officials of the boundaries of human knowledge and knowledge-based control.

Global modeling, in this way, permitted a different way of relating to the future of Soviet society. Although Soviet scientists cautiously avoided direct challenges to the ideological dogma of the superiority of the communist system, the uniqueness of the communist system was simply made redundant. The ideological differences simply did not matter. By the early 1980s the concern with global problems as the metabolism between humans and the biosphere, something which was beyond the Cold War struggle for global hegemony, became legitimate and central in the Soviet Union.[99] This globalist, environmental discourse slowly but steadily accumulated power as the key framework for economic development strategies and, in so doing, as a Russian historian of science Dmitrii Efremenko notes, the global environmental agenda ran parallel to and only rarely intersected with Marxist-Leninist political economy.[100] The focus on long-term global and environmental processes enabled Soviet scholars and policy makers to point out that the Soviet economy and society also had serious problems, which were of a universal and global character and which could not be resolved internally.

Moiseev was especially pointed on this, claiming as early as the 1970s that there was a need to focus on new problems in order to prepare for the new world of advancing computer technologies.[101] We should not dismiss this call as trivial rhetoric: it was, indeed, a smart way of suggesting that the Soviet system was stuck in solving its old problems. To suggest changing the whole system, built on politicized central planning and animosity to the West, would be a claim too revolutionary even for a Soviet scholar as independent-minded as Moiseev. Instead, he suggested turning to new problems, ones of global and long-term character. The attempt to solve these new problems could and did transform the Soviet system.

Most importantly, global models were constitutive to the emerging understanding of the global future as a truly interdependent phenomenon. The discourse of interdependence became a new diplomatic language of a non-zero-sum game. For instance, the GKNT's head of foreign relations would assure his Japanese visitors that the Soviets understood the world "as a system of partners," where "when the system as a whole wins, each partner wins."[102] Deeds, unsurprisingly, did not always follow from the words: Soviet statistical agencies regularly refused to provide data to either Soviet or Western scientists.[103] In spite of these difficulties, the impact of Soviet global modeling on sociopolitical change should not be underestimated, as it was, to use Brian Wynne's words, "more than its final results." Thus in the next chapters I discuss several cases in which global and computer-based modeling was transformed from a mere instrument, producing policy-relevant data, into a large enterprise of "policy argumentation."[104]

6

FROM NUCLEAR WINTER TO THE ANTHROPOCENE

In the previous chapter I showed how the field of computer-based global modeling was constructed as a politically neutral platform that not only enabled scholars to interact across the Iron Curtain, but also to criticize the Soviet regime. Internationally, IIASA positioned itself at the avant-garde of global modeling, and inside the Soviet Union global modeling was a personal pet project of Gvishiani. However, Soviet global modeling was also an arena for fierce, albeit not always explicitly stated, competition: other Soviet scientists challenged Gvishiani's monopoly over global modeling as the East-West platform and organized themselves into networks that were more or less loosely coupled with IIASA.

In this chapter I examine these developments through the particular case of the nuclear winter project, an outcome of global modeling that in its political significance was second only to the Meadows report. A decade after *The Limits to Growth*, it was the nuclear winter report that shook the world of scientific, political, and military elites. Having propelled studies of global environmental change to the top of the political agenda, the nuclear winter project left a deep intellectual legacy on modern governmentality. In this chapter I focus on the nuclear winter study's impact on the Soviet governmental discourses in order to point to the emerging new sociopolitical epistemology, articulating a different relation between the man and nature and positing a need of new institutions and expertise for world government.

The idea that the Earth could be plunged into a "nuclear winter" as the catastrophic outcome of a nuclear war was announced by a group of leading climate and environment scientists from the United States, Western Europe, and the

Soviet Union shortly after Ronald Reagan delivered his "Star Wars" speech in March 1983. Drawing on experiments with data-based computer models, these scholars claimed that a nuclear war, unlike the two world wars, would be not simply a regional, but a truly global disaster. Nuclear missiles, detonated over urban areas, would ignite massive fire storms, which in turn would propel soot particles and aerosols into high levels of the atmosphere. As a result, the computer models predicted, a dust shield would emerge that would be transported by air currents to both the Northern and Southern hemispheres. Hovering in the atmosphere for several months, the dust clouds would bring about dusk at noon, and the air temperature would fall significantly. The lack of sunlight would kill most plant and animal life and, in the long term, a nuclear war would irreversibly change climatic conditions and ecology. In these circumstances, humanity, scholars argued, faced extinction.

The nuclear winter report presented a perfect global disaster. It was illustrated with graphs and maps, showing that both the climate and ecology of the Earth could be irreversibly transformed by a nuclear explosion of 100 megatons, an estimate that was even considered modest given the actual technological capacity. This was no fantasy scenario: in 1961 Khrushchev had refused a request by the military to test a 100-megaton missile.[1] The devastating effects of nuclear warfare had certainly been studied before, but in previous studies the damage had normally been described in terms of the destruction of individuals and infrastructure. The novelty of the nuclear winter study was its focus on the environmental consequences of nuclear war.[2]

The findings were so unexpected and dramatic that the study led to a significant transformation of Cold War defense discourses. For instance, Soviet scientists redefined nuclear arms as "global biospheric arms," "atmospheric bombs," and "global weapons." Meanwhile, the prominent American nuclear strategy mastermind and former secretary of defense Robert McNamara declared that nuclear weapons could no longer be regarded as weapons, meaning that in light of their predicted destructive effects, nuclear missiles would never be deployable.[3] From 1983 onward, the phenomenon of nuclear winter would be invoked time and again in connection with various risks and disasters related to nuclear technologies, be they the India-Pakistan conflict in the late 1990s or the Fukushima meltdown in 2012.[4]

To historians and political scientists, such as Lawrence Badash, who authored the first history of the nuclear winter project, the nuclear winter project seems to mark an extraordinary moment in the history of Cold War international relations and the disarmament movement in the United States.[5] Paul Edwards proposed inscribing the nuclear winter study in the history of (Western) climate change science.[6] However, so far no one has thoroughly addressed the role of the nuclear winter project in the Soviet context, although the very point of the study was that it was jointly pursued by Soviet and US scholars, and despite the feeling that the nuclear winter project influenced Soviet policy rather more significantly than the United States.

Drawing on previously unstudied documents held in the archives of the Russian Academy of Sciences, and specially conducted interviews with the actors involved, this chapter places the nuclear winter report in its wider scientific and political context. It seeks to explain Soviet involvement in the nuclear winter project, the ways in which the nuclear winter report was used inside the Soviet Union, and with what consequences. In contrast to previous work, which situated the nuclear winter project in the context of transnational disarmament movements, I argue that the nuclear winter project had a much wider agenda and impact. In the Soviet Union, but also in the West, the nuclear winter project deeply transformed the understanding of the relationship between mankind and nature by revealing the limits to governability and to the control of human activities' impact on the environment. I suggest that the nuclear winter report showed that nature, previously understood as a "passive opponent" in game theory terms, could in fact be "provoked" by nuclear explosions and retaliate in ways that transgressed superpower interests by making the winner into a loser.

Furthermore, we need to turn back to the history of the nuclear winter project, because it was a path-breaking event that led to some key innovative revisions of the fundamental premises of the historical and social sciences. It was the nuclear winter project that for the first time provided evidence of human activities as geological agency, demonstrating that human activities can lead to irreversible climate change. The nuclear winter study preceded the thesis of global warming that began to gain publicity in the late 1990s. The two strands of research were closely connected, for it was the Nobel laureate Paul Crutzen, one of the key nuclear winter scientists, who coined the term "Anthropocene" in 2002, that is, the epoch of human-caused changes in Earth's geology and ecosystems.

I would like to emphasize this point. Crutzen's thesis on the Anthropocene was so influential that it led to a rethinking of the basic premises of historical and sociological research, most famously by Dipesh Chakrabarty, who outlined the shift from the notion of nature as a backdrop to human activity to human agency as a geological force.[7] However, the beginning of the discussion about globalization in connection to climate change should be dated not to the late 1980s, as Chakrabarty suggests, relying on Bert Bolin's account, but to the year 1983, when the nuclear winter report was released. Second, and more importantly, the role of the sociopolitical and material mechanism of this knowledge production must be brought to the forefront. Mankind did not merely wake up to the fact of climate change. The impact of human activities on the Earth was discovered and made visible through systems sciences, assisted by computer modeling, and it is in the nuclear winter project that this was done for the first time. Humanity did not "fall into the Anthropocene," as Chakrabarty would have it, but, instead, developed special tools to see it and East-West cooperation played an important role in this process.[8]

Thus, the case of the nuclear winter project enables us to begin approaching the idea of the Anthropocene as a product of Cold War scientific technologies and networks. I argue that this is not a mere historical coincidence. It was indeed in the philosophies developed around the nuclear winter project that the coevolution of man and nature was rethought, and this rethinking took place on both sides of the Iron Curtain. Building on Vladimir Vernadskii's idea of the evolution of biosphere into noosphere, Nikita Moiseev, a Russian mathematician and research director of the Soviet Academy of Sciences' Computer Center in Moscow, advanced the thesis of anthropogenic change as a driver of social and political development in the Soviet Union as early as the mid-1980s. But in what follows, I suggest that there is more to the Soviet nuclear winter debate than mere curiosity about the history of ideas, of nuclear winter as a pre-Anthropocene theory. A closer look at the East-West coproduction of the nuclear winter study reveals a surprising porosity in the Iron Curtain, and the transformative power of the study inside the Soviet Union. It also shows the importance of loosely coupled networks for a generation of innovation: although the nuclear winter study was not anchored in IIASA, it was individuals who were loosely coupled with IIASA (and competing with its patron) who developed this study.

Forecasting the Consequences of Nuclear War: The Russians Read Kahn Too

Strictly speaking, the nuclear winter report was not the first to postulate the possibility of a global disaster following a nuclear war: scientists had voiced such warnings from as early as the 1950s. It is the evidence backing this warning and the mode of action that are new. In order to fully appreciate the novelty of the nuclear winter report, a brief review of the earlier estimates of nuclear war damage is therefore necessary.

In the United States, the most prominent forecasts of the consequences of nuclear war had been produced by RAND, a think tank that so far has been attributed a particular role in Cold War historiography. The growing body of literature on RAND's scientists points out that they devised influential schemes and theories of how to solve and rationalize different military and policy problems, developing a wide range of new methods, such as game theory, the scenario and Delphi methods of forecasting, and program budgeting (PPBS). Applications of these tools outside military operations—for instance, in attempting to control dissenting groups in American population, and in social and urban planning—were contested as an illiberal extension of top-down, conservative governance.[9] But it was RAND's contribution to nuclear strategy that attracted the harshest criticism.[10] To briefly recapitulate, in the 1940s RAND scientists Charles Hitch and Robert McNamara formulated the MAD strategy, according to which a sufficiently large nuclear arsenal made possible a speedy and completely devastating retaliation following an incoming strike. The existence of mutually assured destruction (abbreviated to "MAD") formed the basis of deterrence.[11] One interpretation of this intellectual exercise pointed out that it was a typical of the RAND style of thought, according to which even such high-risk, high-stakes problem as nuclear warfare could be and had to be planned with the help of what they regarded as rational methods of cost-benefit analysis. The problem was that the outcome of such intellectual exercises led to considering potential future scenarios that challenged the established moral worldviews, a dilemma most famously explicated in the work of another RAND scholar, Herman Kahn, who published highly controversial scenarios of the development of thermonuclear war, attempting to find a tolerable number of casualties.[12] Liberal critics pointed out that the very availability of nuclear weapons led to the emergence of expertise that appeared to be absurd from the common sense perspective, and thus to a deepening divide between governmental, militarized elites and society.

Although divisive internally in the United States, the nuclearized Cold War governmentality turned out to be an unlikely bridge-builder in East-West relations. Although much of the work done at RAND was classified, one of the goals of nuclear strategy was to serve as an instrument of communication between the great powers.[13] For instance, acknowledging that "Soviet Man" could not be presumed to behave in identical ways to "Rational Man," it was thought that the Soviet government should be socialized into the American strategic thinking mode.[14] Kahn made this particularly clear as his book addressed not only a US audience, but also at least "some of the Soviets." Hoping that his exercise in calculating the damage of nuclear conflict would be read in the Soviet Union, Kahn sought to convert the Soviets to what he understood as the American rational approach to nuclear strategy.[15] Indeed, these expectations seemed to be met: Nikita Khrushchev, according to Walter Clemens, did read a Russian translation of William W. Kaufman's *McNamara Strategy* (1964); an edited translation of Kahn's "On Escalation" (in English, 1965) was also published by Voenizdat, a publishing house in Moscow that published literature for the Soviet Ministry of Defense, in 1966.[16]

Furthermore, US nuclear strategists held that it was useful to share a clear image of disaster with the Soviet enemy: mutual estimation of damage, a shared image of doom, it was thought, could enhance mutual predictability and therefore prevent actual conflict. Public release of such data was certainly carefully controlled: there were secret nuclear defense strategies, constructed around a belief that the nuclear war could be won, albeit if at a high cost. Kahn, for instance, estimated that about one-third of the people living in the United States could perish during a nuclear conflict. The number of predicted casualties increased in American forecasts during the 1970s, but no "serious" nuclear war scenario anticipated a total wipeout of the American population. That the hydrogen bomb explosion could have impacts on the global level was suggested in a closed report by American scientists as early as in 1949; however, a later report (1975) for the US National Academy of Sciences did not foresee substantial climate effects from nuclear war. Kaplan argued that in the United States there was always a secret strategy based on a first strike and the belief in a possible nuclear war victory, but it was only in 1982 that the US government publicly admitted its view of nuclear war as a war that could be fought and won. This statement, made by Reagan's secretary of defense Casper Weinberger, caused outrage among disarmament activists and in part inspired the nuclear winter study.[17]

If many aspects of American nuclear strategies could and have been thoroughly traced and analyzed, little is known about Soviet nuclear strategies that were destined for the internal use of the military-industrial complex. The Soviet government, to be sure, like the US government, made statements on nuclear strategy as part of its public communication in domestic and foreign arenas. However, there are few studies about actual Soviet nuclear strategies for internal use, mainly because this kind of research has been actively suppressed in Russia.[18] It is thought that Soviet nuclear strategic thinking was done at a number of governmental agencies and academic institutes, but we do not know much about the content of these forecasts.[19] Countless Soviet ideological pamphlets warned about the devastating effects of the nuclear arms race and nuclear war, but they never contained any data about possible Soviet losses. The only discernable view was that due to large dispersal, the Soviet population was less vulnerable to nuclear attacks than much denser Western populations.

Beyond Disarmament

Previous studies have examined the nuclear winter project primarily in the context of the disarmament movement. To be sure, the context of nuclear arms negotiations and disarmament activism was fundamentally important for both the conception and dissemination of the nuclear winter report, but this is only one side of a story. Traditionally, the disarmament-oriented narrative inserted the nuclear winter project in the chronology of formal nuclear arms talks between the United States and the Soviet Union. Constructed retrospectively, this narrative was teleological, tracing the buildup of events that led to the deterioration of Soviet-US relations in 1983 and 1984. Thus it begins with the initial success of the Nuclear Test Ban Treaty in 1963 and the ABM and SALT I agreements on October 3, 1972, and then notes how the disarmament negotiations process stalled and deteriorated in the late 1970s. SALT II was signed on July 18, 1979, but President Jimmy Carter withdrew the treaty following the Soviet invasion of Afghanistan in December 1979. Although SALT II was never ratified, both the American and Soviet governments complied with it. The freeze in the arms negotiations was replaced with rapid deterioration in 1983 when the United States launched the Strategic Defense Initiative (SDI), in the same year that the nuclear winter project was publicized. SDI was a program of anti-air missile defense based on technology so sophisticated that the Soviets, presumably, would not be able to match it. For this reason SDI threatened to undermine the mutual vulnerability agreement (the MAD strategy) by making US defense more robust than Soviet defense. The tension was aggravated when the Soviets accidentally shot down a Korean commercial airliner in September 1983. Strategic nuclear arms negotiations were discontinued in December 1983, not to be resumed before Gorbachev ascended to power in 1985.[20]

This context was invoked in order to situate the dance of formal negotiations intertwined with steps undertaken by peace activists. Here disarmament movements are attributed to the field of soft politics that sought to influence governments by shaping public opinion and even devising new, alternative channels for disrupted communication between the opposing regimes.[21] By the time the nuclear winter project was launched, disarmament movements had many years of experience under their belt. One of the key sites was the Pugwash meetings, initiated in 1955; the movement for reducing nuclear arms intensified in the 1960s.[22] Further nongovernmental actors, such as the International Physicians for the Prevention of Nuclear War (IPPNW), joined disarmament activities in the 1970s and 1980s.

In political histories the highest criteria for evaluating the success of the disarmament movement was the signing of arms reduction treaties. This particular measure of success, I argue, has obscured the wider impact of the nuclear winter project. In line with the intentions of activists, disarmament studies put a premium on those actions which led to treaties or other international agreements and subsequent changes in the military arsenal. Here the perceived failure of the nuclear winter project was that it did not lead directly to any treaty, partially because (as Clemens argues), the nuclear winter project was part of "low politics," which could not directly impact on the "high politics" of national security.[23] Matthew

Evangelista, in his influential study of an emerging transnational civil society of scientists, influencing formal policy actions, describes the nuclear winter project as a "fleeting episode" in public diplomacy around arms control.[24] As he was primarily interested in disarmament, Evangelista focuses on the Pugwash movement, whose influence on Gorbachev's decision to reduce the Soviet nuclear arsenal has been well documented. Similarly, even the principal historian of the nuclear winter study, Lawrence Badash, focuses on disarmament outcomes, accordingly interpreting the nuclear winter project as a failure of political activism. Badash details with an archaeologist's attention the many forking paths that the nuclear winter project followed through academic research institutions, US governmental agencies, and the US Congress, and shows convincingly just how multifaceted and complex this undertaking to explore the environmental consequences of nuclear war was. However, Badash rounds off his story with a melancholic note on the scientists' failure to substantially impact defense policy.[25]

In contrast, I argue that the perceived failure of the nuclear winter project is the side effect of an overt focus on disarmament activism, although even this can change with new evidence.[26] In earlier work, voices speaking to the significance of the nuclear winter report, even such as that of the prominent Soviet political scientists and public debater, Georgii Arbatov, are disregarded.[27] Furthermore, some actors involved have recently changed their minds about the significance of this project. For example, Frank von Hippel, an influential mediator between US defense and academic sectors, was quite skeptical about the impact of the nuclear winter report on defense policy in the 1980s,[28] but more recently he has suggested that the Soviet nuclear winter scientists had a strong influence on Gorbachev's decision to drastically reduce the nuclear arsenal.[29] However, for my argument it is most important to understand that the nuclear winter project was conceived not only in order to aid disarmament activists, but also to promote collaborative East-West research on global climate and environment change, something which has been acknowledged only in passing in the previous literature.[30]

Another point to which I want to draw attention is that the focus on disarmament led to the omission from this history of Nikita Moiseev, who was central both to the implementation of the nuclear winter project and to the subsequent development of new notions of governance. It is not possible to overestimate Moiseev's role in both the initiation and the popularization of the nuclear winter project in the Soviet Union: a good hint here is also that Russian historiography normally names (in my view, not entirely correctly) Moiseev as the initiator and director of the Soviet nuclear winter project, whereas Moiseev is absent from Western scholarship on the subject.[31]

In what follows, I show how the production of the nuclear winter prognosis relied on preexisting collaborative networks among Soviet and American scientists involved in global modeling, networks which were forged through Moiseev's effort. The existence of these networks is important for my study, for they illustrate the diverse institutional links between East and West: although much cooperation in systems analysis was channeled through IIASA, there also were other routes, which, as I show, depended on strong personalities. In the last part of this chapter, I detail how Moiseev mobilized the nuclear winter report to advance his own innovative thinking, which extended mathematical modeling of the global climate and environment to a philosophy of a wholly new type of governance, one which had nothing to do with Marxism-Leninism, centralized Party control, or even Cold War confrontation, but shared many concerns with Crutzen's idea of the Anthropocene and what is in recent scholarship described as the government of the unknown.[32]

Cold War Environmental Science

The case of cybernetics, which was shaped and disseminated through the interdisciplinary Macy conferences in New York in the 1940s, demonstrated that breakthroughs in science do not appear out of the blue; instead they tend to be rooted in loosely coupled networks that relate disparate disciplines and enable their cross-fertilization.[33] This was the case for the nuclear winter project, which was born in a very particular institutional milieu and was facilitated by the fact that its key contributors belonged to a new type of scientist. These scientists could relatively easily cross both the geographical borders of the great powers and the boundaries of academic and strategic military research, something that was regarded as disconcerting by some researchers.[34] Surely, a surprising degree of mobility and strategic priority in the state research policy would count as a sign that a science was being manipulated by the government? This was precisely the case where pragmatism intertwined with intellectual ambition.

Some Soviet and American nuclear winter scientists were linked with military research to varying degrees. For instance, a forerunner to the nuclear winter report was commissioned to Stephen Schneider and Michael MacCracken by the US Arms Control and Disarmament Agency (ACDA) via the National Academy of Sciences in 1974. In turn, Richard Turco did work for the Defense Nuclear Agency and had some access to classified data.[35] Being based at one of the foremost research units of the Soviet Academy of Sciences, the Soviet team was understandably coupled to the military complex, albeit not all of them directly. For instance, Moiseev's group was based at the Computer Center of the Soviet Academy of Sciences, which contained a Department for Military Research. On Moiseev's initiative, a unit for operations research (OR) was established at this department in 1966; this unit developed a computer modeling system to enact military operations on particular terrains.[36] However, the Soviet nuclear winter scientists were not based in the OR unit, but at the laboratories for climate and environmental modeling. These laboratories, as it appears from the available sources, were not directly involved in nuclear weapons or defense strategy research. Indeed, this distance from military research turned out to be an asset, because the Soviet scientists who had top secret security clearance and worked directly with military applications were not normally allowed to travel abroad.

However, Moiseev's team worked in direct physical proximity to their OR colleagues. That physical proximity does not necessarily entail intellectual cross-fertilization is a well-known fact in academia, especially its Soviet version. But the Computer Center was a unique organization, because it managed to avoid the notorious compartmentalization and secrecy endemic to Soviet research institutes. Indeed, the center was designed to facilitate informal interaction and ad hoc discussions: its building featured corridors, long and wide enough to accommodate the eight hundred-strong staff strolling and chatting. These peripatetic discussions, my interlocutors told me, were cherished as part of the center's culture. Hence, although the Computer Center climate and environment modelers were never officially supplied with any plausible Soviet war scenarios, it is possible that they had some opportunity to get at least some clues about technical and strategic possibilities of Soviet nuclear defense through these informal channels. Furthermore, other interlocutors hinted that some Soviet scientists involved in the nuclear winter project presumably could access some "really existing" nuclear strategies and the data collected from nuclear tests.[37] This privileged status was enjoyed by a group at the Soviet State Committee of Hydrometeorology and Control of the Environment (Goskomgidromet), directed by Iurii Izrael', a prominent research administrator who was described as a powerful figure and hard-line Stalinist. However, the highly secretive Goskomgidromet never shared these data with the Moscow Computer Center scientists.[38]

Despite being more or less loosely coupled with their respective industrial-military complexes, Soviet and US nuclear scientists were involved in many cooperation programs. One such important area, as previous research shows, was US-Soviet cooperation in the field of climate and environment modeling, which was driven by the insurmountable need for data. Neither Soviet nor American meteorologists, oceanologists, and seismologists could model their national geophysical systems without having historical and current data about world trends. This epistemological need was strong enough to penetrate the Iron Curtain by establishing routes and platforms for direct collaboration, leading to what Edwards describes as infrastructural globalism.[39]

Not only the data, but also the models had to be shared in order to make the studies compatible. However, such international dissemination was not straightforward: special social relations were required to move the data and the computer models. In chapter 5 I detailed that this social mode of transfer involved lengthy stays and face-to-face cooperation, with the aim of generating trust in professional credentials and of acquiring the necessary know-how. It was in these close and lengthy networked collaborations, developed at arm's length from the military-industrial complex, that the nuclear winter report was born. The following section details how Moiseev's team established such connections with the American scientists, which would be later used for the nuclear winter project.

Soviet Climate Modelers Join International Networks

International organizations played a highly important role in mediating US-Soviet relations in the environmental sciences. In 1969 the International Council of Scientific Unions (ICSU) established the Scientific Committee on Problems of the Environment (SCOPE).[40] Linked with UNESCO and the United Nations Environment Program (UNEP), SCOPE provided multiple arenas for East-West collaboration among environmental scientists, including global modelers.[41] The Computer Center at the Soviet Academy of Sciences joined SCOPE activities from the very start of Soviet membership in 1974.[42] Why the Computer Center? Established in 1955, the Computer Center hosted some of the most innovative research, brought together by the need for advanced mathematical applications, ranging from oil and gas extraction to jet fighters, water management, economics, and ecology.[43] The center was equipped with a BESM, at that time the most powerful Russian computer for civilian use (more powerful M-20s were reserved for the military), as well as a smaller STRELA.[44] The center was housed in a specially constructed building, designed in a somber neoclassical Stalinist style, featuring a majestic portico. Situated slightly off busy Vavilov Avenue, the building was surrounded by trees and boasted a prominent and equally somber neighbor: the Steklov Institute of Mathematics.

The first director of the Computer Center was forty-five-year-old Anatolii Dorodnitsyn, a mathematician, who ran the center in a manner that was perceived as excessively authoritarian by some and who did not retire until 1989. In 1957 Nikita Moiseev, then forty, arrived at the center to direct research in the field of hydrodynamics. During the 1960s, Moiseev developed research on optimization, OR, and game theory, finally establishing a department for the study of optimization and theories of control in 1968. In the late 1960s, according to Moiseev, his passion turned to the environmental applications of mathematical methods; a subject that he pursued until his retirement in 1987.[45] It was through Moiseev's personal effort that the Computer Center gained SCOPE membership in 1974.

As mentioned in chapter 5, Moiseev was introduced to global systems thinking and modeling by the biologists Nikolai Timofeev-Resovskii and Viktor Kovda; in fact Moiseev first met Kovda in Paris.[46] An eminent Russian biologist, actively involved in putting research about the biosphere on UNESCO's agenda in the 1960s, Kovda was appointed president of SCOPE from 1973 to 1976.[47] Drawing on these important connections, Moiseev embarked on an entrepreneurial project to promote global modeling in the Soviet Union. In 1976 he created two new laboratories to study global Earth systems, and appointed two mathematicians, Iurii Svirezhev and Vladimir Aleksandrov, to head a laboratory for mathematical ecology and a laboratory on atmosphere research.[48]

Once established, global climate laboratories needed computer models, and this is where Moiseev's networks at SCOPE became indispensable. It was a normal practice in mathematical modeling to borrow well-functioning models. By the 1970s, several general circulation models of the world atmosphere (GCMs) were in use across the world, including in the Soviet Union. Moiseev, however, decided to send Aleksandrov to borrow one particular model from the Americans, the Mintz-Arakawa model. However, the question is, why did he send Computer Center scientists to the United States when there were already several GCMs in the Soviet Union? As argued in chapter 5, one reason was that to borrow a mathematical model did not mean to simply copy it, but rather to "recreate" it. In the process of recreating a model, the receiving scientist both acquired the skills with which to run the model and got the opportunity to develop it. In this particular case there were also pragmatic reasons: the work could be done much faster on the American computer than on the BESM. This acceleration saved the Computer Center more than 100,000 USD, according to Aleksandrov's estimate.[49]

Thus soon after the Computer Center's climate modeling laboratory was inaugurated in 1976, Moiseev contacted Eugene Bierly, then in charge of atmospheric sciences at the National Science Foundation (NSF), asking him to facilitate Aleksandrov's visit to the National Center for Atmospheric Research (NCAR) in Boulder, Colorado.[50] Alongside Livermore National Laboratory, NCAR was a prestigious institute, in which cutting-edge work was performed on global climate modeling. Arranged within the framework of the Soviet-American Cooperation for the Protection of the Environment program (1972), this visit was the first knot in a network that would lead to the East-West cooperation on the nuclear winter report.

A relatively young director of the laboratory of climate modeling, Aleksandrov was a highly distinctive figure. Aleksandrov's easy-going character and his mathematical talent made him a perfect operator in the global modeling field, where the importance of face-to-face interaction was paramount (many Western climate modelers, such as Gerald North, visited his home in Moscow). Accompanied by his colleague Vladimir Sergin from the Russian far east branch of the Soviet Academy of Sciences in Vladivostok, Aleksandrov embarked on his first lengthy trip to the United States in 1978.[51] According to the agreement, the two Soviet scientists were allowed to stay five months in the United States, but as their work progressed well and they earned the trust of their hosts, their stay was extended to eight months. This extension was welcome: as Aleksandrov wrote for the NCAR newsletter, "we could read the results of the American modeling work in your journals, but we can't get a real feeling for what you are doing without trying it ourselves, and so we want to do some of every task connected with building and running such [large global] models."[52] At NCAR Aleksandrov was hosted by Warren Washington, and Aleksandrov's main interest was to work on the Cray-1, a computer which could be fed data from fifty-seven terminals across the United States and Canada, including Oregon State University, and even its own satellite.[53] Although NCAR was explicitly instructed never to let Aleksandrov "anywhere near the computer," the scientists disregarded these security measures. Instead, as one of the most influential atmosphere scientists Stephen Schneider recalled, "Vladimir came, he gave a talk, we had a nice barbecue out in the backyard." In Schneider's memory Aleksandrov emerges as "flipping hamburgers, being a very American guy."[54]

In addition to NCAR, Aleksandrov and Sergin spent two days at Livermore Laboratory, where, unlike at NCAR, the two Soviet scientists were not allowed to see either the experimental equipment or the computer system, but were given loads of printed materials.[55] Their three-week stay at Oregon was more fruitful. Directed by Lawrence Gates, the Climatic Research Institute at Oregon State University was established on the basis of a group of climatic researchers from RAND and university researchers in 1976; the Institute later attracted more scientists from both NCAR and Livermore. Gates, according to Aleksandrov's report, was quite positive about cooperating with the Soviets; for instance, he agreed to give his global circulation model to the Computer Center and even suggested sending two scientists to Moscow to help to adjust this model on the Soviet computer.[56]

The Computer Center's GCM was intended to study the anthropogenic impact on climate, in particular, the emissions of CO_2.[57] Several institutes at the Soviet Academy of Sciences used a compact model designed by Mintz and Arakawa. Therefore Aleksandrov decided to use the Mintz-Arakawa model to develop his own baseline model on Cray-1.[58] In so doing he faced some serious issues that illustrated how the lack of advanced technology made the lives of Soviet scholars quite adventurous. In order to calibrate the model, the NCAR historical weather data were used to simulate the boundary conditions of a January month. The fancy Cray-1 produced a video that showed how weather systems moved around the globe. To check whether these results were meaningful, the data had to be sent back to Moscow. A problem arose: how to transport the results from the new Cray-1 to the archaic BESM-6, which could not support the video interface? Aleksandrov came up with the following solution. He filmed the video on the computer display with a handheld camera and posted the cassette to Moiseev in Moscow.[59] Having received Aleksandrov's tape, Moiseev boarded a flight to travel three thousand kilometers from Moscow to Novosibirsk to consult experts at the Novosibirsk branch of the Soviet Academy of Sciences on Siberian air currents, which are extremely stable and can be used to verify weather simulations.[60] Moiseev recalled that the Novosibirsk scientists promptly recognized that the American computer correctly replicated a "typical Siberian anti-cyclone." The model's calibration was thus verified.[61] Back in Moscow, Aleksandrov spent another year plugging the land and ocean blocks into the model. Finally, in 1980 the Computer Center had a working version of a global biosphere model.[62] It did not have a separate block for simulating human activities: the human activities were fed in through scenarios.[63]

However, Cold War transfer was not a one-way road along which people, ideas, and technologies traveled solely from the West to the East. In 1981 Carl Sagan visited the Soviet Union for the first time as he accompanied Bernard Lown, the founder of the IPPNW. It is unclear whether Sagan met Moiseev's team during this visit.[64] In June 1981, several of the scientists who would later be involved in the nuclear winter study, such as Bierly of NSF, Gates of Oregon State University, and MacCracken, attended a Soviet-American symposium on CO2 emissions. The symposium took place in the Ol'gino hotel, an elegant example of Soviet modernist architecture situated on a picturesque Finnish bay at the outskirts of Leningrad. Bierly and Gates also visited the Computer Center, where they were welcomed by Dorodnitsyn, Moiseev, and Marchuk, then chairman of the GKNT. They also met the meteorologist Izrael'. At the Computer Center a seminar was organized to discuss global biosphere modeling. It was attended by Aleksandrov, Svirezhev, and Tarko. Indeed, Svirezhev and Tarko's talk about CO2 cycles and "general principles of constructing global models" caused so much interest that the seminar ran way over time and Aleksandrov and A. V. Lotov did not even manage to present their talk about the climate and economics model. They had, most probably, occasion to discuss these models during the dinner hosted by Aleksandrov, which was attended by, among others, Bierly, Gates, and Georgii Stenchikov.

During this visit, Bierly and Gates repeatedly confirmed their intention to continue Soviet-American collaboration in global climate modeling. They did not, noted Aleksandrov, propose any concrete measures at that time, "perhaps due to the complicated internal political situation in the United States."[65]

At the same time that Aleksandrov was consolidating his personal connections with Western climate modelers, American scientists began to address the issues that would lead to the nuclear winter idea. In the early 1980s several organizations, including the American Association for Advancement of Science (AAAS), the National Academy of Science (NAS), the World Health Organization, and the Swedish Royal Academy of Sciences, began systematizing research on the environmental effects of nuclear explosions. This process has been detailed in Badash's account, but he did not articulate sufficiently clearly that the idea to study the environmental consequences of a nuclear war originated in a particular scholars' network, the roots of which stretched back to the 1970s.

In an interview, the eminent NCAR atmosphere scientist Stephen Schneider, who was involved in modeling the environmental consequences of nuclear war, modifying the original idea with the hypothesis of a milder environmental effect, a nuclear autumn, described several events which add important pieces to Badash's story. First of all, in 1974 Schneider, MacCracken, and probably Crutzen were asked by NAS to do a study for the ACDA which wanted to know more about the environmental effects of a nuclear explosion. This study, which used data from the Department of Defense (this scenario was later criticized for unrealistically massive explosions), found a slight cooling in air temperature, but this observation did not capture the scholars' attention at that time. Another milieu that brought the future nuclear winter modelers together was a "climate club" that Schneider organized in 1977 with the purpose of discussing the link between CO_2 and deforestation. In these discussions, some curious data discrepancies were observed, which led Crutzen to experiment with burning wood in the Amazon forest and, as a result, discover the importance of the way in which soot aerosols are transported in the atmosphere.[66]

Therefore, when the Swedish journal *Ambio* approached Crutzen with a request for an article about the environmental effects of a nuclear war in 1982, Crutzen, then based at the Max Planck Institute in Mainz, had a eureka moment and connected the cooling of the air and the role of soot. Together with John Birks of the University of Colorado, he conjectured a hypothesis that nuclear explosions would inject soot particles into the atmosphere, which would cause darkening and winter temperatures. Published in *Ambio* (June 1982), this article inspired the idea to test this hypothesis with a GCM, and shortly a group was formed within the SCOPE framework, which included American scientists Richard Turco, Owen

Toon, Thomas Ackerman, and James Pollack and Carl Sagan (known as the TTAPS group). However, it has been overlooked that a Soviet chair of SCOPE, Georgii Skriabin, was also present at the foundational meeting of TTAPS. It is very likely that Skriabin communicated the content of the meeting to the Soviet Academy of Sciences. It is also possible that it was together with Skriabin that Sagan came up with the idea of involving the Soviet Union in the research project. Soviet participation, Sagan believed, would give additional leverage to the geopolitical relevance of the project. Hence Sagan proposed inviting several Soviet scientists to the first in-house screening of the nuclear winter models, planned in April 1983. It was not difficult to choose: at that time the best-connected Soviet climate modeler was Vladimir Aleksandrov.

The TTAPS meeting took place in autumn 1982 and the next meeting was planned for spring of the next year. Although this was hardly a tight deadline, it must be remembered that the process of arranging scientific trips during the Cold War was a lengthy and complicated one. It could take up to six months for the Soviet bureaucracy to process the necessary documents, and there were many forms to be filled and reference letters about a candidate's political characteristics to be written.[67] In this case there was a fortunate coincidence. During Aleksandrov's visit to the United States in November 1982, his American colleagues (not TTAPS) suggested organizing a stay for two Soviet scientists within the framework of the Seventh Working Group of the Soviet-American Commission for the Environment.[68] The invitation was extended by the LaMont-Doherty Earth Observatory at Columbia University.[69] Dorodnitsyn's request to Izrael' that Aleksandrov and his colleague Valerii Parkhomenko be sent to the United States was considered at the commission meeting in Washington in mid-January 1983. Coincidentally, at around the same time Sagan approached Evgenii Velikhov and Roald Sagdeev with the suggestion to invite Soviet scientists to help model the environmental consequences of a nuclear war.[70]

This Washington meeting was highly significant, because it was here that previously unconnected networks converged, just a few months before Reagan's "Star Wars" speech. The arms control scientists were meeting at their own venues, such as the Pontifical Academy of Sciences at the Vatican in 1982.[71] The Soviet peace movement was represented by Velikhov and Sagdeev, both physicists involved in space research and highly positioned as vice presidents of the Soviet Academy of Sciences. Although Aleksandrov, like Moiseev, had little to do with disarmament activism before 1983, both Velikhov and Sagdeev sought to ameliorate the deteriorating US-Soviet relations. Barth described Velikhov as a "prototype of the scientist as political entrepreneur," an example of a strong individual actor, able to initialize and sustain transnational collaboration with American arms control supporters.⁷² It was through Velikhov and Sagdeev that Soviet global climate and ecology modelers became connected with the transnational disarmament policy community.

The interest in making a computer model of the environmental effects of nuclear war was mutual. Environmental modelers wanted to raise the profile of their research, which required a great deal of funding. Arms control activists badly needed some hard data to back their case. Now, to explain the turn of events, I would like to use the insight by an organizational psychologist Karl Weick, who noted that in the organizational context it is extremely difficult to build consensus around something that does not have a material, palpable existence.⁷³ A global damage of nuclear war was just exactly such a phenomenon: never empirically demonstrated. Although nuclear disaster had materialized, of course, through the destruction of Hiroshima and Nagasaki, Hiroshima and Nagasaki were cases of the limited use of nuclear weapons, certainly with horrid, but nevertheless local consequences. The notion of a "local" nuclear war encouraged nuclear optimism, which was acutely perceived as a problem by disarmament activists, particularly because existing statistical projections of nuclear war damage suggested the outcomes of the war to be rather tolerable. For instance, a 1976 American scenario projected that in the case of a nuclear attack dropping 6,559 megatons on the United States, about 80 to 90 percent of the US population would survive.⁷⁴ As such scenarios reinforced the position of the proponents of the nuclear arms race, disarmament activists needed evidence of disaster on a much bigger scale.

Sagan mediated between the scientific and disarmament networks. He quickly grasped that computer simulations could produce the evidence that the disarmament movement needed so badly.⁷⁵ By 1983 the time was right: the key components for simulating the environmental consequences of nuclear war, such as well-functioning transnational networks of scientists, operational computer modeling systems, and an increasing pool of relevant data, were already in place.⁷⁶ But the question remained: how to make these results credible in the eyes of policy makers? Why would one trust a computer simulation of a phenomenon that had never been empirically observed before?

To build such trust, recourse was taken to a classical scientific method of collaboration and replication. The nuclear winter project enrolled many scientists, who already knew each other and had a record of direct collaboration: Aleksandrov knew MacCracken and Gates personally, and he may have met Crutzen at NCAR. Therefore when Aleksandrov arrived at the meeting dedicated to discussing the modeling of the consequences of a nuclear war at the American Academy of Arts and Sciences in Cambridge, Massachusetts (April 22–26, 1983), he was not among strangers.⁷⁷ Plans were already made to present the findings to the public in a "big international conference" in Washington, October 31 to November 1, 1983. The participants at the April meeting also included one of the founders of the Pugwash movement, the British scholar Joseph Rotblat, although, according to Aleksandrov, there were no representatives of such nuclear powers as France or China. In his report to the Moscow Computer Center, Aleksandrov described the discussions as "active and informal."[78] Back in Moscow Aleksandrov argued in his report that the Soviet participation in the autumn conference was absolutely vital from "both political and scientific points of view." Furthermore, Aleksandrov was also impressed with the political implications of this project and wrote that Soviet participation was central to the antinuclear movement of scientists. The conclusion of the conference, he wrote, was a "firm conviction" that the consequences of nuclear war would be "fundamentally more damaging" than stated in the 1975 NAS report.[79]

In parallel to these preparations for modeling, disarmament advocacy networks progressed in the Soviet Union: the Committee of Soviet Scientists for the Defense of Peace against the Nuclear Threat (CSS), chaired by Velikhov, was established during a conference in May 1983.[80] It is obvious that Velikhov was well informed about the ongoing nuclear winter project, and some of its hypotheses were reflected in the agenda of this founding conference, which questioned the idea of a limited nuclear war.[81] It has to be stressed, however, that this committee was a parallel activity and did not originate in the nuclear winter project. The key goal of CCS was to pull together networks and arguments necessary to undermine the American Strategic Defense Initiative (SDI), an expensive undertaking that the Soviet government could not match.

In the summer of 1983, Velikhov sent a letter to the Federation of the American Scientists asking whether the American scientists were in the process of changing their minds about the futility of antinuclear defenses. Having received an answer that no such change was anticipated, and hence, implicitly, that the federation was also against SDI, Velikhov sent an invitation to von Hippel to visit Moscow in late November.[82] This sequence of events shows clearly how the arms control scientists carefully furthered their connections with the view that the soon-to-be-announced nuclear winter project could be instrumental in their anti-SDI efforts. It was this agenda of disarmament activism that brought together Velikhov, Sagdeev, and Sagan (Sagan would later write an introduction to Sagdeev's autobiography, published in English) and, in turn, distanced some of the less activist-oriented scientists like Schneider from Sagan. If Sagan and Velikhov supported the thesis of complete human extinction as a consequence of climate change following nuclear war, other scientists such as Schneider, but also the Soviet team, documented less harsh scenarios.

Simulating a Global Nuclear Disaster in the Soviet Union

Why did Moiseev's team get involved in the nuclear winter project? Personal attempts by Soviet scientists to alert the Soviet government to possible disasters dated back to Igor Kurchatov's classified report about the dangers of nuclear weapons, drafted in March 1954. In this report the scientist warned that the impact of a nuclear war would threaten "all life on Earth." Furthermore, Kurchatov even proposed to publish this report under the names of individuals who were not involved in the atomic weapons industry. Although this idea was not approved by the government, this case, as well as the more famous instances of Andrei Sakharov's and Yulii Khariton's appeal against nuclear weapons, testifies to the public-mindedness of some Soviet scientists, something that would lead Evangelista and David Holloway to identify an island of civil society within the Soviet Academy of Sciences.[83] This said, one should not discount the role of personal interest. When interviewed, several Soviet nuclear winter scientists told me that they were driven both by personal interest in the political implications of the experiment and by scientific curiosity.

The summer of 1983 turned out to be a busy one on both sides of the Iron Curtain. The GCM models crunched the data on the environmental consequences of nuclear war in the hands of the TTAPS group at Livermore, but also of Schneider at NCAR. In Moscow, labor was divided into two groups. The first group, directed by Georgii Golitsyn, focused on climate change. The most important work was done by Georgii Stenchikov and Vladimir Aleksandrov, who adjusted their three-dimensional model for this task. The second group focused on the ecological consequences of nuclear war, with work conducted by Aleksander Tarko under Svirezhev. The climate group investigated how big the dust cloud would be and how it would travel. The ecology modeling group explored the effects of fires, the global dust shield, and radioactivity on plants, animals, and humans.[84]

The language of numbers, as Porter argued, has a magical effect of creating an illusion of order and control, of manageability. However, even numbers are hard to control, especially when it comes to complex calculation: social studies of science have pointed out considerable discrepancy between the neat and coherent front stage and the messy backstage of mathematical studies.[85] Numbers themselves, therefore, need careful management of technologies and social practices, before they can assume an orderly form. This was precisely the case with the nuclear winter project and this is why, I suggest, it is important not to limit our attention to this scientific experiment as an example of numeric rhetoric, used to legitimate a preexisting practice, in this case, disarmament activism.

To make numbers work, lots of management and coordination was required. First of all, many more scientists from various fields and institutes were involved as assistants and consultants to this project than is reflected in the published reports. Second, in line with Soviet hierarchy of scientific patronage, the directors of the projects were not always directly involved in the experiments. For instance, Aleksandrov's key contribution to this project, according to a member of his group, was not so much his hands-on programming but the way he provided the project with international contacts, comparative examples, and data. In a similar way, programmers claimed that little if any hands-on work on the nuclear winter project was done by Svirezhev.[86] It is quite normal for scientists to disagree, sometimes violently, about who actually did "the real" work. It is significant, therefore, that all the scientists whom I interviewed emphasized the importance of Moiseev's contribution: they insisted that without Moiseev's sustained interest and support the Soviet nuclear winter project would never have taken off. Also, my informants pointed out his particular ethical position: to their knowledge, Moiseev never asked to be added as a coauthor to the studies to which he actually did not contribute.

In any case, that machines were central to this process was beyond retrospective dispute: the center's computer BESM-6 was kept truly busy. It took about three and a half hours to simulate processes of one month's duration, and about forty hours to run the simulations for one year.[87] These were forty long hours, because the remaining eight hundred scientists at the center also had work to get done! Stenchikov and his group crafted a model that simulated an injection of soot into the atmosphere, for which they used the *Ambio* scenario of nuclear exchange sequence and power yields. According to this scenario there were two sides involved in the conflict, the strikes occurred almost simultaneously, and less than half of the total US and Soviet nuclear arsenal was used, the total charges amounting to 5,742 megatons. Some attacks were also simulated in third-world countries, so that a total of 5,569 megatons were detonated on the major cities and industrial energy sites, including nuclear industry plants of the Northern hemisphere, and 173 megatons in the Southern hemisphere.

Soviet scientists ran a test covering a whole year, thus a longer time period than Americans, who simulated only one month. The Soviet model also included the ocean, something that the first version of the American model did not. The Soviet forecast was also the first to confirm the idea, voiced at the April conference, that nuclear strikes in the Northern hemisphere would cause climate change in the Southern hemisphere.[88] The first run of Soviet calculations predicted that the spring and summer in Western Europe would turn into a severe winter, and winter into arctic winter; the temperature would drop by 15–40°C over the region extending from Chad to Novosibirsk, the Caspian Sea to Sri Lanka, including India, Pakistan, and Western China.

The results churned out by BESM-6 revealed that a completely different planet would come into being after a nuclear war. It was found that conifer tree forests would be worst affected by the radiation, and that birds would be affected worse than insects, depending on where those birds lived, in the canopy or closer to the ground. Radioactivity would be carried not only by rainclouds, but also by pollen that could be inhaled by mammals.[89] The landscape after nuclear attack would be one with few conifers, but many shrubs, few mammals, but a lot of insects, the latter eventually destroying the surviving conifers. Plants that grew in shade would have better survival rate, given nuclear night and darkness. Should the blast occur in winter, conifers had a better chance of survival. Portraying this post-nuclear landscape, the nuclear winter model did something quite original in the context of nuclear damage studies: it populated what Lynn Eden defines as "asocial" models of the nuclear war damage, that is, models that only featured infrastructure.[90] The nuclear winter study thus spoke eloquently to the public, and its policy implications were clear: in their damage calculations, nuclear strategists had to include such factors as urban fires, irradiation, and sudden and prolonged light deprivation, as well as a drop in temperature. Nature, it seemed, was able to strike back and therefore had to be incorporated into nuclear strategy thinking.

Soviet participation in the nuclear winter project raises many questions about the productive power of informal organizing in Cold War science, because the Soviet scientists involved appeared to be counter-intuitively immune to censorship and ideological control. While it is important to note that it was the production stage of Soviet science, which was less constricted than the dissemination stage, the way Soviet scientists made their findings about the environmental consequences of nuclear war public testifies to an unexpected degree of spontaneity and a clear shift toward more permissibility in Soviet public discourse. But the information was first circulated among elite networks of leading geophysical and mathematical scientists. Documents reveal that nuclear winter modelers just could not wait to share their findings: although for strategic communication reasons it was agreed that no results would be announced before the official conference in Washington, in October 1983, some preliminary findings were informally discussed at several earlier international scientific meetings.

The first public presentation of Soviet findings was made at the international conference "Co-evolution of Man and the Biosphere," organized by l'Institut de la vie in Helsinki, September 5–9, 1983. The Parisian l'Institut de la vie, established by a medical researcher, Maurice Marois, actively pursued its agenda to use scientific argumentation for public diplomacy directed against militarism. In so doing, the institute organized a series of events pertaining to many disciplines of the life sciences, and research that either used computer technologies or engaged with the consequences of computerization. For instance, in 1973 the institute sponsored several meetings dedicated to global modeling. Thus the 1983 Helsinki meeting hosted a well-established network of scholars, many of whom had a decade of cooperation behind them.

Together with the Canadian economist Paul Medow, Moiseev opened this conference with a discussion of Vernadskii's ideas on the biosphere and its coevolution with the technosphere.[91] Although the official Helsinki conference program did not list any presentations on the environmental consequences of nuclear war,[92] according to oral sources and memoirs, Moiseev and Aleksandrov used this event to present the first findings of the nuclear winter report.[93] This suggests that either some improvisation took place or that the Soviet scientists found it expedient not to record their statements for official use. According to Tarko and Parkhomenko, shortly before the seminar Aleksandrov showed Moiseev the curves that demonstrated a fall in temperature and decline in vegetation. Moiseev was so taken aback that he encouraged Aleksandrov to present these findings in Helsinki.[94]

Eyewitnesses recalled that Aleksandrov's talk, although not prearranged, attracted a large crowd: a scientist described to me a fully packed auditorium, in front of which the charismatic speaker Aleksandrov outlined the prospects of global demise illustrated with graphs, drawn by Tarko, which showed the zone

FIGURE 8. Nikita Moiseev, Vladimir Aleksandrov, and Aleksandr Tarko, having first announced their findings about nuclear winter, at the seminar organized by L'institut de la vie, Helsinki, Finland, September 1983. Courtesy of Aleksandr Tarko.

of dying plants extending to the whole northern hemisphere. The audience froze into silence; one of the participants confessed that although he had gone through World War II, he had never been so terrified.[95] Moiseev recalled discussing the implications of the nuclear winter study on nuclear strategy: he drew on the non-zero-sum game model developed by his colleague, the leading Soviet OR scientist Germeier to argue that however scary it was, the nuclear winter reinforced the idea of deterrence. His argument was not well received, because the audience was in favor of complete disarmament.[96] It is interesting that Moiseev would later revise his position and promote nuclear winter as evidence for complete disarmament.

The Helsinki trip was a rich social experience, where Tarko and Moiseev impressed other scholars by taking a dip in the Baltic Sea (this was Finland in September). The junior Soviet scientists had a good opportunity to informally interact with the senior ones, especially when Tarko regained his bottle of vodka, which had been confiscated on the Finnish border on the way to Helsinki but duly given back upon his return in exchange for a receipt. The drink was consumed on the overnight train to Russia, and thus the journey of nuclear winter began.

Nuclear Winter Goes Public

As the Soviet scientists were braving the cold Baltic waters, Sagan carefully orchestrated the first public presentation of the modeling results in Washington. Having obtained support from a number of private foundations, in particular the Kendall Foundation, which funded environmental research and arms control activities, Sagan organized "The World after Nuclear War, the Conference on the Long-term Worldwide Consequences of Nuclear War," an impeccably well-coordinated media event, which attracted five hundred participants and a hundred media representatives. Moreover, the conference included a ninety-minute live television link between the Sheraton in Washington and Ostankino studio in Moscow.

Indeed, this particular medium deserves additional attention. In 1982 several initiatives were launched to connect Soviet and American debating groups via satellite television.[97] For Americans, this medium, known as a simulcast or space bridge (*telemost* in Russian), was intended to contribute toward the development of mutual empathy, if not trust, through what were in truth not entirely orchestrated discussions.[98] The idea of a space bridge was jointly formulated by the Americans and Soviets, including Pavel Korchagin and Sergei Skvortsov, who met up in Moscow in 1981. The first such television link was arranged during a rock festival in California on September 15, 1981. The Soviets used this broadcast as a medium to project a positive image to the West. For instance, in 1979–1980 the first live appearances of the journalist Vladimir Pozner on ABC's *Nightline* were shown only in the United States and not in the Soviet Union. The Soviet broadcast was edited and not broadcasted live.[99]

In a similar way, the Soviet broadcast of the space bridge "A World after Nuclear War" was a semipublic event, targeted at specialist audiences. Thus at 22:00 Moscow time, scholars assembled in the Ostankino studio to see their colleagues on the other side of the Atlantic.[100] The Washington camera revealed a dark hall filled with smartly dressed conference participants with name tags on their lapels. In Moscow, the Ostankino studio seated about forty participants. The directors of leading research institutes sat in the first rows, with heads of departments and prominent scholars behind them. Stenchikov, Parkhomenko, Aleksandrov, Sagdeev, and K. Ia. Kondrat'ev were in Moscow, whereas Moiseev and Golitsyn spoke from Washington. It was not their everyday experience to be rushed to Ostankino, recalled a participating scientist, hence there was a genuine excitement in the air. There was also room for spontaneity: according to my interlocutor, the participants in the audience were not briefed or in any other way instructed beforehand by journalists or special services.[101]

In Ostankino the debate was chaired by Velikhov, who most probably provided a political push to the Internews initiative to organize this event.[102] Present at the round table were the geneticist Alexander Bayev, Iurii Izrael', and the director of the SAS Institute for Genetics Nikolai Bochkov. The US roundtable included Carl Sagan, Paul Erlich, and Stephen Schneider, and was chaired by the deadly serious Thomas Malone, who was also a longstanding member of the US committee for IIASA. Sagan grilled Izrael' on the issue of the Soviet data derived from nuclear test explosions that should be shared in order to advance modeling efforts. Izrael', who, according to my interlocutor, indeed had that kind of data, evaded the question. Soviet scholars showed hand-drawn graphs to the American audience. American scientists, in turn, projected their graphs on computer displays, thus painfully reminding the Soviets how obsolete their computer interfaces were. Speaking from Washington, Moiseev was evidently in high spirits. As he would do on many later occasions, Moiseev insisted that it was vital to widen the studies of the anthropogenic impact on the biosphere and rethink the relationship between man and nature. One could get the impression that Moiseev sensed this was an excellent opportunity to get Vernadskii's theory of the coevolution of humanity and biosphere on a top research agenda.

The national media ran their headlines and the TTAPS report was promptly published in the prominent magazine *Science* (1983). SCOPE understood very well that the perfect storm of publicity caused by the idea of nuclear winter could be used to push climate and environmental modeling into the center of public attention and governmental agendas. Drawing on their long-term project, the study of climate change as a result of CO2 emissions, SCOPE and other organizations used the nuclear winter studies to show the versatility and importance of their scientific field. Shortly thereafter, in 1983, the NAS, the Royal Society of London, and the Soviet Academy of Sciences submitted a request to SCOPE to initiate a collaborative study about the environmental effects of nuclear war.[103] This program, known as ENUWAR, included about three hundred scientists and was the largest single project undertaken by SCOPE so far.[104] Through ENUWAR the nuclear winter project became a genuinely global affair. The program organized meetings in Paris, Stockholm, Delhi, Leningrad, and London in 1984.[105] ENUWAR produced two volumes, and further reports were issued by NAS (December 11, 1984) and various agencies from Canada and New Zealand (1985) as well as the UN. Books and articles discussing the plausibility of the nuclear winter scenario and possible outcomes for military strategy and environment policy were published.[106]

Intense and at times vitriolic debates followed. Not all scientists were pleased with the disarmament focus: some modelers found it frustrating that disarmament activists preferred the worst-case scenario and were unwilling to consider less severe forecasts. For example, the studies focused on disarmament emphasized the importance of an agreement that was reached at the conference at the Pontifical Academy of Sciences at the Vatican on January 23–25, 1984.[107] The point of the Vatican conference was to lower the threshold that would cause dramatic climate change: it was recognized that merely a 100-megaton discharge over urban centers would be fatal for the global system.[108] The models demonstrated that the fires in large cities caused by 100 megatons would change the state of the atmosphere as fundamentally as the ones caused by 5,000 megatons and 10,000 megatons.[109] However, according to other modelers, such as NCAR-based Schneider, the very idea of a threshold was incorrect. The findings testified to the multiple effects, which varied too much to establish any thresholds. For instance, an explosion bigger than 100 megatons would not cause such a drastic climate change if it took place in the Northern hemisphere in winter; but a smaller explosion in connection with massive urban fires could cause much more serious effects.[110] Soviet scientists oscillated between the two positions, the worst-case scenario, preferred by the disarmament activists, and the alternative, more nuanced scientific calculations. Indeed, and to the confusion of historians of nuclear winter, Soviet scientists pragmatically adjusted their position according to their strategic audiences. They saved face before scholars such as Schneider by developing the nuclear autumn hypothesis, yet the Soviets also made strong statements about the extinction of the entirety of humanity in the contexts where they found it rhetorically useful, such as, for instance, popular publications about the danger of nuclear war.

In any case, the claims that Soviet audiences were kept in the dark about the nuclear winter study were not quite correct. In December 1983, and therefore quite soon after the first major public presentation of the nuclear winter thesis, two articles on the environmental consequences of nuclear war were published in *Priroda* (Nature) and *Zemlia i vselennaia* (The Earth and the Universe). In turn, leading scientific milieus were, to be sure, well informed, both in Russian and English: the first Soviet report in English was prepared by Aleksandrov and Stenchikov (1983); this was quite a rushed work. The 1985 report from the Computer Center lists that, in all, the nuclear winter project published ten articles, one edited collection, and a monograph, and submitted to press ten further articles and one monograph.[111] From the mid-1980s too many books, both specialist and popular, were published in the Soviet Union to be listed here. I only want to note that it is quite likely that 1985 was an important threshold opening up space for such publications, possibly facilitated by Gorbachev's accession to the general secretary's position and Velikhov, in turn, had the status of Gorbachev's informal advisor on nuclear matters. The stream of Soviet publications that directly and indirectly concerned the nuclear winter theme continued up until the overhaul of the Soviet system in the 1990s.

As I mentioned above, multiple rationales overlapped in the making and dissemination of the nuclear winter report. Although the study claimed that there would be no winner of a nuclear war, there was an immediate winner in the United States: the science of climate change, as Reagan approved 50 million dollars for atmospheric research in 1984. Not so in the Soviet Union: although the Computer Center flagged the nuclear winter report as its central achievement in 1983–1984, environmental modelers received considerably smaller budgets than the generous funds directed toward the geophysical modeling of oil and gas extraction.[112] It is true that, as one scientist recalled in interview, the work had to be done on a conceptual level, to develop the model further; thus there was a need for more competent researchers and not just a large research budget.[113] In turn, Moiseev successfully lobbied to hire more scientists for geophysical modeling. In 1985 the Computer Center's research plans replaced nuclear winter studies with wider studies of anthropogenic impact (in Russian, *antropogennye trendy*) on the environment.[114] By 1986 there was already a second, improved version of the global biosphere model at work.[115] Here I would only like to note that at the same time related, but different projects were pursued at IIASA, although Moiseev tried, albeit unsuccessfully, to create a joint project on the modeling of the biosphere. Paul Crutzen did become involved with IIASA through the study of acid rain, but I will return to this in chapter 7.

Toward a New Soviet Governmentality of the Noosphere

In contrast with the view prevailing in historiography, I suggest that the nuclear winter prognosis had a rather significant impact on both Soviet science and governance. Some of these impacts, such as on research funds and new policy initiatives, are not easy to trace, as they were not always well documented through formal decisions. Other impacts come to the fore only if one actually considers intellectual governmental techniques to be of any importance.

While I am inclined to emphasize the latter point, arguing that the nuclear winter was an important step in the development of the late Soviet system-cybernetic governmentality, there is also some convincing evidence regarding the first point. First of all, the Soviet nuclear winter scientists recalled receiving an immediate response from the planners of different sectors. For instance, a global modeler would be asked to brief the staff of the tractor institute in order to aid their long-term planning.[116] There were also some hints that the Soviet military was receptive to the nuclear winter concept. In his memoir, Moiseev noted that one of the military strategists remarked that by rendering nuclear weapons unusable, the global modelers "foolishly" made their strategy work obsolete.[117] While these consultations with policy practitioners were, quite possibly, a mere gesture, although still pointing toward awareness of interbranch complexity among some Soviet managers, the nuclear winter report had another much more tangible impact: the project propelled to prominence a particular branch of research, computer-based global modeling, conceived now not just as a tool to generate new data, but as a source of innovative ideas about governability and control. It is on this point that I expand in the remainder of this section.

The Soviet nuclear winter research contributed to an important shift in Soviet governmentality, which can be traced in the emerging new discourse coalition that brought together nuclear winter scientists and some of the key Soviet ideologues. I base this argument on a study of publications in the prominent journal *Voprosy filosofii* (The Issues of Philosophy), a journal that outlined the problems considered to be of high priority in the contemporary research agenda of the Soviet Academy of Sciences. The publicizing of the nuclear winter report in 1983 was followed by a significant change in the themes covered by this journal. Before 1983, global modeling was occasionally covered in *Voprosy filosofii*; the journal also duly published political economic criticisms of the arms race and the US nuclear defense policy. Indeed, the 1983 March and May issues of *Voprosy filosofii* discussed global modeling, but the focus was primarily on the world economy and trade models, developed at the UN and the All-Union Institute for Systems Research (VNIISI) in Moscow, and did not include either geophysical world models or problems of the biosphere. Furthermore, neither the May peace appeal by Soviet scientists nor the October–November conference on nuclear winter in the United States was immediately reflected in the journal's pages; the nuclear winter theme first appeared in September 1984.

Who published in *Voprosy filosofii* mattered as much as what was published. The first article concerning the nuclear winter project was coauthored by no other than Moiseev and Ivan Frolov, one of the key Party philosophers, whose importance has been emphasized in work on the Soviet foreign policy doctrine. I suggest that through Frolov and his colleague Vadim Zagladin, the same Party philosophers who embraced the systems approach patronized by Gvishiani, Moiseev introduced notions derived from Vernadskii's thought into Soviet discourses on foreign policy and globalism. This article claimed that it was imperative to study the interaction of human impact on the environment as an evolution of the biosphere into the noosphere, using the example of the work done at the Computer Center and at Livermore Laboratory on the possible nuclear extinction of the global population.[118]

From that time on, many articles operating with this new discourse of biosphere as an area of global governance followed, a process which also coincided with the ascending *glasnost'* policy.[119] Furthermore, the nuclear winter project was explicitly mentioned as the principal reason for introducing global problems to the Party's agenda. In 1985 "global problems," including the nuclear threat, were for the first time introduced into the program of the twenty-seventh CPSU congress.[120] In 1986 Zagladin wrote that, thanks to the scientists who studied the consequences of nuclear war, "the conclusions which they reached were reflected in the project of a new draft of the CPSU Program, where it states that 'In the end this is a threat of a global military conflict, as a result of which there would be no victors and no losers, but the whole world civilization can perish.'"[121]

If arms control activists like Velikhov used the nuclear winter report to advance disarmament negotiations, Moiseev used it to advance his ideas about a new type of global governance. This new type of global governance was based on the idea of the coevolution of society and the natural environment. In their report, published in 1985, Moiseev, Aleksandrov, and Tarko compared their modeling system with the idea of Gaia, originally formulated by James Lovelock and Lynn Margulis in the 1960s.[122] Indeed, the social networks behind the Gaia idea did intertwine with the nuclear winter project networks in several ways. First, Margulis was the ex-wife of Carl Sagan. Second, Lovelock and Margulis were invited by the prominent anthropologist Margaret Mead to a workshop within the Fogarty Conference in October 1975. This event, dedicated to "The Atmosphere: Endangered and Endangering," also included future nuclear winter scientists such as Schneider and John Holdren.[123] Third, the Gaia theory already had a Russian counterpart: the noosphere theory developed by Vladimir Vernadskii (1863–1945), the founder of Russian environmental science. In *The Biosphere* (1924), Vernadskii claimed that the biosphere, or living matter, mediated between space and the Earth and therefore was a subject of human responsibility (Vernadskii borrowed the term "noosphere" from Teilhard de Chardin, who came up with this idea in the joint seminars with Vernadskii in Paris)."[124] From the late 1960s, Moiseev propagated and developed Vernadskii's theory of the coevolution of the biosphere and noosphere, the implications of which were a melting of boundaries between the social and natural sciences, and computer modeling was one of the technical approaches that allowed scientists to explore the development of these two previously thought separate spheres.[125]

Although some parallels between Vernadskii's biosphere and Lovelock's idea of Gaia have been established, there were significant differences between Moiseev's and Lovelock's thought. If Lovelock regarded Gaia as a giant self-governing system that seeks some kind of equilibrium in a process in which humans have only a very limited role to play, Moiseev regarded the biosphere as a challenge to change the existing modes of rational governance or control. While according to Lovelock, Gaia was a kind of unitary automatic cybernetic system that effectively balanced itself through feedback, Moiseev's developed a more sophisticated approach to the evolution of complex systems, in which cybernetic controls worked at many different levels and not always to the same purpose. According to Vernadskii, the biosphere and human society did not just self-regulate to reach a viable equilibrium, but rather evolved along an open-ended trajectory. Having adopted this insight, Moiseev argued that to govern such a coevolving, complex world the existing principles of "control" (in English) or "*upravlenie*" (in Russian) were not adequate. A new approach was needed, wrote Moiseev, and this was the approach that put a premium on "*napravlenie*" or guiding, pointing in a certain direction. Here the idea of governance as a teleological or goal-oriented process, conceptualized by cybernetic theorists Norbert Wiener, Arturo Rosenblueth, and Julian Bigelow, is maintained, but it is embedded in a vastly complex systemic view of the world.[126] For Moiseev, guidance emphasized the role of human intellect, but this had nothing to do with rational mega schemes to establish a unitary system of goals, thus subordinating all subsystems and leading to a homogenize society. This totalitarian ambition, wrote Moiseev, was simply impracticable. In turn, Moiseev noted that "without goal setting one cannot talk about management (*upravlenie*)." The absence of clear goals, argued Moiseev, did not necessarily result in chaotic development: he compared the role of "guidance" to irrigation structures. To "guide" was to find a way to streamline human energy. To govern through guidance one needs to provide channels, to open up new spaces for future development.[127] It is probably not surprising that Moiseev, originally a specialist in hydromechanics, came up with the metaphor of governance as building canals to irrigate the future.

I suggest that the nuclear winter report found itself torn by a clash between two governmentalities: one of governance as control (*upravlenie*), another of governance as guidance (*napravlenie*). The disarmament activists drew on the older, rather positivist epistemology of governance, one which relied on the establishment of facticity, verification, and control through feedback. This approach worked well for clearly defined, simple, technical tasks, such as the seismological observation project in Semipalatinsk and Nevada that provided the basis for the nuclear test treaty.[128] But the implications of the nuclear winter study were so complex they could not be easily reduced to concrete projects. It is quite possible that one of the reasons why the nuclear winter study was considered a failure was because it simply did not fit this epistemological model of purposive governance through control, leading, instead, to a rethinking of the fundamental premises of the interaction of man and nature.

The nuclear winter report was co-opted from a well-established East-West network of mathematical modelers of climate and ecology. The nuclear winter modelers, to be sure, supported the peace movement. However, their primary task was even more ambitious than paving the road to abolishing the nuclear arsenal.[129] Some Soviet nuclear winter scholars, like Moiseev, wanted to redefine the conceptual premises of the governance of human activities by embedding it in a new, systemic connection with the environment, something that would later be described by Crutzen as the Anthropocene. Furthermore, they sought to replace the notion of national governance with global governance, where the activities of governments would be strictly limited by the natural balances of the biosphere.

The nuclear winter project can be understood as an example of a disruptive science, an attempt to demonstrate loyalty to the government through voice rather than exit, to use Hirschman's terms.[130] The disruption was, however, carefully aligned with scientists' own professional interest of creating both the demand and infrastructure for the new, further scientific expertise. The disruptive effect of the nuclear winter report, to be sure, was not appreciated by all: there were opponents, such as Leon Gouré, a nuclear policy consultant, who in a series of reports to the US government dismissed both the significance of the nuclear winter study and downplayed its importance inside the Soviet Union. In retrospect, Gouré could well be described, following Oreskes and Conway, as a merchant of doubt, as it is difficult to believe that he could have missed the Soviet nuclear winter debate in the major popular and specialist press, like *Priroda* and *Voprosy filosofii*.[131]

While arms control scientists used the nuclear winter prognosis for advocating new defense policy moves, the Soviet modelers of nuclear winter used this prognosis to advocate the need for a substantially new type of governance: something that envisaged a fundamentally different government and society beyond communism, a society which was but an element in the complex system of biosphere. As a result, the old trope of Soviet modernity as a progress where the man conquers nature was redefined: mastery no longer meant conquering nature, but a conscious use of planetary resources in a way that ensured coevolution, using the techniques drawn from cybernetics and the systems approach at that. From this perspective, Soviet society was expected to adapt to the changing natural environment by creating new prohibitive rules to limit human activities, such as armament or development, driven by industrial growth.[132] The nuclear winter project, most importantly, had opened up the closed world: it is a case of how Cold War politics spilled into the politics of nature, and of how technoscientists forged their influence, industry, and power by constructing models of the future of the world and, eventually, creating premises for global change.

7

ACID RAIN
Scientific Expertise and Governance
across the Systemic Divide

In the 1960s Scandinavia and Finland found their fields, forests, and lakes invaded. The invaders were not tanks and soldiers, however, but pollutants. In 1967 Swedish scientist Svante Odén warned the governments of these countries that acid rain was a new problem that could do great damage to the natural environment.[1] Rain infused with sulfur was killing Swedish forests and fish, as pollutants from smokestacks in Poland mixed with pollutants brought by the winds from the Ruhr in Germany and from Britain. The division between the Eastern and Western blocs was literally blown away: a concept of "downwind states," the ones suffering from pollutants that were emitted in other states, began to circulate in scientific and policy circles.

Under pressure from Sweden, the OECD produced its first research report on acid rain in 1968. New terminology was invented to describe this phenomenon, such as "long-range transboundary air pollution." In the 1970s transboundary pollution was traced along the West-West axis; the scope was broadened in the early 1980s to include East-West pollution. Through acid rain the Eastern bloc and the Soviet Union became integrated in the common space of polluted Europe, a space no longer partitioned by national boundaries, but assembled through a grid of a specific number of square miles, from which environmental measurements were taken, consisting of air currents and precipitation. This unprecedented integration of Europe as a complex system in which the environment and industrial outputs interacted without regard for the East-West divide was made possible by a particular technique: computer-based modeling of regional acidification information and simulation, known as RAINS, which was developed at IIASA in 1984.

Why do some models turn out to be influential in policy making when others struggle to establish authority and provide a basis for consensus? Can the answer be found in the results of modeling, or, rather, in the socio-organizational process of modeling? The acid rain case shows that both are equally important. In chapter 5 I showed that the scientific development of global computer models was based to a large extent on lengthy periods of face-to-face communication among the modelers, thus forcing the Soviet government to open up to a sustained, if carefully monitored, cooperation with the West. Then, in chapter 6 I detailed the ways in which global computer modeling was used by different actors to promote disarmament and research into global environmental change, both in their own ways undermining the Cold War divide. In these cases the issues of scientific credibility, public acceptance, policy usefulness, and usability of the computer modeling-based results came to the fore. Scientific hypotheses and evidence were questioned by both peer scientists and the public, and the impact of these studies on the policy process was indirect and therefore difficult to establish. The resolutions, in turn, were not simple fixes, but complex arrangements of interlocking systems of material objects, practices, and institutions, thus inserting global modeling as an important practice in system-cybernetic governmentality. I suggest that the systems approach, instrumentalized by computer modeling, stabilized and facilitated the ongoing sociopolitical change in the organization of both transnational science and politics. This chapter develops this argument further by examining the development of the regional air pollution information and simulation model (RAINS), a project which has been retrospectively described as one of the highest achievements of IIASA, substantiating East-West collaboration beyond scientific diplomacy.

So far the history of RAINS has been explored by historians of environmental science, because this model was fundamental for the implementation of one of the oldest environmental conventions, the United Nations Economic Commission for Europe (UNECE) Geneva Convention on Transboundary Air Pollution. The convention was signed in 1979 and entered into force in Western Europe in 1983, although the Soviet Union had already ratified it back in 1980.

Historians exemplified the development of this convention to advance several different arguments about international cooperation during the Cold War. For instance, Robert Darst argues that the Soviet membership in the Convention on Transboundary Air Pollution revealed the manipulative and hypocritical character of Soviet foreign policy. According to Darst, the Soviets participated in international programs of environmental protection seeking to advance their foreign policy goals, leading to what he describes as a "greening of foreign policy." Because Soviet intentions were cynical—they did not seriously mean to engage in environmental protection, wrote Darst—their participation in international environmental programs did not result in what he called "transnational learning" and did not have any impact on local environmental policies inside the Soviet Union. In joining the convention, argued Darst, the Soviets merely "projected cooperativeness" and did not actually cooperate.[2]

Although Darst makes an important point that the Soviet interest in international cooperation in environmental sciences was reinforced by foreign policy goals, in my view he unfairly downplays the importance of this international cooperation for the internal development of Soviet environmental and policy sciences. Darst's argument also builds on a particular methodological bias, which focuses on a very particular end product (the convention) and disregards the process of its production. Similarly, few scholars have addressed the backstage side of the convention, in particular the complex work of the development of the RAINS model and gathering the required data. Indeed, Darst disregarded the role of IIASA, the RAINS model, and even more importantly, the role of Soviet actors representing lower levels of politics.

Unlike Darst, Stacy VanDeveer focuses on the modeling efforts themselves and argues that the outcomes of the convention extended beyond pollution control, because this convention established a new, regional notion of Europe.[3] In line with VanDeveer, I argue that the case of acid rain was not a mere card in the game of East-West foreign relations, but a part of the emerging new politics of nature, where the very meaning of what constitutes nature was a matter of political negotiation.[4] I suggest that the preparations for the convention should be examined as a significant case of forging and institutionalizing new networks, which not only provided an infrastructure to circulate soft power across the Iron Curtain, but also mobilized a new framework, which was empowered by the systems approach and which merged nature and political action. I argue, therefore, that Soviet involvement in the convention was not merely an expression of the "greening of foreign policy," but a symptom of internal changes in Soviet governance.

All of this makes for an important rationale to reassess the history of RAINS. In spite of the huge volume of specialized literature dedicated to this model, the production of RAINS in the 1980s remained little known outside STS scholarship and environmental history. Yet historical sociology of modern governance has much to benefit from incorporating cases from environmental governance in its mainstream narratives of governmental change. Indeed, Cold War history still has much to discover about the processes that cut across the political divides and shaped new networks, organizations, and practices, all of which contributed toward a peaceful ending of the Cold War. I suggest that the densifying transnational networks that evolved in multiple governmental niche areas provided a certain safety net for post-Soviet institutions. Thus for some of the transnationalized Soviet governmental and scientific elite the collapse of the Soviet Union did not mean looking into an abysmal future of postcommunism but, in contrast, the continuation of business as usual, in this particular case, fighting to secure viable global and regional futures. In this chapter, therefore, I introduce the case of RAINS as an example of rearranging the Cold War Europe, in which the systems approach equipped with computer modeling played a key role, detailing both the consequences and the limits of this process for the transformation of East and West.

Acid Rain

From the 1960s on, the acidification of rain increasingly became recognized as a problem. Pollutants emitted by factories, but also by cars, into the atmosphere were transported by air currents that did not observe national borders and fell on soil and water in countries from which they did not originate. Accordingly, a country that had few polluting industries could suffer from pollution more than a heavily industrialized country. Tall smokestacks resolved the issue of local pollution by injecting poisonous particles into higher layers of the atmosphere, but then those particles were carried by air currents to fall out elsewhere. Furthermore, certain ecological systems were more sensitive to pollution; for instance, conifers were particularly vulnerable to acid rain. Some countries thus appeared net exporters and others net importers of pollution. Nevertheless, according to Rolf Lidskog and Göran Sundqvist, the phenomenon of transboundary pollution was something that scientists only slowly woke up to. It was first posited as a hypothesis, the proof of which required the launching of large research programs.[5] Pollutants, however, do not carry passports, so that externally imposed pollution poses a difficult conceptual and political dilemma: polluters have to be identified and made to compensate for the damage inflicted on the environment in other countries. The first such disputes arose between Canada and the United States, and were soon followed by disputes in West European countries. Political smear campaigns intertwined with scientific debates.[6] In any case, the struggle over the scientific evidence could not mask the actual ongoing damage, caused by pollution, as roofs of houses were corroding in Dresden, Germany, and fish were dying in Canadian lakes.

The phenomenon of acid rain, in this way, emerged as a political hot potato, an issue that could not be dropped but which appeared impossible to solve. Wherever there was an international controversy emerging around an "objective" matter, there was an opportunity for IIASA. Invoking the ideas of Howard Raiffa, Buzz Holling wrote to the US Environmental Protection Agency saying that "when conflict or controversy loomed between two or more nations, they would turn to

IIASA to host a group who would attempt to clarify the technical and factual issues lying behind or triggering controversy."[7] The subsequent events unfolded with typical Cold War ambivalence: although the Soviets supported the idea that IIASA should get involved in modeling acid rain, particular strategies had to be developed to ensure a meaningful Soviet cooperation. Therefore I suggest that the process of developing the RAINS model was just as important as the end product, the model itself which provided international negotiators with the data on which to base their agreement.

In the beginning an alliance to tackle the problem of acid rain was forged between the Soviet Union and Scandinavia. Norwegian prime minister Gro Harlem Brundtland visited Moscow in early 1978. It was agreed that the Norwegians would convince the other Nordic countries about the need for an international agreement on acid rain, and, in turn, the Soviets would mobilize Eastern European governments around this cause. However, the proposal was attacked by the UK, France, and West Germany at the Economic Council of Europe in Geneva. Not only was the proposed agreement contested, but even the very problem of transboundary pollution was questioned. Nevertheless, the Cooperative Program for Monitoring and Evaluation of the Long-Range Transmission of Air Pollutants in Europe (currently known as EMEP) was launched in 1978. The following year, the results of a preliminary study indicated that pollutants could indeed be transferred over long distances and across national borders.

At this initial stage the argument of intertwining foreign policy and international cooperation in the area of environmental protection can explain Soviet involvement. The environment was an important area in which the Soviet government sought to exert its soft power by positioning itself as a globally progressive regime. In the early 1970s the Soviet Union strategically expanded international cooperation through programs for environmental protection, pursuing this direction especially intensely after the Helsinki agreement in 1975. For instance, in 1976 the Soviet government proposed a series of European meetings within the framework of the United Nations Economic Commission for Europe. But enthusiastic Soviet involvement in programs for international cooperation on environmental issues was often met with skepticism by Western governments, because it was regarded as a mere ideological gesturing.[8] It was thought that the Soviet government was attempting to shift the attention of the Western public away from the issue of Soviet violations of human rights by emphasizing their benevolent efforts in environmental protection.

Yet I suggest that the acid rain case was a hybrid project, able to serve simultaneously different agendas in politics and science; just like in the case of the establishment of the East-West institute, where a group of scientists harnessed a foreign policy initiative to advance their own goals. Indeed, acid rain was a perfect example of a universal problem mixed with a global problem, that is, the problem of acid rain was experienced in different countries, but this problem could not be solved from within national borders. The definition of the very problem of acid rain required a systems approach, showing how industrial pollution, the natural environment, and the economy interacted, which in turn required international cooperation to obtain the necessary data. First, mutual vulnerability had to be demonstrated in order to communicate the extent of damage and urgency of concerted governmental action. In the Soviet Union, following the Scandinavian example, the Institute of Applied Geophysics under the State Committee for Hydrometeorology and Control of Natural Environment (*Upravlenie* from 1974, *Committee* from 1978, henceforth Goskomgidromet) published a study showing that acid rain inflicted USD 150 million worth of damage on the European part of the Soviet Union each year.[9]

Once foreign policy goals and the need to advance environmental science were combined, the problem of acid rain was put on the agenda of the Economic Commission for Europe. The 1979 study, conducted under the auspices of the Cooperative Program for Monitoring and Evaluation of the Long-Range Transmission of Air Pollutants in Europe, demonstrated the transboundary flow of pollutants in a "blame matrix" that paved the way to a compromise and the convention.[10] The representatives of East and West achieved an important compromise, however, to put the policy agreement into action, concrete implementation protocols on pollution reduction had to be developed: it had to be decided just how much and at what rate the countries involved in pollution flows should modernize their polluting industries. The decision making required "hard facts," showing the actual level of pollution and the economic effect of abatement measures. It was at precisely this moment that IIASA became involved, as a neutral host for loosely coupled networks, knotted at numerous meetings in Laxenburg, dedicated to the mathematical modeling of both decision aid systems and environmental processes.

In this way, the same logic underpinned the projects to study acid rain and nuclear winter, where scientific experts helped to discover and articulate a new, significant problem and pushed for new governmental action at the same time pursuing their own scientific agenda. But the issue of acid rain was subject to no fewer and perhaps even more security constraints than the nuclear winter prognosis. It might strike the reader as something counterintuitive, but the Soviet scientists found cooperation with Western scientists in simulating the environmental effects of a nuclear war easier than working with them on the effects of acid rain in Europe. Acid rain, being a phenomenon of the present, was much more heavily politicized than a simulated nuclear disaster. Furthermore, the different degree of politicization depended on the different types of information used in the models. Whereas the nuclear winter project used internationally open data and drew on hypothetical scenarios of the course of events, the acid rain model could make sense only with actual data of emissions and damage. As it turned out, much of the environmental data in the Soviet Union was strictly classified, not only because the Soviet government wanted to conceal the extent of environmental damage from its own population, but also for military reasons.

To be sure, the atmosphere sciences were heavily militarized on both sides of the Iron Curtain, but especially so in the Soviet Union, where the key center for the data and infrastructure of meteorological forecasts was Goskomgidromet. Thus when in his study of East-West relations in the acid rain project Darst suggests that Goskomgidromet was a "lowly" meteorological bureau, he disregards the central role that this institution played in the Soviet industrial-military complex for atmosphere science.[11] For instance, the highly strategic status of Goskomgidromet is clearly revealed by the background of the chief Soviet representatives in negotiations on acid rain at the Economic Commission for Europe. The head of the Soviet participation was Iurii Izrael', the chairman of Goskomgidromet, who, just like his deputy Valentin Sokolovskii, was in his mid-fifties at the time of negotiations and claimed solid experience in both military research and high-level administration.[12] Born in Tashkent in 1930, Izrael' was raised in a highly educated family in Central Asia. His father, of Estonian origin, was a military doctor who moved from the army to academia; his Russian mother also had a doctoral degree in medicine and worked in the same department. Beginning in 1954 Izrael' worked on the atmospheric impact of nuclear explosions at Evgenii Fedorov's Institute of Geophysics at the Soviet Academy of Sciences. Retrospectively, Izrael' wrote with pride that he was the first civilian scientist to fly into a radioactive cloud following a test nuclear explosion in Semipalatinsk. Appointed as the head of Goskomgidromet, Izrael' was in charge of a gigantic system, consisting of thirty-four control centers, twenty-two research institutes, and thousands of observation stations and satellites, devised to monitor the environment of the Soviet Union. Although Izrael's expertise was predominantly in radioactivity, he authored a book on acid rain in 1983, thus signaling the importance of this issue and legitimizing research into it.[13] Izrael' was also in charge of the studies of global environmental change and served from 1975 to 1986 as a vice president of the World Meteorological Organization (WMO).[14]

The chief Soviet negotiator, Valentin Sokolovskii, was also brought up in a military family: his father was a marine artillery officer. Trained in hydroengineering and dispatched to Soviet Latvia in the 1950s and 1960s, Sokolovskii was in charge of the mass hydrological improvement program in the Baltic states, something that coincided with forced collectivization and was negatively received by local populations not only because smallholding farms were eliminated to make way for large-scale agriculture, but also because the measures increased water pollution. Ironically, since 1973 Sokolovskii had been in charge of environmental protection programs as a vice chairman of the GKNT, thus nominally holding the same status as Gvishiani. When Sokolovskii was appointed as a senior consultant on the environmental problems of the Soviet Union at the Economic Commission for Europe in 1977, he already had well-established links within the GKNT and environmental agencies, which overlapped with the research agenda pursued at IIASA. In 1979 Sokolovskii also became vice chairman of Goskomgidromet.[15]

In this way, Soviet participation in the international cooperation around acid rain was anchored in Gosgidromet and tightly linked to the military. The determination to control Soviet data was therefore not surprising, and it was expressed in the institutional setup: when in November 1979 the Convention on Long-Range Transboundary Air Pollution was signed by thirty-three countries in Geneva, it was also agreed to appoint two research centers to produce the required data, in Oslo and in Moscow.[16] Thus the Soviet Union committed to disclose some of the data on transboundary pollution, but also made sure that this would be done through a carefully monitored channel. In chapter 6 I mentioned Izrael's maneuvers between his commitment to state secrecy and public support of nuclear winter studies; this engagement indeed overlapped with the Geneva negotiations on policies to combat acid rain. In what follows, I detail how Soviet scientists were torn between the two imperatives: to disclose as few Soviet data as possible to West, but also to meaningfully contribute to the European convention on transboundary pollution. Here IIASA appeared as an important mediator, which helped to resolve these conflicting rationales through highly networked practices.

The Laboratory of Sensitive Facts

As I mentioned earlier, acid rain was a highly controversial issue: the origins, character, and the extent of the damage caused by acid rain were questioned. As a rule, skepticism was voiced by culprit countries. The question was how an agreement could be reached when the economic stakes were high and denial pervasive. This was a perfect opportunity for IIASA to use its neutral status in the service of international agreement; indeed, from as early as 1973 IIASA, according to Koopmans, positioned itself as "an objective commentator on controversial issues."[17]

Scientific objectivity, however, is not something that can be measured against a certain universal standard, but a particular condition, the character of which varies in relation to a particular problem and context: according to sociologists of science, all facts are artifacts, produced by particular scientific communities. Data, for instance, can be viewed as a hybrid object that can never be entirely detached from the infrastructure which was used to produce it and which might be necessary to verify it. The case of acid rain shows that factual information on a controversial subject tends to garner more influence when it is produced in an international institutional setting. But the international setting itself here should be approached as an infrastructure in its own right, which has been strategically assembled; this is precisely what was done at IIASA in relation to the European acid rain study. First, at IIASA the acid rain project was initially developed on the axis of West-West cooperation: the idea of modeling acid rain in Europe was first formulated in discussions among American and Canadian scientists in 1981, at a time when American and Canadian authorities were searching for independent reviewers of transboundary pollution.[18] However, following the Lidingö conference on acidification of the environment, Sweden, and a joint workshop on air pollution arranged by IIASA and World Meteorological Organization, in 1982 IIASA decided to launch a three-year project to study acidification in Europe.[19] At the initial stage, connections with the Nordic countries were forged, as in June 1983, Sweden, Norway, and Finland proposed a schedule to cut emissions by 30 percent by 1990.[20] Eliodoro Runca, an Italian scientist who came to IIASA from the IBM Scientific Center in Venice in 1980, initiated contact with Swedish scientist Uno Svedin, who made sure that IIASA was granted observer's status at Lidingö.[21] Following this, Runca launched discussions with the Economic Commission for Europe and initiated contacts with regulatory and scientific organizations in East European countries, and with the signatories of the convention,[22] including the Central Electricity Generating Board of the United Kingdom and the National Swedish Environmental Protection Board.[23] The US Environmental Protection Agency reported that the East Europeans committed to supply the necessary data and to participate in the project.[24]

Before we proceed, a few words on the United Nations Economic Commission for Europe (ECE) are necessary. Based in Geneva, the ECE was a prominent platform where a new postwar Europe was being constructed as a specific area, brought into being through econometric statistics. To be sure, this version of an economic Europe was clearly marked by the East-West divide, yet it also transcended this divide, because it defined Europe from a global perspective as one of the world's economic regions. As a key meeting place for Soviet, East European, and West European econometricians and policy makers, the ECE was appointed to deal with the problem of acidification under the 1979 Geneva Convention on Transboundary Pollution. The loop was closed in a way that reflected the link that was first explicated in *The Limits to Growth*, that economic growth caused pollution, the solution of which had a financial cost and economic consequences.

As the issue of acid rain was highly politicized around the question, which countries should brace for additional investment to abate the pollution of other countries and to what extent, a premium was put on informal ways of preparing the basis for the international cooperation. In February 1983, IIASA's director Holling sent a very cautious letter to Gvishiani seeking official approval, writing that Runca had assembled a "very carefully developed network of scientists," in this way "quietly and effectively" opening up the possibility of IIASA becoming "a center of synthesis" of existing research on acid rain.[25] The November 1983 meeting at IIASA gathered representatives from meteorological centers in East Europe as well as Scandinavia; the next year, in 1984, the Polish Institute for Meteorology and Water Management and the East German Institute of Cybernetics and Information joined the acid rain project at IIASA. Furthermore, as at that time IIASA was in a precarious financial situation, first because of the withdrawn US NAS membership and then diminished funding, efforts were taken to secure external funding from additional national sources; thus some money came from the Finnish Ministry of the Environment.[26]

It was also at this early stage that the conceptual architecture of the model was developed. The first proposal for the research program emphasized that the computer-based model of transboundary pollution should account for "institutional differences between East and West," although such differences were not specified in this document.[27] Because it specialized in econometric modeling, the Economic Commission for Europe proposed that IIASA should develop a cost-benefit model of abatement policies.[28] Economic cost-benefit modeling was preferred by the US and UK negotiators, who were also quite negative about the possibility that the modelers themselves might offer different policy strategies.[29] The role of scientists, thus, was envisioned as merely auxiliary, a technical role in calculating cost-benefit; scientists were not expected to actively contribute to the development of solutions. However, the appropriateness of a cost-benefit model was questioned by both East and West scientists. I discuss this in greater detail later; here I would only like to note that the idea of a cost-benefit model encountered obstacles of both an ideological and a pragmatic character. Thus the Soviets were not keen on cost-benefit analyses; furthermore, due to the radically decreased budget (as related in chapter 4, this was the period when the US government withdrew its financial support for IIASA), the IIASA team could not afford an economic research assistant.[30] Only in 1985 was a cost-benefit analysis with RAINS included in IIASA's plan.[31]

RAINS consisted of three blocs: pollution generation, atmospheric processes, and environmental impact, with further submodels to investigate emissions, long-range transport, and acidification.[32] The emissions of sulfur were calculated for twenty-seven European countries on the basis of their individual energy pathways, with a time horizon from 1960 to 2030. The model was interactive: a policy maker could select a particular national pathway of energy use, a strategy of pollution control, and environmental impact indicators. On the basis of this information, the computer model simulated the interaction of these three systems, enabling the user to examine the consequences of different alternatives to control acidification.

While the architecture of the model was a subject of scientific debate, access to the data was a subject of intense political lobbying, entailing the leveraging of not only personal contacts, but also the evolving technical and institutional infrastructure of environmental monitoring. As mentioned earlier, the data on transboundary pollution was gathered and processed by the two meteorological centers, one in Oslo and one in Moscow, and IIASA cautiously emphasized that its goal was not to compete with these centers by gathering alternative data, but rather to use these existing data to conduct a systems analysis of transboundary pollution.[33] The model was presented as an instrument enabling the organization of various kinds of information—on energy use, on the atmospheric transport of pollutants, and on the impact of pollution on terrestrial and aquatic ecosystems. In contrast to the computer simulation of the environmental effects of a nuclear war, the goal of RAINS was not a heuristic one; that is, RAINS did not seek to advance scientific knowledge. Instead, the goal of RAINS was pragmatic, to "reconcile existing results" so that they could cast light on problems residing on the borderlines of established disciplinary fields. Typically of computer models of complex, interacting systems, measures were taken to ensure that the model produced plausible results for the future. The choice of time frame was influenced by several constraints, such as the available data, which allowed simulating conditions thirty years ago, and the life cycle of the energy infrastructure, such as power plants and heating systems, which required projecting fifty years into the future. The scientists also chose to model over the long term, because only in this way could they reveal the cumulative effects of acidification, which were not as evident in the short term. Furthermore, IIASA's scientists intended to focus on assessing the probability of different impacts of both acidification and abatement policies on the environment and economy and, in this way, to critically evaluate the existing data.[34] On the basis of this latter aspect, I argue that the RAINS model was equally important as a process and as a final result.

There were some interesting parallels and differences between the projects on acid rain and on nuclear winter, and not only because the study of nuclear winter also showed that acid rains would shower the Earth, damaging conifer forests, after the nuclear blasts. While Soviet atmosphere scientists were bracing themselves for the study of nuclear winter in Moscow, IIASA formally launched the acid rain project, in March, 1983. In both cases the concern with the environment and the future of the populations of Europe and the world was intertwined with institutional interests. Having lost funding from the US National Science Foundation, IIASA badly needed an injection of both symbolic and financial capital to ensure its survival in the future. For instance, Holling expressed a hope that a model of acid rain would help to "enhance the Institute's credibility and visibility."[35] IIASA's burning concern was to prove its relevance to the governments of its member countries. Whereas nuclear winter scientists focused on generating new, hypothetical data about the postnuclear environment and did not pay much attention to the actual usefulness of their model for assisting concrete policy decisions (beyond the impact on public opinion), the initiators of RAINS intentionally and carefully focused on finding a way to prove their model useful for their clients, the national governments. In short, nuclear winter simulation was problem-generating, while simulations of the transboundary acid rain emissions were solution-generating. These different goals shaped governments' trust in the models. The simulation of nuclear winter threatened the status quo by overthrowing the authority of the nuclear "experts," revealing an extreme, long-term uncertainty and establishing the relevance of environmental sciences to nuclear defense strategy. In contrast, the modelers of RAINS were cautious about framing their expertise as mere technical support. In so doing, they strategically relied on the earlier experience, such as the MIT model of seabed mining and tread carefully in the political milieu by adjusting their terminology and claims. For example, the acid rain model was described as "a useful scientific tool" for policy makers, explicating that the authors of the model refrained from taking over the decision making role by offering recommendations.[36] The scientists also assured that they did not intend to propose any particular measures that could possibly compromise the existing policies of individual nations. This intention was communicated to the heads of partner organizations in Poland, Hungary, the Soviet Union, and the United States.

The computer-based model of acid rain was not just a software program. It was a social network bridging scientific and policy-making environments. Having clearly articulated their political stance and distanced themselves from any pretense to a decision-making role, IIASA's team embarked on forging a support network for the model. Given that by 1983 IIASA already had a decade of experience in policy sciences research from both the quantitative and qualitative perspectives, it is not surprising that the environmental modelers were keenly aware of what it takes to make an influential model. Knowing full well that an influential instrument could not be developed solely in isolation inside a laboratory, the modelers cast their nets wide, seeking to enroll supporters from both scientific and extra-scientific fields. The necessary supporters were identified, including influential and distinguished scientists and governmental authorities, and a network was "painstakingly built" by Runca.[37] IIASA provided institutional support and resources for scientists to spread the word about the model face-to-face.

In the spring of 1983 Runca traveled to Moscow, Helsinki, Stockholm, Oslo, Amsterdam, and Frankfurt to brief his colleagues about the idea of a computer-based model of acid rain to governmental authorities. During this trip it was agreed that the participating countries would officially request the Economic Commission for Europe to collaborate with IIASA.[38] Importantly, the executive secretary of this commission, a Finnish-Swede by the name of Klaus Sahlgren, was personally impressed with the idea of modeling transboundary pollution with a computer. The path was successfully broken through this stage of institutional overtures: at the convention meeting in June 1983 several national representatives placed the planned IIASA study on the agenda for negotiations.[39] In September 1983 the Economic Commission for Europe officially confirmed its support for the development of a model of acid rain at IIASA.[40] When Leen Hordijk, the Dutch scientist with whom the RAINS model would become associated in the future, arrived at IIASA, the main components for the acid rain project were already in place. However, it was thanks to the scientific and organizational skills of this Dutch scientist that IIASA would be propelled into the highest levels of East-West cooperation.

A small country whose infrastructure was designed in response to a constant struggle with the ever-encroaching Atlantic, and which had been boasting a great pedigree of systems thinking, dating back to Spinoza's philosophy in the seventeenth century, in the second half of the twentieth century the Netherlands emerged at the forefront of nationwide computer-assisted planning. Long-range planning grew from the postwar spillover of military to civil research in the United States and, as Jenny Andersson notes, long-range governmental programs were transformed into the long term.[41] The Dutch concern with long-range and long-term planning was best expressed in the work of Jan Tinbergen, but interest in the social and economic consequences of technoscientific innovations was also exemplified by the activities of Gerhart Rathenau, the chair of the first public commission on technology assessment of the effects of computerization, in 1978. The Dutch context was not, to be sure, the sole determinant of the future success of the RAINS model, but it is quite important, because it provided a key resource from which scientific expertise in economic and environmental planning could be drawn, as well as the networking skills necessary to mediate between scientific research and governmental policy. Operating on the principle of a balance among the nations represented through the national member organizations, IIASA's council noted that Dutch scientists were underrepresented as project leaders (the Netherlands joined IIASA in 1977), and the secretary of the Dutch member organization, the Dutch Research Council, Eric Ferguson, disseminated a call for candidacies in planning sciences, which would eventually reach Leen Hordijk.

Initially trained in econometrics, Leen Hordijk went on to study environmental economics, and hence became familiar with chemistry and biology. He did not become a specialist in either of these two fields, but learned enough to be able to understand and communicate with chemists and biologists, something that would prove vital in his later career. Hordijk received his first hands-on experience working at the Economic Bureau in Hague, where he examined the environmental consequences of economic development. It was then that, on behalf of the Dutch secretary for IIASA, Eric Ferguson, the economist Peter Nijkamp approached Hordijk, asking whether he might be interested in the opportunity to direct a project on economic planning at IIASA. Hordijk already knew about the institute, because he had visited IIASA for a conference; thus he visited Laxenburg for the second time in 1983 to discuss possible cooperation. However, this engineered meeting did not work: Hordijk realized that he was not interested in the agenda of the economic program, chaired by a Russian scientist, whose approach he found coming "from a different planet." But as a matter of luck, Hordijk was approached by several young scientists, including Joseph Alcamo, who would later become the chief scientist at the United Nations Environment Program. The young IIASA researchers proposed that Hordijk join them in developing an environmental model of acid rain in Europe. Hordijk immediately saw an opportunity to extend the work he was doing in the Netherlands to a larger scale and, consequently, asked IIASA's director if he could collaborate instead on the acid rain project, in whatever role possible. This proposal was accepted and in summer 1983 Hordijk received an offer to join the IIASA as a research scholar, to arrive in Laxenburg to replace Eliodoro Runca in early 1984.[42]

At IIASA Hordijk found himself the leader of a truly international team, made up of scholars from Finland (Pekka Kauppi and others), the United States (Joseph Alcamo), Austria (Maximilian Posch) and Poland (Jerzy Bartnicki).[43] Before his departure, Hordijk got in touch with the Dutch Ministry of Environment requesting a contact who could help him learn more about the problem of acid rain. Hordijk was given a stack of mathematical papers, mathematics being an interdisciplinary language that he could understand, on air quality concentration. Equipped with these materials, Hordijk moved his family to Austria.[44] The IIASA group already had an operational model of European Air Quality, developed in Oslo, Norway. Hordijk's task was to link the atmosphere bloc with other blocs, such as forest and water. According to the initial plan, Hordijk was expected to stay for two years, but his stay was extended to four years before he returned to the Netherlands to become a professor in systems analysis at Wageningen University. In 2002 Hordijk would return to IIASA, now as the director of the institute.

Activating the Coproducers of Knowledge

At the early stage of negotiations on the convention, it was made clear that the model of acid rain was expected to serve as a "neutral" platform for East-West cooperation.[45] However, in this case the meaning of neutrality had nothing to do with laboratory-like isolation, where presumably neutral experts established reliable data, and everything to do with active management of the participating countries. Neutrality, therefore, emerged as an effect of active intervention. The archival documents show that, although IIASA was regarded as an established and, because of its orientation to quantitative methods, a neutral platform for East-West cooperation, partner organizations did not automatically enroll in the acid rain project. Instead, partners had to be actively co-opted through labor-intensive and sometimes, as Runca confessed, painstaking efforts. Like Runca, Hordijk was acutely aware that in order to make the model trustworthy and usable, vast networks had to be forged, including both scientists and high-level policy makers. Indeed, Hordijk meticulously documented his networking efforts through the reports. For instance, at the Munich multilateral conference on the environment, attended by the representatives of thirty-one countries and eighteen ministers, outside of the main program Hordijk briefed the delegates from ECE, UNEP, the UK, the Soviet Union, Sweden, Portugal, Norway, the Netherlands, West Germany, East Germany, Finland, Denmark, Czechoslovakia, Austria, and Canada about the progress of his project, and in all these cases received agreement to support the acid rain modeling at IIASA.[46] In Paris, Hordijk briefed another twenty-eight policy makers and consultants from the OECD Group of Experts on the Environment.[47] Likewise, Hordijk spread the word at the meeting of the Executive Council Panel of Experts in Environmental Pollution of the World Meteorology Organization in Garmisch-Partenkirchen in 1984.[48] Contacts were also pursued with the Dutch headquarters of Shell in a quest for additional funding, and the representatives of Shell came to IIASA to meet the acid rain group, subsequently contributing a small grant to the project.[49] Links were extended across the Atlantic: James Fay of the MIT Energy Laboratory got in touch about possible cooperation.[50]

The Cold War context imposed certain limitations on the selection of relevant partners. For instance, beginning in 1969 environmental issues were studied at the NATO Committee on the Challenges of Modern Society, an institution which was deemed relevant to the acid rain project, but IIASA could not even consider getting involved with any NATO agency.[51] There was an attempt to involve other American collaborators through the US National Acid Precipitation Program, but it was stressed that the model was a European one and therefore Hordijk's networking efforts targeted European meetings.[52] Then, not only international, but also national organizations had to be convinced to participate: over 1983 and 1984 intense correspondence was conducted with the institutes in Poland, East Germany, and the Technical University in Prague. At the Munich meeting in June 1984 the Soviets officially announced their support for the negotiations, and a year later, in July 1985, a protocol on the reduction of sulfur emissions was signed by nineteen states, including the Soviet Union.[53]

Given the financially precarious position of IIASA in the early 1980s, the acid rain project was an astonishing success: the model was developed rather quickly, it was used by high-level policy makers, and it achieved its purpose in just a couple years. It can be argued that this success was the combined result of evident, ongoing environmental damage and the presence of highly motivated individuals, keen to mediate across the East-West divide. For instance, at the Economic Commission for Europe the acid rain group initiated contact with a Swedish civil servant, Johan von Luttemberg, who was extremely helpful in arranging first the presentation of their work and then their participation in negotiations. But this was also the case of a joint transnational scientific effort. Just like with the nuclear winter project, the RAINS model was a result of bricolage rather than creation *ex nihilo*. IIASA's scientists linked a Norwegian atmosphere model of long-range transboundary pollution (known as EMEP), which was developed by the Norwegian modeler Anton Eliassen, with an environmental damage model, adding to it the calculations of abatement procedures.[54] Polish and Dutch scientists collaborated with Eliassen to develop the atmosphere bloc. The contribution of the Finnish scientists was to model pH levels in soil and surface water.

The acid rain model also assumed a public life. The first presentation of the model to the Executive Body of the Economic Commission for Europe Convention was scheduled for the September meeting in 1984.[55] On behalf of the commission, executive secretary Klaus Sahlgren invited Hordijk to present the acid rain model for thirty minutes outside the formal meeting.[56] The model was presented during a lunch break in the negotiations session at the commission on September 26. About twenty-five policy makers attended, a much smaller number than expected, thought to be a consequence of the overlap with other meetings. Coincidentally, a similar study from the UK was presented and the two groups decided to collaborate in the future.[57] From then on the IIASA group became involved in one sublayer of the negotiations, the task force for economic analysis.

According to Hordijk, an important factor in the development of the model was that the chief Soviet, Canadian, and Dutch negotiators quickly became convinced that the model was the only way to reach any agreement. Several representatives at the commission argued that IIASA's team of scientists should not be involved in the negotiations, because IIASA did not have a formal relationship with the UN. However, due to the effort of Russian negotiators, who were first skeptical and then positive, the modelers got the go-ahead. Given that the Russian negotiators were Valentin Sokolovskii and Izrael's deputy chairman of Gidromet, their support was not surprising at all: Izrael' was directly involved in the promotion of the US-Soviet study of the environmental effects of nuclear war, which I detailed in chapter 6. Hordijk also recalled that Sokolovskii and Izrael' pushed the Canadians, and Hordijk himself was personally acquainted with the chief negotiators on behalf of the Netherlands.[58]

In this way, through intense personal efforts and thanks to lucky coincidences, a window for IIASA's modelers was opened into the heart of the policy making world. Beginning in September 1984 the RAINS team would travel to Geneva regularly for a year and a half. It is important to note that even with this approval granted, the relevance of scientists to these high-level negotiations was not self-evident to many negotiators. During their first visit the scientists were still considered a disturbance and kept at a (physical) distance, in an adjacent lounge, because the Economic Commission for Europe was convinced that members of an organization without affiliation with the UN could not be granted access to the hall where negotiations took place. This guarded behavior continued for several months. IIASA's team reacted to this by resorting to their social and technical skills to make their study visible. For instance, whenever possible, the research done at IIASA was presented via remote computer links, such as Datex-P, to high government officials in Amsterdam in February 1985.[59] In doing this, scientists tapped in the symbolic power of a new technology, such as data links, in order to make their case heard at the high policy level. It appears that the use of new technology adds additional legitimacy to new data, just as in the case of nuclear winter study.

But even more important is the point that those principles of the model of acid rain, which made it successful as a tool for an international policy agreement, strongly contradicted the notion of opaque, technocratic decision making empowered by scientific expertise. Governance by scientific experts has been criticized as a complex and arcane activity, shaped by informal customs known only by few and taking place behind tightly shut doors. Although the RAINS model was produced and circulated among scientific and policy elite groups, there were also important moments that revealed the logic of openness and inclusivity. For instance, the description of the acid rain model stated that it had to be "co-designed by analysts and potential users" and "as simple as possible." Occam's principle was at work: the modelers emphasized that more complexity would be introduced only if "necessary and only in conjunction with potential model users."[60] The model also allowed for flexibility, because it was, in fact, an open system of models that could be expanded by adding additional blocs if needed. Furthermore, the principle of openness to external scrutiny was paramount: the modelers wished that RAINS would break away from the image of electronic oracles.[61] The official description stated that the model was intended to "explicitly reflect uncertainty."[62] It was anticipated that the model would be subject to "very close external scrutiny," and therefore the model's uncertainty was evaluated and communicated to the scientific community: the technical specification of the model was available for free to anyone wishing to inspect it.[63] The group organized workshops in which the model was examined by scientists hailing from different disciplines, such as soil science, meteorology, energy, and ecology, but also policy makers from the Economic Commission for Europe and the United States.[64] Also, the creators of the acid rain model were alert to the risk that the claims of their model could be mistaken for reality and therefore dismissed as such. Preventive measures were taken to counteract such criticism: the acid rain model was therefore described as "a decision support system" and "a model for organizing information."

Scientific credibility was to be reinforced by political credibility. Here the institutional context in which the model was produced was of crucial significance. According to Hordijk, as IIASA enjoyed the special status of being a transnational organization it was relatively immune to knee-jerk accusations of national bias that pervaded the ongoing negotiations around acid rain: Nordic countries identified the UK, the Eastern European bloc, and the Soviet Union as culprit polluters, the sources of acid rain that fell on Scandinavia and Finland. But some British scientists dismissed the data, denying that the damage was caused by acid rain or that the UK had anything to do with it. National studies were accused of being biased, their results questioned. Furthermore, scholars "trembled at the simplifications" that they had to make in order to communicate their results to the media.[65] The biochemical processes of the acidification of forests, soil, and water were complex, varied, and sometimes insufficiently understood.

However, there was an acute feeling that action had to be taken sooner rather than later. This sense of urgency was also shared by national negotiators, who needed some kind of mutually acceptable data set in order to reach an international agreement. The RAINS model responded to this need, first and foremost by providing negotiators with a system that showed, visually, the interrelating causes and effects. The maps and graphs, nicknamed "the Alps of Europe," as they showed the curves peaking and dropping down sharply, illustrated different scenarios of actions from which a policy maker could chose an energy pathway for a country. In response, the model calculated the sulfur emissions and the resulting environmental impact over the whole European area, including the Soviet Union, for a fifty-year horizon.[66] The policy makers, wrote IIASA scientists, could see how a problem "evolves and can be corrected with time."[67] Visualized in, as one scholar put it, "maps over time," the problem was assembled as an amenable process, which required action and intervention.[68]

Nevertheless, it was easier to ensure openness to external scientific scrutiny than to arrange access to the data without which the model made no sense. Here accessing the Soviet data on pollution was a particularly difficult problem, which was further exacerbated by the methodological requirements of the modelers. In order to establish the precise areas of origins and fallout of pollutants, the model required data taken from a grid of many square kilometers, covering all of Western Europe, Eastern Europe, and the European part of the Soviet Union. At that time the data for Europe were aggregated for 150/150-km grid cells (at the moment of writing in 2015 they are 50/50 km in size). This seemingly harmless requirement immediately clashed with Cold War secrecy. According to Sokolovskii, the Soviet government refused to reveal such data of localized pollution, because this could indirectly reveal the location of heavy industry factories, which constituted strategic objects in the case of military conflict. For this reason, only the data on total national emissions were initially submitted to the commission's atmosphere transport model, although it was also agreed that the Soviets would supply some data on the fluxes that crossed the western borders of the Soviet Union.[69] Further data were pooled from the databases of the WMO, the UNEP, and the ECE Collaborative Program on the Monitoring and Evaluation of the Long-Range Transmission of Air Pollutants in Europe.[70]

Here I would like to add that, while the environment was deemed to be apolitical and therefore a suitable area for East-West cooperation, some environmental data were subject to tight security. Such was, for instance, the case for tree pulp samples, which were used for dendrochronological studies of climate change. Different chemical processes left marks on a tree's rings and in this way a tree constituted a document, a record of the changes in the immediate environment, be it the fluctuation in CO_2 or radioactive emissions. Yet, because such samples were collected from a rather small, four-by-four kilometer grid in the European part of the Soviet Union, an actual sample would enable a dendrochronologist to detect the location of, for example, nuclear missile silos.[71] Nature, in this way, appeared to have a potential to tell stories about military defense systems and industrial accidents, something which was never explicitly acknowledged in the discussions on East-West data sharing, but rather ran in between the lines, being a source of continuous delays and evasive answers.

How did IIASA scientists deal with the Soviets, the "masters of openness without disclosure?"[72] This difficulty was anticipated, and collaboration with East European scientists was not self-evident from the beginning of the acid rain project: the early research plans did not place a strong emphasis on the Eastern European contribution.[73] Originally oriented toward the Canada-US axis, then Europe-Scandinavia, the project came to include the Eastern Bloc only at a later stage. Polish scientists were brought in first, because they cooperated in conducting an uncertainty study of the model. East Germany and Czechoslovakia also cooperated. Part of the Soviet participation in the acid rain project, as in the case of nuclear winter study, was organized within the framework of the UNESCO program on the sustainable development of the biosphere. Although Soviet representatives at the Economic Commission for Europe were instrumental in getting the acid rain model on the agenda, the development of actual contacts with the Soviet institutes was not straightforward.[74] Predictably, VNIISI was listed as a collaborating institute, but it was through Izrael' that IIASA sought official permission to contact Soviet atmosphere scientists. There were hardly any horizontal relations involved at this point. At a meeting in Warsaw, for instance, members of the acid rain project met a scholar from the EMEP Meteorological Synthesizing Center-East of the Institute of Applied Geophysics in Moscow (this Center-East was a counterpart of the Center-West in Oslo). Then the director of IIASA, Thomas Lee, approached Izrael' with a request to cooperate by providing the data produced at the Center-East for further use in the RAINS model.[75] This chain of command is telling: whereas Hordijk always directly corresponded with Western scientists, UNECE, and other international organizations, he needed support from his superiors in order to achieve cooperation with the Soviets.

Furthermore, from the Soviet point of view the project on acid rain was a small piece in a larger puzzle, which probably partially explains the rather lenient and inflexible approach to data supply, as such requests may have fallen through the cracks. Soviet participation in IIASA's acid rain project was pursued within a wider framework of the program on sustainable development of the biosphere, which involved quite a few prominent names. In the mid-1980s there were several high-profile meetings bringing together the world's leading environmental scientists in Soviet Russia. Thus the August 27–31, 1984 meeting brought together Izrael', Viktor Kovda, Anatolii Dorodnitsyn, Georgii Zavarzin, and Dmitrii Zviagintsev, as well as Thomas Schelling, Thomas Malone, oceanologist McElroy, mathematician Jeremy Ravetz, Paul Crutzen, and Harvey Brooks, the chair of the US committee for IIASA.[76] Another meeting in Suzdal, March 11–15, 1985, included Izrael', Thomas Lee, Ted Munn, Hordijk, Buzz Holling, McElroy, and Crutzen; Bert Bolin and Martin Holdgate were also invited. The Soviet side was represented by Izrael' and Gvishiani and other scientists, who included such prominent climatologists as Mikhail Budyko, Iu. Aniukhin, and the microbiologist Zavarzin.[77] Although Nikita Moiseev and Kovda were mentioned in earlier correspondence, they were absent from the final list.[78]

I invoke these meetings as examples of the Soviet will to cooperate, which turned out to be constrained by unknown factors, possibly by faulty administration. According to the archival documents at IIASA, the organization of these meetings resembled a roller coaster. The Soviets, it seemed, were slow with absolutely everything: issuing visas for participants, making their own participant list known, and preparing the final program. Throughout the turbulent period, IIASA's leaders were anxious to avoid any further blots on the reputation of the institute. For instance, William Clark stated this in a confidential letter to Kaftanov, saying that there was a risk that the Soviet Union would fail to ensure the participation of senior scientists and hence even further compromise IIASA's reputation. He also firmly insisted that Soviet scientists supply their papers beforehand, even if they were only available in Russian, making it clear that the stage of science diplomacy was over, and that the substance of East-West cooperation must prevail over the form.[79]

Here, as in any cases where official organizing ran into difficulties, informal routes were taken to compensate for the slow and unpredictable machinery of Soviet bureaucracy. Indeed, informality played an important role throughout the entire process of creating and inserting RAINS into the policy process. For instance, that the RAINS model was first demonstrated outside formal sessions was an asset and not an obstacle, because contrasting and critical views were almost never exchanged in the formal sessions. But there was also a straightforward, centuries-old function of informality as an ice-breaker. The Soviet negotiators were cautious about providing data, but lavished vodka and caviar on the Westerners. Such was the case, for instance, at the Munich meeting in 1986, where after a four-and-a half-hour dinner, Izrael' invited then-EPA administrator William Ruckelshaus, together with two aides, to his suite at the Four Seasons Hotel to discuss bilateral programs. The party included Izrael' himself, Sokolovskii, and I. Kazakov. Reportedly, it was during this long and well-lubricated-with-vodka meeting that Ruckelshaus and Izrael' agreed to personally manage the planned agreement.[80]

Informal ways were also used to get the internal mechanism of the model, not only the external social and institutional machine, running. The acid rain project constructed its own database, which brought together previously scattered data, and that in turn posed the question of whether the data could be trusted. The data pertained to both energy structures in the countries involved and emissions of pollutants, as well as the costs of reducing the emissions. The data sets did not always correspond: for instance, the size of the industry and the supplied data on pollution might not appear to match. To deal with such cases, the following practice was adopted: once the modelers suspected that the data had been tweaked, they made hypothetical calculations of what more probable data could be. Then they confronted the national officials with their alternative data. This was the case of Poland, for example, but also Italy and Romania. While this method of data correction was obviously a sensitive issue, and probably a time-consuming one, scholars benefited enormously from being based at IIASA, because they did not have to travel far to get to Warsaw from Vienna; it was also easier to locate the right contacts through IIASA's networks. I was told that these investigations usually revealed not so much falsification as methodological flaws, although my interlocutor told me that in some cases the modelers felt that it was a question of good manners not to dig too deeply if the methods had been tweaked to obtain smaller emission numbers.[81]

Another difficult issue that emerged concerned the question of whether RAINS was to be primarily a geophysical or an economic model. Hordijk personally was extremely cautious about the use of cost-benefit analysis in policy making, and, indeed, he removed this cost-benefit bloc at a later stage, because he saw that policy makers had a propensity to extract a single number from a range of uncertainty. In Hordijk's view, this habit of using discrete numbers rather than ranges threatened to undermine the scientific credibility of the model. For different reasons, the Soviets were also against cost-benefit analysis, because, as Atsushi Ishii noted, the cost-benefit analysis was based on market economy principles, thus disagreeing with the fundamental ideological principles of Soviet political economy.[82] Also, as explicated by Anthony Patt, cost-benefit analysis presupposed aggregated preferences of a given population despite the values differences across the political spectrum. Different national cultures, for instance, may place a different value on nature, or inhabitants of one remote region might not agree to pay for cleaning lakes in another remote region. In all, it was thought that this kind of analysis could not enable international comparisons of utility between capitalist and communist regimes.

Later in the 1980s a new concept of "critical loads" was forged by Swedish scientists. Applied only to geophysical systems, "critical loads" constructed nations as nonpolitical geophysical systems. The limits of changing these systems were determined by natural scientists, and the measures taken to limit the impact of industries on them could be agreed upon by policy makers, thus effectively eliminating the problem of public choice. As a result, RAINS allowed the costs associated with abatement policies to be identified, but this was not a full-fledged cost-benefit analysis.[83]

The case of the acid rain model supports the argument made by Marie-Laure Djelic that in order to succeed transnationally, experts need to be well anchored in and reinforced by their national organizations.[84] The nuclear winter scientists largely disregarded the importance of the embedding their project in their respective national bureaucracies, engaging instead in a horizontal, transnational cooperation. This was both an asset and an obstacle: in consequence, although the nuclear winter study produced spectacular results, it had limited direct usability in policy making. In comparison to Lynn Eden's study of the organization of the US research into postnuclear fire damage, the nuclear winter scientists had much more room for experimentation, because, unlike fire research scientists, they were not entrenched in a well-institutionalized organization, such as the US Department of Defense.[85] But the nuclear winter scientists faced a different problem: being organized in horizontal networks of research teams, they had but limited possibility to translate their expertise into organizational routines. Here the position of acid rain modelers was somewhere in between: they were organized in a network, but they were also hosted by a well-established organization, IIASA. Furthermore, the acid rain model was carefully grafted onto the agenda of top national authorities in charge of international negotiations. Positioned as a neutral tool rather than a set of results and recommendations, the acid rain model could perform and be used in actual decision making. In 1985 in Helsinki, sixteen countries signed a protocol to reduce SO2 emissions, which was followed with the 1988 Sofia protocol on nitrogen emissions.

The acid rain modeling exercise also had a conserving effect that reaffirmed the existing power structure: attached to the top decision makers, the modelers did not engage with the civil society activists altogether. Scientific authority and credibility was at stake. Who produced the model mattered as much as the modeling results and, as the nuclear winter study revealed, scientists preferred to carefully manage the involvement of activists, because activists tended to prefer more radical versions of forecasts. And yet the RAINS model was also subversive because, strictly speaking, it was not merely a tool in the hands of policy makers. The modeling effort was a performative process in that it facilitated the establishment of new East-West networks and helped move the data across borders. Some efforts spilled over from the acid rain model to further East-West collaborations; such was the case of Jerzy Bartnicki of the Institute for Meteorology and Water Management in Poland and Joop den Tonkelaar of the Royal Netherlands Meteorological Institute.[86] As in the case of the nuclear winter project, cooperation around the issue of acid rain added to the change in Soviet thinking: that environmental security entered the ranks of highly prioritized issues, being listed alongside national defense in the Soviet was a result not only of a series of environmental disasters, but also an outcome of transnational East-West cooperation.[87] The case of acid rain thus becoming another component in the system-cybernetic governmentality, which, through a series of studies, posited that the biosphere set limits to the Soviet government.

Epilogue
THE AVANT-GARDE OF SYSTEM-CYBERNETIC GOVERNMENTALITY

This book has outlined the transnational career of systems analysis as a science of governance as it was coproduced by liberal democratic and authoritarian regimes. Developed by East and West scientists, the systems approach evolved from military operations research (OR) into a set of governmental techniques and was used across different sectors, in particular for global governance concerned with the issues of energy, population, and the environment. Easy to understand even for nonspecialists, systems analysis rendered disparate practices meaningful, offering a framework for the understanding and control of a complex and fast-changing world. As such, I argue, systems analysis formed a vitally important resource for the emergence of global governance, where Cold War tension appeared to be an opportunity and not an obstacle. Cold War confrontation led the US and Soviet governments to look for apolitical channels of communication, and, as a result, some areas of technoscience were deemed suitable to be used as a tool for East-West diplomacy. Influential communities of OR scholars used the diplomatic momentum to position the emergent field of systems analysis as a priority area, thus gaining resources for the intellectual advancement and institutionalization of what would become known as the systems approach.

But, as I have shown in this book, the history of systems analysis was not just about intellectual innovation or academic power grabbing. Because the systems approach was developed through East-West cooperation, it led to many crucial innovations that changed not only the conceptual, but also the institutional composition of the governmental worlds on both sides of the Iron Curtain. Such innovations include, but are not limited to, the new idea of apolitical steering that drew on systems analysis (later, policy analysis); new institutions such as an international think tank (IIASA); new tools such as regional and global computer-based models of intertwined economic, social, and geophysical processes; new objects of governance such as the biosphere; and, most importantly, a new language and conceptual principles of steering, building on the ideas of complex systems, self-regulation, uncertainty, and reflexivity, all of which posited the fundamental intertwining of scientific expertise and government.

I have demonstrated that these new ideas emerged in relation to particular scientific, organizational, social, and political contexts. One such context was the emergence of a group of Soviet governmental elites who acknowledged the importance of scientific expertise and East-West transfer for the future of the Soviet system. Another context entailed the establishment of IIASA as a "bridge between East and West." A third context involved the everyday tactics of the making of systems analysis as an apolitical science of governance inside IIASA. I argued that the impact of systems analysis was not limited to its end products, such as the scientific expertise expressed in reports, data, or images. All of these were, of course, significant, but my point is that the very *process* of the production of systems analysis mattered, because it was during this process that transformation was generated.

As a transformative instrument of governance, systems analysis was deeply ambivalent: this became particularly evident in the case of Soviet governance. Top Soviet government officials, such as Dzhermen Gvishiani, promoted East-West cooperation in the area of systems analysis, because they saw systems analysis as a legitimate channel for transferring high-tech expertise and know-how from the West. This transfer was expected to be fully controllable, leading to the strengthening of the Soviet economy and thus maintaining the existing power structure inside the Soviet Union. Yet other Soviet actors had rather different expectations for the East-West coproduction of systems analysis. I showed, for instance, that the mathematician Nikita Moiseev drew on systems analysis to articulate fundamentally different epistemological principles and an ethos of government as guidance (in Russian, *napravlenie*) of complex systems that, underscoring uncertainty, rejected the idea of the human control of the nature.

In this epilogue, I expand on the ambivalent role of systems analysis and consider its legacy in the post-Soviet period. I begin by discussing the implications of transnational system-cybernetic governmentality for the understanding of the bipolar Cold War world, proposing the idea of the system-cybernetic avant-garde of governance. Following this, I address the complex question of the link between system-cybernetic governmentality and the neoliberal transformation of post-Soviet Russia. I argue that although the system-cybernetic governmentality and economic neoliberalism did not share institutional origins, they were linked during the post-Soviet transformation as a result of historical momentum: the members of the Soviet systems approach community were best positioned to conduct the transfer of the models of the market economy from the West at a time when neoliberal ideas on the free market economy were gaining popularity. However, I also suggest that this should not mean that the pre-1980 history of system-cybernetic governmentality should be tainted as neoliberal; rather, I argue that this reveals the extent to which scientific governance can be appropriated by different economic and political regimes. If anything, the pre-1980 history of system-cybernetic governmentality is a history of a rather liberal, in the classic sense, governmental technology, underscoring the conditions of autonomy, self-regulation, and government at a distance. I wrap up my argument with consideration of the implications of my case of East-West system-cybernetic governmentality for studies of governance and sociopolitical change, proposing that the seeds for transformation can be found both at the margins and at the center of power.

Beyond the Cold War Panopticon: The System-Cybernetic Avant-Garde

In his influential account of the technical infrastructure of globality, Paul Edwards argues that computer technology was a constitutive part of the Cold War "closed world," because it enabled a political system relying on practices of surveillance and control.[1] In the same way many scholars explained the worldwide appeal of the systems approach by its military roots, interpreting the spread of the systems approach as a symptom of a pan-military, elitist mentality that, following paranoid Cold War logic, sought to render the population visible and amenable to perfect control.

But this view does not exhaust the reasons behind the international spread of the systems approach. Strongly dependent on computer technology, systems analysis was not just a tool of military competition. The values and the politics that the systems approach contained were not limited to the pan-military mentality. As I show in chapters 2, 3, and 4, it was due to a particular episode in Cold War diplomacy that policy sciences such as the systems approach assumed the particular role of a bridge between East and West. However, neither its military origins nor this diplomatic role solely determined the contents and uses of the systems approach as a policy science. Rooted in the OR tradition, the systems approach was used as a tool for East-West diplomacy and technology transfer, but then it morphed into a more ambitious venture for policy argumentation. The systems approach did not merely solve existing governmental problems, but *con-*

structed problems. As I show in chapter 4, systems analysts were as much problem *makers* as problem *solvers*. Their original contribution was the invention of "common problems" requiring new modes of sharing data, coproducing expert knowledge and new institutional frameworks for action. The very idea of common problems invites us to question the hypothesis of a paranoid, closed Cold War world.

Furthermore, system-cybernetic governmentality does not fit the image of the global panopticon.[2] I detail in chapters 3 and 4 that the shift to common problems was not mere diplomatic rhetoric. The production of common problems was only made possible by a complex organizational effort that carefully made and remade boundaries between technoscience and the political, a process which was a matter of everyday, pragmatic negotiation. Soviet policy sciences, based on cybernetics and systems analysis, were depoliticized with the aim of propelling Soviet military and industrial might to a bright future. But the system-cybernetic governmentality smuggled into Soviet governance a new epistemology, a new understanding of both the world and control.[3] This new epistemology undermined both the Marxist-Leninist view of stage-driven development and high modernist beliefs in control. According to the classical definition, liberal governance is "a limited government that operates through theoretical and scientific knowledge of immanent social and other processes external to the institutions of formal political authority."[4] Imposing limits on governmental optimism, system-cybernetic governmentality could be interpreted as a version of an organized skepticism which, in turn, liberalized Soviet governance.

How can a science of control have a liberalizing effect? According to Andrew Pickering, the ontology of cybernetics builds on "nonknowability," that is, an assumption that we can never fully represent and thus understand a complex system. This idea can be extended to describe both the content and the form of the organization of systems analysis as a field of international transfer. For instance, at IIASA pretentions to omniscience were rejected in the internal debate on the use of mathematical methods in scientific governance.[5] In its plan for the 1990s, IIASA acknowledged the limitations of its initial optimism toward the ability to solve policy issues with the help of mathematical decision aid tools and called for greater use of qualitative approaches.[6] Furthermore, cybernetic governmentality presupposes not a perfect knowledge of the world out there, but rather performativity: even under conditions of uncertainty, we can still figure out how the complex systems behave and interact with them.[7] Pickering also notes that the cybernetic notion of control did not historically develop as an instrument enabling straightforward domination or surveillance, although cybernetic control defines control as an informational, feedback-based process. Instead, argues Pickering,

> The entire task of cybernetics was to figure out how to get along in a world that was not enframable, that could not be subjugated to human designs—how to build machines and construct systems that could adapt performatively to whatever happened to come their way.[8]

In this way, the notion of cybernetic control allows for the areas of opacity and self-regulation. Applied to the Soviet context, this deeply challenges the notion of totalitarian control. Pickering's thesis of nonknowability as a central premise of cybernetic ontology is helpful to understand the central mechanism driving the East-West exchange in policy sciences. At IIASA, East-West scientists did not strive to accumulate detailed knowledge about each other. It was not a precise representation that both sides were striving after, for had one gone too deeply into details, the risk of espionage emerged. Instead of *knowing*, East-West scientists were *doing*: creating an environment that enabled them to perform, to work together. It is in this process that a new world emerged, one of global problems and complex interdependence, IIASA being, to be sure, just one site out of many, but a very important one nonetheless. It is on this basis that I insist on the idea of East-West coproduction of governance and not a mere "exchange" of preexisting models and ideas.

Moreover, the system-cybernetic emphasis on performative adaptability strongly disagrees with what scholars describe as the high modernist approach to governance, expressed in the large technological projects pursued by Soviet and US planners. It is widely documented that Soviet experts implemented some ill-conceived large-scale projects at enormous human and environmental cost, many of which dated back to Stalin's period, such as Magnitogorsk, the White Sea Canal, and Norilsk. It is on the basis of these examples, as described in the work of Stephen Kotkin, Sheila Fitzpatrick, and Orlando Figes, that Scott builds his thesis of high modernist expertise-based governance, equally blind to the principle of uncertainty and localized forms of knowledge. But as long as we restrict ourselves to this demonized view of Soviet technocracy, we cannot explain why Soviet rule lasted as long as it did and, furthermore, enjoyed a considerable degree of domestic and international legitimacy. I propose that a missing part of the explanation is Soviet system-cybernetic governmentality, which offered the hope of more enlightened governance, both for the governors and the governed, as well as an equally important promise of adaptability.

In this way, system-cybernetic governmentality entailed both revolutionary and conservative effects, where different actors mobilized it to achieve different goals. Indeed, it is thanks to this ambivalence that the systems approach could be presented as a "mere" instrument that did not threaten but reinforced the Communist Party's monopoly of power. Accordingly, new systems of control and even scientific expertise would performatively adapt to the existing hierarchies and conserve them by serving as their extensions.

The relationship between these two qualities, limiting and conserving the existing power structures, I propose, can be explained through a particular dynamic relation between the mainstream and the avant-garde. Back in the 1950s, and with reference to the artistic world, the French semiotician Roland Barthes observed that the avant-garde subsists on mainstream elite power and consumption networks, albeit at the same time avant-garde production seeks explicitly to overthrow elite mainstream habits.[9] I suggest that Barthes's notion of the interdependence of the avant-garde and mainstream can be used to understand the double role of system-cybernetic governmentality in the Soviet Union. Although seeking to fundamentally transform Soviet governance, systems analysis could not be practiced without organizational and financial support from the Soviet government. This mode of expertise required powerful computers, large data sets and, most importantly, the pooling of multidisciplinary expertise; thus it depended upon well-established scientific milieus with institutionalized links among them. All of these could not exist without state approval and support. In turn, the very existence of the system-cybernetic community conferred legitimacy on the otherwise bureaucratic and inefficient Soviet governmental system, as this community literally embodied the promise for a better future as well as symbolized a commitment to participate in the global networks of cutting-edge policy sciences. But I want to add that as an avant-garde approach, system-cybernetic governmentality conferred a degree of legitimacy on the Soviet government, only as long as it was seen as actively supporting efforts to think beyond national borders and narrow instrumentalism. Matthew Evangelista and Walter Clemens describe the significant efforts of Soviet antinuclear arms control scientists to reduce the world nuclear arsenal. In a similar way, the system-cybernetic research community of Soviet scientists actively participated in the development of global governance, which they saw as an antidote to short-term government concerned with quick fixes.

Indeed, the legitimizing role of the system-cybernetic avant-garde is confirmed by Russia's approach to IIASA after the collapse of the Soviet Union, when many Western countries, such as the Britain, France, and Italy, left IIASA in the 1980s—Russia continued paying its IIASA membership dues. On the other hand, considering the post-1990 period, there was also an evident discrepancy in Russian policy between "keeping face" before foreign partners and at the same time neglecting domestic communities of systems analysis to such an extent that they largely disintegrated.

The Decline of the System-Cybernetic Avant-Garde

The systems approach reached maturity in the Soviet Union in the second half of the 1980s, that is, just before the Soviet empire began to crumble. The volume of specialized academic journals, teaching programs, institutes, and academic literature on the systems approach was growing, and some of the affiliates of the movement finally entered the ranks of top decision makers, such as the econometrician Abel' Aganbegian, who participated in the drafting of Gorbachev's program for restructuring the Soviet economic system. Was this a chance for the avant-garde to become mainstream? Apparently not: Foucault's observation that "the art of government can only spread, be reflected, and take on and increase its dimensions in a period of expansion free from the great military, economic and political emergencies" applies well to the case of Soviet system-cybernetic governmentality, which appeared to thrive during the period normally described as "the stagnation," from the mid-1960s to the late 1980s.[10] But post-Soviet Russia in the 1990s was torn by many political and economic emergencies, which effectively disrupted the established networks of system-cybernetic expertise.

The success of the Soviet systems approach was entrenched in a particular social setting, that, on the one hand was dependent on stable access to generous governmental funding and, on the other hand, was a rather autonomous collective that fostered an ethos of responsibility for global issues that went beyond the boundaries of a discipline, a branch, or a polity. The Cold War divide was crucial to assuring the former and, probably, it was a generational cohort that ensured the latter. Both factors appeared to wither away during the 1980s. Prime Minister Kosygin retired in 1980 and died soon thereafter. During the next seven years, Kosygin's son-in-law, Gvishiani, continued to occupy important posts, retiring as a vice chairman of IIASA only in 1987. Briefly appointed to the State Planning Committee in 1985, Gvishiani disagreed with Mikhail Gorbachev's agenda and, judging from his memoirs, was neither invited nor wished to become deeper involved in the reconstruction.[11] It is likely that Gvishiani's political importance also diminished for health reasons (only in his fifties, he reported frequent illness) and the changing political climate. Following Kosygin's death, the GKNT's chairman Kirillin immediately retired. The axis of Kosygin-Kirillin-Gvishiani was therefore broken and many new actors, who did not necessarily share the same vision and mission, stepped in. Furthermore, in the late 1980s the Soviet Union was increasingly opening up to Western trade, establishing direct links between Western and Soviet companies. Accordingly, the GKNT had been losing its exceptional status as the East-West gatekeeper. In turn, the Soviet systems community was also losing the rationale to justify its priority status in East-West transfer.

Changes—some political others purely inexplicable—were also affecting the lower levels of the Soviet systems community. The Soviet nuclear winter scholars were struggling to come to terms with the mysterious disappearance of the atmospheric scientist Vladimir Aleksandrov, who went missing during his trip to an urban governance conference in Cordoba, Spain, in April 1985. Last seen in Madrid, from where he was supposed to fly back to Moscow to defend his doctoral dissertation in twenty days' time, Aleksandrov never boarded the aircraft and was never seen again. (At the moment of writing in 2015 his wife was still hoping to hear about him).[12] Despite the many unknowns and allegations, some alluding that the sociable Aleksandrov was involved in espionage, Aleksandrov's colleagues stayed loyal him: his tragic disappearance and scientific contribution was acknowledged in the 1987 edition of Velikhov's volume, dedicated to the study of the environmental consequences of nuclear war.[13] However, it is arguable that this unfortunate event did cast a shadow over the so far rather strikingly smooth transnational cooperation among East-West global modelers.

If political and security issues were understandably important, it was the state of the economy that posed insurmountable difficulties. As the economic situation continued deteriorating, the Soviet funding for science shrank, to almost completely vanish following the dissolution of the Soviet Union in 1991. Nikita Moiseev left his post as research director of the Computer Center in 1986, directing his efforts to publishing prolifically on the idea of the noosphere that set limits to government and the need for a new approach to government, emphasizing guidance and not control. In his memoir, published in 1993, Moiseev expressed bitter disappointment with the fate of the Academy of Sciences. Personally, he saw his livelihood drastically reduced by the collapsing economy and, once again, just like in the late 1940s, the eminent scientist could not afford to buy a decent suit.[14] Moiseev published his memoir before the US government, in partnership with several foundations and the philanthropist George Soros, launched their program intended to soften the hard landing of Soviet scientists during the transformation into a market economy. In the last pages, Moiseev documented the deep disappointment of the leading Soviet scientists, seeing their lifetime work going down the drain.[15] Sadly, Moiseev did not live to see the rise of the concept of the Anthropocene, of which he would have approved, as the governmental implications of the Anthropocene were in many ways so close to Moiseev's own theory of the noosphere.[16]

If the older scientists lamented the past, the younger scholars were facing an uncertain future. The Soviet nuclear winter group fragmented during the post-Soviet transformation. The head of the ecological modeling team, Iurii Svirezhev, left Moscow first for Hungary and then, in 1992, to take up a leading position at the Potsdam Institute for Climate Impact Research in Germany. A workaholic who did not stop even after retirement, Svirezhev would die on his way home from the office in 2007.[17] The designer of the general circulation model, Georgiy Stenchikov, also left the Computer Center in 1992. He recalled having decided to emigrate when his car was stolen from the center's car parking lot, this being "the last drop."[18] Stenchikov first went to work at Maryland and Rutgers universities and later to the King Abdullah University of Science and Technology in Saudi Arabia. However, some members of the team stayed in Moscow, such as the modeler of ecological systems, Aleksander Tarko, who enjoys cross-country skiing and photography when he does not teach and research at the Computer Center and runs the virtual museum dedicated to Nikita Moiseev. Although Tarko also replaced Skriabin as the scientific secretary of the Russian national committee at SCOPE and participated in the US-Russian modeling of the environmental consequences of a hypothetical nuclear conflict between India and Pakistan, one gets the feeling that the status of this research does not play quite the same significant role as it did in the early 1980s.

This somewhat depressing end illustrates the importance of the symbiotic relationship between informal, transnational scientists' collectives, strong governmental agencies, and well-funded organizational platforms for the international transfer of knowledge. The system-cybernetic ethos fell to pieces only when the storm died—when the Cold War ended following the collapse of the Soviet Union and the Russian economy. Although Gvishiani was mainly concerned with international trade, he also provided an institutional shelter for system-cybernetic scholarship, particularly for nonmilitary applications. The excessive, high modernist belief of the Soviet government in scientific fixes also led to the development of the institutional framework that enabled systems scientists to work at arm's length from the Party. The archival documents pertaining to Dzhermen Gvishiani's activities in the government cannot be accessed, so we are not able to fully evaluate personal contributions behind the stage. Nevertheless, it is important that, as one of my interlocutors told me, Gvishiani "genuinely respected science." Their proximity to the government, as my sources show, was indeed valued, even by the reformist Soviet systems scholars.

There was, in this way, a special social contract between the mainstream Soviet political bureaucracy and the system-cybernetic avant-garde. Whereas the original intentions of the Soviet leaders of the trade and military complex could well have been exploitative and limited to the short-term needs of their departments, these top leaders at least were politically intelligent enough to grant a carefully managed autonomy to system-cybernetic scholars. In turn, these scholars directed their efforts to global and pragmatic issues, the ones which were expected not to raise controversy inside the Soviet Union, thus neglecting such topics as human rights. The setup was seen as practical by both sides. In 1998 Nikita Moiseev wrote that both the United States and the Soviet Union benefited from the "hostile unity," but by this he did not simply refer to the bipolar geopolitical stability, but also to a joint commitment to shape the world beyond the Cold War divide.[19]

System-Cybernetic Governmentality and Neoliberalism

Looking back at the development of system-cybernetic governance from the perspective of the current debate on neoliberal technologies of government, an obvious question is how we can understand the link between the decline of the Soviet system-cybernetic governmentality and the onset of neoliberal reforms and globalization that followed the collapse of the Soviet regime. There is, as I mentioned earlier, a certain chronological overlap between the emergence of the Foucauldian studies of (neo)liberal governance and the rise of the systems approach in policy sciences. Furthermore, neoliberal economic ideas about the market and privatization entered high governmental circles in the early 1980s, precisely at the time when the systems approach—then increasingly framed as policy analysis—was becoming a mainstream subject in management education.[20] The two—neoliberal economic principles and policy analysis—became entangled in what would be called neoliberal governmentality.[21]

There is no consensus about the definition of neoliberalism; however, commentators appear to agree on at least one point—that neoliberal governance seeks to depoliticize governmental processes and keenly relies on techniques of calculation in doing this.[22] From this perspective, policy sciences might appear as obvious components of neoliberal governance. As I show in this book, policy scientists explicitly depoliticized systems analysis and developed approaches that could be viewed as predecessors to the evidence-based policy that drew on quantitative methods of evaluation in the 1990s.[23] However, the link between the systems approach and neoliberal governance is not straightforward: in the next section I suggest that the East-West partnership in the making of system-cybernetic governmentality complicates the interpretation of the systems approach as neoliberal.

There is an influential conversation going on among historians of Soviet political economy about its links with neoliberalism, the first and most distinct studies in this direction being conducted by Johanna Bockman and Gil Eyal. According to Bockman, the networks of neoliberal economic thinkers exploited the institutional and intellectual resources produced by left-oriented economists.[24] In her study of East European economic thought, Bockman argues that state socialist economic thinking was not limited to Marxist political economy, but also engaged with neoclassical economic thought, a development that took place under the conceptual umbrella of mathematical economics (econometrics). As East European economists were familiar with theories of market systems, the post-1989 transformation did not entirely catch them by surprise.[25] A more surprising moment was that the actual implementation of the transformation of the centrally commanded economy to a market economy was limited to a package of neoliberal reforms. This choice, according to Bockman, happened because the transnational right had effectively decoupled the idea of the socialist system from the idea of the market, thus rendering the combination of these two ideas politically bankrupt.[26]

Now, the systems-approach in policy sciences was developed outside neoliberal circles, originating instead in the circles of the Cowles Commission and Keynesian economists, who closely cooperated with the Soviet mathematical economists. This specific origin, to be sure, did not render system-cybernetic governmentality immune to different political appropriations: history shows that system-cybernetic governmentality appealed equally to liberal democratic capitalists, Soviet state socialists and, as we have seen over recent decades, neoliberals. How can we explain this? One possible explanation is that there is an inflexible supply of policy sciences and the system-cybernetic assemblage was simply understood as "the best available." Toward the end of the 1980s system-cybernetic governmentality became widespread globally and institutionalized in the fast-growing fields of management and policy studies and education, as well as private consulting. Positioned as a toolbox—and thus *not* a general, consistent theory—for planning at the international, state, and firm levels, systems analysis was equally welcome in centrally planned systems but also included in the repertoire of neoliberal governance, which put a premium on quantitative methods.

But also, one should be careful not to fall into the trap of epistemological realism. I am therefore skeptical about the usefulness of the attempt to search for the "roots" or "origins" of neoliberal governmental techniques. One reason is, as I demonstrate in this book, it does not make sense to talk about an intrinsic meaning of policy sciences, for meanings and outcomes differ in different contexts, being the subject of a laborious semiotic and institutional construction. The use of neoliberalism as an "–ism" word is misleading in itself, because it suggests a consistent and durable phenomenon. In contrast, the meanings and practices of systems analysis as a governmental technique were locally negotiated, heterogeneous, ambiguous, and more often than not contradictory.

A more fitting way of approaching this complex situation is to acknowledge the importance of the changing contexts of the articulation, institutionalization, and application of policy sciences. Linking system-cybernetic governance with neoliberal reforms was due to one such historically contingent context. The transnational East-West networks of system-cybernetic policy scientists began to overlap with the evolving networks of so-called neoliberal economists toward the late 1980s. When in 1986 Robert McNamara, former director of the World Bank, delivered the second distinguished lecture in IIASA's Kreisky lecture series, he spoke not about the economy but about nuclear security, as its condition was transformed by the study of nuclear winter.[27] The change took place in a few years, when in 1989 the prominent Russian economist Stanislav Shatalin nominated IIASA to be the platform for devising a program for economic restructuring of the Soviet Union. Starting in 1990 IIASA hosted a series of workshops for the development of a blueprint of East European transition to a market economy, which gathered the future minister of foreign economic relations and the influential oligarch, Petr Aven, future minister of economics, Evgenii Iasin, Gregorii Iavlinskii, and Stanislav Shatalin, among others.

It was at these events that the IIASA community established direct links with the organizations and individuals associated with neoliberal market ideology, espousing the values of a lean state, market economy, and "structural adjustment" policies.[28] From the West, Jacques Attali, then François Mitterand's advisor, and Jérôme Vignon, the director of the European Commission's Department for Prospective Studies, assured their support.[29] Some of these workshops were arranged with the support of the key British liberal think-tank, the Institute of Economic Affairs in London.[30] Also, Jeffrey Sachs, who devised shock therapy economic policies for Poland and Russia, was involved. The program, "500 Days," which involved privatization, liberalization of prices, and stabilization of the market, all followed with economic growth, was developed at IIASA. This program combined transformation with conservation as it retained the idea of the political integrity of the Soviet Union, but was never adopted by the Central Committee.

This is just a sketch of this turbulent period and the actual mechanism linking systems analysis and neoliberal reform of the Russian economy remains to be explored. Future research is needed to examine the role of long-term planning, the branch with which global modeling was most readily associated, during the volatile process of privatization in Russia in the first half of the 1990s, where leading industries were transferred from the state to private ownership and when economic decline prevented any commitment to large infrastructure projects.

On the other hand, during the same period Russia was entering the world of international finance. Here, long-term planning and systematic studies were delegated to the established international organizations, such as the World Bank and the International Monetary Fund, and to IIASA, where regional programs for transitioning from centrally commanded to market economies were developed.

Yet local agency should not be discarded beforehand. It would be interesting, for instance, to trace the knowledge and experience transfer from Soviet systems research communities to post-Soviet management consultants.[31] For a Western investor, the Russian industries that emerged in the 1990s were probably even less comprehensible than the old Soviet enterprises: in the 1990s ex-Soviet companies continued barter exchanges, but now the ownership of many was unclear, with some companies changing hands through armed takeovers. In this context, as Susanne Wengle shows, the importance of managerially trained experts was paramount in the privatization of Russian companies, because these managerial experts made the ex-Soviet industries legible for Western investors.[32] Thus, during the post-Soviet transformation, policy sciences once again provided a common language and linked East and West.

One thing is clear: the institutional landscape, where system-cybernetic governmentality was developed, was changing. After 1991 the production of policy expertise was no longer limited to the former members of the Soviet Academy of Sciences, but was instead fragmented into the hybrid and private field of management training and consultancy.[33] It is quite remarkable that the old research institutes were retained, but it was also obvious that the power shifted elsewhere. During my visit to the Computer Center and the Institute for Systems Research in Moscow in 2013, I noticed obvious signs of struggling organizations: dilapidated corridors and large office spaces that housed fewer scientists than originally intended. Professors complained about the difficulty of attracting doctoral students, as talented scientists often embarked on lucrative commercial careers rather than toiling, underpaid, in academia. However, the pride in the past was still present and the staff fondly remembered the pioneers in their field. The Computer Center, now named after its director Anatolii Dorodnitsyn, kept Moiseev's office as a memorial museum. Similarly, Gvishiani's office was maintained in the Institute for Systems Analysis (formerly VNIISI, now ISA): his coat had been left on a hanger, a pack of his favorite blue Pall Malls lay waiting, and neatly dusted book shelves displayed Western publications on policy analysis.

But the center of power in Russian scientific expertise on the future appeared to have shifted to other institutional environments, such as Rosnano, the agency in charge of the development of nanotechnologies, established in 2011 and situated just a stone's throw from ISA, and the Skolkovo innovation center, established in 2009, a controversial project that directly cooperates with MIT and IBM, among others. Although there is no space to expand on these developments, I would like to add that the ascension to power of Vladimir Putin in 2000 coincided with the return of macro planning, new infrastructure projects, and eventually a new expansionism in foreign policy. Whereas currently it seems completely unlikely that the Russian elites will embark on the route to democratization, they once again rely heavily on policy sciences and intellectual military technologies, such as reflexive control, in the conduct of so-called hybrid warfare.[34] Industries and technologies, though described as "just business" in the 1990s and the early 2000s, have once again become a matter of political prestige, particularly in the domestic context.[35] Recently the Polytechnic Museum, a venerable institution established in the nineteenth century in Moscow, mounted a new exposition entitled "Russia Can Do It Herself" (*Rossia delaet sama*). Furthermore, according to some conservative critics, the Russian foreign policy mobilized the very idea of global interdependence to set the new rules of international relations, seeking to claim back its great power status.[36] In this context, the ideas of uncertainty and the utopia of control, which played an important critical role during the Cold War, might once again hold significant critical potential.

Should we conclude, then, that the system-cybernetic avant-garde was ultimately a failure to liberalize government, both in East and West, ridden by their own versions of authoritarianisms, what Alena Ledeneva describes as the Putin *sistema* and what is described as neoliberalism? If anything, I hope to have shown in this book that that the liberalizing effect of system-cybernetic governmentality is always context specific. At IIASA, the systems approach to governance evolved toward the incorporation of qualitative methods in policy sciences, at the same time emphasizing informality, reflexivity, and social aspects of science and technology. Furthermore, during the Cold War the process of East-West coproduction of scientific expertise mattered at least as much as its end products, because in this process new, unanticipated practices, networks, ideas, and projects, some of which radically departed from the initial rationale, were generated. Finally, the history of system-cybernetic governmentality shows that sources for critical thinking and action can be found not only in what is described as the margins or practices of resistance, but also rooted in the very center of power and, furthermore, narrow, functionalist applications. The instrumental can become the critical and vice versa. Perhaps the system-cybernetic avant-garde has not been exhausted yet.

Notes

INTRODUCTION

1. Russian mathematician and research director of the Computer Center at the Soviet Academy of Sciences, Nikita Moiseev wrote in his memoir that he began to be embarrassed about his military jacket and was only able to buy his first civil suit in 1951, adding that at the moment of writing, in the mid-1990s, he once again could not afford to buy a suit. Nikita Moiseev, *Kak daleko do zavtreshnego dnia: svobodnye razmyshleniia, 1917–1993* (Moscow: ASPEKT, 1994).

2. Archive of the Russian Academy of Sciences (henceforth ARAN), documents of the discussion at the Council of the Soviet Academy of Sciences, 1972.

3. Robert R. Kline, *The Cybernetics Moment: Or Why We Call Our Age the Information Age* (Baltimore, MD: Johns Hopkins University Press, 2015); Hunter Heyck, *Age of System: Understanding the Development of Modern Social Science* (Baltimore, MD: Johns Hopkins University Press, 2015); Paul Edwards, *A Vast Machine: Computer Models, Climate Data, and the Politics of Global Warming* (Cambridge, MA: MIT Press, 2010). See also Stephen Collier and Andrew Lakoff, "Vital Systems Security: Reflexive Biopolitics and the Government of Emergency," *Theory, Culture and Society* 32, no. 2 (2015): 19–51.

4. Slava Gerovitch, *From Newspeak to Cyberspeak: A History of Soviet Cybernetics* (Cambridge, MA: MIT Press, 2002).

5. See, for instance, a novel by Carl A. Posey, *Red Danube* (London: St Martin's, 1986).

6. Giuliana Gemelli, ed., *The Ford Foundation and Management Education in Western and Eastern Europe (1950s–1970s)* (Brussels: European Interuniversity Press, 1998); Giuliana Gemelli, ed., *American Foundations and Large-Scale Research: Construction and Transfer of Knowledge* (Bologna: Clueb, 2001); Johan Heilbron, Nicolas Guilhot, and Laurent Jeanpierre, "Toward a Transnational History of the Social Sciences," *Journal of the History of the Behavioral Sciences* 44, no. 2 (2008): 146–160; Roger E. Backhouse and Philippe Fontaine, eds., *A Historiography of the Modern Social Sciences* (Cambridge: Cambridge University Press, 2014); Mark Solovey, ed., *Shaky Foundations: The Politics-Patronage-Social Science Nexus in Cold War America* (New Brunswick, NJ: Rutgers University Press, 2013); Jenny Andersson, "The Great Future Debate and the Struggle for the World," *American Historical Review* 117 (2012): 1411–1430.

7. Mark Sandle, "Russian Think Tanks, 1956–1996," in *Think Tanks Across Nations: A Comparative Approach*, ed. Diane Stone, Andrew Dedham, and Mark Garnett (Manchester, UK: Manchester University Press, 1998), 202–222. See also Marion Fourcade, *Economists and Societies: Discipline and Profession in the United States, Britain and France, 1890s–1990s* (Princeton, NJ: Princeton University Press, 2009).

8. Fernando Elichirigoity, *Planet Management: Limits to Growth, Computer Simulation, and the Emergence of Global Spaces* (Evanston, IL: Northwestern University Press, 1999); Leena Riska-Campbell, *Bridging East and West: The Establishment of the International Institute for Applied Systems Analysis (IIASA) in the United States Foreign Policy of Bridge Building, 1964–1972* (Helsinki: The Finnish Society of Science and Letters, 2011).

9. Stacy D. VanDeveer, "Ordering Environments: Regions in European International Environmental Cooperation," in *Earthly Politics: Local and Global in Environmental Governance*, ed. Sheila Jasanoff and Marybeth Martello (Cambridge, MA: MIT Press, 2004),

309–334; Duncan Liefferink, *Environment and the Nation State: The Netherlands, the European Union and Acid Rain* (Manchester, UK: Manchester University Press, 1996). See also Rolf Lidskog and Göran Sundkvist, eds., *Governing the Air: The Dynamics of Science, Policy, and Citizen Interaction* (Cambridge, MA: MIT Press, 2011).

10. It is quite possible that the relative obscurity of this organization, at least in Cold War and Soviet histories, is due rather to the fact that its target audience constituted of a particular set of elite research and political organizations, an orientation which, according to Stone and Garnett, was indeed typical of the majority of Western think tanks. Diane Stone and Mark Garnett, "Introduction: Think Tanks, Policy Advice and Governance," in *Think Tanks Across Nations: A Comparative Approach*, ed. Diane Stone, Andrew Denham, and Mark Garnett (Manchester, UK: Manchester University Press. 1998), 13–14.

11. Barbara Czarniawska-Joerges and Guje Sevón, eds., *Translating Organizational Change* (Berlin: de Gruyter, 1996).

12. While I am not the first to suggest this, I am not aware of any other study of the activities pursued at IIASA. Some scholars, like Elichirigoity, Schwartz, and Riska-Campbell point out the relevance of IIASA to the emergence of a new type of global thinking beyond the Cold War in US foreign policy from the 1960s, but I am not aware of other thorough studies on this. Fernando Elichirigoity, *Planet Management, Limits to Growth, Computer Simulation, and the Emergence of Global Spaces* (Evanston, IL: Northwestern University Press, 1999); Francis J. Gavin and Mark Atwood Lawrence, eds., *Beyond the Cold War: Lyndon Johnson and the New Global Challenges of the 1960s* (Oxford: Oxford University Press, 2014).

13. In this respect, my study is a kind of history of the present transnational policy entrepreneurship. See, for instance, Andrew Moravcsik, "A New Statecraft? Supranational Entrepreneurs and International Cooperation," *International Organization* 53, no. 2 (1999): 267–306.

14. See also Oscar Sanchez-Sibony, who underscores the importance of international trade for the Soviet government, suggesting that East-West relations were based less on head-on confrontation than on mutual accommodation and cooperation. Oscar Sanchez-Sibony, *Red Globalization: The Political Economy of the Soviet Cold War from Stalin to Khrushchev* (Cambridge: Cambridge University Press, 2014), 4–7.

15. These are two bodies of literature that only occasionally overlap. Some have attempted to draw the disparate fields into one, system-cybernetic paradigm; the roots of this intellectual project of field-building go back to the 1970s. I refer here only to the publications in English, although there is extensive literature on the paradigm of system-cybernetic sciences in French and Swedish. For an example, see Darrell P. Arnold, ed., *Traditions of Systems Theory: Major Figures and Contemporary Developments* (New York: Routledge, 2014). The other type of scholarship reflects on the elements of what I call system-cybernetic governmentality and, drawing on the history of science and technology, critically examines it. Early examples include Daniel Bell's writings on the postindustrial society, Yoneji Masuda's work on information society, and David Noble's writing on the social consequences of automation. Later and highly influential examples include Katherine Hayles, *How We Became Posthuman: Virtual Bodies in Cybernetics, Literature, and Informatics* (Chicago: University of Chicago Press, 1999); Manuel Castells and Emma Kiselyova, *The Collapse of Soviet Communism: A View from the Information Society* (Berkeley: University of California Press, 1995). A third body of literature involves those social and political theories that (either explicitly or implicitly) incorporated elements of a system-cybernetic approach to advance social science. Examples are very many, the most prominent being the works of Karl Deutsch, Gregory Bateson, Amitai Etzioni, Nikolas Luhmann, and François Lyotard. See Céline Lafontaine, *L'empire cybernétique: des machines à penser à la pensée machine* (Paris: Seuil, 2004). More recently, studies have begun to appear scrutinizing the impact

and legacy of system cybernetic sciences in governance and culture from a historical perspective. See Eglė Rindzevičiūtė, *Constructing Soviet Cultural Policy: Cybernetics and Governance after World War II* (Linköping, Sweden: Linköping University Press, 2008); David Crowley and Jane Pavitt, eds., *Cold War Modern* (London: V&A, 2010); Eden Medina, *Cybernetic Revolutionaries Technology and Politics in Allende's Chile* (Cambridge, MA: MIT Press, 2011); Orit Halpern, *Beautiful Data: A History of Vision and Reason since 1945* (Durham, NC: Duke University Press, 2014).

16. Obviously, systems thinking in governance has much older roots, considering which is beyond the scope of this book. I have limited my analysis to the Cold War period, largely because precisely at this time the newly invented computer technology and cybernetics informed new notions of governance and control. However, there is an interesting argument to be made regarding efforts to develop East-West scientific cooperation, efforts which could well be seen as an attempt to re-create the international world scientific community of the nineteenth century regardless of the ideological divisions imposed on the Cold War world. Further research is necessary to fully understand to what extent the Cold War was a driver and obstacle of scientific cooperation.

17. The key works that touch on the East-West transfer of systems analysis are Paul Erickson et al., *How Reason Almost Lost Its Mind: The Strange Career of Cold War Rationality* (Chicago: University of Chicago Press, 2013); David Holloway, *Stalin and the Bomb: The Soviet Union and Atomic Energy, 1939–1956* (New Haven, CT: Yale University Press, 1996); Walter C. Clemens, *Can Russia Change? The USSR Confronts Global Interdependence* (Boston: Unwin Hyman, 1990); David Holloway, "The Political Uses of Scientific Models: The Cybernetic Model of Government in Soviet Social Science," in *The Use of Models in the Social Sciences*, ed. L. Collins (Boulder, CO: Westview Press, 1976); Mark R. Beissinger, *Scientific Management, Socialist Discipline, and Soviet Power* (Cambridge, MA: Harvard University Press, 1988); Loren Graham, *Science, Philosophy, and Human Behaviour in the Soviet Union* (New York: Columbia University Press, 1987); Ilmari Susiluoto, *The Origins and Development of Systems Thinking in the Soviet Union: Political and Philosophical Controversies from Bogdanov and Bukharin to Present-Day Re-Evaluation* (Helsinki: Suomalainen tiedeakatemia, 1982); F. J. Fleron, ed. *Technology and Communist Culture: The Socio-Cultural Impact of Technology under Socialism* (New York: Praeger, 1977).

18. Albeit previously criticized for its lack of a critical position in the 1990s and throughout the first decade of the twenty-first century, the governmentality perspective appears to be well-established as a mainstream approach across the disciplines of sociology, political science, and cultural studies. Recently the critical thrust of the governmentality perspective became evident in the studies of neoliberal governance. William Davies, *The Limits of Neoliberalism: Authority, Sovereignty and the Logic of Competition* (London: Sage, 2014); Nicholas Gane, "The Governmentalities of Neoliberalism: Panopticism, Post-Panopticism and Beyond," *The Sociological Review* 60, no. 4 (2012): 611–634; Nicholas Gane, "Sociology and Neoliberalism: A Missing History," *Sociology* 48, no. 6 (2014): 1092–1106.

19. Mitchell Dean, *Governmentality: Power and Rule in Modern Society* (London: Sage, 1999), 1.

20. Foucault's own definition states "First, by 'governmentality' I understand the ensemble formed by institutions, procedures, analyses, and reflections, calculations, and tactics that allow the exercise of this very specific, albeit very complex power that has the population as its target, political economy as its major form of knowledge and apparatuses of security as its essential technical instrument. Second, by 'governmentality' I understand the tendency, the line of force, that for a long time, and throughout the West, has constantly led towards the pre-eminence over all other types of power—sovereignty, discipline, and so on—of the type of power that we can call 'government' and which has led

to the development of specific of a series of specific governmental apparatus (*appareils*) on the one hand, [and on the other] to the development of a series of knowledges (*savoirs*). Finally, by 'governmentality' I think we should understand the process, or rather the result of the process by which the state of justice of the Middle Ages became the administrative state in the fifteenth and sixteenth centuries and was gradually 'governmentalised'." Michel Foucault, *Security, Territory, Population: Lectures at the Collège de France, 1977–1978*, trans. Graham Burchell, ed. Michael Senallart (Basingstoke, UK: Palgrave Macmillan, 2009), 108–109.

21. Foucault, *Security, Territory, Population*, 122, 92, 99.

22. For the history of a rational agent, see Nicola Giocoli, *Modelling Rational Agents: From Interwar Economics to Early Modern Game Theory* (Cheltenham, UK: Edward Elgar, 2003). For a definition of governmental rationality in the Foucauldian sense, see Dean, *Governmentality*, 10–11. For a concise exposition of the research agenda of governmentality studies see Nikolas Rose and Peter Miller, "Political Power beyond the State: Problematics of Government," *The British Journal of Sociology*, 43, no. 2 (1992): 173–205.

23. Ian Hacking, "How Should We Do the History of Statistics?" in *Foucault's Effect: Studies in Governmentality*, ed. Graham Burchell, Colin Gordon, and Peter Miller (Chicago: University of Chicago Press, 1991), 181–196.

24. For the focus of governmentality studies on the "art of governance" see Dean, *Governmentality*, 18. The longstanding internal debate on systems analysis as an art of governance is vast, but see Aaron Wildavsky, *Speaking Truth to Power: The Art and Craft of Policy Analysis* (Boston: Little, Brown, 1979); and Giandomenico Majone, *Evidence, Argument and Persuasion in the Policy Process* (New Haven, CT: Yale University Press, 1989).

25. Alan McKinlay and Philip Taylor, *Foucault, Governmentality, and Organization* (New York: Routledge, 2014), 2–3. I thank Colin Gordon for the commentary on whether Foucault borrowed the term from Barthes.

26. Céline Lafontaine suggests that Michel Foucault's theory of dispersed and distributed power apparatuses draws on "the relational logic of cybernetics." Although she does not offer substantiating proof of Foucault's readings on cybernetics, there is indeed a good deal of overlap between system-cybernetic ontology and Foucault's idea of power and episteme. Also, Lafontaine makes a strong argument by indicating the contemporaneous criticism of structuralists as "cybermen" and "technocrats," as in Henri Lefebvre's *Position: Against Technocrats* (1967). Lafontaine, *L'empire cybernétique*, 110. See also Céline Lafontaine, "The Cybernetic Matrix of French Theory," *Theory, Culture & Society* 24, no. 5 (2007): 27–46.

27. See, for instance, David Holloway, "Innovation in Science—The Case of Cybernetics in the Soviet Union," *Science Studies* 4, no. 4 (1974): 299–337; but also Erik Hofmann and Robin F. Laird, *Technocratic Socialism: The Soviet Union in the Advanced Industrial Era* (Durham, NC: Duke University Press, 1985).

28. Gerovitch, *From Newspeak to Cyberspeak*.

29. Karl Polanyi, *The Great Transformation: The Political and Economic Origins of Our Time* (New York: Farrar & Rhinehart, 1944). The term "social technology" was also used by Olaf Helmer, who proposed changing human behavior by amending the material settings rather than changing people's views. This understanding of social technology was welcome in the Soviet Union, as in, for instance, Edvard Arab-Ogly, *V labirinte prorochestv* (Moscow: Molodaia gvardiia, 1973), 105.

30. Rindzevičiūtė, *Constructing Soviet Cultural Policy*.

31. This perspective is advanced in the studies on large technical infrastructures. See Thomas P. Hughes, *Networks of Power: Electrification of Western Society, 1880–1930* (Baltimore, MD: Johns Hopkins University Press, 1983); Andrew Barry, *Material Politics: Disputes along the Pipeline* (Oxford: Wiley-Blackwell, 2013); and Penny Harvey and Hannah

Knox, *Roads: An Anthropology of Infrastructure and Expertise* (Ithaca, NY: Cornell University Press, 2015).

32. The classic studies are Otto Mayr, *The Origins of Feedback Control* (Cambridge, MA: MIT Press, 1970); Stuart Bennett, *A History of Control Engineering 1800–1930* (Stevenage, UK: Peregrinus, 1979); David A. Mindell, *Between Human and Machine: Feedback, Control, and Computing before Cybernetics* (Baltimore, MD: Johns Hopkins University Press, 2002); John Agar, *The Government Machine: A Revolutionary History of the Computer* (Cambridge, MA: MIT Press, 2003); Gerovitch, *From Newspeak to Cyberspeak*.

33. Bruno Latour, *Reassembling the Social: An Introduction to Actor-Network-Theory* (Oxford: Oxford University Press, 2005).

34. In much scholarship "technocracy" is often used as synonymous with technical totalitarianism and belief in a determinist world and, thus simplified, used to contrast different forms of either reflexive governance or complex organizational reality. I suggest that in such cases "technocracy" is used as a critical and not a descriptive concept. However, I would argue that there is more complexity to technocracy, which in some cases is able to embrace complexity and reflexivity, as revealed in the history of Soviet systems approach. For a similar argument see Michael Power, *Organized Uncertainty: Designing a World of Risk Management* (Oxford: Oxford University Press, 2007).

35. S. M. Amadae, *Rationalizing Capitalist Democracy: The Cold War Origins of Rational Choice Liberalism* (Chicago: University of Chicago Press, 2003); Paul Erickson et al., *How Reason almost Lost its Mind*; Philip Mirowski, *Machine Dreams: Economics Becomes a Cyborg Science* (Chicago: University of Chicago Press, 2010); Jennifer Light, *From Warfare to Welfare: Defense Intellectuals and Urban Problems in Cold War America* (Baltimore, MD: Johns Hopkins University Press, 2004).

36. The importance of East-West relations is acknowledged in recent studies on transnational governmentalities, such as neoliberal economics. Johanna Bockman, *Markets in the Name of Socialism: The Left-Wing Origins of Neoliberalism* (Stanford, CA: Stanford University Press, 2011). However, my case of the development of systems analysis questions Bockman's and Bernstein's thesis that the onset of neoliberalism put East-West coproduction of governance to an end, making way for a "monologue" of neoliberal governance. This is because the impact of system-cybernetic governmentality should be traced in wider sectors of governance and not only in the struggles over the institutionalization of markets or a planned economy. Johanna Bockman and Michael Bernstein, "Scientific Community in a Divided World: Economists, Planning, and Research Priority during the Cold War," *Comparative Studies in Society and History* 50, no. 3 (2008): 581–613.

37. Joy Rohde, *Armed with Expertise: The Militarization of American Social Research during the Cold War* (Ithaca, NY: Cornell University Press, 2013); Erickson et al., *How Reason Almost Lost Its Mind*.

38. Marie-Laure Djelic and Kerstin Sahlin-Andersson, eds., *Transnational Governance: Institutional Dynamics of Regulation* (Cambridge: Cambridge University Press, 2006).

39. Scholars, like Timothy Mitchell, turned to colonial history in the search of the origins of expertise-based governance. Timothy Mitchell, *Rule of Experts: Egypt, Techno-Politics, Modernity* (Berkeley: University of California Press, 2002). For a first study of Soviet governmentality of selfhood see Oleg Kharkhordin, *The Collective and the Individual in Russia: A Study of Practices* (Berkeley: University of California Press, 1999). Foucault himself commented on Soviet biopolitics; for more on this, see Sergei Prozorov, "Foucault and Soviet Biopolitics," *History of the Human Sciences* (2014): 1–20.

40. Dean, *Governmentality*, 145; Mitchell Dean, "Liberal Government and Authoritarianism," *Economy and Society* 31, no. 1 (2002): 37–61.

41. The notion of coproduction was popularized in the social sciences by Bruno Latour, *We Have Never Been Modern* (Cambridge, MA: Harvard University Press, 1991).

From at least the 1950s the many principles of coproduction have been explicitly discussed in practice-oriented disciplines, such as management, social engineering, security research, and particularly, as I show in this book, systems approach.

42. Sheila Jasanoff, "The Idiom of Co-production," in *States of Knowledge: The Co-production of Science and Social Order*, ed. Sheila Jasanoff (New York: Routledge, 2004), 2–3.

43. Jasanoff, "The Idiom," 3, 4.

44. Latour, *We Have Never Been Modern*. I first proposed to study the history of Soviet cybernetics as an intertwining process of hybridization and purification of cybernetics with/from the political in Eglė Rindzevičiūtė, "Purification and Hybridisation of Soviet Cybernetics: The Politics of Scientific Governance in an Authoritarian Regime," *Archiv für sozialgeschichte* 50 (2010): 289–309.

45. Thomas F. Gieryn, *Cultural Boundaries of Science: Credibility on the Line* (Chicago: University of Chicago Press, 1999), 23.

46. Nikolas Rose, *Powers of Freedom: Reframing Political Thought* (Cambridge: Cambridge University Press, 1999).

47. Loren Graham, "Introduction: The Impact of Science and Technology on Soviet Politics and Society," in *Science and the Soviet Social Order*, ed. Loren Graham (Cambridge, MA: Harvard University Press, 1990), 15.

48. Graham, "The Impact of Science," 10–12.

49. Eglė Rindzevičiūtė, "A Struggle for the Soviet Future: The Birth of Scientific Forecasting in the Soviet Union," *Slavic Review*, 75, no. 1 (2016): 52–76.

50. For more about Soviet technocracy, see Kendall E. Bailes, "The Politics of Technology: Stalin and Technocratic Thinking among Soviet Engineers," *The American Historical Review* 79, no. 2 (1974): 445–469; D. K. Rowney, *Transition to Technocracy: The Structural Origins of the Soviet Administrative State* (Ithaca, NY: Cornell University Press, 1989). New work on the modernization of Russia and the Soviet Union has appeared, mainly as part of the revision of Cold War studies. See Markku Kangaspuro and Jeremy Smith, eds., *Modernisation in Russia since 1900* (Helsinki: Finnish Literature Society, 2006); Sari Autio-Sarasmo and Katalin Miklóssy, eds., *Reassessing Cold War Europe* (New York: Routledge, 2011).

51. For more on technocracy, see Frank Fischer, *Technocracy and the Politics of Expertise* (Newbury Park, CA: Sage, 1990); Gabrielle Hecht, "Planning a Technological Nation: Systems Thinking and the Politics of National Identity in Postwar France," in *Systems, Experts, and Computers: The Systems Approach in Management and Engineering, World War II and After*, ed. Agatha C. Hughes and Thomas P. Hughes (Cambridge, MA: MIT Press, 2000), 133–160.

52. Fischer, *Technocracy and the Politics of Expertise*, 17.

53. Research shows that not all technically educated bureaucrats are prone to what is described as "technocratic" decision making. In all, debates on how to identify a technocrat go back at least fifty years. See Robert D. Putnam, "Elite Transformation in Advanced Industrial Societies: An Empirical Assessment of the Theory of Technocracy," *Comparative Political Studies* 10, no. 3 (1977): 383–412.

54. Loren Graham, *Science in Russia and the Soviet Union: A Short History* (Cambridge: Cambridge University Press, 1993), 161.

55. For studies of Soviet scientific management in the context, see Loren Graham, *The Ghost of an Executed Engineer: Technology and the Fall of the Soviet Union* (Cambridge, MA: Harvard University Press, 1996); Stephen Hanson, *Time and Revolution: Marxism and the Design of Soviet Institutions* (Chapel Hill: University of North Carolina Press, 1997).

56. Beissinger, *Scientific Management, Socialist Discipline and Soviet Power*; Kendall Bailes, "Alexei Gastev and the Soviet Controversy over Taylorism, 1918–24," *Soviet Studies* 29, no. 3 (1977): 373–394.

57. Nikita Moiseev, *Sotsializm i informatika* (Moscow: izdatel'stvo politicheskoi literatury, 1988), 67.

58. Stephen Fortescue, *Science Policy in the Soviet Union* (New York: Routledge, 1990); Pekka Sutela, *Socialism, Planning and Optimality: A Study in Soviet Economic Thought* (Helsinki: Finnish Society of Science and Letters, 1984).

59. Graham, *Science in Russia and the Soviet Union*, 160–165.

60. The seminal works are Theodore Porter, *Trust in Numbers: The Pursuit of Objectivity in Science and Public Life* (Princeton, NJ: Princeton University Press, 1995); Mary Poovey, *A History of the Modern Fact: Problems of Knowledge in the Sciences of Wealth and Society* (Chicago: University of Chicago Press, 1998); Ian Hacking, *The Taming of Chance* (Cambridge: Cambridge University Press, 1990).

61. Vivien A. Schmidt, *Democracy in Europe: The EU and National Polities* (Oxford: Oxford University Press, 2006). For an overview of the link between the foundational debates on technocracy and more recent discussions, see Christina Ribbhagen, *Technocracy within Representative Democracy: Technocratic Reasoning and Justification among Bureaucrats and Politicians* (Gothenburg: University of Gothenburg Press, 2013); Claudio M. Radaelli, *Technocracy in the European Union* (New York: Longman, 1999).

62. For informality in centralized planning, see Paul R. Gregory, *The Political Economy of Stalinism: Evidence from the Soviet Secret Archives* (Cambridge: Cambridge University Press, 2003). Here I am drawing on the important work on the ambivalent role of informal practices in the Russian economy and society by Alena V. Ledeneva, *How Russia Really Works: The Informal Practices that Shaped the Post-Soviet Politics and Business* (Ithaca, NY: Cornell University Press, 2006). For the importance of informality in the organization of scientific expertise in the EU agencies, see Andrew Barry, *Political Machines: Governing a Technological Society* (London: Athlone, 2001), 93–101.

63. See the argument in Steven Brint, *In an Age of Experts: The Changing Role of Professionals in Politics and Public Life* (Princeton, NJ: Princeton University Press, 1994).

64. James C. Scott, *Seeing Like a State: How Certain Schemes to Improve the Human Condition Have Failed* (New Haven, CT: Yale University Press, 1998), 4.

65. Scott, *Seeing Like a State*, 96.

66. Ibid., 5.

67. Scott, *Seeing Like a State*, 98–99; Richard Stites, *Revolutionary Dreams: Utopian Vision and Experimental Life in the Russian Revolution* (New York: Oxford University Press, 1989).

68. Loren Graham, *Moscow Stories* (Bloomington: Indiana University Press, 2006).

69. Richard F. Vidmer, "Soviet Studies of Organization and Management: A 'Jungle' of Competing Views," *Slavic Review* 40, no. 3 (1981): 404–422.

70. Chapter 5 is a revised version of my article, "Toward a Joint Future Beyond the Iron Curtain: East-West Politics of Global Modelling," in *A Struggle for the Long-Term in Transnational Science and Politics: Forging the Future*, eds. Jenny Andersson and Eglė Rindzevičiūtė (New York: Routledge, 2015).

71. Graham, "The Impact of Science," 13.

1. GRAY EMINENCES OF THE SCIENTIFIC-TECHNICAL REVOLUTION

1. Such a simplistic division between political and technocratic power is described and criticized by Frank Fischer in *Technocracy and the Politics of Expertise*, 110–111.

2. Ronald Grigor Suny, *The Soviet Experiment: Russia, the USSR and the Successor States* (New York: Oxford University Press, 1998).

3. Fischer, *Technocracy and the Politics of Expertise*, 19.

4. For a concise overview of the Soviet military-industrial complex, see Audra J. Wolfe, *Competing with the Soviets: Science, Technology and the State in Cold War America* (Baltimore, MD: Johns Hopkins University Press, 2013), and for a comprehensive review of Soviet environmental programs and disasters, see Paul Josephson et al., *An Environmental History of Russia* (Cambridge: Cambridge University Press, 2013).

5. Fischer, *Technocracy and the Politics of Expertise*.

6. See Josephson et al., *An Environmental History of Russia*; Laurent Coumel and Marc Elie, "A Belated and Tragic Ecological Revolution: Nature, Disasters, and Green Activists in the Soviet Union and the Post-Soviet States, 1960s–2010s," *Soviet and Post-Soviet Review* 40, no. 2 (2013): 157–165.

7. Bruno Latour, *We Have Never Been Modern*. Translated by Catherine Porter (Cambridge, MA: Harvard University Press, 1993).

8. Louise Amoore, *The Politics of Possibility: Risk and Security Beyond Probability* (Durham and London: Duke University Press, 2013), 34–39.

9. Stephen Fortescue, *Science Policy in the Soviet Union* (New York: Routledge, 1990), 27.

10. The role of Gvishiani as an internationalizer of Soviet governance is discussed in Clemens, *Can Russia Change?* and in Matthew Evangelista, *Unarmed Forces: The Transnational Movement to End the Cold War* (Ithaca, NY: Cornell University Press, 1999).

11. Kosygin supported the ousting of Khrushchev and, indeed, it was he who granted permission to erect a monument to Khrushchev after his death. William Taubman, *Khrushchev: The Man and His Era* (New York: W. W. Norton, 2004), 647.

12. For example, Khrushchev's son-in-law, Aleksei Adzhubei, became chief editor of *Izvestii*, and the son-in-law of Brezhnev, Iurii Churbanov, served as a deputy minister of Interior Affairs.

13. The Russian State Archive of the Economy (henceforth RGAE), f.99, op.1, d.890, l.33.

14. This argument has been defended in a vast body of work: Michael E. Latham, *Modernization as Ideology: American Social Science and "Nation Building" in the Kennedy Era* (Chapel Hill: University of North Carolina Press, 2000); David Engerman et al., eds., *Staging Growth: Modernization, Development and the Global Cold War* (Amherst: University of Massachusetts Press, 2003); Nils Gilman, *Mandarins of the Future: Modernization Theory in Cold War America* (Baltimore, MD: Johns Hopkins University Press, 2004); Michael E. Latham, *The Right Kind of Revolution: Modernization, Development, and U.S. Foreign Policy from the Cold War to the Present* (Ithaca, NY: Cornell University Press, 2010).

15. See also Latham, *The Right Kind of Revolution*, 7; and Nils Gilman, "Modernization Theory, the Highest Stage of American Intellectual History," in *Staging Growth: Modernization, Development and the Global Cold War*, ed. David Engerman et al. (Amherst: University of Massachusetts Press, 2003), 50.

16. Gilman, "Modernization Theory, the Highest Stage," 54–55.

17. For Bernal's role in the development of postwar policy sciences in Britain, see William Thomas, *Rational Action: The Sciences of Policy in Britain and America, 1940–1960* (Cambridge, MA: MIT Press, 2015) and Andrew Jamison, "Technology's Theorists: Conceptions of Innovation in Relation to Science and Technology Policy," *Technology and Culture* 30, no. 3 (1989): 505–533. For a biography of Bernal, see Andrew Brown, *J. D. Bernal: The Sage of Science* (Oxford: Oxford University Press, 2007).

18. J. D. Bernal, *The Social Function of Science* (London: Routledge, 1939), 379, 383.

19. Ibid., 409.

20. For the US version of technological modernization as both solution and problem, see Latham, *The Right Kind of Revolution*.

21. Mikuláš Teich, "The Scientific-Technical Revolution: An Historical Event in the Twentieth Century?" in *Revolution in History*, ed. Roy Porter and Mikuláš Teich (Cambridge: Cambridge University Press, 1986), 317–319.

22. J. P. Snow, *The Two Cultures and the Scientific Revolution* (New York: Cambridge University Press, 1959).

23. Leonard Silk, *The Research Revolution* (New York: McGraw-Hill, 1960).

24. Donald N. Michael, *Cybernation: The Silent Contest* (Santa Barbara, CA: Center for the Study of Democratic Institutions, 1962); Marshall McLuhan, "Cybernation and Culture," in *The Social Impact of Cybernetics*, ed. Charles R. Dechert (Notre Dame, IN: University of Notre Dame Press, 1966), 95–108. See also Daniel Bell, *The End of Ideology: The Exhaustion of Political Ideas in the 1950s*, 2nd ed. (Cambridge, MA: Harvard University Press, 2000); Daniel Bell, *The Coming of Post-Industrial Society: A Venture in Social Forecasting* (New York: Basic Books, 1976); Malcolm Waters, *Daniel Bell* (New York: Routledge, 1996), 106.

25. Silk, *The Research Revolution*, 106.

26. Gilman, "Modernization Theory, the Highest Stage," 54–55.

27. Discussed in Thomas, *Rational Action*.

28. According to Dmitrii Efremenko, the term "scientific-technical revolution" emerged in Soviet discourse in 1954. Dmitrii Efremenko, *Ekologo-politicheskie diskursy: vozniknovenie i evoliutsiia* (Moscow: INION, 2006).

29. Anatolii Zvorykin, *Sozdanie material'no-tekhnicheskoi bazy kommunizma v SSSR* (Moscow: Sotsekgiz, 1959). Importantly, Zvorykin includes electronic and automatic technologies in the material-technical basis of communism, outlining the East-West development in the following way: material-technical basis first originates in capitalism, and is then taken over to make the material-technical basis for socialism and, eventually, communism. Zvorykin discusses the importance of automatic machinery, which developed from rigid control mechanisms to reflexive, digital servomechanisms, based on informational control, where, ultimately, complex systems of machines emerge. Note that from the 1950s through the early 1960s, Zvorykin focuses exclusively on technoscientific progress and only later expands his interests to include social change. Anatolii Zvorykin, "Material'no-tekhnicheskaia baza kommunizma," *Voprosy filosofii* 4 (1960): 26–40. Others, however, mention the social consequences of STR as early as 1960: see V. S. Naidenov, "Sotsial'no-ekonomicheskie posledstvie tekhnicheskogo progressa pri sotsializme," *Voprosy filosofii* 8 (1960): 14–24.

30. Bernal was translated into Russian: His *Science in History* (1954) was published in Moscow in 1956. For more on the importance of Bernal in the Soviet thinking on STR, see V. G. Marakhov and Iu. S. Meleshchenko, "Sovremennaia nauchno-tekhnicheskaia revoliutsiia i ee sotsialnye posledstviia v usloviiakh sotsializma," *Voprosy filosofii* 3 (1966): 130.

31. Anatolii A. Zvorykin, "Nauka i proizvodstvo," *Kommunist* 4 (1962): 37.

32. V. S. Semenov, "Na V vsemirnom sotsiologicheskom kongrese," *Voprosy filosofii* 11 (1962): 19–35.

33. L. V. Smirnov, "Matematicheskoe modelirovanie razvitiia," *Voprosy filosofii* 1 (1965): 67–73.

34. M. B. Mitin and V. S. Semenov, "Dvizhenie chelovechestva k komunizmu i burzhuaznaia kontseptsiia 'edinogo industrial'nogo obshchestva,'" *Voprosy filosofii* 5 (1965): 35–45.

35. Aleksandr Kuzin, Ivan Negodaev, and V. I. Belolipetskii, eds. *Sovremennaia nauchno-tekhnicheskaia revoliutsiia: Istoricheskoe issledovanie* (Moscow: Nauka, 1967).

36. For early versions of Soviet techno-optimism coupled with STR, see Genadii M. Dobrov and Anton Iu. Golian-Nikol'skii, *Vek velikih nadezhd: sud'by nauchno-tehnicheskogo progressa XX stoletiia* (Kiyv: Naukova dumka, 1964).

37. The key East European authorities of STR were, in GDR, Kurt Tessman; in Czechoslovakia, Radovan Richta, who published *Človĕk a technika v revoluci našich dnů* (Prague: Čs. společ, 1963); and in Romania, Valter Roman, who authored *Revoluția industrială în dezvoltarea societății* (Bucharest: Editura Ştiințifică, 1965).

38. For more on Richta, see Vítězslav Sommer, "Forecasting the Post-Socialist Future: Prognostika in Late Socialist Czechoslovakia, 1970–1989," in *The Struggle for the Long Term in Transnational Science and Politics: Forging the Future*, ed. Jenny Andersson and Eglė Rindzevičiūtė, 144–168 (New York: Routledge, 2015).

39. These were the volumes *Človĕk-vĕda-technika* [*Man, Science and Technology*] (1974) and *Vĕdecko-technická revoluce a socialismus* [*Scientific-Technical Revolution and Socialism*] (1971). Richta's *Civilizace na rozcestí* [*Civilization at the Crossroads*] (1966) was not translated into Russian until 1977 and was published in Prague under the title *The Freedom of Which We Talk* (Svoboda, o kotoroi idet rech'!).

40. Anatolii P. Kudriashov, *Sovremennaia nauchno-tekhnicheskaia revoliutsiia i ee osobennosti* (Moscow: Mysl, 1965).

41. Dzhermen Gvishiani, "Problemy upravleniia sotsialisticheskoi promyshlennost'iu," *Voprosy filosofii* 11 (1966): 4.

42. Arab-Ogly, *V labirinte prorochestv*, 65.

43. As early as in 1986 Mikuláš Teich had suggested that STR was a state socialist development theory. Teich, "The Scientific-Technical Revolution," 323.

44. Barbara Czarniawska, *Narrating the Organization: Dramas of Institutional Identity* (Chicago: University of Chicago Press, 1997).

45. For instance, see the argument of Michael Burawoy, "The End of Sovietology and the Renaissance of Modernization Theory," *Contemporary Sociology* 21, no. 6 (1992): 774–785.

46. For a concise overview of the background to Kosygin's reforms, which aimed to change the incentives of firms, shaped in response to faulty centralized planning, see Mark Harrison, "Economic Growth and Slowdown," in *Brezhnev Reconsidered*, ed. Edwin Bacon and Mark Sandle (Basingstoke, UK: Palgrave Macmillan, 2002), 55–58.

47. The key source is the biography of Aleksei Kosygin produced by his grandson. Aleksei Gvishiani, *Fenomen Kosygina: zapiski vnuka* (Moscow, Fond kul'tury Ekaterina, 2004), 20–32.

48. Gvishiani, *Fenomen Kosygina*, 20–32.

49. Ibid., 41–59.

50. In his memoir, Dzhermen Gvishiani briefly describes the Leningrad purge, writing that they only had an intuition that "something terrible" was going on because Kosygin was especially quiet at home and said final good-byes before going to work. It is difficult to even begin to imagine what was really happening. Historians such as Khlevniuk and Gorlizki oppose the groups of Kosygin and Beria, for whom Mikhail Gvishiani's group worked. Oleg Khlevniuk and Yoram Gorlizki, *Cold Peace: Stalin and the Soviet Ruling Circle, 1945–1953* (Oxford: Oxford University Press, 2004), 73–75; Dzhermen Gvishiani, *Mosty v budushchee* (Moscow: Editorial URSS, 2004), 24.

51. Gvishiani, *Fenomen Kosygina*, 98.

52. Kosygin reportedly personally checked on the progress of the development of Siberian oil and gas field projects. Dmitry Travin and Otar Marganiya, "Resource Curse: Rethinking the Soviet Experience," in *Resource Curse and Post-Soviet Eurasia: Oil, Gas and Modernization*, ed. Vladimir Gel'man and Otar Marganiya (New York: Lexington Books, 2010), 31–32.

53. Nataliya Kibita, *Soviet Economic Management under Khrushchev: The Sovnarkhoz Reform* (New York: Routledge, 2013), 92–93.

54. Gvishiani, *Fenomen Kosygina*, 90.

55. Ibid., 105.

56. Vladislav M. Zubok, *A Failed Empire: The Soviet Union in the Cold War from Stalin to Gorbachev* (Chapel Hill: University of North Carolina Press, 2007), 194–195, 200–202. Zubok describes Kosygin as a "red director" who not only was not keen on international relations, but was also not receptive to nuclear thinking, as expressed in his outrage over McNamara's suggestion at the Glassboro meeting.

57. Zubok, *A Failed Empire*, 194.

58. Jonathan Haslam, *Russia's Cold War: From the October Revolution to the Fall of the Wall* (New Haven, CT: Yale University Press, 2012), 214.

59. Odd Arne Westad, *The Global Cold War: Third World Interventions and the Making of Our Times* (Cambridge: Cambridge University Press, 2007), 315–316.

60. David Rockefeller, *Memoirs* (London: Random House, 2004).

61. Gvishiani surfaces in writings about the CIA and technological espionage, as a source of the information about the failing development of Soviet ICBMs in 1961. See Haslam, *Russia's Cold War*, 196.

62. Exceptions to this include the work of Matthew Evangelista and Walter Clemens, who both point to the importance of Gvishiani. However, although the significance of Aleksei Kosygin is recognized by some leading historians, such as Moshe Lewin, Kosygin's role in the introduction of scientific expertise into Soviet governance remains to be explored. Moshe Lewin, *The Soviet Century* (London: Verso, 2005).

63. Gvishiani, *Mosty*, 70–71. Following this meeting, Gvishiani established a lasting contact with Knox. Another prominent businessman whom Gvishiani lists as a good friend is Armand Hammer of Occidental Petroleum.

64. Olga Kryshtanovskaya and Stephen White, "From Soviet Nomenklatura to Russian Elite," *Europe-Asia Studies*, 48, no. 5 (1996): 711–733.

65. Robert Conquest, *The Great Terror: A Reassessment* (Oxford: Oxford University Press, 1990), 438.

66. Vladislav Zubok and Constantine Pleshakov, *Inside the Kremlin's Cold War: From Stalin to Khrushchev* (Cambridge, MA: Harvard University Press, 1996).

67. For more on Mikhail Gvishiani, see Michael Parrish, *The Lesser Terror: Soviet State Security, 1939–1953* (Westport, CT: Praeger, 1996).

68. Riska-Campbell, *Bridging East and West*, 60. In any case, the Leningrad affair took place after the marriage between Dzhermen Gvishiani and Liudmila Kosygina.

69. Gregory, *The Political Economy of Stalinism*, 17.

70. Interview 1, conducted September 30, 2009. Here and elsewhere, my interviews are completely anonymized.

71. Riska-Campbell, *Bridging East and West*, 53.

72. Willem Oltmans, "A Life of Science: Six Conversations with Dr. Philip Handler" (draft manuscript, most probably from 1981, p. 93), IIASA Archives, Laxenburg, Austria.

73. Gvishiani accompanied Wiesner on his trip to explore the presumed Soviet superiority in cybernetic technologies. Wiesner wrote that he could not identify any traces of such superiority, though Gvishiani wrote that he tried to show Wiesner "the most interesting" things. Spurgeon M. Keeny Jr., "The Search for Soviet Cybernetics," in *Jerry Wiesner: Scientist, Statesman, Humanist: Memories and Memoirs*, ed. Judy Rosenblith (Cambridge, MA: MIT Press, 2003), 86–87; Gvishiani, *Mosty*, 86.

74. Yale Richmond, *Practising Public Diplomacy: A Cold War Odyssey* (Oxford: Berghahn Books, 2008), 139.

75. Howard Raiffa, *The Art and Science of Negotiation: How to Resolve Conflicts and Get the Best of Bargaining* (Cambridge, MA: Belknap Press, 1985), 4–5.
76. Riska-Campbell, *Bridging East and West*, 55; Solly Zuckerman, *Men, Monkeys and Missiles* (New York: W. W. Norton, 1989).
77. Gvishiani, *Mosty*, 18.
78. Ibid., 20–21.
79. See the discussion of Nazi engineers in Dolores L. Augustine, *Red Prometheus: Engineering and Dictatorship in East Germany, 1945–1990* (Cambridge, MA: MIT Press, 2007), 28–29.
80. Nikolai Zen'kovich, *Samye sekretnye rodstvenniki: entsiklopedia biografii* (Moscow: Olma Medis Group, 2005).
81. Iurii Popkov, Vadim Sadovskii, Aleksandr Seitov, "Mosty v budushchee: 'ezda v neznaemoe,'" in Gvishiani, *Mosty*, 6, 21.
82. Gvishiani, *Mosty*, 21.
83. Zubok and Pleshakov, *Inside the Kremlin's Cold War*, 176.
84. At the end of her career Liudmila Gvishiani directed the Library of Foreign Literature in Moscow. Gvishiani, *Fenomen Kosygina*, 107.
85. Gvishiani, *Fenomen Kosygina*, 93; Iankovich and Zen'kovich, *Samye sekretnye*, 195.
86. I thank Marija Drėmaitė for her comment on the Soviet residential architecture.
87. For more on this area, see Graham, *Moscow Stories*, 243.
88. Gvishiani, *Fenomen Kosygina*; Gvishiani, *Mosty*; Ekaterina Zhiritskaia, "O kodekse zhizni na Nikolinoi Gore," *Nezavisimaia gazeta*, February 15, 2008.
89. Moshe Lewin, "Rebuilding the Soviet nomenklatura 1945–1948," *Cahiers du monde Russe* 44 nos. 2–3 (2003): 219–252.
90. Gvishiani, *Fenomen Kosygina*, 94–95.
91. Gvishiani, *Mosty*, 26–29, 31.
92. Fortescue, *Science Policy*, 22.
93. Even top scientists from the VNIISI, an institute under the personal patronage of Gvishiani, complained of being unable to have an impact on the Central Committee. Interview 28, April 15, 2013; Interview 29, April 15, 2013.
94. Another important channel for bringing US management into the Soviet Union was Valerii Tereshchenko, who returned to Ukraine and gave a talk on US management theories; his book was published in 1965. Popkov, Sadovskii, Seitov, "Mosty v budushchee," 11.
95. Gvishiani, *Mosty*, 51.
96. Ibid., 103.
97. This was the opinion of Yegor Gaidar, who worked at VNIISI and emphasized that, due to Gvishiani's formal role and informal connections, VNIISI could enjoy some autonomy from the ideological restrictions. Yegor Gaidar, *Days of Defeat and Victory* (Seattle: University of Washington Press, 1999), 20.
98. This was suggested both by my informants and by some historians. See, for example, Robert Wellington Campbell, *A Bibliographical Dictionary of Russian and Soviet Economists* (New York: Routledge, 2012), 131–132.
99. Popkov, Sadovskii, Seitov, "Mosty v budushchee," 11–13.
100. Gvishiani, *Mosty*, 109.
101. Zubok, *A Failed Empire*, 102–103.
102. Gvishiani, *Mosty*, 34. In 1955 the Soviet government allowed Soviet citizens to travel abroad; 700,000 of them did so in 1957. Zubok, *A Failed Empire*, 172.
103. Riska-Campbell, *Bridging East and West*, 54.
104. Gvishiani, *Mosty*, 43.

105. Gvishiani, *Fenomen Kosygina*, 94–95. For more on the signing of the Soviet-FIAT deal see Riska-Campbell, *Bridging East and West*, 86–89.

106. Gvishiani, *Mosty*, 61.

107. Clemens, *Can Russia Change?*, 162.

108. Interview 13, October 18, 2010.

109. Viacheslav V. Sychev, "Vospominaniia o V. A. Kirilline," in *Akademik Vladimir Alekseevich Kirillin: Biografiia, vospominaniia, dokumenty*, ed. by Kirillin, A. V. et al. (Moscow, MEI, 2008).

110. Kirillin, Vladimir, et al., eds. *Akademik Vladimir Alekseevich Kirillin: Biografiia, vospominaniia, dokumenty* (Moscow, MEI, 2008), 32–36.

111. For more on Kosygin's reforms and management science, see Beissinger, *Scientific Management*, 172–178.

112. For more on the predecessors of the GKNT, see Eugène Zaleski, *Planning Reforms in the Soviet Union, 1962–1966* (Chapel Hill: University of North Carolina Press, 2012). One of the first such organizations was the Commission for the Studies of Natural Productive Forces, established at the Academy of Sciences by Vladimir Vernadskii in 1915. I thank Oleg Genisaretskii for this reference.

113. For an overview, see Fortescue, *Science Policy*, 22–54.

114. This amounts on average to 250 rubles per employee, which was considered to be a good monthly salary in the Soviet Union. If a cleaner received 60 rubles, Gvishiani's salary amounted to 585 rubles, not so much more than the salary of the head of department (450 rubles). "Shtatnoe raspisanie," GKNT, 1976, the Russian State Archives of the Economy (henceforth RGAE), f.9480, op.12, d.328, l.1–19.

115. When Kosygin died in 1980, Kirillin immediately resigned from his post at the GKNT.

116. RGAE, f.9480, op.9, l.6–7.

117. The project OGAS was criticized from early on by both insiders and Western commentators. For an example, see Ben Peters, *How Not to Network a Nation* (Cambridge, MA: MIT Press, 2016).

118. Issues discussed at the collegium of the GKNT, October 9, 1971, prot. 56, RGAE, f.9480, op.9, d.1291, l.30.

119. RGAE, f.9480, op.9, d.1291, l.10.

120. RGAE, f.9480, op.9, l.6–7.

121. "Ob itogah vypolneniia plana po osnovnym nauchno-issledovatelskim problemam i vnedreniiu dostizhenii nauki i tehniki v narodnoe khoziaistvo za 1971 god," RGAE, f.9480, op.9, d.1434, 1–8.

122. For a discussion of what constituted high-technology in East-West relations, see Gary K. Bertsch, ed., *Controlling East-West Trade and Technology Transfer: Power, Politics and Policies* (Durham, NC: Duke University Press, 1988).

123. Donald F. Hornig, Lyndon B. Johnson's science advisor, to K. N. Rudnev, April 15, 1965, RGAE, f.9480, op.9, d.439, l.16; Vladimir Kirillin to Donald F. Hornig, RGAE, f.9480, op.9, d.439, l.18–19.

124. Meeting with the US science attaché Glenn Schweitzer at the GKNT, May 17, 1966, RGAE, f.9480, op.9, d.439, l.38.

125. A. Mironov, "Spravka," March 17, 1966, RGAE, f.9480, op.9, d.439, l.25–6.

126. For instance, Marchuk wrote to Gvishiani that Hewlett Packard was not only interested in selling smaller computer systems to the Soviet Union, but also in organizing campaigns to soften the embargo. Gurii Marchuk to Dzhermen Gvishiani, confidential, May 16, 1971, RGAE, f.9480, op.9, d.1964, l.1–3; "Spravka," April 12, 1973, RGAE, f.9480, op.9, d.1964, l.51.

127. Foy D. Kohler to Rudnev, April 29, 1965, RGAE, f.9480, op.9, d.439, l.20; "Spravka," November 13, 1965, RGAE, f.9480, op.9, d.439, l.24.

128. "Protocol," November 4, 1972, Russian State Archives of the Russian Academy of Sciences (henceforth ARAN), f.579, op.13, d.200, l.36.

129. RGAE, f.9480, op.9, d.439, l.55; RGAE, f. 9480, op.9, d.932, l.116.

130. RGAE, f-9480, op.9, d.1238, l.2–3.

131. Travin and Marganiya, "Resource Curse," 32–33.

132. Beginning in 1968, decision sciences and control systems were included among the key priorities for long-term research at the Academy of Sciences. ARAN, f.2, op.6m, d.435, l.180.

133. Stephen Fortescue, ed., *Russian Politics from Lenin to Putin* (Basingstoke, UK: Palgrave, 2010).

2. BRIDGING EAST AND WEST

1. The envisioned center had many working titles; thus I refer to it as the East-West Institute before it was formally established in October 1972, and as IIASA, after that date. The name IIASA began to figure in the documents in 1969, such as in Howard Raiffa's memoir of the meeting in Moscow on July 10–11, 1969.

2. Karl E. Weick, *The Social Psychology of Organizing* (New York: McGraw-Hill, 1979), 89–118.

3. Schwartz makes this point strongly and correctly, yet because of his methodological angle he underestimates the impact that IIASA would have beyond diplomacy. Thomas A. Schwartz, "Moving Beyond the Cold War: The Johnson Administration, Bridge-Building and Détente," in *Beyond the Cold War: Lyndon Johnson and the New Global Challenges of the 1960s*, ed. Francis Gavin and Mark Atwood Lawrence (Oxford: Oxford University Press, 2014), 76–96.

4. See a detailed discussion of this announcement in Riska-Campbell, 29–31.

5. See Schwartz's chapter for an excellent reconstruction of the US foreign policy context, within which the idea of the East-West institute was formulated. Schwartz, 80–81.

6. Raiffa refers to an "unpublished unfinished manuscript to Mark Thompson," which suggests that the collaboration effort was seen as an attempt by the undersecretary, George Ball, and the Council of Presidential Advisors to ease the Cold War. McGeorge Bundy invited Henry Rowen, the president of RAND Corporation, and commissioned a draft proposal from two RAND administrators, Roger Levien and Sid Winters. Howard Raiffa, "Analytical Roots of a Decision Scientist: A Memoir" (unpublished manuscript, IIASA Archives, Laxenburg, Austria, June 28, 2005), 85.

7. Andersson, "The Great Future Debate."

8. Some actors, such as Solly Zuckerman, Louis Armand, and Pierre Piganiol, involved in the MIT for Europe project, would resurface in the organization of the East-West Institute. John Krige, *American Hegemony and the Postwar Reconstruction of Science in Europe* (Cambridge, MA: MIT Press, 2006), 210–211.

9. John Krige and Helke Rausch, eds., *American Foundations and the Coproduction of World Order in the Twentieth Century* (Götingen: Vanderhoeck & Ruprecht, 2012).

10. Gemelli, "Building Bridges," 174. Note that it was Walt Rostow who convinced Johnson to establish the UN Economic Commission for Europe.

11. Dzhermen Gvishiani, *Mosty*, 133; Interview 1, September 30, 2009.

12. I am referring to the GKNT files kept at RGAE.

13. RGAE, f.579, op.13, d.199, l.170.

14. Raiffa wrote about meeting secretly with Gvishiani without staff during 1967. Bundy also told Raiffa that the first meeting was scheduled in late June 1968. Raiffa, "Analytical Roots," 85–86.

15. In 1979 OMENTO gained the status of an agency (*upravlenie*), hence its new acronym, UMENTO. RGAE, f.9480, op.12, d.58, l.74.

16. For instance, in his report on the negotiations on the East-West Institute, Raiffa listed the following Soviet representatives, whom he met during one of his last trips to Europe: Aleksandr Letov from the Soviet Academy of Sciences, an assistant for foreign affairs Andrei Bykov, Ananichev's deputy Genrik Shvedov, Viktor Krylov of the GKNT, then Boris Mil'ner of the Academy's Institute for the US and Canada Studies. Documentation of Howard Raiffa's trip appears on page 1 of "Persons met in Europe in 1972" (IIASA Archives, Laxenburg, Austria). Other meetings, such as the one in Paris, 1971, included Ananichev of the GKNT. A list of the delegates to the Paris, October 11–12, 1972 meeting appears in the IIASA Archives, Laxenburg, Austria.

17. Ronald E. Doel and Kristine C. Harper, "Prometheus Unleashed: Science as a Diplomatic Weapon in the Lyndon B. Johnson Administration," *Osiris* 21, no. 2 (2006): 66–85.

18. A report about Soviet participation at the Economic Commission of the UN, "Otchet," Geneva, October 2–7, 1967, RGAE, f.99, op.1, d.890, l.32–63.

19. Jenny Andersson, "RAND Goes to France: Genèse de la prospective française" (paper presented at *Writing the History of the 'Neoliberal Turn,'* Sciences Po in Paris, October 17, 2014).

20. Wassily Leontief, "Proposal for the establishment by the United Nations of an international scientific agency for technical economics," August 11, 1964, ARAN, f.1959, op.1, d.92, l.13–14.

21. Ibid.

22. Riska-Campbell, *Bridging East and West*, 73–4. Gvishiani forwarded Leontief's proposal to Fedorenko at the Central Institute for Mathematical Economics (TsEMI). Fedorenko expressed an interest, but no further steps were taken. ARAN, f.1959, op.1, d.92, l.11–12.

23. For more on the Club of Rome, see Elodie Vieille-Blanchard, "Les limites à la croissance dans un monde global: modélisations, prospectives, réfutations" (PhD diss., École des Hautes Études en Sciences Sociales, Paris, 2011).

24. Aurelio Peccei, *The Human Quality* (New York: Pergamon, 1977), 51; cf. Elichirigoity, *Planet Management*, 84.

25. Raiffa, "Analytical Roots," 98.

26. Herbert A. Simon, *Models of My Life* (New York: Basic Books, 1991), 301.

27. Gvishiani, *Mosty*, 161–164. Raiffa noted in 1973 that Gvishiani joined Zuckerman to criticize *The Limits to Growth* when it was published. Both Gvishiani's and American views softened, however, and Raiffa had a free hand to develop global modeling at the IIASA. See "Rapporteurs notes—advisory meeting re U.S. participation in IIASA," March 9, 1973, 12, IIASA Archives, Laxenburg, Austria.

28. "Memo of Conversation on the International Institute of Systems Analysis" December 17, 1970, IIASA Archives, Laxenburg, Austria. Peccei was, however, kept in the loop until the signing of the IIASA charter; for example, Raiffa visited Peccei on his European trip in June 1972.

29. Gvishiani, *Mosty*, 89–90.

30. Thomas Medvetz, *Think Tanks in America* (Chicago: University of Chicago Press, 2012); Christina Garsten and Adrienne Sörbom, *Think Tanks as Policy Brokers in Partially Organized Fields: The Case of World Economic Forum* (Stockholm: Scores rapportserier, 2014).

31. Akira Irye, *Global Community: The Role of International Organizations in the Making of the Contemporary World* (Berkeley: University of California Press, 2004).

32. Roger Levien, "RAND, IIASA, and the Conduct of Systems Analysis," in *Systems, Experts and Computers: The Systems Approach in Management and Engineering, World*

War II and After, ed. Agatha Hughes and Thomas Hughes (Cambridge, MA: MIT Press, 2000), 448; Raiffa, "Analytical Roots," 85–86.

33. For instance, a highly positioned US negotiator told me that the euphemism "advanced industrial society" was used to please and comfort the Soviet Union. (Interview 1.) I suggest that there may have also been another use: to prevent Third World countries from entering the East-West Institute, in part because their financial contribution was doubted, in part because they were amenable to Soviet manipulation. The hint to this is the Russian insistence that the phrase "modern societies" be removed from IIASA's preamble, which the Americans refused to do. The GDR representative did not like this term either. See Raiffa's reports, "Meeting in Moscow with GKNT representatives (June 6, 1972)," 5; "Meeting in East Berlin" (June 7, 1972), 11–12 (IIASA Archives, Laxenburg, Austria). India, for instance, wished to join IIASA until they "saw the price tag" in 1973. "Rapporteurs notes of an advisory meeting," March 9, 1973, 3, IIASA Archives, Laxenburg, Austria.

34. Ronald E. Powaski, *The Cold War: The United States and the Soviet Union, 1917–1991* (New York: Oxford University Press, 1998), 165.

35. This suggests that Gvishiani either forgot about or chose not to mention his earlier talk with Leontief in his memoir.

36. Gvishiani, *Mosty*, 124–125.

37. McGeorge Bundy to Henry Kissinger, memo, April 4, 1969, 1–2, IIASA Archives, Laxenburg, Austria.

38. "Moscow travel plans for Bundy group," n.d., probably July 1969, IIASA Archives, Laxenburg, Austria. The document does not list Carl Kaysen, who was part of the group. This group also included Joseph Bower and Howard Swearer.

39. Not all experts involved were indifferent to Czechoslovakia. For instance, Schelling was reported to have grown quite skeptical about further collaboration with "the Russians." Joseph Bower to McGeorge Bundy, May 14, 1969, IIASA Archives, Laxenburg, Austria.

40. McGeorge Bundy, memorandum of conversation with Dzhermen Gvishiani, April 3, 1969, Ford Foundation, IIASA Archives, Laxenburg, Austria.

41. "Planning for the Institute of the Systems Methodology," aide-memoire, Vienna meeting, December 8, 1969, IIASA Archives, Laxenburg, Austria. The name of the center or institute for "the study of common problems of industrialized societies" would resurface in the American documents in 1970, but by the end of the year the name IIASA made a return. "Proposed center for the study of common problems of industrialized societies," draft prepared for the NAS, November 1970, IIASA Archives, Laxenburg, Austria; "Notes on the December 3 London Meeting to Discuss the Proposed Center for the Study of the Problems of Advanced Societies," December 3, 1970, IIASA Archives, Laxenburg, Austria, 1.

42. Willem Oltmans, *A Life of Science* (unpublished manuscript, IIASA Archives, Laxenburg, Austria, n.d.), 100.

43. Philip Handler to Edward David, president's science advisor, May 18, 1972, IIASA Archives, Laxenburg, Austria.

44. ARAN, f.579, op.13, d.200, l.135.

45. Letter from unknown to Raiffa, "For heaven's sake let us get the Institute set up in such a way that it can be relied upon to achieve its purpose, as opposed to being an indiscernible ornament in a major package deal with the Russians," May 18, 1972, Cabinet Office, London, IIASA Archives, Laxenburg, Austria.

46. Gvishiani, *Mosty*, 47.

47. Ibid., 201–202.

48. "Excerpt from Dr Handler's trip report of May 1970," July 1970, 2–3, IIASA Archives, Laxenburg, Austria.

49. "Zapis' besedy," November 29, 1972, RGAE, f.9480, op.9, d.1716 (1), l.109.

50. In turn, mathematical methods and computers in planning and management were classified under "Economic Sciences." "Proekt," 1972, ARAN, f.2, op.1, d.2, l.14, 19–20.

51. US-Soviet agreement on scientific exchange, signed by Mstislav Keldysh and Philip Handler, November 4, 1972, New York, ARAN, f.579, op.13, d.200, l.137.

52. See the introduction in Gavin and Lawrence, *Beyond the Cold War*, 17–43 and Schwartz, "Moving Beyond the Cold War," 78, 80–81.

53. See, for example, the argument in Heyck, *Age of System*, 81–125; Jenny Andersson and Eglė Rindzevičiūtė, "Introduction," in *The Struggle for the Long-Term in Transnational Science and Politics: Forging the Future*, ed. Jenny Andersson and Eglė Rindzevičiūtė, 1–15 (New York: Routledge, 2015).

54. John Lewis Gaddis, *Strategies of Containment: A Critical Appraisal of American National Security Policy during the Cold War* (Oxford: Oxford University Press, 2005), 275–279.

55. "Background information provided by Professor Bower," attachment C1, for the Woods Hole, Massachusetts meeting, (August 13–14, 1970), 3–8, IIASA Archives, Laxenburg, Austria.

56. For instance, Levien and Winter drew inspiration from some of the organizational principles of the International Geophysical Year and the International Year of the Quiet Sun. Roger Levien and S. G. Winter Jr., "Draft Proposal for an International Research Center and International Studies Program for Systematic Analysis of the Common Problems of Advanced Societies," The RAND Corporation, April 1967, 17, IIASA Archives, Laxenburg, Austria.

57. Audra J. Wolfe, *Competing with the Soviets: Science, Technology, and the State in Cold War America* (Baltimore, MD: Johns Hopkins University Press, 2013).

58. Gvishiani, *Mosty*, 146–147, 149.

59. "Rapporteurs Notes—Advisory Meeting. Re: U.S. Participation in IIASA," March 9, 1973, 9, IIASA Archives, Laxenburg, Austria.

60. Oltmans, *A Life of Science*, 75–80. Under his presidency, Philip Handler reorganized NAS and NCR into many subcommittees and made sure that it was NAS members who made decisions at NCR.

61. Simon, *Models of My Life*, 291.

62. "Notes from the NAS Advisory Committee Meeting on Center for Study of the Common Problems of Industrialized Societies," October 23, 1970, 5, IIASA Archives, Laxenburg, Austria.

63. Levien and Winter, "Draft Proposal," 1–8, 15–16.

64. Simon, *Models of My Life*, 291–292.

65. "Notes from the NAS Advisory Committee Meeting," 5.

66. "Eight months summary," 1969, IIASA Archives, Laxenburg, Austria.

67. Levien and Winter, "Draft Proposal," 20–21, IIASA Archives, Laxenburg, Austria.

68. "Notes from the NAS Advisory Committee Meeting," 5.

69. Guidelines addressed to or from Joseph Bower, "The Director," November 13, 1970, IIASA Archives, Laxenburg, Austria.

70. Joseph L. Bower to Mr. McGeorge Bundy, April 11, 1969, IIASA Archives, Laxenburg, Austria.

71. Ibid.

72. Jacques Dreze was the director of the Center for Operations Research and Econometrics at Université Catholique in Louvain, Belgium. This center, established in 1965, was an important channel for transferring American game theory to Europe; for instance, Koopmans visited it. See Mirowski, *Machine Dreams*, 490.

73. Bower to Bundy, 2.

74. McGeorge Bundy, to Dr. Henry Kissinger, memorandum, April 4, 1969, 2, IIASA Archives, Laxenburg, Austria. In his memoir Simon wrote that after the case of Sakharov he did not meet to any Russian scientists, against which he was discouraged as a member of NAS, and he never visited Moscow before 1987 (Simon, *Models of My Life*, 356). Nevertheless, Arrow still suggested Simon as a candidate for IIASA's director in 1971. Kenneth Arrow to Philip Handler, April 12, 1971, IIASA Archives, Laxenburg, Austria.

75. "Notes from the NAS Advisory Committee Meeting," 5.

76. Bundy to Kissinger, 1.

77. "Meeting and luncheon," May 12, 1969, IIASA Archives, Laxenburg, Austria.

78. Russell L. Ackoff to McGeorge Bundy, May 28. 1969, 1, IIASA Archives, Laxenburg, Austria.

79. Robert Dorfman to Joseph L. Bower, May 13, 1969, 1, IIASA Archives, Laxenburg, Austria.

80. For more on Kremlinologists, see David C. Engerman, *Know Your Enemy: The Rise and Fall of America's Soviet Experts* (Oxford: Oxford University Press, 2009); and for more on conservative neoliberals, see Philip Mirowski and Dieter Plehwe, eds., *The Road from Mont Pèlerin: The Making of the Neoliberal Thought Collective* (Cambridge, MA: Harvard University Press, 2009).

81. Oltmans, *A Life of Science*, 81. In this interview, Handler adds that NAS had built in "carefully enforced institutional procedures to see to it that the standards are always rigorously maintained."

82. Robert Dorfman to Joseph L. Bower, May 13, 1969, 1, IIASA Archives, Laxenburg, Austria. The economist Dorfman envisioned this center as "a long two-storey building in a pleasant park easily accessible to the northern suburbs of London" and "a squarish building with lounge, library, refectory, and rooms for transient visitors" and a conference center nearby.

83. Gvishiani noted that the Soviet government limited international cooperation to "scientific and technical" spheres. Any cooperation that dealt with issues of humanities was "treated very skeptically." Gvishiani, *Mosty*, 150.

84. Raiffa's notes from his trip to Moscow, June 6, 1972, 6, IIASA Archives, Laxenburg, Austria. These notes suggest that both Shvedov and Mil'ner had a mandate to negotiate the research agenda and some organizational matters pertaining to the charter.

85. Howard Raiffa, "Recent trip to the member institutions of IIASA," Cambridge, Massachusetts, June 22, 1972, 4, IIASA Archives, Laxenburg, Austria.

86. "Rapporteurs notes—advisory meeting," March 9, 1973, 11, IIASA Archives, Laxenburg, Austria.

87. "Predlozheniie Akademii nauk SSSR po rasshireniiu nauchnogo sotrudnichestva s SShA," ARAN, f.579, op.13, d.196, l.82, 114.

88. McGeorge Bundy to Wassily Leontief, September 25, 1969, IIASA Archives, Laxenburg, Austria.

89. "Institute for Applied Systems Analysis: Site Considerations (Privileges and Immunities)," memorandum, March 16, 1972, IIASA Archives, Laxenburg, Austria; Howard Raiffa to Friedrich Schneider, June 14, 1972, IIASA Archives, Laxenburg.

90. See papers in relation to Raiffa's trip to Europe and Moscow in June 1972, particularly his notes from Moscow, dated June 5, 1972, IIASA Archives, Laxenburg, Austria.

91. Howard Raiffa, "Recent trip to the member institutions of IIASA," Cambridge, Massachusetts, June 22, 1972, 2, IIASA Archives, Laxenburg, Austria.

92. *Charter of the International Institute of Applied Systems Analysis* (IIASA Archives, Laxenburg, Austria, 1972).

93. "Notes on the December 3 London Meeting to Discuss the Proposed Center for the Study of the Problems of Advanced Societies," December 3, 1970, 3, IIASA Archives, Laxenburg, Austria.

94. Louis Levin, Assistant Director for Institutional Programs at NAS, to Philip Handler, October 6, 1971, IIASA Archives, Laxenburg, Austria.

95. Interview 1, September 30, 2009.

96. Jenny Andersson and Eglė Rindzevičiūtė, "The Political Life of Prediction: The Future as a Space of Scientific World Governance in the Cold War Era." *Les Cahiers européens de Sciences Po*, 4 (2012): 1–25.

97. Eden Medina, *Cybernetic Revolutionaries: Technology and Politics in Allende's Chile* (Cambridge, MA: MIT Press, 2011).

3. SHAPING A TRANSNATIONAL SYSTEMS COMMUNITY (1)

1. McGeorge Bundy and Jermen Gvishiani, "Foreword," in *Organization for Forecasting and Planning: Experience in the Soviet Union and the United States*, ed. W. R. Dill and G. Kh. Popov (New York: Wiley, 1979), vi–ix.

2. James Beniger, *The Control Revolution: Technological and Economic Origins of the Informational Society* (Cambridge, MA: Harvard University Press, 1989); JoAnne Yates, *Control through Communication: The Rise of System in American Management* (Baltimore, MD: Johns Hopkins University Press, 1993).

3. Peter Galison, "The Ontology of the Enemy: Norbert Wiener and the Cybernetic Vision," *Critical Inquiry* 21, no. 1 (1994): 228–266.

4. See Ida R. Hoos, *Systems Analysis in Public Policy: A Critique* (Berkeley: University of California Press, 1972).

5. As early as in 1967 Yezhekel Dror argued for a shift from systems analysis to a more diversified policy analysis that would be more sensitive to political struggles and issues of agenda setting. Yezhekel Dror, "Policy Analysts: A New Professional Role in Government Service," *Public Administration Review* 27, no. 3 (1967): 197–203. For a good overview of the changing institutional role of policy analysts, see Beryl A. Radin, *Beyond Machiavelli: Policy Analysis Comes of Age* (Washington, DC: Georgetown University Press, 2000).

6. Scott, *Seeing Like a State*; Josephson et al., *An Environmental History of Russia*.

7. Heyck, *Age of System*, 3–5.

8. A similar revision of the history of cybernetics, a field which split into highly different approaches to control, where some followed Wiener to underscore uncertainty and futility to apply cybernetic control to complex social systems, whereas others believed in such applications, was proposed by Robert Kline in *The Cybernetics Moment*.

9. Here I am in agreement with a similar suggestion to acknowledge a higher heterogeneity of Cold War culture, in Paul Erickson, "Mathematical Models, Rational Choice, and the Search for Cold War Culture," *Isis* 101, no. 2 (2010): 386–392.

10. Hoos, 15–17, 86.

11. Ibid., 15.

12. Aihwa Ong and Stephen Collier, *Global Assemblages: Technology, Politics, and Ethics as Anthropological Problems* (Oxford: Wiley-Blackwell, 2004); Nigel Thrift, Adam Tickell, Steve Woolgar, and William Roop, eds., *Globalization in Practice* (Oxford: Oxford University Press, 2014).

13. Kunda's ethnography of a high-tech company offers many valuable insights into the organizational logic that guided the development of the IIASA. Gideon Kunda, *Engineering Culture: Control and Commitment in a High-Tech Corporation*, rev. ed. (Philadelphia: Temple University Press, 2006).

14. Michael Thompson, "Among the Energy Tribes: The Anthropology of the Current Policy Debate," Working Paper WP-82-059 (Laxenburg, Austria: International Institute for Applied Systems Analysis, 1982).

15. See David Mindell, *Between Human and Machine: Feedback, Control, and Computing Before Cybernetics* (Baltimore: John Hopkins University Press, 2002); Heyck, *Age of System*; Thomas, *Rational Action*.

16. Agatha C. Hughes and Thomas P. Hughes, eds. "Introduction," in *Systems, Experts and Computers: The Systems Approach in Management and Engineering, World War II and After* (Cambridge, MA: MIT Press, 2000), 1–26.

17. According to Majone, in the 1970s systems analysis applied to public issues was reframed as policy analysis. Giandomenico Majone, *Evidence, Argument and Persuasion in the Policy Process* (New Haven, CT: Yale University Press, 1989), 14.

18. James J. Kay, "An Introduction to Systems Thinking," in *The Ecosystem Approach: Complexity, Uncertainty, and Managing for Sustainability*, ed. David Waltner-Toews, James J. Kay, and Nina-Marie E. Lister (New York: Columbia University Press, 2008), 3–14; Igor' V. Blauberg, Vadim N. Sadovskii, and Erik G. Yudin, *Systems Theory: Philosophical and Methodological Problems* (Moscow: Progress, 1977); Kenneth Boulding, "General Systems Theory: A Skeleton of Science," *Management Science* 2, no. 3 (1956): 197–208. Cf., Silvio Funtowicz and Jerome Ravetz, "Science for the Post-Normal Age," *Futures* 25, no. 7 (1993): 739–755.

19. Susiluoto, *Origins and Development of Systems Thinking*; Georgii Gloveli, "The Sociology of Aleksandr Bogdanov," in *Aleksandr Bogdanov Revisited*, ed. Vesa Oittinen (Helsinki: Aleksanteri Institute, 2009), 47–80; for an attempt at contextualizing Bogdanov's thought and at assessing its relevance to the contemporary theory of self-organization, see John Biggart, Peter Dudley, and Francis King, eds., *Alexander Bogdanov and the Origins of Systems Thinking in Russia* (Aldershot, UK: Ashgate, 1998).

20. See Philip Mirowski's argument in *Machine Dreams*, 177–184; Thomas, *Rational Action*, 199–209. These approaches pervaded or rather posed research problems to many disciplines and led to the formulation of the policy sciences. The first academic journal, *Policy Sciences*, was founded in 1970 and featured articles by Harold D. Lasswell and E. S. Quade, who would later write his *Handbook of Systems Analysis* when at IIASA.

21. Mirowski, *Machine Dreams*, 177–189, 314–319.

22. Here I draw on the Swedish systems thinker Lars Ingelstam, a mathematician, appointed as head of a unit for planning theory at the Royal Institute of Technology in Stockholm, who was deeply involved in setting up future studies and promoting systems approach in Sweden. Lars Ingelstam, *System: Att Tänka över samhälle och teknik* (Stockholm: Energimyndigheten, 2002), 12.

23. Collier and Lakoff, "Vital Systems Security," 26.

24. Here I draw heavily on Ingelstam's outline of systems thinking.

25. Lewis Mumford, *Technics and Civilization* (Chicago: University of Chicago Press, 2010), 52.

26. Lewis Mumford, "Authoritarian and Democratic Technics," *Technology and Culture* 5, no. 1 (1964), 2–5.

27. Jürgen Habermas, *The Theory of Communicative Action*, vol. 2, *Lifeworld and System: A Critique of Functionalist Reason*, trans. Thomas McCarthy (Boston: Beacon Press, 1987). See also Ingelstam, *System*.

28. Dror, "Policy Analysts," 199–200.

29. Andrew Pickering, *The Cybernetic Brain: Sketches of Another Future* (Chicago: University of Chicago Press, 2010).

30. Michael Ruse, *The Gaia Hypothesis: Science on a Pagan Planet* (Chicago: University of Chicago Press, 2013).

31. Celine Lafontaine, *L'empire cybernétique*; Gregory Bateson, *Steps to an Ecology of Mind* (Northvale, NJ: Jason Aronson, 1987).

32. Key works on infrastructure systems include Thomas P. Hughes, *Networks of Power: Electrification in Western Society, 1880–1930* (Baltimore: Johns Hopkins University Press, 1983); Susan Leigh Star, "The Ethnography of Infrastructure," *American Behavioral Scientist* 43, no. 3 (1999): 377–391; Paul Edwards, "Infrastructure and Modernity: Force, Time, and Social Organization in the History of Sociotechnical Systems," in *Modernity and Technology*, ed. Thomas Misa, Philip Brey, and Andrew Feenberg (Cambridge, MA: MIT Press, 2004), 185–225; Paul Edwards, S. J. Jackson, G. C. Bowker, and C. P. Knobel, *Understanding Infrastructure: Dynamics, Tensions, and Design* (Ann Arbor: Deep Blue, 2007).

33. A similar argument is pursued by Hunter Heyck; however, Heyck is inclined to treat the systems approach as a coherent field, at least in social sciences, and proposes that the systems approach can be understood as an expression of high modern science. Heyck, *Age of System*.

34. Ingelstam, *System*, 49–50.

35. E. S. Quade, "Introduction," in *Systems Analysis and Policy Planning: Applications in Defence*, ed. E. S. Quade and W. I. Boucher (New York: American Elsevier, 1968), 2; Giandomenico Majone, "Systems Analysis: A Genetic Approach," in *Handbook of Systems Analysis: Overview of Uses, Procedures, Applications and Practice*, ed. Hugh J. Miser and Edward S. Quade, Chapter 2 (Chichester, UK: John Wiley, 1985); Mirowski, *Machine Dreams*; Arne Kaijser and Joar Tiberg, "From Operations Research to Futures Studies: The Establishment, Diffusion, and Transformation of the Systems Approach in Sweden, 1945–1980," in *Systems, Experts and Computers: The Systems Approach in Management and Engineering, World War II and After*, edited by Agatha C. Hughes and Thomas P. Hughes (Cambridge, MA: MIT Press, 2000), 385–412. For a good overview of US and British OR, see John Krige, *American Hegemony and the Postwar Reconstruction of Science in Europe* (Cambridge, MA: MIT Press, 2006), 162–251; and the more recent study by Thomas, *Rational Action*.

36. For Arrow, planning equaled rational choice under uncertainty in the conditions of a Walrasian economy. Mirowski, *Machine Dreams*, 298.

37. Schelling would go on to work at IIASA only after the end of the Cold War, in 1994–1999. Amy Dahan, "Axiomatiser, modéliser, calculer: les mathématiques, instrument universel et polymorphe d'action," in *Les sciences pour la guerre: 1940–1960*, ed. Amy Dahan and Dominique Pestre (Paris: Éditions de l'École des Haute Études en Sciences Sociales, 2004), 49–82.

38. Mirowski, *Machine Dreams*, 256–257, 290.

39. "Rapporteurs notes," NAS, Washington, D.C., March 9, 1973, IIASA Archives, Laxenburg, Austria. Malone, for instance, was directly involved in negotiations with Gvishiani. RGAE, f. 9480, op.9, d.1716, l.211–212.

40. Mirowski, *Machine Dreams*, 289.

41. Ingelstam, *System*, 72. Ackoff's volume *On Purposeful Systems* (1972), coauthored with Fred Emery, was quickly translated into Russian in 1974. See also his programmatic article: Russell Ackoff, "The Systems Revolution," *Long Range Planning* 7, 6 (1974): 2–20.

42. Kenneth E. Boulding, "General Systems Theory—the Skeleton of Science," *Management Science* 2, no. 3 (1956): 197–208.

43. For more see Gemelli, *The Ford Foundation and Management Education*; Krige, *American Hegemony*.

44. Gemelli, "Building Bridges," 177–179. For more on Blackett, see Thomas, *Rational Action*, chapters 5, 7, and 17; and Erik P. Rau, "Technological Systems, Expertise, and

Policy Making: The British Origins of Operational Research," in *Technologies of Power: Essays in Honor of Thomas Parke Hughes and Agatha Chipley Hughes*, ed. Michael Thad Allen and Gabrielle Hecht (Cambridge, MA: MIT Press, 2001), 215–252.

45. Bernal, together with Zuckerman, contributed a study of blast damage during World War II and was directly involved in the debate on the expanding the role of the British government in funding science and technology after the war. Rau, "Technological Systems, Expertise, and Policy Making," 62; William Thomas, *Rational Action*, 53, 155–159.

46. Franck Cochoy, *Une histoire du marketing: Discipliner l'économie de marché* (Paris: La Découverte, 1999).

47. Gabrielle Hecht, "Planning a Technological Nation: Systems Thinking and the Politics of National Identity in Postwar France," in *Experts, Systems and Computers*, 133–160.

48. Dominique Pestre, "Le nouvel univers des sciences et des techniques: une proposition générale," in *Les sciences pour la guerre: 1940–1960*, ed. Amy Dahan and Dominique Pestre (Paris: Éditions de l'École des Haute Études en Sciences Sociales, 2004), 22.

49. Riska-Campbell, *Bridging East and West*, 295.

50. Mirowski, *Machine Dreams*, 490.

51. Rindzevičiūtė, "A Struggle for the Soviet Future."

52. For instance, Nikolai Vorob'ev, a prominent Leningrad-based Soviet game theorist, published his first work on game theory and control processes in 1955, and established the first research unit in the Soviet Union dedicated to game theory and OR in 1961. See his biographical profile on the website *Istoriia Matematiki*, http://www.math.ru/history/people/vorobev_nn (Russian), accessed March 18, 2016.

53. Gerovitch, *From Newspeak to Cyberspeak*, 179; Sergei Sobolev, Anatolii Kitov, Aleksei Liapunov, "Osnovnye cherty kibernetiki," *Voprosy filosofii* 4 (1955): 136–148.

54. Gerovitch, *From Newspeak to Cyberspeak*, 267.

55. In 1970 the Russian translation of von Neumann and Morgenstern's *Game Theory and Economic Behavior* was published by Nauka.

56. In November 1964, W. Ross Ashby visited the editorial offices of the influential journal *Issues of Philosophy*, where he spoke with members of the Moscow Methodological Circle and philosophers Erik Iudin, Oleg Genisaretskii, and Igor' Blauberg.

57. Gerovitch, *From Newspeak to Cyberspeak*, 272.

58. Krige, *American Hegemony*, 233.

59. E. B. Ianovskaia, "Pervaia Vsesoiuznaia konferentsiia po teorii igr," *Uspekhi matematicheskikh nauk* 24 (4, no. 148) (1969): 216–220.

60. "Norbert Viner v redaktsii nashego zhurnala," *Voprosy filosofii* 9 (1960): 164–168.

61. I have outlined the history of the Moscow Methodological Circle elsewhere: see Eglė Rindzevičiūtė, "The Future as an Intellectual Technology in the Soviet Union: From Centralised Planning to Reflexive Management," *Cahiers du monde Russe* 56, no. 1 (2015): 111–134.

62. Aksel I. Berg, "O nekotorykh problemakh kibernetiki," *Voprosy filosofii* 4 (1960): 58.

63. Vladislav A. Lektorskii and Vadim N. Sadovskii, "O printsipakh issledovaniia system (V sviazi s 'obshchei teoriei sistem' L. Bertalanfi)," *Voprosy filosofii* 8 (1960): 67–78.

64. Lektorskii and Sadovskii, "O printsipakh issledovaniia system," 74.

65. Georgii Shchedrovitskii, "Problemy metodologii sistemnogo issledovaniia (1964)," in G. P. Shchedrovitskii, *Izbrannye Trudy*, 155–196 *(Moscow:* Izd-vo Shkoly kul'turnoi politiki, 1995).

66. Igor' Blauberg, Vadim Sadovskii, and Erik Iudin, *Sistemnyi podhod: predposylki, problemy, trudnosti* (Moscow: Znanie, 1969).

67. Rindzevičiūtė, *Constructing Soviet Cultural Policy*.

68. Rindzevičiūtė, "The Future as an Intellectual Technology."

69. Per Angelstam et al., "Biodiversity and Sustainable Forestry in European Forests: How East and West Can Learn from Each Other," *Wildlife Society Bulletin* 25, no. 1 (1997): 38–48.

70. Radin, *Beyond Machiavelli*, 16–17.

71. B. G. Iudin, "Iz istorii sistemnykh issledovanii: mezhdu metodologiei i ideologiei," *Vestnik TGPU* 1, no. 75 (2008): 28–33.

72. V. N. Volkova and A. A. Denisov, *Osnovy teorii sistem i sistemnogo analiza* (St Petersburg: SPbGTU, 2001). Optner's volume was translated by the effort of TsEMI.

73. Their key works, published in Russian over that period, include Sadovskii and Iudin, *Research on General Systems Theory* (1969). Iudin and Blauberg published their monograph *The Development and Essence of Systems Approach* in 1973, and Sadovskii published his *The Foundations of General Systems Theory: Logico-methodological Analysis* in 1974.

74. Iudin, "Iz istorii," 29.

75. Ibid., 32.

76. Gvishiani made sure that his protégés would not unnecessarily suffer from ideological attacks, as, for instance, the sociologist Nikolai Lapin.

77. Notes from Gvishiani's meeting with Raiffa in Moscow, "Zapis' besedy" (November 27, 1972), RGAE, f. 9480, op.9, d.1716 (1), l.107–110.

78. Volkova and Denisov, *Osnovy teorii sistem*.

79. In general IIASA signed bilateral cooperation agreements with many Soviet research institutes, predominantly the ones in the system of the Academy of Sciences. For an overview of the Institute of Automation and Control, where the most advanced mathematical calculations for control purposes were developed, see A. B Kurzhanskii, "50 Years of Coexistence in Control: The Contributions of the Russian Community," *European Journal of Control* 13, no. 1 (2007): 49–60.

80. GKNT, "Prikaz," December 15, 1976, RGAE, f.9480, op.12, d.58, l.73.

81. "Poiasnitelnaia zapiska," RGAE, f.9480, op.12, d.343, l.13.

82. Nikolai Lapin, *Teoriia i praktika innovatiki* (Moscow: Logos, 2013), 18–19.

83. "Postanovlenie," ARAN, f.2, op.6m, d.435, l.108–10; RGAE, f.9480, op.12, d.58, l.73.

84. RGAE, f.9480, op.12, d.343, l.4; RGAE, f.9480, op.12, d.1865, l.4.

85. In the late 1970s the prevailing view at VNIISI was that it was pointless to develop a general systems theory; instead a loosely defined systems analysis was proposed. Interview 24, December 11, 2012.

86. RGAE, f.9480, op.12, d.343, l.9.

87. Stuart A. Umpleby and Vadim N. Sadovsky, *A Science of Goal Formulation: American and Soviet Discussions of Cybernetics and Systems Theory* (New York: Hemisphere, 1991).

88. Roger Levien to Dzhermen Gvishiani, October 21, 1977, 6, IIASA Archives, Laxenburg, Austria.

89. Raiffa, memo, September 20, 1973, 3, IIASA Archives, Laxenburg, Austria.

90. IIASA internal seminars, 1973–1974, 6, IIASA Archives, Laxenburg, Austria. The stay of Stafford Beer overlapped with those of Abel' Aganbegian, L. Evenko, and V. Tokhadze of the Soviet Academy of Science. "Project Review: Design and Management of Large Organizations," n.d., but likely 1976, IIASA, 11–12, IIASA Archives, Laxenburg, Austria.

91. Roger Levien, "IIASA after Five Years: Retrospect and Prospect," Laxenburg, November 1977, 2, IIASA Archives, Laxenburg, Austria.

92. Interview 13, October 18, 2010.

93. Levien, "IIASA after Five Years," 8.

94. Roger Levien, "Survey/Handbook Project," November 1974, 1–12, IIASA Archives, Laxenburg, Austria. This survey led to a series of publications, with Gvishiani as the chairman of the publishing board.

95. Annual Task Report, 1978, 1, IIASA Archives, Laxenburg, Austria.

96. Quade, "Introduction," 2.

97. Minutes from the twenty-fourth meeting of the IIASA Council, June 19–20, 1985, 16, IIASA Archives, Laxenburg, Austria.

4. SHAPING A TRANSNATIONAL SYSTEMS COMMUNITY (2)

1. Paul Edwards, *The Closed World: Computers and the Politics of Discourse in Cold War America.* (Cambridge, MA: MIT Press, 1996), 317.

2. As described by Nathan Ensmenger, *The Computer Boys Take Over: Computers, Programmers, and the Politics of Technical Expertise* (Cambridge, MA: MIT Press, 2010); Mirowski, *Machine Dreams*; Fred M. Kaplan, *The Wizards of Armageddon,* (Stanford, CA: Stanford University Press, 1991); Sharon Ghamari-Tabrizi, *The Worlds of Herman Kahn: The Intuitive Science of Thermonuclear War* (Cambridge, MA: Harvard University Press, 2005).

3. For instance, a Russian scientist named Mikhail Lopukhin stayed at RAND for almost one year and as a result of this stay published *PATTERN Method for Planning and Forecasting Science* (1971). Volkova and Denisov *Osnovy teorii sistem.*

4. Nils Gilman, "The Cold War as an Intellectual Force Field," *Modern Intellectual History*, First View Article (2015), 17.

5. Howard Raiffa, "Can IIASA survive?" confidential, first draft, November 19, 1981, 24, IIASA Archives, Laxenburg, Austria.

6. Mats Alvesson and Per-Olof Berg, *Corporate Culture and Organizational Symbolism: An Overview* (Berlin: de Gruyter, 1992), 16.

7. Catherine Casey, "'Come, Join Our Family': Discipline and Integration in Corporate Organizational Culture," *Human Relations* 52, no. 1 (1999): 155–178.

8. Raiffa, "Analytical Roots," 117. Another initiative pursued by Raiffa was to get Israel and Egypt to join IIASA. Interview 13, October 18, 2010.

9. Interview 3, November 2010.

10. Raiffa, "Analytical Roots," 106.

11. Raiffa's address to the IIASA staff, "Farewell," 1975, 11, IIASA Archives, Laxenburg, Austria.

12. My informant recalled that his contract for a three-year fellowship at IIASA was drawn with the GKNT. Interview 37, October 22, 2014.

13. Raiffa, "Can IIASA Survive?" confidential, first draft, November 19, 1981, 14, IIASA Archives, Laxenburg, Austria.

14. Raiffa, "Analytical Roots," 118.

15. Interview 19, October 11, 2010.

16. Raiffa, "Analytical Roots," 112.

17. Ibid., 116.

18. This is clear from the comments by Soviets and Raiffa in the archival documents stored in RGAE and IIASA. See also chapter 2.

19. Interview 6, October 22, 2010.

20. Interview 10, October 20, 2010.

21. Unsigned letter to McGeorge Bundy, April 12, 1977, 1–3, IIASA Archives, Laxenburg, Austria.

22. Martha Wohlwendt, "IIASA Employee Number 1," http://blog.iiasa.ac.at/2014/02/18/alumni-iiasa-employee-number-1/.

23. Interview 18, October 12, 2010. On the other hand, according to Slava Gerovitch only a few circles of Soviet mathematicians fostered internal, informal democratic interaction, whereas the mathematics institutes both administratively and architecturally sought to establish control over any activities of their students and staff.

24. Interview 3, November 2010.

25. Holloway, *Stalin and the Bomb*.

26. Conversation with IIASA library staff, October 2010.

27. Interview 10, October 20, 2010; Interview 37, October 22, 2014.

28. Interview 13, October 18, 2010; Raiffa, "Can IIASA Survive?" 15.

29. Interview 3, November 2010.

30. Interview 37, October 22, 2014.

31. Interview 37, October 22, 2014.

32. Interview 25, March 21, 2013.

33. "Stenograma," December 14, 1972, ARAN, f.579, op.13, d.199, l.212–213.

34. Kirillin, A. V. et al., eds. *Akademik Vladimir Alekseevich Kirillin*, 118.

35. Moiseev, *Kak daleko*.

36. The Tallinn workshop within the framework of the UN Conference on Science and Technology for Development was organized by Gvishiani. Further workshops in the series followed, in Singapore, Kuala Lumpur, and Mexico. Jermen Gvishiani, ed., *Science, Technology, and Global Problems: Trends and Perspectives in Development of Science and Technology and Their Impact on Contemporary Global Problems* (Oxford: Pergamon, 1979).

37. Interview 36, May 12, 2014.

38. Interview 3, November 2010.

39. Radin, *Beyond Machiavelli*, 21.

40. Ibid., 14–16.

41. Engerman et al., *Staging Growth*.

42. Patrick O. Cohrs, "Towards a New Deal for the World? Lyndon Johnson's Aspirations to Renew the Twentieth Century's Pax Americana," in *Beyond the Cold War: Lyndon Johnson and the New Global Challenges of the 1960s*, ed. by Francis J. Gavin and Mark Atwood Lawrence (Oxford: Oxford University Press, 2014), 58.

43. Carl Schmitt, *The Concept of the Political* (Chicago: University of Chicago Press, 1996).

44. Letter from B. E. Freeman, "Proposal to establish a US/USSR working group to model the economic and military interactions of the two countries," February 1975, 1–3, IIASA Archives, Laxenburg, Austria.

45. James H. Bigelow to T. A. Brown, March 11, 1975, IIASA Archives, Laxenburg, Austria.

46. Augustine adds that the German notion of technology was attached to irrational creativity, coupled with ideas of national greatness, and in this way removed from economic rationality. Augustine, *Red Prometheus*, 22–24.

47. For an example of politically motivated socialist engineers, see the study on Palchinskii by Graham, *The Ghost*.

48. Daniel Bell, *The End of Ideology*, 419.

49. Ibid., 419. See also John F. Kennedy, "Commencement Address at Yale University," June 11, 1962, *The American Presidency Project.* http://www.presidency.ucsb.edu/ws/?pid=29661.

50. Hermann et al., *History of CERN*, 789.

51. The IIASA archives contain documents in which Raiffa requested CERN to send him a report on their organizational structure and salary system. Similar information was

received from a representative of UNIDO, which also shared (positive) experience about Austrian support for their Vienna operations. Handwritten notes, Mark Thompson's meeting with John Birkhead (UNIDO), June 29, 1972, Vienna. These notes included a meticulous list of the long shelves and other kinds of furniture seen in the UNIDO offices.

52. Hermann et al., *History of CERN*, 345.

53. Howard Raiffa, director's farewell address, November 24, 1975, Laxenburg, Austria, 6, IIASA Archives, Laxenburg, Austria.

54. Raiffa, "IIASA's Long Range Options," November 1974, IIASA Archives, Laxenburg, Austria.

55. Raiffa, "IIASA's Long Range Options," November 1974, 15.

56. Raiffa, "IIASA's Long Range Options," November 1974, 17. Dantzig and Koopmans were in charge of the methodology project, where they developed the multiattribute utility theory, to be used to make decisions with many different objectives, such as pest control, siting a nuclear reprocessing facility, and setting standards. Tjalling Koopmans, "Methodology Project," November 1974, IIASA Archives, Laxenburg, Austria.

57. Interview 19, October 11, 2010.

58. Interview 21, May 29, 2012.

59. For more on the Soviet Aesopian discourse see Irina Sandomirskaja, "Aesopian Language: The Politics and Poetics of Naming the Unnameable," in *The Vernaculars of Communism: Language, Ideology and Power in the Soviet Union and Eastern Europe*, ed. Petre Petrov and Lara Ryazanova-Clarke (New York: Routledge, 2015), 63–88.

60. "Rapporteur notes," March 9, 1973, NAS, Washington, DC, IIASA Archives, Laxenburg, Austria.

61. Interview 3, November 2009.

62. Interview 13, October 18, 2010.

63. Interview 6, October 22, 2010.

64. Roger Levien to Dzhermen Gvishiani, June 6, 1979, 4, IIASA Archives, Laxenburg, Austria.

65. Brian Arthur, "On Competing Technologies and Historical Small Events: The Dynamics of Choice under Increasing Returns," (working paper 83-090, 1983), IIASA Archives, Laxenburg, Austria; W. Brian Arthur, *Increasing Returns and Path Dependency in the Economy* (Ann Arbor: University of Michigan Press, 1994).

66. W. Brian Arthur, "Competing Technologies and Economic Prediction," *Options* 2 (1984): 1–3; Paul A. David, "Clio and the Economics of QWERTY," *American Economic Review Proceedings* 75, no. 2 (1985): 332–337.

67. Brian Arthur to C. S. Holling, February 11, 1982, 1, IIASA Archives, Laxenburg, Austria.

68. "From QWERTY to Microsoft," *Options* (Winter 2007): 20–21.

69. The idea of cyclical development of the economy emerged in the late 1800s, when several economists, such as Clement Juglar and William Stanley Jevons, proposed statistical evidence of cycles. See Mary Morgan, *The History of Econometric Ideas* (Cambridge: Cambridge University Press, 1990).

70. N. D. Kondratieff, "The Long Waves in Economic Life [1926]," *Review (Ferdinand Braudel Center)* 2, no. 4 (1979): 519–562.

71. Dennis Meadows, "Tools for Understanding the Limits to Growth: Comparing a Simulation and a Game," *Simulation and Gaming* 32, no. 4 (2001): 526–527.

72. The Balaton Bulletin, January 1984, IIASA Archives, Laxenburg, Austria.

73. Dennis Meadows, "A Brief and Incomplete History of Operational Gaming in Systems Dynamics," *System Dynamics Review* 33, nos. 2–3 (2007): 199–203. Available at systemsdynamics.org.

74. "Mezhdunarodnyj 16-yi seminar IFAK/ISAGA po delovym igram i imitatsionnomu modelirovaniiu," *Avtomatika i telemekhanika* 10 (1986): 173–175.

75. John Sterman and Dennis Meadows, "STRATAGEM-2: A Microcomputer Simulation Game of the Kondratiev Cycle," *Simulation & Gaming* 16, no. 2 (June 1985): 174–202.

76. John Sterman and Dennis Meadows, "STRATAGEM-2: A Microcomputer Based Operational Game on the Kondratiev Cycle," (working paper, WP-84-60, IIASA, Laxenburg, Austria, August 1984), 12.

77. Sterman and Meadows, "STRATAGEM-2," 13.

78. Raiffa, memo, IIASA, September 20, 1973, 5, IIASA Archives, Laxenburg, Austria.

79. J. Curry, "IIASA Computer Services," report, November 1974, 4, IIASA Archives, Laxenburg, Austria; Gary Bertsch, ed., *Controlling East-West Trade and Technology Transfer: Power, Politics and Policies* (Durham, NC: Duke University Press, 1988), 210.

80. István Sebestyén, ed., *Experimental and Operational East-West Computer Connections: The Telecommunication Hardware and Software, Data Communication Services, and Relevant Administrative Procedures* (Laxenburg, Austria: International Institute for Applied Systems Analysis, 1983), vii.

81. For more on Soviet computer networks see Eglė Rindzevičiūtė, "Internal Transfer of Cybernetics and Informality in the Soviet Union: The Case of Lithuania," in *Reassessing Cold War Europe*, ed. Sari Autio-Sarasmo and Katalin Miklossy (New York: Routledge, 2011), 119–137; Slava Gerovitch, "InterNyet: Why the Soviet Union Did Not Build a Nationwide Computer Network," *History and Technology* 24, no. 4 (2008): 335–350; Peters, *How Not to Network a Nation*.

82. Alexandr Butrimenko, "Computer Sciences Project," report, November 1974, 8, IIASA Archives, Laxenburg, Austria.

83. Alexandr Butrimenko and I. Sebestyén, "Data Communication in the USSR: The Telecommunication Infrastructure and Relevant Administrative Procedures," in *Experimental and Operational East-West Computer Connections: The Telecommunication Hardware and Software, Data Communication Services and Relevant Administrative Procedures*, ed. István Sebestyén (Laxenburg, Austria: IIASA, 1983), 291–292.

84. Interview 5, October 22, 2010.

85. Global modeling of long-term oil demand was actively developed in Soviet research institutes beginning in the 1970s, for instance, by IIASA-based Aleksandr Papin of Novosibirsk.

86. Interview 16, October 14, 2010.

87. The Director's report on IIASA's activities, November 1976–July 1977, 12, IIASA Archives, Laxenburg, Austria.

88. *Oral Testimony to the Subcommittee for HUD and Independent Agencies, Committee on Appropriations,* 100th Cong. (29 April 1987) (statement of vice president of the Institute of Defense Analysis Chester Cooper), 1–2, IIASA Archives, Laxenburg, Austria. In his testimony Cooper described the measures that he took to consult the CIA and DOD as to the safety of his cooperation with IIASA. Both agencies confirmed that the work at IIASA posited no danger for the United States; a DOD technical expert described IIASA computer equipment as outdated.

89. Transcript of Sir Hermann Bondi's Statement to the IIASA Council, June 3, 1982, 1–4, IIASA Archives, Laxenburg, Austria. For a brief account of the Royal Society's involvement, see Peter Collins, *The Royal Society and the Promotion of Science Since 1960* (Cambridge: Cambridge University Press, 2015), 178–181.

90. Howard Raiffa, "Can IIASA Survive?" 1–4, IIASA Archives, Laxenburg, Austria. The decision was first relayed by Thomas Malone to Gvishiani via phone, at the instruction of the president of NAS, Frank Press.

91. "Can IIASA Survive?" 17–18.

92. "Can IIASA Survive?" 33.

93. Draft minutes, 19th meeting of the IIASA Council, November 11–12, 1982, 1, IIASA Archives, Laxenburg, Austria.

94. "IIASA-UK," notes from the 23rd meeting of the IIASA Council, November 21–22, 1984, IIASA Archives, Laxenburg, Austria; Robert Maxwell to Tom Lee, November 15, 1984, IIASA Archives, Laxenburg, Austria. But in November 1984 China decided to apply for a membership at IIASA; see Wu Dalan to Dzhermen Gvishiani, November 17, 1984, IIASA Archives, Laxenburg, Austria.

95. Notes from the 24th meeting of the IIASA Council, June 19–20, 1985, 8–9, IIASA Archives, Laxenburg, Austria.

96. See the correspondence between Hugh Miser and Howard Raiffa from 1988 to 1990, particularly the memo from Hugh Miser to Pry, Salewicz, and Raiffa, July 10, 1990; and letter from Howard Raiffa to Hugh Miser, March 3, 1989, and from Hugh Miser to Robert H. Pry, as well as Howard Raiffa, "A response to Raiffa's challenge to create regional IIASAs," November 8, 1988, IIASA Archives, Laxenburg, Austria.

97. Other Russian scientists involved include Danilov-Danilian, D. N. Bobryshev, and D. Levchuk of VNIISI. Documentation of East-West Symposium on Corporate Planning Practices, Fontainebleau, France February 8–11, 1978, 1–4, IIASA Archives, Laxenburg, Austria; Paul Josephson, *Red Atom: Russia's Nuclear Power Program from Stalin to Today* (New York: W. H. Freeman, 1999), 94–95.

98. Thomas Lee, "Long-Term Strategy for IIASA," June 19–20, 1985, 8, IIASA Archives, Laxenburg, Austria.

99. Draft of "Training programme on international economics, scientific and technological relations for East-West executives," IIASA Council meeting, June 19, 1985, 10, IIASA Archives, Laxenburg, Austria.

100. Stuart A. Umpleby and Vadim N. Sadovsky, *A Science of Goal Formulation: American and Soviet Discussions of Cybernetics and Systems Theory* (New York: Hemisphere, 1991).

101. Kunda, *Engineering Culture.*

102. Interview 19, October 11, 2010; Interview 11, October 19, 2010.

103. This is also the argument suggested by Jardini, who pointed out that the Great Society program of welfare sought to remove what was conceived as "political issues" from the planning process; David R. Jardini, "Out of the Blue Yonder: The Transfer of Systems Thinking from the Pentagon to the Great Society, 1961–1965," in *Systems, Experts, and Computers: The Systems Approach in Management and Engineering, World War II and After,* ed. Agatha C. Hughes and Thomas P. Hughes (Cambridge, MA: MIT Press, 2000), 385–412.

104. Importantly, this is an internal, practitioner's view; for instance, see the book by IIASA scholar, Andrzej P. Wierzbicki, *Technen: Elements of Recent History of Information Technologies with Epistemological Conclusions* (Berlin: Springer, 2014), 36.

105. See William C. Clark and C. S. Holling, "Sustainable Development and Biosphere: Human Activities and Global Change," July 1984, IIASA Archives, Laxenburg, Austria. In this draft of a paper for the First ICSU "Multidisciplinary Symposium on Global Change," Ottawa, Canada, September 22–25, 1984, Clark refers to Charles Lindblom and David K. Cohen, *Usable Knowledge: Social Science and Social Problem Solving* (New Haven, CT: Yale University Press, 1979). See also Donella Meadows, John Richardson, and Gerhart Bruckmann, eds., *Groping in the Dark: The First Decade of Global Modelling* (New York: Wiley, 1982).

106. Keyfitz thus replaced Andrei Rogers as the head of the population program. The twentieth IIASA Council meeting, June 1, 1983, 8, IIASA Archives, Laxenburg, Austria.

107. Mirowski, *Machine Dreams*, 307.
108. Ibid., 304.
109. Amadae, *Rationalizing Capitalist Democracy*, particularly Chapter 2.

5. THE EAST-WEST POLITICS OF GLOBAL MODELING

1. UNESCO was a central platform for the articulation of these views. See Perrin Selcer, "Patterns of Science: Developing Knowledge for a World Community at UNESCO" (PhD diss., University of Pennsylvania, 2011); and Sibylle Duhautois, "The Future of World Problems" (PhD diss., Sciences Po, Paris, in progress).

2. See, for example, Dzhermen Gvishiani, "Methodological Problems of Global Development Modelling," in *Science, Technology and the Future: Soviet Scientists' Analysis of the Problems of and Prospects for the Development of Science and Technology and their Role in Society*, ed. E. P. Velikhov, J. M. Mikhaiilovich Gvishiani, and S. R. Mikulinskii (Oxford: Pergamon, 1980), 21–35.

3. For instance, see Elichirigoity, *Planet Management*; Giuliana Gemelli, "Building Bridges in Science and Societies During the Cold War: The Origins of the International Institute for Applied Systems Analysis (IIASA)," in *American Foundations and Large Scale Research: Construction and Transfer of Knowledge*, ed. Giuliana Gemelli (Bologna: Clueb, 2001), 159–198. The lack of empirical research was pointed out in Michael Barnett and Martha Finnemore, *Rules for the World: International Organizations in Global Politics* (Ithaca, NY: Cornell University Press, 2004). The subject is touched upon but not fully explored in the transnational histories of science, especially with regard to the Club of Rome activities and the development of earth sciences. See Néstor Herran, Soraya Boudia, and Simone Turchetti, *Transnational History and the History of Science* (Cambridge: Cambridge University Press, 2012); and Bentley B. Allan, "Producing the Climate: States, Scientists and the Constitution of Global Governance Objects," *International Organization*, forthcoming.

4. One possible reason may be, building on Tatarchenko, the excessive focus on hardware in the histories of computing. In contrast, global modeling is principally about software. Ksenia Tatarchenko, "'A House with a Window to the West': The Akademgorodok Computer Center (1958–1993)" (PhD diss., Princeton University, 2013). For historiography, see Martin Campbell-Kelly, William Aspray, Nathan Ensmenger, and Jeffrey R. Yost, *Computer: A History of the Information Machine*, 2nd ed. (Boulder, CO: Westview, 2004); Paul Ceruzzi, *A History of Modern Computing*, 2nd ed. (Cambridge, MA: MIT Press, 2003); and Agar, *The Government Machine*.

5. See Jon Agar, "'Future Forecast—Changeable and Probably Getting Worse': The UK Government's Early Response to Anthropogenic Climate Change," *Twentieth Century British History* 26, no. 4 (2015): 602–628; Bentley Allan, "Producing the Climate: States, Scientists, and the Constitution of Global Governance Objects," *International Organization* (forthcoming); Ola Uhrqvist, *Seeing and Knowing the Earth as a System: An Effective History of Global Environmental Change Research as Political and Scientific Practice* (PhD diss., Linköping University, Sweden, 2014); and ongoing work by Kevin Baker at Northwestern University.

6. United Nations, 1084th Plenary Meeting, December 19, 1961. See the full text of this resolution at http://www.un.org/documents/ga/res/16/ares16.htm.

7. Peter Galison and Bruce W. Hevly, eds., *Big Science: The Growth of Large-Scale Research* (Stanford, CA: Stanford University Press, 1992).

8. Brian Wynne, *Models, Muddles and Megapolicies: The IIASA Energy Study as an Example of Science for Public Policy*, IIASA Reports WP-83-127 (Laxenburg, Austria: International Institute for Applied Systems Analysis, 1983).

9. Ludwik Fleck, *Genesis and Development of a Scientific Fact*, trans. Frederick Bradley and Thaddeus J. Trenn (Chicago: University of Chicago Press, 1979).

10. See also the argument by Bruce Allyn, "Fact, Value, and Science," in *Science and the Soviet Social Order*, ed. Loren Graham (Cambridge, MA: Harvard University Press, 1990), 238.

11. I base this statement on the use of the term "global" in the Gosplan documents, kept at the Russian State Archive of the Economy (RGAE).

12. Vadim Zagladin and Ivan Frolov, *Global'nye problemy sovremennosti: nauchnye i sotsial'nye aspekty* (Moscow: Mezhdunarodnye otnosheniia, 1981).

13. Viktor Los', "Global'nye problem kak predmet kompleksnykh nauchnykh issledovanii (Nekotorye itogi izucheniia global'nykh protsessov mirovogo razvitiia)," *Voprosy filosofii* 12 (1985): 3–17.

14. The Club of Rome was one of the several transnational elite networks that appeared in the postwar era. An examples of a similar associations would be the Mont Pelerin Society. For more on the organizational power of transnational elites, see Andrew Kakabadse and Nada Kakabadse, eds., *Global Elites: The Opaque Nature of Transnational Policy Determination* (Basingstoke, UK: Palgrave Macmillan, 2012).

15. For more, see Elodie Vieille-Blanchard, "Technoscientific Cornucopian Futures versus Doomsday Futures: The World Models and *The Limits to Growth*," in *The Struggle for the Long- Term in Transnational Science and Politics: Forging the Future*, ed. Jenny Andersson and Eglė Rindzevičiūtė (New York: Routledge, 2015), 92–114.

16. Paul Edwards, "The World in a Machine: Origins and Impacts of Early Computerized Global Systems Models," in *Systems, Experts and Computers: The Systems Approach in Management and Engineering, World War II and After*, ed. Agatha C. Hughes and Thomas P. Hughes (Cambridge, MA: MIT Press, 2000), 221–254.

17. Immediately criticized as flawed and imperfect, this experiment of projecting world development up to the year 2050 nonetheless stirred huge interest from the scientific community: in just four years a further nine major world development models were created. Gvishiani, "Methodological Problems," 22–27. For a discussion of concerns about world population and scientific planning of global systems, see Matthew Connelly, *Fatal Misconception: The Struggle to Control World Population* (Cambridge, MA: Harvard University Press, 2010).

18. Gvishiani, *Mosty*, 77.

19. Forrester's model was discussed in a symposium on trends in mathematical modeling, organized by the Italian National Research Council and UNESCO in December 1971. In addition to Dennis Meadows, participants included prominent Russian scientists, such as the mathematician Nikita Moiseev and the specialist in economic modeling Kirill Bagrinovskii, as well as the leading American futurologists Olaf Helmer and Alvin Toffler. Nigel Hawkes, ed. *International Seminar on Trends in Mathematical Modelling, Venice, 13–18 December 1971* (Berlin: Springer Verlag, 1973).

20. Interview 35, March 4, 2014; Meadows et al., *Groping in the Dark*; Gvishiani, *Mosty*.

21. Jay Forrester, "System Dynamics and the Lesson of 35 Years," in *A Systems-Based Approach to Policymaking*, ed. Kenyon De Greene (Berlin: Springer, 1993): 199–240.

22. Viktor Gelovani, Vladimir Britkov, and Sergei Dubovskii, *SSSR i Rossiya v global'noy sisteme (1985–2030): rezultaty globalnogo modelirovaniia* (Moscow: Librokom, 2009), 48; Efremenko, *Ekologo-politicheskie*, 104; Interview 29, April 15, 2013.

23. Interview 22, December 13, 2012.

24. Sergei Dubovskii, "Global'noe modelirovanie: voprosy teorii i praktiki," *Vek globalizatsii* 2 (2010), 57; Sergei Dubovskii and O. A. Eismont, "Long-Range Modelling of the USSR Economy," in *The Future of the World Economy*, ed. Wilhelm Krelle (Berlin: Springer Verlag, 1989), 311–324.

25. Gvishiani, *Mosty*, 141.

26. H. S. D. Cole, C. Freeman, M. Jahoda, and K. Pavitt, eds., *Thinking about the Future: A Critique of "The Limits to Growth"* (Brighton, UK: Sussex University Press, 1973).

27. Barbara Ward et al., *Science, Technology and Management: Who Speaks for Earth?* ed. Maurice F. Strong (New York: W. W. Norton, 1973).

28. Carl Kaysen, "The Computer that Printed Out W*O*L*F," *Foreign Affairs* 50, no. 4 (July 1972): 660–668.

29. "Rapporteur notes," March 9, 1973, Washington, DC, NAS, IIASA Archives, Laxenburg, Austria.

30. "Rapporteur notes," March 9, 1973; Raiffa, *Analytical Roots*; Meadows et al., *Groping in the Dark*.

31. Howard Raiffa, *An Initial Research Strategy for the International Institute of Applied Systems Analysis*, February 1973, IIASA Archives, Laxenburg, Austria.

32. The IIASA global modeling conferences scrutinized the Mesarovic-Pestel model (1974), the Latin American labor model (Bariloche, 1974), the Dutch model of international relations in agriculture (MOIRA, 1975), and the British Systems Analysis Research Unit model (SARU), which was developed by the Environment Agency (1976) and hence the only one funded by governmental body. Its Version, SARUM 76, was used by OECD Interfutures scenarios. Other models discussed at IIASA included the MRI (Polish national model, 1976), as well as the UN world model and the Futures of Global Interdependence model (FUGI, 1977) (Meadows et al., *Groping in the Dark*, 2–4).

33. The inability of global models to produce conclusive results led to a redefinition of the purpose of modeling, from policy prescription to less formal insight. For instance, in 1979 at IIASA Olaf Helmer created the Global Economic Model (GEM), not to "solve the problems directly," but to lead to "a better intuitive understanding of the problem structure." Olaf Helmer and L. Blencke, "GEM: An Interactive Simulation Model of the Global Economy" (working paper RR-79-4, IIASA Archives, Laxenburg, Austria, 1979), 2.

34. A. G. Ivakhnenko and V. G. Lapa, *Cybernetics and Forecasting Techniques* (New York: Elsevier, 1967); cf. Reuben Hersh, "Mathematics Has a Front and a Back," *Synthese*, 88, no. 2 (1991): 127–133. See also an internal debate in the VNIISI yearbook, *Modelirovanie protsessov global'nogo razvitiia: sbornik trudov VNIISI*, 8 (Moscow: VNIISI, 1979).

35. Interview 31, April 10, 2013.

36. Nikita N. Moiseev to Dzhermen Gvishiani, 1980, ARAN, f.1918, op.1, d.463, l.4.

37. See Wynne, *Models, Muddles and Megapolicies*, 5; Bill Keepin and Brian Wynne, "Technical Analysis of IIASA Energy Scenarios," *Nature* 319 (December 20, 1984): 691–695.

38. See United Nations Statistics Division, http://unstats.un.org/unsd/statcom/stacom_archive/brochures/for%20web/Brochure%20-%20IT.pdf. Accessed March 19, 2016.

39. Wassily Leontief, Ann Carter, and Peter A. Petri, *The Future of the World Economy: A United Nations Study* (Oxford: Oxford University Press, 1977), 1.

40. The archival documents reveal active correspondence between the leaders of the newly established TsEMI, the UN, and Western economists. Jakob Mosak to Nikolai Fedorenko, February 5, 1965, ARAN, f.1959, op.1, d.92, l.19–20.

41. Nikolai Fedorenko to Jakob Mosak, UN HQ Bureau of General Economic Research and Policies, ARAN, f.1959, op.1, d.92, l.18; Nikolai Fedorenko to Wassily Leontief, n.d., ARAN, f.1959, op.1, d.92, l.60. These documents are not dated, but both are filed in folders dated 1965.

42. Dzhermen Gvishiani to Nikolai Fedorenko, February 17, 1966, ARAN, f.1959, op.1, d.129, l.15.

43. Ibid.

44. Leontief's father was a professor who organized strikes in his grandfathers' factories. Bernard Rosier, ed., *Wassily Leontief: Textes et Itinéraire* (Paris: Éditions la Découverte, 1986), 78–80.

45. Wassily Leontief, "The Decline and Rise of Soviet Economic Science," *Foreign Affairs* (January 1960): 261–272; Rosier, *Wassily Leontief*, 80, 90–92; Engerman, *Know Your Enemy*, 97.

46. The Soviet philosophers appreciated Leontief's world model, calling it "more realistic" than the models sponsored by the Club of Rome. Zagladin and Frolov, *Global'nye problem sovremennosti*, 11, 182, 189.

47. Bockman, *Markets in the Name of Socialism*, 18.

48. Rosier, *Wassily Leontief*.

49. Leontief's study involved demographic, economic, and environmental spheres with benchmark years of 1980, 1990, and 2000. The world was divided into fifteen regions, each region comprising forty-five sectors of activities. The regions were linked via imports and exports of forty classes of goods and monetary transfers.

50. Leontief et al., *The Future*, 1–3.

51. Ibid., 2, 34–35.

52. Nikita Moiseev, *Algoritmy razvitiia. . . . Akademicheskie chteniia* (Moscow: Nauka, 1987), 5.

53. Nikolai Timofeev-Resovski was a pioneering population geneticist. For more about him, see Vasilii Babkov and Elena Sakanian, *Nikolai Timofeev-Resovskii* (Moscow: Pamiatniki istoricheskoi mysli, 2002); and Yakov G. Rokityanskij, "N. V. Timofeef-Resovski in Germany, July 1925–September 1945," *Journal of Bioscience* 30, no. 5 (2005): 573–580. For more about Vladimir Vernadskii, see Jonathan Oldfield and Denis Shaw, "V. I. Vernadskii and the Development of Biogeochemical Understandings of the Biosphere, c. 1880s–1968," *British Journal for the History of Science* 46, no. 2 (2013): 287–310.

54. Interview 34, April 5, 2013.

55. A. A. Petrov, *Nikita Nikolaevich Moiseev: sud'ba strany v sudbe uchenogo* (Moscow: Ekologiia i zhizn, 2011), 56.

56. Moiseev, *Kak daleko*.

57. Moiseev was skeptical about econometrics in general and even more so about Soviet econometrics, yet for him economic modeling was a lesser evil. Moiseev wrote that in order to succeed, Soviet economic forecasting had to be based on "strictly scientific modelling systems" and not "unreliable expert surveys." Nikita Moiseev, *Prosteishie matematicheskie modeli ekonomicheskogo prognozirovaniia* (Moscow: Znanie, 1975), 62; Nikita Moiseev to Dzhermen Gvishiani, 1980, ARAN, f.1918, op.1, d.463, l.16.

58. Curiously, even at VNIISI global modeling was split into the environmental and the economic, and these two groups worked in parallel and did not directly collaborate. (Interview 29, April 15, 2013.)

59. Other milieus where Soviet global models of various kinds were developed included econometric modeling at IMEMO, under Mylishka at the Main Geophysical Laboratory in Leningrad, under Marchuk and Dynikov in the Novosibirsk branch of the Soviet Academy of Sciences, even at the Moscow State University (Dubovskii, "Global'noe," 55). It was Stanislav Men'shikov, the vice director of IMEMO, who conducted econometric research at IMEMO as early as 1968 and later in Novosibirsk. (Interview 34, April 5, 2013.)

60. Nikita Moiseev, V. V. Aleksandrov, V. F. Krapivin, A. V. Lotov, Iu. M. Svirezhev, A. M. Tarko, "Global Models: The Biospheric Approach (Theory of the Noosphere)," *Collaborative Papers*, Laxenburg, Austria: IIASA Archives, July 1983.

61. In 1987 Gelovani was also appointed as the head of the Soviet branch of the World Laboratory. The World Laboratory was an interesting Cold War effort: established in 1986, it was an NGO initiated by Paul Dirac, Petr Kapitsa, and Antonino Zichichi. It was recognized by the UN and dedicated to facilitating East-West and North-South scientific exchanges. Stanislav Emel'ianov, ed., *30 let institute sistemnogo analiza Rossiiskoi akademii nauk: istoriia sozdaniia i razvitiia Institutea sistemnogo analiza, 1976–2006 gg* (Moscow: URSS, 2006), 129.

62. Interview 34, April 5, 2013.

63. "Otchet," 1982, ARAN, f.1918, op.1, d.492, l.4.

64. Lawrence Gates developed a model called OSU AGCM, which was detailed, but also faster and, unlike other American models, did not require that much of computer memory (only 100 Kb), which was very important for Soviet scientists who worked on the slow BESM-6. "Otchet," 1978, ARAN, f.1918, op.1, d.421, l.88.

65. Ibid., l.89.

66. Interview 31, April 10, 2013.

67. For an early publication discussing human impact on environmental change, see William L. Thomas, *Man's Role in Changing the Face of the Earth* (Chicago: University of Chicago Press, 1956).

68. Interview 33, February 14, 2014.

69. I draw on my interviews with the scientists who work or used to work in the Soviet Academy of Sciences' Computer Center.

70. Moiseev kept close connections with French scholars: taught French by his grandmother, he was less comfortable with English and there were many Russian exile scientists in Paris who were keen to welcome him. Petrov, *Nikita Nikolaevich Moiseev*, 50.

71. "Otchetnyi balans," RGAE, f.9480, op.12, d.343, l.9.

72. "Poiasnitel'naia zapiska," RGAE, f.9480, op.12, d.343, l.13, 18.

73. Clemens's interview with Alexander King, February 4, 1987 (Clemens, *Can Russia Change?* 138). See also Dzhermen Gvishiani, "Methodological Problems of Global Development Modelling," 33.

74. VNIISI was created on Gvishiani's initiative and in alliance with systems theoretician Boris Mil'ner, economist Stanislav Shatalin, and OR specialist Stanislav Emel'ianov. Stanislav Emel'ianov and A. Porshnev, "Vklad B.Z. Mil'nera v razvitiiu nauki upravleniia," *Rosiiskii zhurnal menedzhmenta* 4 (2004): 156.

75. Emel'ianov, *30 let*, 132–135.

76. For example, Gvishiani invited Vadim Sadovskii and Stanislav Emel'ianov to the meeting with Raiffa at the GKNT in November, 1972. RGAE, f. 9480, op.9, d.1716, l.110.

77. RGAE, f.9480, op.12, d.343, l.20; RGAE, f.9480, op.12, d.1865, l.4.

78. Dubovskii, "Global'noe," 56. Given that VNIISI's computer was produced by a major American computer producer, Digital Equipment Corporation, and the embargo on exporting computer technology to the Soviet Union, its road to VNIISI must had been an interesting one. Frank Cain, "Computers and the Cold War: United States Restrictions on the Export of Computers to the Soviet Union and Communist China," *Journal of Contemporary History* 40, no. 1 (2005): 131–147.

79. Gelovani et al., *SSSR i Rossiya*, 16.

80. Andersson, "The Great Future Debate."

81. Gelovani et al., *SSSR i Rossiya*, 18.

82. Men'shikov also knew J. K. Galbraith, whom he met at a lunch with David Rockefeller in the US Embassy in Moscow in the mid-1960s. In 1988 Men'shikov and Galbraith coauthored the book *Socialism, Capitalism and Co-existence: From a Bitter Path to a Better Prospect.* Stanislav Men'shikov, *O vremeni i o sebe* (Moscow: Mezhdunarodnye otnosheniia, 2007).

83. Leontief et al., *The Future*, iii; Men'shikov, *O vremeni*.

84. VNIISI was informed by Krelle's study, a joint project between the IIASA and the University of Bonn, 1985–1987. Wilhelm Krelle, *The Future of the World Economy: Economic Growth and Structural Change* (Berlin: Springer Verlag, 1989). Between 1984 and 1989, by Krelle's invitation, VNIISI took part in this project, where Brekke, Gelovani, and Kay developed scenarios of global development on the basis of American, Soviet, and Japanese models (Dubovskii, "Global'noe," 57; Emel'ianov, *30 let*, 141).

85. Interview 28, April 15, 2013.

86. Gelovani, Britkov and Dubovskii, *SSSR i Rossiya*, 64; Dubovskii and Eismont, "Long-Range Modelling."

87. Gelovani, Britkov and Dubovskii, *SSSR i Rossiya*, 7.

88. Nikolai Fedorenko, *Vspominaia proshloe, zagliadyvaiu v budushchee* (Moscow: Nauka, 1999), 387.

89. Interview 31, April 10, 2013.

90. Michael Ellman and Vladimir Kontorovich, eds., *The Destruction of the Soviet Economic System: An Insiders' History* (Armonk, NY: M. E. Sharpe, 1998): 76–85.

91. Efremenko, *Ekologo-politicheskie*.

92. D. Chernikov, A. Batizi, N. Volkov, and A. Ivanov to Thomas Lee, November 28, 1986, IIASA Archives, Laxenburg, Austria.

93. Gelovani, Britkov, and Dubovskii, *SSSR i Rossiya*, 48, 80.

94. Dubovskii, "Global'noe," 56–57.

95. Ibid., 58.

96. Interview 28, April 15, 2013.

97. Nikita Moiseev to Dzhermen Gvishiani, 1980, ARAN, f.1918, op.1, d.463, l.12.

98. Donald MacKenzie, *Mechanizing Proof: Computing, Risk, and Trust* (Cambridge, MA: MIT Press, 2001).

99. P. N. Fedoseyev, "Topical Problems of Our Time," in *Science, Technology and the Future: Soviet Scientists' Analysis of the Problems of and Prospects for the Development of Science and Technology and Their Role in Society*, ed. Evgenii Velikhov, M. Gvishiani, and S. R. Mikulinsky (Oxford: Pergamon, 1980), 3–20.

100. Efremenko, *Ekologo-politicheskie*.

101. Petrov, *Nikita Nikolaevich Moiseev*.

102. K. V. Ananichev's meeting with the Japanese delegation, "Zapis' besedy," GKNT (April 13, 1972), RGAE, f.9480, op.9, d.1716, l.37.

103. Gvishiani, *Mosty*, 239.

104. Wynne, *Models, Muddles and Megapolicies*," 12–13.

6. FROM NUCLEAR WINTER TO THE ANTHROPOCENE

1. Evangelista, *Unarmed Forces*, 73.

2. I use the terms "nuclear winter study" and "nuclear winter project" interchangeably. There were many outcomes to the project on the environmental consequences of nuclear war, and some of them pointed to milder effects, which were not described as a nuclear winter. However, as the nuclear winter became a distinct brand of this project, and for the sake of brevity, I decided to use "nuclear winter" throughout the chapter, although strictly speaking this is not an entirely correct expression.

3. Iurii M. Svirezhev, *Ecological and Demographic Consequences of Nuclear War* (Moscow: Computer Center of the USSR Academy of Sciences, 1985), 6; Evgenii Velikhov, "Sovetskaia programma mira i zadachi sovetskih uchenykh," in *Klimaticheskie i biologicheskie posledstviia iadernoi voiny*, ed. Evgenii Velikhov (Moscow: Nauka, 1987), 24; Robert McNamara, *Blundering into Disaster: Surviving the First Century of the Nuclear Age* (London: Bloomsbury, 1987).

4. See the 2012 issue of *The Bulletin of the Atomic Scientists*.

5. Lawrence Badash, *A Nuclear Winter's Tale: Science and Politics in the 1980s* (Cambridge, MA: MIT Press, 2009); Paul Rubinson, "The Global Effects of Nuclear Winter: Science and Antinuclear Protest in the United States and the Soviet Union in the 1980s," *Cold War History* 14, no. 1 (2014): 47–69. Badash cites the work of Lynn Eden in passing, but does not engage more deeply with the issue of the status of fire research in the United States in the 1970s and 1980s. Extrapolating from Eden's study, it can be suggested that the prognosis of nuclear winter was met with skepticism partially because of the prevailing view on the unpredictability of fire. In turn, had Eden paid more attention to the nuclear winter study, perhaps she would have traced a link between the growing evidence of the environmental consequences of nuclear war, caused by fires, and the US government's sudden support for fire research. Lynn Eden, *Whole World on Fire: Organizations, Knowledge, and Nuclear Weapons Devastation* (Ithaca, NY: Cornell University Press, 2004).

6. Paul Edwards, "Entangled Histories: Climate Science and Nuclear Weapons Research," *Bulletin of the Atomic Scientists* 68, no. 4 (2012): 28–40.

7. Dipesh Chakrabarty, "The Climate of History: Four Theses," *Critical Inquiry* 35, no. 2 (2008): 197–222.

8. Chakrabarty, for instance, wrote "the industrial way of life has acted much like the rabbit hole in Alice's story; we have slid into a state of things." Chakrabarty, "The Climate," 217.

9. David R. Jardini, *Out of the Blue Yonder: The RAND Corporation's Diversification into Social Welfare Research, 1946–1968* (PhD dissertation, Carnegie Mellon University, 1996); Rohde, *Armed With Expertise*; Andersson, "The Great Future Debate."

10. S. M. Amadae, *Prisoners of Reason: Game Theory and Neoliberal Political Economy* (Cambridge: Cambridge University Press, 2016).

11. The essence of nuclear strategy is articulated in a chain of strikes and retaliations: the preemptive strike or first strike, the counter strike or launch-on-warning strike, and the retaliatory strike. Pavel Podvig, *Russian Strategic Nuclear Forces* (Cambridge, MA: MIT Press, 2001), 50; Francis J. Gavin, *Nuclear Statecraft: History and Strategy in America's Atomic Age* (Ithaca, NY: Cornell University Press, 2012).

12. Herman Kahn, *On Thermonuclear War* (Princeton, NJ: Princeton University Press, 1960). For more about the rationalization of nuclear strategy at RAND, see Kaplan, *The Wizards of Armageddon*, and Ghamari-Tabrizi, *The Worlds of Herman Kahn*.

13. Evangelista emphasized the importance of this point, arguing that Soviet-Western interaction had a substantial effect in institutionalizing the notion that scientists were important actors, messengers between the opposing governments. Evangelista refers to Jeremy Stone for explication of this rationale. The empowerment, it seems, was mutual. Evangelista, *Unarmed Forces*, 138; Jeremy J. Stone, *Strategic Persuasion: Arms Limitations through Dialogue* (New York: Columbia University Press, 1967).

14. Snyder, Jack L. *The Soviet Strategic Culture: Implications for Limited Nuclear Operations.* RAND Report R-2154-AF, September 1977. Available online at https://www.rand.org/content/dam/rand/pubs/reports/2005/R2154.pdf.

15. Kahn, *On Thermonuclear War*.

16. Clemens, *Can Russia Change?* 78. Nevertheless, nuclear calamities were, at least publicly, held at an optimistic minimum: in the 1960s US nuclear strategists claimed that about 80 percent of the American population would survive a nuclear exchange. Lee Clarke, *Mission Improbable: Using Fantasy Documents to Tame Disaster* (Chicago: University of Chicago Press, 1999).

17. Badash, *A Nuclear Winter's Tale*, 8.

18. See Podvig, *Russian Strategic Nuclear Forces*; Jonathan Coopersmith, "The 'Normalcy' of Russian, Soviet, and Post-Soviet Science and Technology Studies," *Technology and Culture* 47, no. 3 (2006): 623–637.

19. In the 1960s the Politbureau of CPSU assumed a form of the top nuclear warfare commanding organization; the specific elements were worked out by the Ministry of Defense and General Staff. The nuke tests in the Soviet Union were conducted under the umbrella of the Ministry of Medium Machine Building (Minsredmash) and the Ministry of Defense. The Defense Industry Department at the Computer Center was mainly excluded from decision-making, while foreign policy was devised by the Ministry of Foreign Affairs. For a full overview, see Podvig, *Russian Strategic Nuclear Forces*, 39–40. Some research groups at the Academy of Sciences' institutes were also involved. For instance, nuclear strategy for the balance of powers was developed at the Institute for Systems Research in Moscow. Emel'ianov, *30 let*, 133–136.

20. Podvig, *Russian Strategic Nuclear Forces*, 9, 14, 16, 18–20. The negotiations were resumed with Gorbachev in power in 1985. In 1988 Gorbachev renounced Brezhnev's doctrine or intervention into other countries, and international class struggle was no longer the foundation of Soviet foreign policy. The START I treaty was signed in July 1991.

21. Kai-Henrik Barth, "Catalysts of Change: Scientists as Transnational Arms Control Advocates in the 1980s," *Osiris* 21, no. 1 (2006), 187.

22. One of the first postwar East-West scientists' meetings took place in the Conference on the Peaceful Uses of Atomic Energy in Geneva, 1955. In the same year, the American physicist Victor Weisskopf was invited to visit Dubna, one of the key Soviet military research towns. The 1955 events that set the path for Pugwash already included a group of four Soviet scientists led by Aleksandr Topchiev, who endorsed Russell-Einstein's statement. For more, see Evangelista, *Unarmed Forces*, 29, 31.

23. Clemens, *Can Russia Change?* 121–122.

24. Evangelista, *Unarmed Forces*, 88.

25. Badash, *A Nuclear Winter's Tale*.

26. A similar argument is pursued by Kelly Moore, who points out that not all social movements aim to change legislation. Instead, wrote Moore, social movements often seek to change norms or behavior, the effect on which may be revealed only in the long term. Kelly Moore, *Disrupting Science: Social Movements, American Scientists, and the Politics of the Military, 1945–1975* (Princeton, NJ: Princeton University Press, 2008), 15.

27. For instance, Arbatov referred to both ecological crises and the nuclear winter study as the key reasons to look for a new US-Soviet strategic agreement. Georgy A. Arbatov, "Where Should We Go from Here: A Soviet View," in *Windows of Opportunity: From Cold War to Peaceful Competition in U.S.-Soviet Relations*, ed. Graham T. Allison, William L. Ury, and Bruce J. Allyn (Cambridge, MA: Ballinger, 1989), 297.

28. Badash, *A Nuclear Winter's Tale*.

29. Frank von Hippel, "Gorbachev's Unofficial Arms-Control Advisers." Soviet scientists were quite confident that the nuclear winter report would convince the Soviet government that a nuclear arms' race was a waste of resources. Gelovani et al., *SSSR i Rossiia v global'noi sisteme* (Moscow: Librokom, 2009).

30. With the exception of Paul Edwards. Paul Edwards, "Entangled Histories."

31. A prominent commentator on Russian society, Masha Gessen, described Moiseev as a rare example of a nonconformist Soviet intellectual who enjoyed a high status in both academic and governmental circles. See Masha Gessen, *Dead Again: The Russian Intelligentsia After Communism* (London: Verso, 1997), 27. Gessen, however, was not correct on several important details: Moiseev was not involved hands-on in the design of the nuclear winter model and his travels abroad did not appear to be restricted; indeed, Moiseev traveled widely in the West both before and after the nuclear winter report.

32. See Collier and Lakoff, "Vital Systems Security"; and Claudia Aradau and Rens van Munster, *Politics of Catastrophe: Genealogies of the Unknown* (New York: Routledge, 2011).

33. See Kline, *Cybernetics Moment*.

34. Rohde, *Armed with Expertise*.

35. Stephen Schneider, interview by Robert M. Chervin, January 10–13, 2002, 75–76, transcript, American Meteorological Society, University Corporation for Atmospheric Research, available online at http://nldr.library.ucar.edu/repository/assets/ams/AMS-000-000-000-191.pdf.

36. M. K. Kerimov, "Kratkaia istoriia Vychislitel'nogo tsentra imeni akademika A. A. Dorodnitsyna Rossiiskoi Akademii Nauk (k 50-desiletiiu so vremeni osnovaniia)," *Zhurnal vychislitel'noi matematiki i matematicheskoi fiziki* 46, no. 7 (2006): 1178. Also, the scientists at the Computer Center designed a game to simulate military actions among three (unnamed) states, which, according to Moiseev, was intercepted by the CIA. "Protokol" (December 14, 1983), ARAN, f.1918, op.1, d.537, l. 66–67.

37. Interview 33, February 14, 2014.

38. Vassily Sokolov et al., "Turning Points: The Management of Global Environmental Risks in the Soviet Union," in *Learning to Manage Global Environmental Risks*, vol. 1, *A Comparative History of Social Responses to Climate Change, Ozone Depletion, and Acid Rain,* ed. The Social Learning Group (Cambridge, MA: MIT Press, 2001), 139–166.

39. Edwards, *A Vast Machine*. The first meeting of East and West seismologists was organized to discuss the control of nuclear tests, in July 1958. According to Evangelista, in this meeting it appeared that Western and Soviet scientists knew so much about each other that they did not need an introduction. In addition to the seismologists' meeting, one should mention that the World Meteorological Organization, established in 1947, sponsored a global atmospheric research program in 1967. The World Weather Watch, established in 1963, was another important organization facilitating East-West contacts. Evangelista, *Unarmed Forces*, 60–61.

40. SCOPE was funded through national membership, but its projects received support from various UN agencies, WHO, business corporations such as Exxon and Shell, and Ford, Carnegie, and other American foundations. Gilbert White, "SCOPE: The First Sixteen Years," *Environmental Conservation* 14, no. 1 (1987): 7–13.

41. The collaborations based at SCOPE led to the setting up of the Intergovernmental Panel for Climate Change.

42. Soviet side was represented by the scientific secretary N. K. Lukianov and G. A. Zavarzin.

43. In 1948 the Computer Center belonged to the Institute of Precision Mechanics and Computer Technology; in 1956 it was transferred to the Steklov Institute of Mathematics, although even then the center was an independent unit with its own directorship and budget. Kerimov, "Kratkaia."

44. Gregory D. Crowe and Seymour E. Goodman, "S. A. Lebedev and the Birth of Soviet Computing," *IEEE Annals of the History of Computing* 16, no. 1 (1994): 4–24.

45. Kerimov, "Kratkaia."

46. Nikita Moiseev, *Byt' ili ne byt'... chelovechestvu?* (Moscow: n.p. 1999), 7; Moiseev, "Otchet" (February 13–17, 1978, March 2, 1978), ARAN, f.1918, op.1, no.421, l.85–87, 92.

47. For more on Kovda, see Oldfield and Shaw, "V. I. Vernadskii."

48. This, and the fact that the figure of a founding father is very popular in the Russian scientific and literary culture, may well explain why Russian historiography nominates Moiseev as the central figure in the nuclear winter project. See, for instance, V. G. Gorokhov,

ed., *Sotsialnaia i ekologicheskaia otsenka nauchno-tekhnicheskogo razvitiia* (Moscow: Rossiskoe filosofskoe obshchestvo, 2007), 4. Indeed, although Moiseev never detail-managed the project, his personal support was vital. Interview 31, April 10, 2013; Interview 34, April 5, 2013.

49. Having dedicated many pages to detail his experience of the new and powerful Cray-1 computer (installed at NCAR in 1977), Aleksandrov pointed out huge American investments in the atmosphere sciences. He referred to a decision by the National Ocean and Atmosphere Administration to provide the laboratory of Geophysical Dynamics at Princeton University with the Cray-2, an expensive supercomputer, to argue that the studies of the interaction of ocean and atmosphere were of extreme importance. ARAN, f.1918, op.1, d.421, l. 84–112.

50. Nikita Moiseev, *Kak daleko*, 211.

51. ARAN, f.1918, op.1, d.421, l.84–86. The idea of sending Soviet atmosphere scientists to the United States was voiced as early as 1976. The length of stay was to be one year due to the complexity of the work, but in 1977 the American side insisted on cutting this stay to six months. When the scientists arrived in the United States in 1978, the stay was further shortened to five months, so short a time that, wrote Aleksandrov, it was impossible to complete his task on an "unfamiliar computer system."

52. Vladimir Aleksandrov, "NCAR is Host to Two Soviet Scientists," *Staff Notes* (NCAR's internal newsletter) 13, no. 21 (June 2, 1978): 1–2.

53. ARAN, f.1918, op.1, d.421, l. 87–91, 125–126.

54. Schneider, interview, 136.

55. ARAN, f.1918, op.1, d.421, l.92.

56. Ibid., l.112.

57. Anatolii A. Dorodnitsyn to Georgii K. Skriabin, January 6, 1983. ARAN, f.1918, op.1, no.522, l.189.

58. ARAN, f.1918, op.1, d.421, l.85.

59. Ibid., l.150–151; Moiseev, *Kak daleko*.

60. According to the report kept at ARAN, the title of the film is "The General Circulation of the Atmosphere in January as Computed by Cray-1." ARAN, f.1918, op.1, d.421, l.150–151.

61. Moiseev, *Kak daleko*, 242–243.

62. Anatolii Dorodnitsyn, ed. *Matematicheskie modeli ekosistem: ekologicheskie i demograficheskie posledstviia iadernoi voiny* (Moscow: Nauka, 1986), 9.

63. There was also a simpler version, in which marshland was substituted for ocean. Nikita Moiseev, V. V. Aleksandrov, and A. M. Tarko, *Chelovek i biosfera: opyt sistemnogo analiza i eksperimenty s modeliami* (Moscow: Nauka, 1985), 5, 109.

64. Evangelista, *Unarmed Forces*, 154.

65. V. V. Aleksandrov, "Otchet," n.d. ARAN, f.1918, op.1, no. 485, l.23.

66. Schneider, interview, 74–79.

67. For a description of the cumbersome process of traveling abroad during the Soviet era, see Paul R. Josephson, *Lenin's Laureate: Zhores Alferov's Life in Communist Science* (Cambridge, MA: MIT Press, 2010), 139–146.

68. The US-Soviet agreement to collaborate in the protection of environment was concluded in 1972.

69. A. A. Dorodnitsyn to G. K. Skriabin, January 6, 1983, ARAN, f.1918, op.1, d.522, l.190.

70. ARAN, f.1918, op.1, d.522, l.191. The same proposal asked for permission for the American scientists from Livermore Laboratory, NYU in Stony Brook, and Gates of Oregon University to visit the Computer Center.

71. In September 1982 a declaration was signed at the *Pontifical Academy* of Sciences by representatives of thirty-six science academies, including the United States, the United Kingdom, France, and the Soviet Union, stating that nuclear weapons should not be either instruments of politics or war. Velikhov, "Sovetskaia programma," 24.

72. Later Velikhov became an informal science advisor for Gorbachev on nuclear issues. Velikhov and Moiseev were put in charge of a scientific council that dealt with the consequences of Chernobyl. Barth, "Catalysts of Change," 185, 195.

73. Weick, *The Social Psychology of Organizing*.

74. Clarke, *Mission Improbable*, 36.

75. Badash, *A Nuclear Winter's Tale*, 47–116.

76. The empirical data and causal relations were provided by experimental studies in atmosphere and ecology research, but drawn by way of analogy from rather exotic studies, such as the investigations of dust clouds on Mars and in the stratosphere, related to the project Mariner 9 (1971) and historical cases of smoke emissions, such as Tambora volcanic eruptions and large urban fires.

77. I base this account on Aleksandrov's report, filed in the archives of the Russian Academy of Sciences. Oddly, the files do not seem to be complete; for instance, other sources mention the participation of Moiseev and Golitsyn, although this was not indicated by Aleksandrov or other documents. Also, the consulted files do not contain reports from the Washington conference launching the nuclear winter report. ARAN, f.1918, op.1, d.522.

78. ARAN, f.1918, op.1, d.522, l.7, 8.

79. Aleksandrov was also receptive to Sagan's note that there may be a migration of dust clouds from the Northern hemisphere to the Southern hemisphere. ARAN, f.1918, op.1, d.522, l. 13.

80. The interviews testify to the fact that Velikhov was inspired to establish this committee by Lown, who insisted that Velikhov needed "a think tank" in order to have better access to policy makers. Evangelista, *Unarmed Forces*, 160.

81. Velikhov, "Sovetskaia programma," 3, 19.

82. von Hippel, "Gorbachev's Unofficial Arms-Control Advisors," 41.

83. Evangelista, *Unarmed Forces*, 51–52; Holloway, *Stalin and the Bomb*.

84. Velikhov, "Sovetskaia programma," 6. See also Anatolii Dorodnitsyn, ed., *Ekologicheski i demograficheskie posledstviia iadernoi voiny* (Moscow: Nauka, 1986).

85. Hersh, "Mathematics Has a Front and a Back."

86. Interview 34, April 5, 2013; Interview 31, April 10, 2013.

87. Moiseev et al., *Chelovek i biosfera*, 108.

88. Moiseev, *Kak daleko*, 245.

89. Svirezhev, *Ecological and Demographic Consequences*, 31–52.

90. Eden, *Whole World on Fire*, 290.

91. Maurice Marois, ed., *Documents pour l'histoire*, vol. 3, *Les grandes conférences internationales: l'homme et la planète* (Paris: Editions Rive Droite, 1997), 249.

92. Marois, *Documents pour l'histoire*, 250.

93. Because I did not find support for this in the archival records of the Computer Center, I base this statement on my interview with a member of the group (Interview 31, April 10, 2013). Also, in his memoir Moiseev wrote that he spoke about nuclear winter at the Helsinki meeting. See Moiseev, *Kak daleko*.

94. Aleksandr Tarko and Valerii Parkhomenko, "Iadernaia zima: istoriia voprosa i prognozy," *Biosfera* 3, no. 2 (2011): 164–173.

95. Interview 31, April 10, 2013.

96. Nikita Moiseev, *Razmyshlenie o sovremennoi politologii* (Moscow, 1999).

97. Another roundtable discussing the international physicians' movement was broadcast by Ostankino in June 1982. Evangelista, *Unarmed Forces*, 155.

98. The project was implemented by Gosteleradio and the Unison Corporation. For more, see Helene Keyssar, "Space Bridges: The U.S.-Soviet Space Bridge Resource Center," *PS: Political Science and Politics* 27, no. 2 (1994): 247–253. At that time the broadcasted Soviet-American discussions were not completely glossed, but often featured quite sharp debates and disagreements; see Ellen Mickiewicz, *Split Signals: Television and Politics in the Soviet Union* (Oxford: Oxford University Press, 1992), 50–53.

99. Vladimir Pozner, *Parting with Illusions* (New York: Atlantic Monthly Press, 1990), 253, 228; V. V. Mukusev, *Razberemsia: fragmenty interv'u, vystuplenii, stati, stsenarii i rassledovaniia raznykh let* (Moscow: Nauka, 2007), 56.

100. Erlich et al., *The Cold and the Dark: The World after Nuclear War* (New York: W. W. Norton, 1984).

101. Interview 33, February 14, 2014.

102. On the initiative of Allen, with representatives of Internews, Kim Spencer of Internews negotiated with Gosteleradio. Erlich et al., *The Cold and the Dark*, xviii–xix.

103. According to Greenaway, Thomas Malone was instrumental in convincing SCOPE to undertake the project which was to become ENUWAR, using his informal method of telephoning. Greenaway also noted that SCOPE only sought to deliver "objective" and "hard data" to the policy makers, as opposed to concrete policy guidelines. Frank Greenaway, *Science International: A History of the International Council of Scientific Unions* (Cambridge: Cambridge University Press, 1996), 179.

104. White, "SCOPE," 9.

105. "Otchet," May 1984, ARAN, f.1918, op.1, d.546, l.15–16.

106. See, for instance, Peter C. Sederberg, ed., *Nuclear Winter, Deterrence and the Prevention of Nuclear War* (Westport, CT: Praeger: 1986).

107. It was Leo Szilard who in 1964 voiced the idea that scientists' meetings that would not be torn by political tensions should be funded by the Vatican. In 1982 the *Pontifical Academy of Sciences* held a meeting on the nuclear arms race at which Velikhov represented the Soviet side. Evangelista, *Unarmed Forces*, 158.

108. Velikhov, "Sovetskaia programma," 21, 23.

109. Moiseev et al., *Chelovek i biosfera*, 126.

110. Schneider, interview.

111. "Otchet," 1985, ARAN, f.1918, op.1, d.568, l.2.

112. "Otchet," ARAN, f.1918, op.1, d.546, l.2–3.

113. Interview 31, April 10, 2013.

114. ARAN, f.1918, op.1, d.585, l.3, 17.

115. The total five-year budget for the project was 137,200 / 77,700 rubles. Svirezhev's group received 68,700 / 49,000 rubles. ARAN, f.1918, op.1, d.540, l.2, 25; Dorodnitsyn, *Matematicheskie modeli ekosistem*, 9.

116. Interview 31, April 10, 2014.

117. Moiseev, *Kak daleko*.

118. Nikita Moiseev and I. T. Frolov, "Vysokoe soprikosnovenie: obshchesto, chelovek, i priroda v vek mikroelektroniki, informatiki i biotekhnologii," *Voprosy filosofii* 9 (1984): 40.

119. For instance, a commentary on Gorbachev's "new thinking" stated that the United States posed nothing less than an "anthropogenic threat" and explicitly referred to Vernadskii in describing the world as a noosphere. V. M. Gavrilov and M. Iu. Sitnina, "Militarizatsiia kosmosa: novaia global'naia ugroza," *Voprosy filosofii* 11 (1985): 98–99.

120. Viktor Los', "Global'nye problem kak predmet kompleksnykh nauchnykh issledovanii (Nekotorye itogi izucheniia global'nykh protsessov mirovogo razvitiia)," *Voprosy filosofii* 12 (1985): 3–17.

121. Vadim Zagladin, "Programmnye tseli KPSS i global'nye problemy," *Voprosy filosofii* 2 (1986): 3.

122. Moiseev et al., *Chelovek i biosfera*, 5.

123. Schneider, interview, 110.

124. Moiseev et al., *Chelovek i biosfera*, 9. For more on Vernadskii, see Vaclav Smil, *The Earth's Biosphere: Evolution, Dynamics and Change* (Cambridge, MA: MIT Press, 2003). Some environmental modelers were acutely aware of the implications of this instrument on the notions of human agency and control. Science intertwined with philosophy and the history of ideas in a serendipitous way: for instance, it was during his stay at the IIASA in 1984 that Rafal Serafin, a Polish scientist, wrote the report connecting the ideas of Vernadskii, de Chardin, Lovelock, and Moiseev.

125. Moiseev, *Kak daleko*, 235.

126. Norbert Wiener, Arturo Rosenblueth, and Julian Bigelow, "Behavior, Purpose and Teleology," *Philosophy of Science* 10, no. 1 (1943): 18–24.

127. Moiseev et al., *Chelovek i biosfera*, 9.

128. Barth, "Catalysts of Change."

129. Focusing on the role of Sagan, Lynn Eden suggests that the nuclear winter campaign was mainly directed toward the "outside," building "public and political support" for the reduction of nuclear arms, whereas fire researchers, such as Hal Brode, played "an inside game," addressing the internal needs of this research area. However, this thesis suffers from "the Sagan effect": the nuclear winter study was also part of the inside game, as it was successfully used to increase the priority status of atmosphere research. Eden, *Whole World on Fire*, 240–241.

130. Moore, *Disrupting Science*; Albert O. Hirschman, *Exit, Voice, and Loyalty: Responses to Decline in Firms, Organizations, and States* (Cambridge, MA: Harvard University Press, 1970).

131. Naomi Oreskes and Erik M. Conway, *Merchants of Doubt: How a Handful of Scientists Obscured the Truth on Issues from Tobacco Smoke to Global Warming* (New York: Bloomsbury, 2010). I base this on the study of Leon Gouré's file at the Hoover Institution Archives.

132. Moiseev et al., *Chelovek i biosfera*, 11.

7. ACID RAIN

1. Göran Sundqvist, "Fewer Boundaries and Less Certainty: The Role of Experts in European Air Policy," in *Governing the Air: The Dynamics of Science, Policy, and Citizen Interaction*, ed. Rolf Lidskog and Göran Sundqvist (Cambridge, MA: MIT Press, 2011), 203–207.

2. Robert G. Darst, *Smokestack Diplomacy: Cooperation and Conflict in East-West Environmental Politics* (Cambridge, MA: MIT Press, 2001), 15, 21.

3. VanDeveer, "Ordering Environments"; Duncan Liefferink, *Environment and the Nation State: The Netherlands, the European Union and Acid Rain* (Manchester, UK: Manchester University Press, 1996). See also Lidskog and Sundqvist, eds., *Governing the Air*, and Anthony Patt, "Separating Analysis from Politics: Acid Rain in Europe," *Review of Policy Research* 16, nos. 3–4 (1999), 104–137. For documentation, see Joseph Alcamo, Roderick Shaw, and Leen Hordijk, *The RAINS Model of Acidification: Science and Strategies at Europe* (Dordrecht: Kluwer Academic, 1990).

4. Albert Weale, *The New Politics of Pollution* (Manchester, UK: Manchester University Press, 1992).
5. Lidskog and Sundqvist, *Governing the Air*.
6. Interview 26, March 20, 2013.
7. C. S. Holling to Allan Hirsch, October 29, 1981, Folder Resources & Environment Core/Acid Rain, IIASA Archives, Laxenburg, Austria.
8. Lidskog and Sundqvist, *Governing the Air*.
9. Valentin Sokolovskii, "Fruits of a Cold War," in *Clearing the Air: 25 Years of the Convention on Long-Range Transboundary Air Pollution*, ed. Johan Sliggers and Willem Kakebeeke (New York: UN Economic Commission for Europe, 2004), 7–14.
10. Sokolovskii, "Fruits of a Cold War"; Alcamo et al., *The RAINS Model*.
11. Darst, *Smokestack Diplomacy*, 99.
12. "USSR's participation in IIASA's transboundary air pollution study," Eliodoro Runca, February 4, 1983, IIASA Archives, Laxenburg, Austria; C. S. Holling to Iurii Izrael', February 17, 1983, IIASA Archives, Laxenburg, Austria.
13. Iurii Izrael' et al., *Kislotnye dozhdi* (Leningrad: Gidrometeoizdat, 1983).
14. "Izrael' Iurii Antonievich," *The Ministers of the Soviet Era*. http://www.minister.su/article/1248.html. Accessed March 19, 2016.
15. "Valentinu Georgievichu Sokolovskomu 85 let," *Priroda Rossii*. http://www.priroda.ru/events/detail.php?ID=10865. Accessed March 19, 2016.
16. Darst, *Smokestack Diplomacy*, 95.
17. "Rapporteur notes," NAS meeting, Washington, DC, March 9, 1973, IIASA Archives, Laxenburg, Austria.
18. John M. R. Stone to M. Kirby, December 3, 1981, folder "Resources & Environment Core/Acid Rain." IIASA Archives, Laxenburg, Austria.
19. Eliodoro Runca to C. S. Holling, August 16, 1982, IIASA Archives, Laxenburg, Austria.
20. Darst, *Smokestack Diplomacy*, 96.
21. Eliodoro Runca and T. Jozseffi to C. S. Holling, June 16, 1982, IIASA Archives, Laxenburg, Austria; "Acid Rain," *Options* 1 (1984), 4.
22. The IIASA scientists simultaneously developed a proposal to model a decision-aid for US-Canadian transboundary pollution. A model to address North American acid rains was developed at NCAR in the summer of 1983, funded by the Environmental Protection Agency and the National Science Foundation.
23. I base this on the correspondence kept in the folder "1983, Env-Tasks Acid Rain," IIASA Archives, Laxenburg, Austria.
24. Allan Hirsch to Chester Cooper, January 28, 1983, IIASA Archives, Laxenburg, Austria.
25. C. S. Holling to Dzhermen Gvishiani, February 10, 1983, IIASA Archives, Laxenburg, Austria.
26. Kauppi to Leen Hordijk, October 9, 1984, IIASA Archives, Laxenburg, Austria.
27. Project description by C. S. Holling, "Transboundary Air Pollution: Acid Rain," February 11, 1983, 2, IIASA Archives, Laxenburg, Austria.
28. Klaus A. Sahlgren to C. S. Holling, March 1, 1983, IIASA Archives, Laxenburg, Austria.
29. Allan Hirsch to Janusz Kindler and Eliodoro Runca, February 14, 1983, IIASA Archives, Laxenburg, Austria.
30. Leen Hordijk to Thomas Lee, October 25, 1984, IIASA Archives, Laxenburg, Austria.
31. Report by Leen Hordijk, "Acid Rain," January 1985, 1, IIASA Archives, Laxenburg, Austria.

32. The long-range transport model was produced by EMEP, which refers to the Cooperative Program for Monitoring and Evaluation of the Long-Range Transmission of Air Pollutants in Europe.

33. Göran Persson to Eliodoro Runca, February 7, 1983, 2, IIASA Archives, Laxenburg, Austria.

34. Outline of IIASA study, "Acid Rain," draft, circa April 1983, 1–5, IIASA Archives, Laxenburg, Austria.

35. C. S. Holling to research leaders, March 17, 1983, IIASA Archives, Laxenburg, Austria.

36. Allan Hirsch to Igor' Ganin, May 10, 1983, IIASA Archives, Laxenburg, Austria.

37. Eliodoro Runca to C. S. Holling, September 8, 1983, IIASA Archives, Laxenburg, Austria.

38. Eliodoro Runca to J. Kindler, memo report, June 9, 1983, IIASA Archives, Laxenburg, Austria.

39. Allan Hirsch to Eliodoro Runca, June 13, 1983, IIASA Archives, Laxenburg, Austria.

40. United Nations Economic Community for Europe to C. S. Holling, September 1, 1983, IIASA Archives, Laxenburg, Austria.

41. Jenny Andersson, "The Great Future Debate."

42. Leen Hordijk to Vitalii Kaftanov, October 6, 1983, folder "Env-Tasks Acid Rain." IIASA Archives, Laxenburg, Austria.

43. C. S. Holling, Program/Project Summary Sheet, February 1983, 1–2, IIASA Archives, Laxenburg, Austria.

44. I base this and other personal details on my conversation with the scientist involved in the acid rain project.

45. Eliodoro Runca to J. Kindler, a memo report, June 9, 1983, IIASA Archives, Laxenburg, Austria.

46. Leen Hordijk to C. S. Holling, July 2, 1984, IIASA Archives, Laxenburg, Austria.

47. Jag S. Maini to Chester Cooper, May 29, 1984, IIASA Archives, Laxenburg, Austria.

48. Leen Hordijk to Alcamo et al., May 3 1984, WMO Meeting in Garmisch-Partenkirchen, April 30 through May 4, 1984, IIASA Archives, Laxenburg, Austria.

49. Shell transferred 34,800 Austrian schillings to the acid rain project. Leen Hordijk to ACI members, September 6, 1984; Leen Hordijk to Chester Cooper, August 3, 1984, IIASA Laxenburg; Outside Funds Report, March 26, 1985, IIASA Archives, Laxenburg, Austria.

50. James Fay to Thomas Lee, 10 November 1984, IIASA Archives, Laxenburg, Austria.

51. Allan Hirsch to Chester Cooper, September 27, 1984, IIASA Archives, Laxenburg, Austria.

52. Leen Hordijk to Chester Cooper, September 7, 1984, IIASA Archives, Laxenburg, Austria.

53. Darst, *Smokestack Diplomacy*, 96.

54. Leen Hordijk to C. S Holling, February 9, 1984, IIASA Archives, Laxenburg, Austria.

55. Leen Hordijk to C. S Holling, July 30, 1984, IIASA Archives, Laxenburg, Austria.

56. Klaus A. Sahlgren to C. S Holling, August 30, 1984, IIASA Archives, Laxenburg, Austria.

57. The British study was led by C. S. Watson of Cambridge. Leen Hordijk to ACI Group, October 2, 1984, IIASA Archives, Laxenburg, Austria.

58. C. S Holling to Eliodoro Runca, July 11, 1983, IIASA Archives, Laxenburg, Austria.

59. Leen Hordijk to Paul Medow, February 13, 1985, IIASA Archives, Laxenburg, Austria.

60. "Abstract of IIASA Acid Rain Project," January–July 1984, 1–3, IIASA Archives, Laxenburg, Austria.

61. Donella Meadows and J. M. Robinson, *The Electronic Oracle: Computer Models and Social Decisions,* reprinted with forward by Dennis Meadows and John Sterman. (Albany, NY: System Dynamics Society, 2007).

62. "The IIASA Acid Rain Interactive Model: A Brief Overview and Some Very Preliminary Results," February 10, 1984, IIASA Archives, Laxenburg, Austria.

63. Leen Hordijk to Thomas Lee, September 30, 1984, IIASA Archives, Laxenburg, Austria.

64. Leen Hordijk to Chester Cooper, "Briefing for T. Lee," July 30, 1984, 1–2, IIASA Archives, Laxenburg, Austria.

65. F. Kenneth Hare to C. S. Holling, July 11, 1984, IIASA Archives, Laxenburg, Austria.

66. "Abstract of IIASA Acid Rain Project," January–July 1984, 5, IIASA Archives, Laxenburg, Austria.

67. "Outline of IIASA study 'Acid Rain'" (draft, circa April 1983), 4, IIASA Archives, Laxenburg, Austria.

68. The term "maps over time" was used to describe computer-generated images of scenarios, see letter from Wolf-Dieter Grossmann to Boris Segerstahl, March 7, 1984, IIASA Archives, Laxenburg, Austria.

69. Sokolovskii, "Fruits of a Cold War," 12.

70. C. S. Holling to Godwin Obasi, May 7, 1984, IIASA Archives, Laxenburg, Austria.

71. Interview 37, October 22, 2014.

72. Brenda Marder, "A Master of Openness without Disclosure," *Brandeis Review* 7, no. 1 (1987).

73. See letter from Leen Hordijk to Andersson, August 3, 1984, IIASA Archives, Laxenburg, Austria.

74. Leen Hordijk to Chester Cooper, "Briefing for T. Lee," July 30, 1984, 1–2, IIASA Archives, Laxenburg, Austria.

75. Thomas Lee to Iurii Izrael', September 26, 1985, IIASA Archives, Laxenburg, Austria.

76. Chester Cooper to Ganin, July 31, 1984, IIASA Archives, Laxenburg, Austria. Bert Bolin and Paul Crutzen participated in the IIASA feasibility study for ICSU/SCOPE.

77. "Sostav," June 10, 1985, IIASA Archives, Laxenburg, Austria.

78. Thomas Lee to Iurii Izrael', January 17, 1985, IIASA Archives, Laxenburg, Austria; Vitalii Kaftanov to Thomas Lee, January 14, 1985, IIASA Archives, Laxenburg, Austria.

79. William Clark to Vitalii Kaftanov, January 11, 1985, IIASA Archives, Laxenburg, Austria; William Clark, "Organization of the USSR Biosphere Meeting: Tasks in Need of Attention," January 11, 1985, IIASA Archives, Laxenburg, Austria.

80. Fitzhugh Green, "Sparks of Bilateral Congeniality," *EPA Journal* 13, no. 1 (1987): 38.

81. Interview 26, March 20, 2013.

82. Atsushi Ishii, "Scientists Learn Not Only Science but Also Diplomacy: Learning Processes in the European Transboundary Air Pollution Regime," in *Governing the Air: The Dynamics of Science, Policy, and Citizen Interaction,* ed. Rolf Lidskog and Göran Sundqvist (Cambridge, MA: MIT Press, 2011), 183.

83. As in the case of the nuclear winter project, the RAINS model was criticized by the Americans who had a more sophisticated model, but theirs took much longer to run than the IIASA model.

84. Marie-Laure Djelic and Sigrid Quack, eds. *Transnational Communities: Shaping Global Economic Governance* (Cambridge: Cambridge University Press, 2010).

85. Eden, *Whole World on Fire*.

86. Leen Hordijk to C. S. Holling, February 9, 1984, IIASA Archives, Laxenburg, Austria.

87. Arbatov, "Where Should We Go from Here." For more about the institutionalization of environmental crisis management in the Soviet Union as a result of the series of disasters, see Marc Elie, "Late Soviet Responses to Disasters, 1989–1991: A New Approach to Crisis Management or the Acme of Soviet Technocratic Thinking?" *Soviet and Post-Soviet Review* 40, no. 2 (2013): 214–238.

EPILOGUE

1. Edwards, *The Closed World*, 1.

2. Stephen Gill, "The Global Panopticon? The Neoliberal State, Economic Life, and Democratic Surveillance," *Alternatives: Global, Local, Political* 20, no. 1 (1995): 1–49.

3. The systems approach, in this way, is an example of what sociologist Tony Bennett calls a "liberal government via milieu," an idea that involves technical infrastructure and material settings. However, if for Bennett government via milieu is a top-down strategy, where the elites steer subordinate subjects who were unable to self-regulate themselves, the Soviet system-cybernetic governmentality may be called bottom-up governance via milieu, wherein scientific experts seek to set limits on the activities of the Communist Party. See Tony Bennett, *Making Culture, Changing Society* (New York: Routledge, 2013), 36–37.

4. Dean, "Liberal Government," 42.

5. Here I refer, first and foremost, to the work of Aaron Wildavsky and Russell Ackoff, specializing in "mess" or ill-structured problems. See also David Dery, *Problem Definition in Policy Analysis* (Lawrence: University Press of Kansas, 1984); Peter deLeon, *Advice and Consent: The Development of the Policy Sciences* (London: Russell Sage, 1989); and studies conducted by Mark Thompson at IIASA.

6. "An Assessment of IIASA's Position and Potential in Today's World," September 1987, 4, IIASA Archives, Laxenburg, Austria.

7. Pickering, *The Cybernetic Brain*, 19.

8. Ibid., 32.

9. Roland Barthes, *Mythologies* (London: Vintage, 1993), 139.

10. Foucault, *Security, Territory, Population*, 101.

11. On restructuring policies and Gvishiani, see Anders Åslund, "Gorbachev's Economic Advisors," in *Milestones in Glasnost and Perestroyka: Politics and People*, ed. Edward A. Hewett and Victor Winston (Washington, DC: Brookings Institution, 1991), 74–94.

12. See an interview by David Todd and David Weisman with Gerald North, Part 3 of 3, March 4, 2008, Conservation History Association of Texas, Texas Legacy Project Records. http://av.cah.utexas.edu/index.php?title=TexLegacyProj:North_gerald_2438&gsearch=gerald%20north. Accessed March 18, 2016. North visited the Soviet Union for the first time in 1976 and then again to participate at Aleksandrov's seminar in Vilnius, Lithuania, in 1981.

13. Evgenii Velikhov, "Sovetskaia programma mira," 9–10.

14. Moiseev, *Kak daleko*.

15. Loren Graham and Irina Dezhina, *Science in the New Russia: Crisis, Aid, Reform* (Bloomington: Indiana University Press, 2008).

16. Eglė Rindzevičiūtė, "The Birth of the Soviet Anthropocene: Nikita Moiseev and the Transformation of Soviet Governmentality" (paper presented at the Ninth World Congress

of the International Council for East European Studies, Makuhari, Japan, August 3–8, 2015).

17. Sven Erik Jørgensen, "Obituary for Yuri Svirezhev," *Ecological Modelling* 216, no. 2 (2008): 81–88.

18. Dmitrii Pisarenko, "Utechka 'mozgov': kak vernut' rosiiskikh uchenykh?" *Argumenty i fakty* (March 21, 2012). http://www.aif.ru/society/education/31975. Accessed March 18, 2016.

19. Nikita Moiseev, *To Be or Not To Be: Humanity's Dilemma* (Moscow: Noosphere, 2002), 21.

20. For a discussion of bureaucracy and new modes of management, see Paul du Gay, "New Spirits of Public Management . . . 'Post-Bureaucracy,'" in *New Spirits of Capitalism? Crises, Justifications, and Dynamics,* ed. Paul du Gay and Glenn Morgan (Oxford: Oxford University Press, 2013), 274–293. For privatization of expertise see Diane Stone, *Knowledge Actors and Transnational Governance: The Private-Public Policy Nexus in the Global Agora* (Basingstoke, UK: Palgrave, 2013).

21. Alexandr Styhre, *Management and Neoliberalism: Connecting Policies and Practices* (New York: Routledge, 2014).

22. Davies, *The Limits of Neoliberalism*; Stephen Collier, *Post-Soviet Social: Neoliberalism, Social Modernity, Biopolitics* (Princeton, NJ: Princeton University Press, 2011).

23. For an outline of the history of evidence-based policy in the area of public health, see Katherine Smith, *Beyond Evidence-Based Policy in Public Health: The Interplay of Ideas* (Basingstoke, UK: Palgrave Macmillan, 2013).

24. Bockman, *Markets in the Name of Socialism*, 2; Johanna Bockman and Gil Eyal, "Eastern Europe as a Laboratory for Economic Knowledge: The Transnational Roots of Neoliberalism," *American Journal of Sociology* 108, no. 2 (2002): 310–352.

25. Bockman, *Markets in the Name of Socialism*, 216–217.

26. Bockman attributes the following reforms as a neoliberal package: deregulation, liberalization of trade and capital flows, anti-inflationary stabilization, and privatization of state enterprises. Bockman, *Markets in the Name of Socialism*, 4.

27. The first IIASA distinguished lecture was delivered by the Russian economist Abel' Aganbegian, the public face of Gorbachev's economic reforms.

28. Daniel Stedman Jones, *Masters of the Universe: Hayek, Friedman, and the Birth of Neoliberal Politics* (Princeton, NJ: Princeton University Press, 2013), 7–8. For the central role of the Institute of Economic Affairs in the development of a network of neoliberal experts, see Marie-Laure Djelic, "Spreading Ideas to Change the World: Inventing and Institutionalizing the Neoliberal Think Tank." http://papers.ssrn.com/sol3/papers.cfm?abstract_id=2492010. Accessed March 18, 2016.

29. P. O. Aven, S. S. Shatalin, and F. Schmidt-Bleek, "Economic Reform and Integration, Proceedings of March 1–3, 1990 Meeting" (CP-90-4, July 1990), iii–iv, IIASA Archives, Laxenburg, Austria.

30. In his memoir, Richard Rose writes that it was at IIASA that he was persuaded by Russian economist Petr Aven to conduct a comparative survey on public opinion in Russia and Eastern Europe. Then the neoliberal Institute of Economic Affairs gave him an initial grant to conduct a Russian study. Richard Rose, *Learning about Politics in Time and Space* (Colchester, UK: ECPR, 2013), 133–134.

31. I have begun this inquiry in Rindzevičiūtė, "The Future as an Intellectual Technology."

32. Susanne A. Wengle, "Engineers versus Managers: Experts, Market-Making and State-Building in Putin's Russia," *Economy and Society* 41, no. 3 (2012): 435–467.

33. For more on Georgii Schedrovitskii, see Rindzevičiūtė, "The Future as an Intellectual Technology."

34. Iver B. Neumann, "Russia as a Great Power, 1815–2007," *Journal of International Relations and Development* 11, no. 2 (2008): 128–151; Rindzevičiūtė, "The Future as an Intellectual Technology."

35. Wengle, "Engineers versus Managers," 444.

36. Edward Lucas, *The New Cold War: Putin's Russia and the Threat to the West* (London: Bloomsbury, 2009).

Bibliography

ARCHIVES

Archives of the International Institute of Applied Systems Analysis, Laxenburg, Austria
Hoover Institution Archives, Stanford University
Russian State Archive of the Economy (RGAE)
Archive of the Russian Academy of Sciences (ARAN)

BIBLIOGRAPHY

Ackoff, Russell. "The Systems Revolution." *Long Range Planning* 7, no. 6 (1974): 2–20.
Agar, John. "'Future Forecast—Changeable and Probably Getting Worse': The UK Government's Early Response to Anthropogenic Climate Change." *Twentieth Century British History* 26, no. 4 (2015): 602–628. doi: 10.1093/tcbh/hwv008.
——. *The Government Machine: A Revolutionary History of the Computer*. Cambridge, MA: MIT Press, 2003.
Alcamo, Joseph, Roderick Shaw, and Leen Hordijk. *The RAINS Model of Acidification: Science and Strategies at Europe*. Dordrecht: Kluwer Academic, 1990.
Allan, Bentley. "Producing the Climate: States, Scientists, and the Constitution of Global Governance Objects." *International Organization* (forthcoming).
Allyn, Bruce. "Fact, Value, and Science." In *Science and the Soviet Social Order*, edited by Loren Graham, 225–255. Cambridge, MA: Harvard University Press, 1990.
Alvesson, Mats, and Per-Olof Berg. *Corporate Culture and Organizational Symbolism: An Overview*. Berlin: de Gruyter, 1992.
Amadae, S. M. *Prisoners of Reason: Game Theory and Neoliberal Political Economy*. Cambridge: Cambridge University Press, 2016.
——. *Rationalizing Capitalist Democracy: The Cold War Origins of Rational Choice Liberalism*. Chicago: University of Chicago Press, 2003.
Amoore, Louise. *The Politics of Possibility: Risk and Security Beyond Probability*. Durham, NC: Duke University Press, 2013.
Andersson, Jenny. "The Great Future Debate and the Struggle for the World." *American Historical Review* 117 (2012): 1411–1430.
——. "RAND Goes to France: Genèse de la prospective française." Paper presented at *Writing the History of the 'Neoliberal Turn,'* Sciences Po, Paris, October 17, 2014.
Andersson, Jenny, and Eglė Rindzevičiūtė. "The Political Life of Prediction: The Future as a Space of Scientific World Governance in the Cold War Era." *Les Cahiers européens de Sciences Po* 4 (2012): 1–25.
——, eds. "Introduction: Toward a New History of the Future." In *The Struggle for the Long-Term in Transnational Science and Politics: Forging the Future*, 1–15. New York: Routledge, 2015.
Angelstam, Per, Vladimir Anufriev, Linas Balciauskas, et al. "Biodiversity and Sustainable Forestry in European Forests: How East and West Can Learn from Each Other." *Wildlife Society Bulletin* 25, no. 1 (1997): 38–48.
Arab-Ogly, Edvard. *V labirinte prorochestv*. Moscow: Molodaia gvardiia, 1973.

Aradau, Claudia, and Rens van Munster. *Politics of Catastrophe: Genealogies of the Unknown.* New York: Routledge, 2011.
Arbatov, Georgy A. "Where Should We Go from Here: A Soviet View." In *Windows of Opportunity: From Cold War to Peaceful Competition in U.S.-Soviet Relations*, edited by Graham T. Allison, William L. Ury, and Bruce J. Allyn, 285–308. Cambridge, MA: Ballinger, 1989.
Arnold, Darrell P., ed. *Traditions of Systems Theory: Major Figures and Contemporary Developments.* New York: Routledge, 2014.
Arthur, W. Brian. "Competing Technologies and Economic Prediction." *Options* 2 (1984): 1–3.
———. *Increasing Returns and Path Dependency in the Economy.* Ann Arbor: University of Michigan Press, 1994.
Augustine, Dolores L. *Red Prometheus: Engineering and Dictatorship in East Germany, 1945–1990.* Cambridge, MA: MIT Press, 2007.
Autio-Sarasmo, Sari, and Katalin Miklóssy, eds. *Reassessing Cold War Europe.* New York: Routledge, 2011.
Backhouse, Roger E., and Philippe Fontaine, eds. *A Historiography of the Modern Social Sciences.* Cambridge: Cambridge University Press, 2014.
Babkov, Vasilii, and Elena Sakanian. *Nikolai Timofeev-Resovskii.* Moscow: Pamiatniki istoricheskoi mysli, 2002.
Badash, Lawrence. *A Nuclear Winter's Tale: Science and Politics in the 1980s.* Cambridge, MA: MIT Press, 2009.
Bailes, Kendall E. "Alexei Gastev and the Soviet Controversy over Taylorism, 1918–24." *Soviet Studies* 29, no. 3 (1977): 373–394.
———. "The Politics of Technology: Stalin and Technocratic Thinking among Soviet Engineers." *The American Historical Review* 79, no. 2 (1974): 445–469.
Barnett, Michael, and Martha Finnemore. *Rules for the World: International Organizations in Global Politics.* Ithaca, NY: Cornell University Press, 2004.
Barry, Andrew. *Material Politics: Disputes along the Pipeline.* Oxford: Wiley-Blackwell, 2013.
———. *Political Machines: Governing a Technological Society.* London: Athlone, 2001.
Barth, Kai-Henrik. "Catalysts of Change: Scientists as Transnational Arms Control Advocates in the 1980s." *Osiris* 21, no. 1 (2006): 182–206.
Barthes, Roland. *Mythologies.* London: Vintage, 1993, 139. First published in 1957 by Editions du Seuil, Paris. Translation 1972 by Jonathan Cape.
Bateson, Gregory. *Steps to an Ecology of Mind.* Northvale, NJ: Jason Aronson, 1987. First published in 1972 by Chandler.
Beissinger, Mark R. *Scientific Management, Socialist Discipline, and Soviet Power.* Cambridge, MA: Harvard University Press, 1988.
Bell, Daniel. *The Coming of Post-Industrial Society: A Venture in Social Forecasting.* New York: Basic Books, 1976.
———. *The End of Ideology: The Exhaustion of Political Ideas in the 1950s.* 2nd ed. Cambridge, MA: Harvard University Press, 2000. First published in 1962 by Free Press.
Beniger, James. *The Control Revolution: Technological and Economic Origins of the Informational Society.* Cambridge, MA: Harvard University Press 1989.
Bennett, Stuart. *A History of Control Engineering 1800–1930.* Stevenage, UK: Peregrinus, 1979.
Bennett, Tony. *Making Culture, Changing Society.* New York: Routledge, 2013.
Berg, Aksel I. "O nekotorykh problemakh kibernetiki." *Voprosy filosofii* 4 (1960): 58.
Bernal, John Desmond. *The Social Function of Science.* London: Routledge, 1939.
Bertsch, Gary, ed. *Controlling East-West Trade and Technology Transfer: Power, Politics and Policies.* Durham, NC: Duke University Press, 1988.
Biggart, John, Peter Dudley, and Francis King, eds. *Alexander Bogdanov and the Origins of Systems Thinking in Russia.* Aldershot, UK: Ashgate, 1998.

Blauberg, Igor, Vadim Sadovskii, and Erik Yudin. *Sistemnyi podkhod: predposylki, problemy, trudnosti.* Moscow: Znanie, 1969.

——. *Systems Theory: Philosophical and Methodological Problems.* Moscow: Progress, 1977.

Brint, Steven. *In an Age of Experts: The Changing Role of Professionals in Politics and Public Life.* Princeton, NJ: Princeton University Press, 1994.

Bockman, Johanna. *Markets in the Name of Socialism: The Left-Wing Origins of Neoliberalism.* Stanford, CA: Stanford University Press, 2011.

Bockman, Johanna, and Michael Bernstein. "Scientific Community in a Divided World: Economists, Planning, and Research Priority during the Cold War." *Comparative Studies in Society and History* 50, no. 3 (2008): 581–613.

Bockman, Johanna, and Gil Eyal. "Eastern Europe as a Laboratory for Economic Knowledge: The Transnational Roots of Neoliberalism." *American Journal of Sociology* 108, no. 2 (2002): 310–352.

Boulding, Kenneth. "General Systems Theory: A Skeleton of Science," *Management Science* 2, no. 3 (1956): 197–208.

Brown, Andrew. *J. D. Bernal: The Sage of Science.* Oxford: Oxford University Press, 2007.

Bundy, McGeorge, and Jermen Gvishiani. "Foreword." In *Organization for Forecasting and Planning: Experience in the Soviet Union and the United States*, edited by W. R. Dill and G. Kh. Popov, vii–ix., New York: Wiley, 1979.

Burawoy, Michael. "The End of Sovietology and the Renaissance of Modernization Theory." *Contemporary Sociology* 21, no. 6 (1992): 774–785.

Butrimenko, A., and I. Sebestyén. "Data Communication in the USSR: The Telecommunication Infrastructure and Relevant Administrative Procedures." In *Experimental and Operational East-West Computer Connections: The Telecommunication Hardware and Software, Data Communication Services and Relevant Administrative Procedures*, edited by István Sebestyén, 267–298. Laxenburg, Austria: International Institute for Applied Systems Analysis, 1983.

Cain, Frank. "Computers and the Cold War: United States Restrictions on the Export of Computers to the Soviet Union and Communist China." *Journal of Contemporary History* 40, no. 1 (2005): 131–147.

Campbell-Kelly, Martin, William Aspray, Nathan Ensmenger, and Jeffrey R. Yost. *Computer: A History of the Information Machine.* 2nd ed. Boulder, CO: Westview, 2004.

Campbell, Robert W. *A Bibliographical Dictionary of Russian and Soviet Economists.* New York: Routledge, 2012.

Casey, Catherine. "'Come, Join Our Family': Discipline and Integration in Corporate Organizational Culture." *Human Relations* 52, no. 1 (1999): 155–178.

Castells, Manuel, and Emma Kiselyova. *The Collapse of Soviet Communism: A View from the Information Society.* Berkeley: University of California Press, 1995.

Casti, John L. *Linear Dynamical Systems.* rev. ed. Orlando: Academic, 1987.

Ceruzzi, Paul. *A History of Modern Computing.* 2nd ed. Cambridge, MA: MIT Press, 2003.

Chakrabarty, Dipesh. "The Climate of History: Four Theses." *Critical Inquiry* 35, no. 2 (2008): 197–222.

Clarke, Lee. *Mission Improbable: Using Fantasy Documents to Tame Disaster.* Chicago: University of Chicago Press, 1999.

Clemens, Walter. *Can Russia Change? The USSR Confronts Global Interdependence.* Boston: Unwin Hyman, 1990.

Cochoy, Franck. *Une histoire du marketing: Discipliner l'économie de marché.* Paris: La Découverte, 1999.

Cohrs, Patrick O. "Towards a New Deal for the World? Lyndon Johnson's Aspirations to Renew the Twentieth Century's Pax Americana." In *Beyond the Cold War: Lyndon*

Johnson and the New Global Challenges of the 1960s, edited by Francis J. Gavin and Mark Atwood Lawrence, 44–75. Oxford: Oxford University Press, 2014.

Cole, H. S. D., C. Freeman, M. Jahoda, and K. Pavitt, eds. *Thinking about the Future: A Critique of "The Limits to Growth."* Brighton, UK: Sussex University Press, 1973.

Collier, Stephen. *Post-Soviet Social: Neoliberalism, Social Modernity, Biopolitics.* Princeton, NJ: Princeton University Press, 2011.

Collier, Stephen, and Andrew Lakoff. "Vital Systems Security: Reflexive Biopolitics and the Government of Emergency." *Theory, Culture and Society* 32, no. 2 (2015): 19–51.

Collins, Peter. *The Royal Society and the Promotion of Science since 1960.* Cambridge: Cambridge University Press, 2015.

Connelly, Matthew. *Fatal Misconception: The Struggle to Control World Population.* Cambridge, MA: Harvard University Press, 2010.

Conquest, Robert. *The Great Terror: A Reassessment.* Oxford: Oxford University Press, 1990.

Coopersmith, Jonathan. "The 'Normalcy' of Russian, Soviet, and Post-Soviet Science and Technology Studies." *Technology and Culture* 47, no. 3 (2006): 623–637.

Coumel, Laurent, and Marc Elie. "A Belated and Tragic Ecological Revolution: Nature, Disasters, and Green Activists in the Soviet Union and the Post-Soviet States, 1960s–2010s." *Soviet and Post-Soviet Review* 40, no. 2 (2013): 157–165.

Crowe, Gregory D., and Seymour E. Goodman. "S. A. Lebedev and the Birth of Soviet Computing." *IEEE Annals of the History of Computing* 16, no. 1 (1994): 4–24.

Crowley, David, and Jane Pavitt, eds. *Cold War Modern.* London: V&A, 2010.

Czarniawska, Barbara. *Narrating the Organization: Dramas of Institutional Identity.* Chicago: University of Chicago Press, 1997.

Czarniawska-Joerges, Barbara, and Guje Sevón, eds. *Translating Organizational Change.* Berlin: de Gruyter, 1996.

Dahan, Amy. "Axiomatiser, modéliser, calculer: les mathématiques, instrument universel et polymorphe d'action." In *Les sciences pour la guerre: 1940–1960,* edited by Amy Dahan and Dominique Pestre, 49–82. Paris: Éditions de l'École des Haute Études en Sciences Sociales, 2004.

Darst, Robert G. *Smokestack Diplomacy: Cooperation and Conflict in East-West Environmental Politics.* Cambridge, MA: MIT Press, 2001.

David, Paul A. "Clio and the Economics of QWERTY." *American Economic Review* 75, no. 2, Papers and Proceedings of the Ninety-Seventh Annual Meeting of the American Economic Association. (1985): 332–337.

Davies, William. *The Limits of Neoliberalism: Authority, Sovereignty and the Logic of Competition.* London: Sage, 2014.

Dean, Mitchell. *Governmentality: Power and Rule in Modern Society.* London: Sage, 1999.

———. "Liberal Government and Authoritarianism." *Economy and Society* 31, no. 1 (2002): 37–61.

deLeon, Peter. *Advice and Consent: The Development of the Policy Sciences.* London: Russell Sage, 1989.

Dery, David. *Problem Definition in Policy Analysis.* Lawrence: University Press of Kansas, 1984.

Djelic, Marie-Laure. "Spreading Ideas to Change the World: Inventing and Institutionalizing the Neoliberal Think Tank." March 18, 2016. Available online at http://papers.ssrn.com/sol3/papers.cfm?abstract_id=2492010.

Djelic, Marie-Laure, and Sigrid Quack, eds. *Transnational Communities: Shaping Global Economic Governance.* Cambridge: Cambridge University Press, 2010.

Djelic, Marie-Laure, and Kerstin Sahlin-Andersson, eds. *Transnational Governance: Institutional Dynamics of Regulation.* Cambridge: Cambridge University Press, 2006.

Doel, Ronald E., and Kristine C. Harper. "Prometheus Unleashed: Science as a Diplomatic Weapon in the Lyndon B. Johnson Administration." *Osiris* 21, no. 2 (2006): 66–85.

Dorodnitsyn, Anatolii, ed. *Ekologicheski i demograficheskie posledstviia iadernoi voiny.* Moscow: Nauka, 1986.

———, ed. *Matematicheskie modeli ekosistem: ekologicheskie i demograficheskie posledstviia iadernoi voiny.* Moscow: Nauka, 1986.

Dror, Yezhekel. "Policy Analysts: A New Professional Role in Government Service." *Public Administration Review* 27, no. 3 (1967): 197–203.

Dobrov, Genadii M., and Anton Iu. Golian-Nikol'skii. *Vek velikih nadezhd: sud'by nauchnotehnicheskogo progressa XX stoletiia.* Kiev: Naukova dumka, 1964.

Dubovskii, Sergei. "Global'noe modelirovanie: voprosy teorii i praktiki." *Vek globalizatsii* 2 (2010): 47–67.

Dubovskii, Sergei, and O. A. Eismont. "Long-Range Modelling of the USSR Economy." In *The Future of the World Economy*, edited by Wilhelm Krelle, 311–324. Berlin: Springer Verlag, 1989.

du Gay, Paul. "New Spirits of Public Management . . . 'Post-Bureaucracy.'" In *New Spirits of Capitalism? Crises, Justifications, and Dynamics*, edited by Paul du Gay and Glenn Morgan, 274–293. Oxford: Oxford University Press, 2013.

Duhautois, Sibylle. "The Future of World Problems." PhD diss., Sciences Po, Paris, in progress.

Eden, Lynn. *Whole World on Fire: Organizations, Knowledge, and Nuclear Weapons Devastation.* Ithaca, NY: Cornell University Press, 2004.

Edwards, Paul. *The Closed World: Computers and the Politics of Discourse in Cold War America.* Cambridge, MA: MIT Press, 1996.

———. "Entangled Histories: Climate Science and Nuclear Weapons Research." *Bulletin of the Atomic Scientists* 68, no. 4 (2012): 28–40.

———. "Infrastructure and Modernity: Force, Time, and Social Organization in the History of Sociotechnical Systems." In *Modernity and Technology*, edited by Thomas Misa, Philip Brey, and Andrew Feenberg, 185–225. Cambridge, MA: MIT Press, 2004.

———. *A Vast Machine: Computer Models, Climate Data, and the Politics of Global Warming.* Cambridge, MA: MIT Press, 2010.

———. "The World in a Machine: Origins and Impacts of Early Computerized Global Systems Models." In *Systems, Experts and Computers: The Systems Approach in Management and Engineering, World War II and After*, edited by Agatha C. Hughes and Thomas P. Hughes, 221–254. Cambridge, MA: MIT Press, 2000.

Edwards, Paul, Steven Jackson, Geoffrey Bowker, and Cory Knobel. *Understanding Infrastructure: Dynamics, Tensions, and Design.* Ann Arbor: Deep Blue, 2007.

Efremenko, Dmitrii. *Ekologo-politicheskie diskursy: vozniknovenie i evoliutsiia.* Moscow: Academic Institute of Scientific Information on Social Sciences, 2006.

Elichirigoity, Fernando. *Planet Management: Limits to Growth, Computer Simulation, and the Emergence of Global Spaces.* Evanston, IL: Northwestern University Press, 1999.

Elie, Marc. "Late Soviet Responses to Disasters, 1989–1991: A New Approach to Crisis Management or the Acme of Soviet Technocratic Thinking?" *Soviet and Post-Soviet Review* 40, no. 2 (2013): 214–238.

Ellman, Michael, and Vladimir Kontorovich, eds. *The Destruction of the Soviet Economic System: An Insiders' History.* Armonk, NY: M.E. Sharpe, 1998.

Emel'ianov, Stanislav, ed. *30 let institute sistemnogo analiza Rossiiskoi akademii nauk: istoriia sozdaniia i razvitiia Instituta sistemnogo analiza, 1976–2006 gg.* Moscow: URSS, 2006.

Emel'ianov, Stanislav, and A. Porshnev. "Vklad B.Z. Mil'nera v razvitiiu nauki upravleniia." *Rosiiskii zhurnal menedzhmenta* 4 (2004): 156.

Engerman, David C. *Know Your Enemy: The Rise and Fall of America's Soviet Experts.* Oxford: Oxford University Press, 2009.

Engerman, David, Nils Gilman, Mark H. Haefele, and Michael E. Latham, eds. *Staging Growth: Modernization, Development and the Global Cold War.* Amherst: University of Massachusetts Press, 2003.

Ensmenger, Nathan L. *The Computer Boys Take Over: Computers, Programmers, and the Politics of Technical Expertise.* Cambridge, MA: MIT Press, 2010.

Erickson, Paul. "Mathematical Models, Rational Choice, and the Search for Cold War Culture." *Isis* 101, no. 2 (2010): 386–392.

Erickson, Paul, Judy L. Klein, Lorraine Daston, Rebecca Lemov, Thomas Sturm, and Michael D. Gordin. *How Reason Almost Lost Its Mind: The Strange Career of Cold War Rationality.* Chicago: University of Chicago Press, 2013.

Erlich, Paul, Carl Sagan, Donald Kennedy, and Walter Orr Roberts. *The Cold and the Dark: The World after Nuclear War.* New York: W. W. Norton, 1984.

Evangelista, Matthew. *Unarmed Forces: The Transnational Movement to End the Cold War.* Ithaca, NY: Cornell University Press, 1999.

Fedorenko, Nikolai P. *Vspominaia proshloe, zagliadyvaiu v budushchee.* Moscow: Nauka, 1999.

Fedoseyev, Petr. "Topical Problems of Our Time." In *Science, Technology and the Future: Soviet Scientists' Analysis of the Problems of and Prospects for the Development of Science and Technology and Their Role in Society,* edited by Evgenii Velikhov, M. Gvishiani, and S. R. Mikulinsky, 3–20. Oxford: Pergamon, 1980.

Fischer, Frank. *Technocracy and the Politics of Expertise.* Newbury Park, CA: Sage, 1990.

Fleck, Ludwik. *Genesis and Development of a Scientific Fact.* Translated by Frederick Bradley and Thaddeus J. Trenn. Chicago: University of Chicago Press, 1979.

Fleron, Frederic J., ed. *Technology and Communist Culture: The Socio-Cultural Impact of Technology under Socialism.* New York: Praeger, 1977.

Forrester, Jay. "System Dynamics and the Lesson of 35 Years." In *A Systems-Based Approach to Policymaking,* edited by Kenyon De Greene, 199–240. Berlin: Springer, 1993.

Fortescue, Stephen, ed. *Russian Politics from Lenin to Putin.* Basingstoke, UK: Palgrave, 2010.

———. *Science Policy in the Soviet Union.* New York: Routledge, 1990.

Foucault, Michel. *Security, Territory, Population: Lectures at the Collège de France, 1977–1978.* Translated by Graham Burchell. Edited by Michael Senallart. Basingstoke, UK: Palgrave Macmillan, 2009.

Fourcade, Marion. *Economists and Societies: Discipline and Profession in the United States, Britain and France, 1890s–1990s.* Princeton, NJ: Princeton University Press, 2009.

"From QWERTY to Microsoft," *Options* (Winter 2007): 20–21.

Funtowicz, Silvio, and Jerome Ravetz. "Science for the Post-Normal Age." *Futures* 25, no. 7 (1993): 739–755.

Gaddis, John Lewis. *Strategies of Containment: A Critical Appraisal of American National Security Policy during the Cold War.* Oxford: Oxford University Press, 2005.

Gaidar, Yegor. *Days of Defeat and Victory.* Translated by Jane Miller. Seattle: University of Washington Press, 1999.

Galison, Peter. "The Ontology of the Enemy: Norbert Wiener and the Cybernetic Vision." *Critical Inquiry* 21, no. 1 (1994): 228–266.

Galison, Peter, and Bruce W. Hevly, eds. *Big Science: The Growth of Large-Scale Research.* Stanford, CA: Stanford University Press, 1992.

Gane, Nicholas. "The Governmentalities of Neoliberalism: Panopticism, Post-Panopticism and Beyond." *The Sociological Review* 60, no. 4 (2012): 611–634.

———. "Sociology and Neoliberalism: A Missing History." *Sociology* 48, no. 6 (2014): 1092–1106.

Gavin, Francis J. *Nuclear Statecraft: History and Strategy in America's Atomic Age*. Ithaca, NY: Cornell University Press, 2012.

Gavin, Francis J., and Mark Atwood Lawrence, eds. *Beyond the Cold War: Lyndon Johnson and the New Global Challenges of the 1960s*. Oxford: Oxford University Press, 2014.

Gavrilov, V. M., and M. Iu. Sitnina. "Militarizatsiia kosmosa: novaia global'naia ugroza." *Voprosy filosofii* 11 (1985): 98–99.

Gelovani, Viktor, Vladimir Britkov, and Sergei Dubovskii. *SSSR i Rossiia v global'noi sisteme (1985–2030): rezultaty globalnogo modelirovaniia*. Moscow: Librokom, 2009.

Gemelli, Giuliana, ed. *American Foundations and Large-Scale Research: Construction and Transfer of Knowledge*. Bologna: Clueb, 2001.

———. "Building Bridges in Science and Societies During the Cold War: The Origins of the International Institute for Applied Systems Analysis (IIASA)." In *American Foundations and Large Scale Research: Construction and Transfer of Knowledge*, edited by Giuliana Gemelli, 159–198. Bologna: Clueb, 2001.

———, ed. *The Ford Foundation and Management Education in Western and Eastern Europe (1950s–1970s)*. Brussels: European Interuniversity Press, 1998.

Gerovitch, Slava. *From Newspeak to Cyberspeak: A History of Soviet Cybernetics*. Cambridge, MA: MIT Press, 2002.

———. "InterNyet: Why the Soviet Union Did Not Build a Nationwide Computer Network." *History and Technology* 24, no. 4 (2008): 335–350.

Gessen, Masha. *Dead Again: The Russian Intelligentsia After Communism*. London: Verso, 1997.

Ghamari-Tabrizi, Sharon. *The Worlds of Herman Kahn: The Intuitive Science of Thermonuclear War*. Cambridge, MA: Harvard University Press, 2005.

Gieryn, Thomas F. *Cultural Boundaries of Science: Credibility on the Line*. Chicago: University of Chicago Press, 1999.

Gill, Stephen. "The Global Panopticon? The Neoliberal State, Economic Life, and Democratic Surveillance." *Alternatives: Global, Local, Political* 20, no. 1 (1995): 1–49.

Gilman, Nils. "The Cold War as an Intellectual Force Field." *Modern Intellectual History* (2015): 1–17. doi:10.1017/S1479244314000420.

———. *Mandarins of the Future: Modernization Theory in Cold War America*. Baltimore, MD: Johns Hopkins University Press, 2004.

———. "Modernization Theory, the Highest Stage of American Intellectual History." In *Staging Growth: Modernization, Development and the Global Cold War*, edited by David C. Engerman, Nils Gilman, Mark Haefele, and Michael E. Latham, 47–80. Amherst, MA: University of Massachusetts Press, 2003.

Giocoli, Nicola. *Modelling Rational Agents: From Interwar Economics to Early Modern Game Theory*. Cheltenham, UK: Edward Elgar, 2003.

Gloveli, Georgii. "The Sociology of Aleksandr Bogdanov." In *Aleksandr Bogdanov Revisited*, edited by Vesa Oittinen, 47–80. Helsinki: Aleksanteri Institute, 2009.

Gorokhov, V. G., ed. *Sotsialnaia i ekologicheskaia otsenka nauchno-tekhnicheskogo razvitiia*. Moscow: Rossiskoe filosofskoe obshchestvo, 2007.

Graham, Loren. *The Ghost of an Executed Engineer: Technology and the Fall of the Soviet Union*. Cambridge, MA: Harvard University Press, 1993.

———. "Introduction: The Impact of Science and Technology on Soviet Politics and Society." In *Science and the Soviet Social Order*, edited by Loren Graham, 1–16. Cambridge, MA: Harvard University Press, 1990.

———. *Moscow Stories*. Bloomington: Indiana University Press, 2006.
———. *Science, Philosophy, and Human Behaviour in the Soviet Union*. New York: Columbia University Press, 1987.
———. *Science in Russia and the Soviet Union: A Short History*. Cambridge: Cambridge University Press, 1993.
Graham, Loren, and Irina Dezhina. *Science in the New Russia: Crisis, Aid, Reform*. Bloomington: Indiana University Press, 2008.
Greenaway, Frank. *Science International: A History of the International Council of Scientific Unions*. Cambridge: Cambridge University Press, 1996.
Green, Fitzhugh. "Sparks of Bilateral Congeniality," *EPA Journal* 13, no. 1 (1987): 38.
Gregory, Paul R. *The Political Economy of Stalinism: Evidence from the Soviet Secret Archives*. Cambridge: Cambridge University Press, 2003.
Gvishiani, Aleksei. *Fenomen Kosygina: zapiski vnuka*. Moscow: Fond kul'tury Ekaterina, 2004.
Gvishiani, Dzhermen. "Methodological Problems of Global Development Modelling." In *Science, Technology and the Future: Soviet Scientists' Analysis of the Problems of and Prospects for the Development of Science and Technology and their Role in Society*, edited by E. P. Velikhov, J. M. Mikhaiilovich Gvishiani, and S. R. Mikulinskii, 21–35. Oxford: Pergamon, 1980.
———. *Mosty v budushchee*. Moscow: Editorial URSS, 2004.
———. "Problemy upravleniia sotsialisticheskoi promyshlennost'iu." *Voprosy filosofii* 11 (1966): 3–13.
Gvishiani, Jermen, ed. *Science, Technology, and Global Problems: Trends and Perspectives in Development of Science and Technology and Their Impact on Contemporary Global Problems*. Oxford: Pergamon, 1979.
Habermas, Jürgen. *The Theory of Communicative Action*. Vol. 2, *Lifeworld and System: A Critique of Functionalist Reason*. Translated by Thomas McCarthy. Boston: Beacon Press, 1987.
Hacking, Ian. "How Should We Do the History of Statistics?" In *Foucault's Effect: Studies in Governmentality*, ed. Graham Burchell, Colin Gordon, and Peter Miller, 181–196. Chicago: University of Chicago Press, 1991.
———. *The Taming of Chance*. Cambridge: Cambridge University Press, 1990.
Halpern, Orit. *Beautiful Data: A History of Vision and Reason since 1945*. Durham, NC: Duke University Press, 2014.
Hanson, Stephen. *Time and Revolution: Marxism and the Design of Soviet Institutions*. Chapel Hill: University of North Carolina Press, 1997.
Harrison, Mark. "Economic Growth and Slowdown." In *Brezhnev Reconsidered*, edited by Edwin Bacon and Mark Sandle, 38–67. Basingstoke, UK: Palgrave Macmillan, 2002.
Harvey, Penny, and Hannah Knox. *Roads: An Anthropology of Infrastructure and Expertise*. Ithaca, NY: Cornell University Press, 2015.
Haslam, Jonathan. *Russia's Cold War: From the October Revolution to the Fall of the Wall*. New Haven, CT: Yale University Press, 2012.
Hawkes, Nigel, ed. *International Seminar on Trends in Mathematical Modelling, Venice, 13–18 December 1971*. Berlin: Springer Verlag, 1973.
Hayles, Katherine. *How We Became Posthuman: Virtual Bodies in Cybernetics, Literature, and Informatics*. Chicago: University of Chicago Press, 1999.
Hecht, Gabrielle. "Planning a Technological Nation: Systems Thinking and the Politics of National Identity in Postwar France." In *Systems, Experts, and Computers: The Systems Approach in Management and Engineering, World War II and After*, edited by Agatha C. Hughes and Thomas P. Hughes, 133–160. Cambridge, MA: MIT Press, 2000.

Heilbron, Johan, Nicolas Guilhot, and Laurent Jeanpierre. "Toward a Transnational History of the Social Sciences." *Journal of the History of the Behavioral Sciences* 44, no. 2 (2008): 146–160.
Hermann, Armin, J. Krige, U. Mersits, and D. Pestre. *History of CERN*. Vol. 2, *Building and Running the Laboratory, 1954–1965*. Amsterdam: North-Holland, 1990.
Herran, Néstor, Soraya Boudia, and Simone Turchetti. *Transnational History and the History of Science*. Cambridge: Cambridge University Press, 2012.
Hersh, Reuben. "Mathematics Has a Front and a Back." *Synthese* 88, no. 2 (1991): 127–133.
Heyck, Hunter. *Age of System: Understanding the Development of Modern Social Science*. Baltimore, MD: Johns Hopkins University Press, 2015.
Hirschman, Albert O. *Exit, Voice and Loyalty: Responses to Decline in Firms, Organizations and States*. Cambridge, MA: Harvard University Press, 1970.
Hitch, Charles, and Roland McKean, eds. *The Economics of Defense in the Nuclear Age*. Rand Report R-346 (1960). Available online at http://www.rand.org/pubs/reports/R346.html.
Hofman, Erik, and Robin F. Laird. *Technocratic Socialism: The Soviet Union in the Advanced Industrial Era*. Durham, NC: Duke University Press, 1985.
Holloway, David. "Innovation in Science—The Case of Cybernetics in the Soviet Union." *Science Studies* 4, no. 4 (1974): 299–337.
———. "The Political Uses of Scientific Models: The Cybernetic Model of Government in Soviet Social Science." In *The Use of Models in the Social Sciences*, ed. Lyndurst Collins, 110–129. Boulder, CO: Westview Press, 1976.
———. *Stalin and the Bomb: The Soviet Union and Atomic Energy, 1939–1956*. New Haven, CT: Yale University Press, 1996.
Hoos, Ida R. *Systems Analysis in Public Policy: A Critique*. Berkeley: University of California Press, 1972.
Hughes, Agatha C., and Thomas P. Hughes, eds. "Introduction." In *Systems, Experts and Computers: The Systems Approach in Management and Engineering, World War II and After*, 1–26. Cambridge, MA: MIT Press, 2000.
Hughes, Thomas P. *Networks of Power: Electrification of Western Society, 1880–1930*. Baltimore, MD: Johns Hopkins University Press, 1983.
Ianovskaia, E. B. "Pervaia Vsesoiuznaia konferentsiia po teorii igr," *Uspekhi matematicheskikh nauk* 24, no. 4, (1969): 216–220.
Ingelstam, Lars. *System: Att Tänka över samhälle och teknik*. Stockholm: Energimyndigheten, 2002.
Irye, Akira. *Global Community: The Role of International Organizations in the Making of the Contemporary World*. Berkeley: University of California Press, 2004.
Ishii, Atsushi. "Scientists Learn Not Only Science but Also Diplomacy: Learning Processes in the European Transboundary Air Pollution Regime." In *Governing the Air: The Dynamics of Science, Policy, and Citizen Interaction*, edited by Rolf Lidskog and Göran Sundqvist, 163–194. Cambridge, MA: MIT Press, 2011.
Iudin, B. G. "Iz istorii sistemnykh issledovanii: mezhdu metodologiei i ideologiei." *Vestnik TGPU* 1, no. 75 (2008): 28–33.
Iudin, Erik, and Igor' Blauberg. *Stanovlenie i sushchnost' sistemnogo podkhoda*. Moscow: Nauka, 1973.
Ivakhnenko, A. G., and V. G. Lapa. *Cybernetics and Forecasting Techniques*. New York: Elsevier, 1967.
Izrael', Iurii, et al. *Kislotnye dozhdi*. Leningrad: Gidrometeoizdat, 1983.
Jamison, Andrew. "Technology's Theorists: Conceptions of Innovation in Relation to Science and Technology Policy." *Technology and Culture* 30, no. 3 (1989): 505–533.

Jardini, David R. "Out of the Blue Yonder: The Transfer of Systems Thinking from the Pentagon to the Great Society, 1961–1965." In *Systems, Experts, and Computers: The Systems Approach in Management and Engineering, World War II and After*, edited by Agatha C. Hughes and Thomas P. Hughes, 311–358. Cambridge, MA: MIT Press, 2000.

——. *Out of the Blue Yonder: The RAND Corporation's Diversification into Social Welfare Research, 1946–1968*. PhD diss., Carnegie Mellon University, 1996.

Jasanoff, Sheila. "The Idiom of Co-production." In *States of Knowledge: The Co-production of Science and Social Order*, edited by Sheila Jasanoff, 1–12. New York: Routledge, 2004.

Jones, Daniel Stedman. *Masters of the Universe: Hayek, Friedman, and the Birth of Neoliberal Politics*. Princeton, NJ: Princeton University Press, 2013.

Jørgensen, Sven Erik. "Obituary for Yuri Svirezhev." *Ecological Modelling* 216, no. 2 (2008): 81–88.

Josephson, Paul R. *Lenin's Laureate: Zhores Alferov's Life in Communist Science*. Cambridge, MA: MIT Press, 2010.

——. *Red Atom: Russia's Nuclear Power Program from Stalin to Today*. New York: W. H. Freeman, 1999.

Josephson, Paul, Nicolai Dronin, Rubin Mnatsakanian, et al. *An Environmental History of Russia*. Cambridge: Cambridge University Press, 2013.

Kahn, Herman. *On Thermonuclear War*. Princeton, NJ: Princeton University Press, 1960.

Kaijser, Arne, and Joar Tiberg. "From Operations Research to Futures Studies: The Establishment, Diffusion, and Transformation of the Systems Approach in Sweden, 1945–1980." In *Systems, Experts, and Computers: The Systems Approach in Management and Engineering, World War II and After*, edited by Agatha C. Hughes and Thomas P. Hughes, 385–412. Cambridge, MA: MIT Press, 2000.

Kakabadse, Andrew, and Nada Kakabadse, eds. *Global Elites: The Opaque Nature of Transnational Policy Determination*. Basingstoke, UK: Palgrave Macmillan, 2012.

Kangaspuro, Markku, and Jeremy Smith, eds. *Modernisation in Russia since 1900*. Helsinki: Finnish Literature Society, 2006.

Kaplan, Fred M. *The Wizards of Armageddon*. Stanford: Stanford University Press, 1991.

Kay, James J. "An Introduction to Systems Thinking." In *The Ecosystem Approach: Complexity, Uncertainty, and Managing for Sustainability*, edited by David Waltner-Toews, James J. Kay, and Nina-Marie E. Lister, 3–14. New York: Columbia University Press, 2008.

Kaysen, Carl. "The Computer that Printed Out W*O*L*F." *Foreign Affairs* 50, no. 4 (July 1972): 660–668.

Keeny, Spurgeon M. Jr. "The Search for Soviet Cybernetics." In *Jerry Wiesner: Scientist, Statesman, Humanist: Memories and Memoirs*, edited by Judy Rosenblith, 81–88. Cambridge, MA: MIT Press, 2003.

Keepin, Bill, and Brian Wynne. "Technical Analysis of IIASA Energy Scenarios." *Nature* 312 (December 20, 1984): 691–695.

Kerimov, M. K. "Kratkaia istoriia Vychislitel'nogo tsentra imeni akademika A. A. Dorodnitsyna Rossiiskoi Akademii Nauk (k 50-desiletiiu so vremeni osnovaniia)." *Zhurnal vychislitel'noi matematiki i matematicheskoi fiziki* 46, no. 7 (2006): 1144–1183.

Keyssar, Helene. "Space Bridges: The U.S.-Soviet Space Bridge Resource Center." *PS: Political Science & Politics* 27, no. 2 (1994): 247–253.

Kharkhordin, Oleg. *The Collective and the Individual in Russia: A Study of Practices*. Berkeley: University of California Press, 1999.

Khlevniuk, Oleg, and Gorlizki, Yoram. *Cold Peace: Stalin and the Soviet Ruling Circle, 1945–1953*. Oxford: Oxford University Press, 2004.
Kibita, Nataliya. *Soviet Economic Management under Khrushchev: The Sovnarkhoz Reform*. New York: Routledge, 2013.
Kirillin, A. V., V. L. Kirillina, A. V. Iurasova, N. A. Iurasova, eds. *Akademik Vladimir Alekseevich Kirillin: Biografiia, vospominania, dokumenty*. Moscow: MEI, 2008.
Kline, Robert R. *The Cybernetics Moment: Or Why We Call Our Age the Information Age*. Baltimore, MD: Johns Hopkins University Press, 2015.
Kondratieff, N. D. "The Long Waves in Economic Life [1926]." *Review (Ferdinand Braudel Center)* 2, no. 4 (1979): 519–562.
Krelle, Wilhelm. *The Future of the World Economy: Economic Growth and Structural Change*. Berlin: Springer Verlag, 1989.
Krige, John. *American Hegemony and the Postwar Reconstruction of Science in Europe*. Cambridge, MA: MIT Press, 2006.
Krige, John, and Helke Rausch, eds., *American Foundations and the Coproduction of World Order in the Twentieth Century*. Götingen: Vanderhoeck & Ruprecht, 2012.
Kryshtanovskaya, Olga, and Stephen White. "From Soviet Nomenklatura to Russian Elite." *Europe-Asia Studies* 48, no. 5 (1996): 711–733.
Kudriashov, Anatolii, P. *Sovremennaia nauchno-tekhnicheskaia revoliutsiia i ee osobennosti*. Moscow: Mysl, 1965.
Kunda, Gideon. *Engineering Culture: Control and Commitment in a High-Tech Corporation*. Rev. ed. Philadelphia: Temple University Press, 2006.
Kurzhanskii, A. B. "50 Years of Coexistence in Control: The Contributions of the Russian Community." *European Journal of Control* 13, no. 1 (2007): 49–60.
Kuzin, Aleksandr, Ivan Negodaev, and V. I. Belolipetskii, eds. *Sovremennaia nauchnotekhnicheskaia revoliutsiia: Istoricheskoe issledovanie*. Moscow: Nauka, 1967.
Lafontaine, Céline. "The Cybernetic Matrix of French Theory." *Theory, Culture & Society* 24, no. 5 (2007): 27–46.
———. *L'empire cybernétique: des machines à penser à la pensée machine*. Paris: Seuil, 2004.
Lapin, Nikolai. *Teoriia i praktika innovatiki*. Moscow: Logos, 2013.
Latour, Bruno. *Reassembling the Social: An Introduction to Actor-Network-Theory*. Oxford: Oxford University Press, 2005.
———. *We Have Never Been Modern*. Translated by Catherine Porter. Cambridge, MA: Harvard University Press, 1993.
Latham, Michael E. *Modernization as Ideology: American Social Science and "Nation Building" in the Kennedy Era*. Chapel Hill: University of North Carolina Press, 2000.
———. *The Right Kind of Revolution: Modernization, Development, and U.S. Foreign Policy from the Cold War to the Present*. Ithaca, NY: Cornell University Press, 2010.
Ledeneva, Alena V. *How Russia Really Works: The Informal Practices that Shaped the Post-Soviet Politics and Business*. Ithaca, NY: Cornell University Press, 2006.
Lektorskii, V. A., and V. N. Sadovskii. "O printsipakh issledovaniia system (V sviazi s 'obshchei teoriei sistem' L. Bertalanfi)." *Voprosy filosofii* 8 (1960): 67–78.
Leontief, Wassily. "The Decline and Rise of Soviet Economic Science." *Foreign Affairs* (January 1960): 261–272.
Leontief, Wassily W., Ann Carter, and Peter A. Petri. *The Future of the World Economy: A United Nations Study*. Oxford: Oxford University Press, 1977.
Levien, Roger. "RAND, IIASA, and the Conduct of Systems Analysis." In *Systems, Experts and Computers: The Systems Approach in Management and Engineering, World War II and After*, edited by Agatha Hughes and Thomas Hughes, chapter 14. Cambridge, MA: MIT Press, 2000.

Lewin, Moshe. "Rebuilding the Soviet nomenklatura 1945–1948." *Cahiers du monde Russe* 44, nos. 2–3 (2003): 219–252.
———. *The Soviet Century*. Edited by Gregory Elliot. London: Verso, 2005.
Lidskog, Rolf, and Göran Sundqvist, eds. *Governing the Air: The Dynamics of Science, Policy, and Citizen Interaction*. Cambridge, MA: MIT Press, 2011.
Liefferink, Duncan. *Environment and the Nation State: The Netherlands, the European Union and Acid Rain*. Manchester, UK: Manchester University Press, 1996.
Light, Jennifer S. *From Warfare to Welfare: Defense Intellectuals and Urban Problems in Cold War America*. Baltimore, MD: Johns Hopkins University Press, 2004.
Lindblom, Charles, and David K. Cohen, *Usable Knowledge: Social Science and Social Problem Solving*. New Haven, CT: Yale University Press, 1979.
Los', Viktor. "Global'nye problem kak predmet kompleksnykh nauchnykh issledovanii (Nekotorye itogi izucheniia global'nykh protsessov mirovogo razvitiia)." *Voprosy filosofii* 12 (1985): 3–17.
Lucas, Edward. *The New Cold War: Putin's Russia and the Threat to the West*. London: Bloomsbury, 2009.
MacKenzie, Donald. *Mechanizing Proof: Computing, Risk, and Trust*. Cambridge, MA: MIT Press, 2001.
Majone, Giandomenico. *Evidence, Argument and Persuasion in the Policy Process*. New Haven, CT: Yale University Press, 1989.
———. "Systems Analysis: A Genetic Approach." In *Handbook of Systems Analysis: Overview of Uses, Procedures, Applications and Practice*, edited by Hugh Miser and Edward Quade, chapter 2. Chichester, UK: John Wiley, 1985.
Marakhov, V. G., and Iu. S. Meleshchenko, "Sovremennaia nauchno-tekhnicheskaia revoliutsiia i ee sotsialnye posledstviia v usloviiakh sotsializma," *Voprosy filosofii* 3 (1966): 129–140.
Marder, Brenda. "A Master of Openness without Disclosure." *Brandeis Review* 7, no. 1 (1987).
Marois, Maurice, ed. *Documents pour l'histoire*. Vol. 3, *Les grandes conferences internationales: l'homme et la planète*. Paris: Editions Rive Droite, 1997.
Mayr, Otto. *The Origins of Feedback Control*. Cambridge, MA: MIT Press, 1970.
McKinlay, Alan, and Philip Taylor. *Foucault, Governmentality, and Organization*. New York: Routledge, 2014.
McLuhan, Marshall. "Cybernation and Culture." In *The Social Impact of Cybernetics*, edited by Charles R. Dechert, 95–108. Notre Dame, IN: University of Notre Dame Press, 1966.
McNamara, Robert. *Blundering into Disaster: Surviving the First Century of the Nuclear Age*. London: Bloomsbury, 1987.
Meadows, Dennis. "A Brief and Incomplete History of Operational Gaming in System Dynamics." *System Dynamics Review* 33, nos. 2–3 (2007): 199–203.
———. "Tools for Understanding the Limits to Growth: Comparing a Simulation and a Game." *Simulation & Gaming* 32, no. 4 (2001): 522–536.
Meadows, Donella, John Richardson, and Gerhart Bruckmann, eds. *Groping in the Dark: The First Decade of Global Modelling*. New York: Wiley, 1982.
Meadows, Donella, and J. M. Robinson. *The Electronic Oracle: Computer Models and Social Decisions*. Reprinted with foreword by Dennis Meadows and John Sterman. Albany, NY: System Dynamics Society, 2007.
Medina, Eden. *Cybernetic Revolutionaries: Technology and Politics in Allende's Chile*. Cambridge, MA: MIT Press, 2011.
Medvetz, Thomas. *Think Tanks in America*. Chicago: University of Chicago Press, 2012.
Men'shikov, Stanislav. *O vremeni i o sebe*. Moscow: Mezhdunarodnye otnosheniia, 2007.

"Mezhdunarodnyi 16-yi seminar IFAK/ISAGA po delovym igram i imitatsionnomu modelirovaniiu," *Avtomatika i telemekhanika* 10 (1986): 173–175.
Michael, Donald N. *Cybernation: The Silent Contest.* Santa Barbara, CA: Centre for the Study of Democratic Institutions, 1962.
Mickiewicz, Ellen. *Split Signals: Television and Politics in the Soviet Union.* Oxford: Oxford University Press, 1992.
Mindell, David A. *Between Human and Machine: Feedback, Control, and Computing before Cybernetics.* Baltimore, MD: Johns Hopkins University Press, 2002.
Mirowski, Philip. *Machine Dreams: Economics Becomes a Cyborg Science.* Chicago: University of Chicago Press, 2010.
Mirowski, Philip, and Dieter Plehwe, eds. *The Road from Mont Pèlerin: The Making of the Neoliberal Thought Collective.* Cambridge, MA: Harvard University Press, 2009.
Miser, Hugh J., and Edward S. Quade. *Handbook of Systems Analysis: Craft Issues and Procedural Choices.* Chichester, UK: Wiley, 1988.
Mitchell, Timothy. *Rule of Experts: Egypt, Techno-Politics, Modernity.* Berkeley: University of California Press, 2002.
Mitin, M. B., and V. S. Semenov, "Dvizhenie chelovechestva k komunizmu i burzhuaznaia kontseptsiia 'edinogo industrial'nogo obshchestva,'" *Voprosy filosofii* 5 (1965): 35–45.
Modelirovanie protsessov global'nogo razvitiia: sbornik trudov VNIISI, vol. 8. Moscow: VNIISI, 1979.
Moiseev, Nikita. *Algoritmy razvitiia. . . . Akademicheskie chteniia.* Moscow: Nauka, 1987.
———. *Byt' ili ne byt' . . . chelovechestvu?* Moscow: Ulianovskii dom pechati, 1999.
———. *Kak daleko do zavtreshnego dnia: svobodnye razmyshleniia, 1917–1993.* Moscow: ASPEKT, 1994.
———. *Prosteishie matematicheskie modeli ekonomicheskogo prognozirovaniia.* Moscow: Znanie, 1975.
———. *Razmyshlenie o sovremennoi politologii.* Moscow: MNEPU, 1999.
———. *Sotsializm i informatika.* Moscow: Izdatel'stvo Politicheskoi Literatury, 1988.
———. *To Be or Not To Be: Humanity's Dilemma.* Moscow: Noosphere, 2002.
Moiseev, Nikita, V. V. Aleksandrov, and A. M. Tarko. *Chelovek i biosfera: opyt sistemnogo analiza i eksperimenty s modeliami.* Moscow: Nauka, 1985.
Moiseev, Nikita, and I. T. Frolov. "Vysokoe soprikosnovenie: obshchesto, chelovek, i priroda v vek mikroelektroniki, informatiki i biotekhnologii." *Voprosy filosofii* 9 (1984): 24–41.
Moore, Kelly. *Disrupting Science: Social Movements, American Scientists, and the Politics of the Military, 1945–1975.* Princeton, NJ: Princeton University Press, 2008.
Moravcsik, Andrew. "A New Statecraft? Supranational Entrepreneurs and International Cooperation." *International Organization* 53, no. 2 (1999): 267–306.
Morgan, Mary. *The History of Econometric Ideas.* Cambridge: Cambridge University Press, 1990.
Mukusev, V. V. *Razberemsia: fragmenty interv'iu, vystuplenii, stati, stsenarii i rassledovaniia raznykh let.* Moscow: Nauka, 2007.
Mumford, Lewis. "Authoritarian and Democratic Technics." *Technology and Culture* 5, no. 1 (1964): 1–8.
———. *Technics and Civilization.* Chicago: University of Chicago Press, 2010. First published in 1934 by Routledge & Kegan Paul.
Naidenov, V. S. "Sotsial'no-ekonomicheskie posledstvie tekhnicheskogo progressa pri sotsializme," *Voprosy filosofii* 8 (1960): 14–24.
Neumann, Iver B. "Russia as a Great Power, 1815–2007." *Journal of International Relations and Development* 11, no. 2 (2008): 128–151.

"Norbert Viner v redaktsii nashego zhurnala," *Voprosy filosofii* 9 (1960): 164–168.

Oldfield, Jonathan, and Denis Shaw. "V. I. Vernadskii and the Development of Biogeochemical Understandings of the Biosphere, c. 1880s–1968." *British Journal for the History of Science* 46, no. 2 (2013): 287–310.

Ong, Aihwa, and Stephen Collier, eds. *Global Assemblages: Technology, Politics, and Ethics as Anthropological Problems.* Oxford: Wiley-Blackwell, 2004.

Optner, Stanford L. "Introduction." In *Systems Analysis*, edited by Stanford L. Optner, 9–16. Harmondsworth, UK: Penguin, 1973.

Oreskes, Naomi, and Erik Conway. *Merchants of Doubt: How a Handful of Scientists Obscured the Truth on Issues from Tobacco Smoke to Global Warming.* New York: Bloomsbury, 2010.

Parrish, Michael. *The Lesser Terror: Soviet State Security, 1939–1953.* Westport, CT: Praeger, 1996.

Patt, Anthony. "Separating Analysis from Politics: Acid Rain in Europe." *Review of Policy Research* 16, nos. 3–4 (1999): 104–137. New York: Routledge, 2014.

Peccei, Aurelio. *The Human Quality.* New York: Pergamon, 1977.

Pestre, Dominique. "Le nouvel univers des sciences et des techniques: une proposition générale." In *Les sciences pour la guerre: 1940–1960*, edited by Amy Dahan and Dominique Pestre, 11–47. Paris: Éditions de lÉcole des Haute Études en Sciences Sociales, 2004.

Peters, Ben. *How Not to Network a Nation.* Cambridge, MA: MIT Press, 2016.

Petrov, A. A. *Nikita Nikolaevich Moiseev: sud'ba strany v sudbe uchenogo.* Moscow: Ekologiia i zhizn', 2011.

Pickering, Andrew. *The Cybernetic Brain: Sketches of Another Future.* Chicago: University of Chicago Press, 2011.

Pisarenko, Dmitrii. "Utechka 'mozgov': kak vernut' rosiiskikh uchenykh?" *Argumenty I fakty* (March 21, 2012). Available online at http://www.aif.ru/society/education/31975.

Podvig, Pavel, ed. *Russian Strategic Nuclear Forces.* Cambridge, MA: MIT Press, 2001.

Polanyi, Karl. *The Great Transformation: The Political and Economic Origins of Our Time.* New York: Farrar & Rhinehart, 1944.

Poovey, Mary. *A History of the Modern Fact: Problems of Knowledge in the Sciences of Wealth and Society.* Chicago: University of Chicago Press, 1998.

Popkov, Iurii, Vadim Sadovskii, Aleksandr Seitov. "Mosty v budushchee: 'ezda v neznaemoe.'" In Dzhermen Gvishiani, *Mosty v budushchee*, 1–14. Moscow: Editorial URSS, 2004.

Porter, Theodore. *Trust in Numbers: The Pursuit of Objectivity in Science and Public Life.* Princeton, NJ: Princeton University Press, 1995.

Posey, Carl A. *Red Danube.* London: St Martin Press, 1986.

Powaski, Ronald E. *The Cold War: The United States and the Soviet Union, 1917–1991.* New York: Oxford University Press, 1998.

Power, Michael. *Organizing Uncertainty: Designing a World of Risk Management.* Oxford: Oxford University Press, 2007.

Pozner, Vladimir. *Parting with Illusions.* New York: Atlantic Monthly Press, 1990.

Prozorov, Sergei. "Foucault and Soviet Biopolitics." *History of the Human Sciences* 27, no. 5 (2014): 6–25.

Putnam, Robert D. "Elite Transformation in Advanced Industrial Societies: An Empirical Assessment of the Theory of Technocracy." *Comparative Political Studies* 10, no. 3 (1977): 383–412.

Quade, E. S. "Introduction." In *Systems Analysis and Policy Planning: Applications in Defence*, edited by E. S. Quade and W. I. Boucher, 1–18. New York: American Elsevier, 1968.

Radaelli, Claudio Maria. *Technocracy in the European Union.* New York: Longman, 1999.
Radin, Beryl A. *Beyond Machiavelli: Policy Analysis Comes of Age.* Washington, DC: Georgetown University Press, 2000.
———. *The Art and Science of Negotiation: How to Resolve Conflicts and Get the Best of Bargaining.* Cambridge, MA: Belknap, 1985.
Rau, Erik P. "Technological Systems, Expertise, and Policy Making: The British Origins of Operational Research." In *Technologies of Power: Essays in Honor of Thomas Parke Hughes and Agatha Chipley Hughes,* edited by Michael Thad Allen and Gabrielle Hecht, 215–252. Cambridge, MA: MIT Press, 2001.
Ribbhagen, Christina. *Technocracy within Representative Democracy: Technocratic Reasoning and Justification among Bureaucrats and Politicians.* Gothenburg: University of Gothenburg Press, 2013.
Richta, Radovan. *Člověk a technika v revoluci našich dnů.* Prague: Čs. společ, 1963.
Richmond, Yale. *Practising Public Diplomacy: A Cold War Odyssey.* Oxford: Berghahn Books, 2008.
Rindzevičiūtė, Eglė. "The Birth of the Soviet Anthropocene: Nikita Moiseev and the Transformation of Soviet Governmentality." Paper presented at the 9th World Congress of the International Council for East European Studies, Makuhari, Japan, August 3–8, 2015.
———. *Constructing Soviet Cultural Policy: Cybernetics and Governance after World War II.* Linköping, Sweden: Linköping University Press, 2008.
———. "The Future as an Intellectual Technology in the Soviet Union: From Centralised Planning to Reflexive Management." *Cahiers du monde Russe* 56, no. 1 (2015): 113–134.
———. "Internal Transfer of Cybernetics and Informality in the Soviet Union: The Case of Lithuania." In *Reassessing Cold War Europe,* edited by Sari Autio-Sarasmo and Katalin Miklossy, 119–137. New York: Routledge, 2011.
———. "Purification and Hybridisation of Soviet Cybernetics: The Politics of Scientific Governance in an Authoritarian Regime." *Archiv für sozialgeschichte* 50 (2010): 289–309.
———. "A Struggle for the Soviet Future: The Birth of Scientific Forecasting in the Soviet Union." *Slavic Review* 75, no. 1 (2016): 52–76.
———. "Toward a Joint Future Beyond the Iron Curtain: East-West Politics of Global Modelling." In *A Struggle for the Long-Term in Transnational Science and Politics: Forging the Future,* eds. Jenny Andersson and Eglė Rindzevičiūtė, 115–143. New York: Routledge, 2015.
Riska-Campbell, Leena. *Bridging East and West: The Establishment of the International Institute for Applied Systems Analysis (IIASA) in the United States Foreign Policy of Bridge Building, 1964–1972.* Helsinki: The Finnish Society of Science and Letters, 2011.
Rockefeller, David. *Memoirs.* New York: Random House, 2004.
Rohde, Joy. *Armed with Expertise: The Militarization of American Social Research during the Cold War.* American Institutions and Society. Ithaca, NY: Cornell University Press, 2013.
Rokityanskij, Yakov G. "N. V. Timofeeff-Resovski in Germany, July 1925–September 1945." *Journal of Bioscience* 30, no. 5 (2005): 573–580.
Roman, Valter. *Revoluția industrială în dezvoltarea societății.* Bucharest: Editura Științifică, 1965.
Rose, Nikolas. *Powers of Freedom: Reframing Political Thought.* Cambridge: Cambridge University Press, 1999.

Rose, Nikolas, and Peter Miller. "Political Power beyond the State: Problematics of Government." *The British Journal of Sociology* 43, no. 2 (1992): 173–205.
Rose, Richard. *Learning about Politics in Time and Space.* Colchester, UK: ECPR, 2013.
Rosier, Bernard, ed. *Wassily Leontief: Textes et Itinéraire.* Paris: Éditions la Découverte, 1986.
Rowney, Don Karl. *Transition to Technocracy: The Structural Origins of the Soviet Administrative State.* Ithaca, NY: Cornell University Press, 1989.
Rubinson, Paul. "The Global Effects of Nuclear Winter: Science and Antinuclear Protest in the United States and the Soviet Union in the 1980s." *Cold War History* 14, no. 1 (2014): 47–69.
Ruse, Michael. *The Gaia Hypothesis: Science on a Pagan Planet.* Chicago: University of Chicago Press, 2013.
Sadovskii, Vadim. *Osnovaniia obshchei teorii system: logiko-metodologicheskii analiz.* Moscow: Nauka, 1974.
Sadovskii, Vadim, and Erik Iudin. *Issledovaniia po obshchei teorii sistem.* Moscow: Progress, 1969.
Sanchez-Sibony, Oscar. *Red Globalization: The Political Economy of the Soviet Cold War from Stalin to Khrushchev.* Cambridge: Cambridge University Press, 2014.
Sandle, Mark. "Russian Think Tanks, 1956–1996." In *Think Tanks Across Nations: A Comparative Approach,* edited by Diane Stone, Andrew Denham, and Mark Garnett, 202–222. Manchester, UK: Manchester University Press, 1998.
Sandomirskaja, Irina. "Aesopian Language: The Politics and Poetics of Naming the Unnameable." In *The Vernaculars of Communism: Language, Ideology and Power in the Soviet Union and Eastern Europe,* edited by Petre Petrov and Lara Ryazanova-Clarke, 63–88. New York: Routledge, 2015.
Schmidt, Vivien A. *Democracy in Europe: The EU and National Polities.* Oxford: Oxford University Press, 2006.
Schmitt, Carl. *The Concept of the Political.* Translated by George Schwab. Chicago: University of Chicago Press, 1996. Translation based on the 1932 edition published by Dunker & Humbolt.
Schwartz, Thomas A. "Moving Beyond the Cold War: The Johnson Administration, Bridge-Building and Détente." In *Beyond the Cold War: Lyndon Johnson and the New Global Challenges of the 1960s,* edited by Francis Gavin and Mark Atwood Lawrence, 76–96. Oxford: Oxford University Press, 2014.
Schneider, Stephen. "Interview of Stephen H. Schneider." By Robert M. Chervin. American Meteorological Society, University Corporation for Atmospheric Research. January 10–13, 2002. Available online at http://nldr.library.ucar.edu/repository/assets/ams/AMS-000-000-000-191.pdf.
Scott, James C. *Seeing Like a State: How Certain Schemes to Improve the Human Condition Have Failed.* Yale Agrarian Studies Series. New Haven, CT: Yale University Press, 1998.
Sebestyén, István, ed. *Experimental and Operational East-West Computer Connections: The Telecommunication Hardware and Software, Data Communication Services, and Relevant Administrative Procedures.* Laxenburg, Austria: International Institute for Applied Systems Analysis, 1983.
Sederberg, Peter C., ed. *Nuclear Winter, Deterrence and the Prevention of Nuclear War.* Westport, CT: Praeger, 1986.
Selcer, Perrin. "Patterns of Science: Developing Knowledge for a World Community at Unesco." PhD diss., University of Pennsylvania, 2011. Available at http://repository.upenn.edu/dissertations/AAI3463035/.
Semenov, V. S. "Na V vsemirnom sotsiologicheskom kongresse." *Voprosy filosofii* 11 (1962): 19–35.

Shchedrovitskii, Georgii. "Problemy metodologii sistemnogo issledovaniia (1964)." In G. P. Shchedrovitskii, *Izbrannye Trudy*, 155–196. Moscow: Izd-vo Shkoly kul'turnoi politiki, 1995.
Silk, Leonard. *The Research Revolution*. New York: McGraw-Hill, 1960.
Simon, Herbert A. *Models of My Life*. New York: Basic Books, 1991.
Smil, Vaclav. *The Earth's Biosphere: Evolution, Dynamics and Change*. Cambridge, MA: MIT Press, 2003.
Smirnov, L. V. "Matematicheskoe modelirovanie razvitiia." *Voprosy filosofii* 1 (1965): 67–73.
Smith, Katherine. *Beyond Evidence-Based Policy in Public Health: The Interplay of Ideas*. Basingstoke, UK: Palgrave Macmillan, 2013.
Smolian, Georgii L. *Issledovanie operatsii: instrument effektivnogo upravleniia*. Moscow: Znanie, 1967.
Snow, J. P. *The Two Cultures and the Scientific Revolution*. New York: Cambridge University Press, 1959.
Snyder, Jack L. *The Soviet Strategic Culture: Implications for Limited Nuclear Operations*. RAND Report R-2154-AF, September 1977. Available online at https://www.rand.org/content/dam/rand/pubs/reports/2005/R2154.pdf.
Sobolev, Sergei, Anatolii Kitov, Aleksei Liapunov. "Osnovnye cherty kibernetiki." *Voprosy filosofii* 4 (1955): 136–148.
Sokolovskii, Valentin. "Fruits of a Cold War." In *Clearing the Air: 25 Years of the Convention on Long-range Transboundary Air Pollution*, edited by Johan Sliggers and Willem Kakebeeke, 7–14. New York: UN Economic Commission for Europe, 2004.
Sokolov, Vassily, Jill Jäger, Vladimir Pisarev, et al. "Turning Points: The Management of Global Environmental Risks in the Soviet Union." In *Learning to Manage Global Environmental Risks*. Vol. 1, *A Comparative History of Social Responses to Climate Change, Ozone Depletion, and Acid Rain*, edited by The Social Learning Group, 139–166. Cambridge, MA: MIT Press, 2001.
Solovey, Mark, ed. *Shaky Foundations: The Politics-Patronage-Social Science Nexus in Cold War America*. New Brunswick, NJ: Rutgers University Press, 2013.
Sommer, Vítězslav. "Forecasting the Post-Socialist Future: Prognostika in Late Socialist Czechoslovakia, 1970–1989." In *The Struggle for the Long Term in Transnational Science and Politics: Forging the Future*, edited by Jenny Andersson and Eglė Rindzevičiūtė, 144–168. New York: Routledge, 2015.
Star, Susan Leigh. "The Ethnography of Infrastructure." *American Behavioral Scientist* 43, no. 3 (1999): 377–391.
Sterman, John, and Dennis Meadows. "STRATAGEM-2: A Microcomputer Simulation Game of the Kondratiev Cycle." *Simulation & Gaming* 16, no. 2 (June 1985): 174–202.
Stigler, Stephen M. *Statistics on the Table: The History of Statistical Concepts and Methods*. Cambridge, MA: Harvard University Press, 1999.
Stites, Richard. *Revolutionary Dreams: Utopian Vision and Experimental Life in the Russian Revolution*. New York: Oxford University Press, 1989.
Stone, Diane. *Knowledge Actors and Transnational Governance: The Private-Public Policy Nexus in the Global Agora*. Basingstoke, UK: Palgrave, 2013.
Stone, Diane, and Mark Garnett. "Introduction: Think Tanks, Policy Advice and Governance." In *Think Tanks Across Nations: A Comparative Approach*, edited by Diane Stone, Andrew Denham, and Mark Garnett, 1–16. Manchester, UK: Manchester University Press, 1998.
Stone, Jeremy J. *Strategic Persuasion: Arms Limitations through Dialogue*. New York: Columbia University Press, 1967.

Styhre, Alexandr. *Management and Neoliberalism: Connecting Policies and Practices*. New York: Routledge, 2014.
Sundqvist, Göran. "Fewer Boundaries and Less Certainty: The Role of Experts in European Air Policy." In *Governing the Air: The Dynamics of Science, Policy, and Citizen Interaction*, edited by Rolf Lidskog and Göran Sundqvist, 195–221. Cambridge, MA: MIT Press, 2011.
Suny, Ronald Grigor. *The Soviet Experiment: Russia, the USSR and the Successor States*. New York: Oxford University Press, 1998.
Susiluoto, Ilmari. *The Origins and Development of Systems Thinking in the Soviet Union: Political and Philosophical Controversies from Bogdanov and Bukharin to Present-Day Re-Evaluations*. Helsinki: Finnish Academy of Science and Letters, 1982.
Sutela, Pekka. *Socialism, Planning and Optimality: A Study in Soviet Economic Thought*. Helsinki: Finnish Society of Science and Letters, 1984.
Svirezhev, Iurii M. *Ecological and Demographic Consequences of Nuclear War*. Moscow: Computer Center of the USSR Academy of Sciences, 1985.
Sychev, Viacheslav V. "Vospominaniia o V. A. Kirilline." In *Akademik Vladimir Alekseevich Kirillin: biografiia, vospominaniia, dokumenty*. Moscow: MEI, 2008.
Tarko, Aleksandr, and Valerii Parkhomenko. "Iadernaia zima: istoriia voprosa i prognozy." *Biosfera* 3, no. 2 (2011): 164–173.
Tatarchenko, Ksenia. "'A House with a Window to the West': The Akademgorodok Computer Centre (1958–1993)." PhD diss., Princeton University, 2013.
Taubman, William. *Khrushchev: The Man and His Era*. New York: W. W. Norton, 2004.
Teich, Mikuláš. "The Scientific-Technical Revolution: An Historical Event in the Twentieth Century?" In *Revolution in History*, edited by Roy Porter and Mikuláš Teich, 317–330. Cambridge: Cambridge University Press, 1986.
Thomas, William. *Rational Action: The Sciences of Policy in Britain and America, 1940–1960*. Cambridge, MA: MIT Press, 2015.
Thomas, William L. *Man's Role in Changing the Face of the Earth*. Chicago: University of Chicago Press, 1956.
Thompson, Michael. "Among the Energy Tribes: The Anthropology of the Current Policy Debate." Working Paper WP-82-059. Laxenburg, Austria: International Institute for Applied Systems Analysis, 1982.
Thrift, Nigel, Adam Tickell, Steve Woolgar, and William H. Roop, eds. *Globalization in Practice*. Oxford: Oxford University Press, 2014.
Travin, Dmitry, and Otar Marganiya. "Resource Curse: Rethinking the Soviet Experience." In *Resource Curse and Post-Soviet Eurasia: Oil, Gas and Modernization*, edited by Vladimir Gel'man and Otar Marganiya, 23–48. New York: Lexington Books, 2010.
Umpleby, Stuart A., and Vadim N. Sadovsky. *A Science of Goal Formulation: American and Soviet Discussions of Cybernetics and Systems Theory*. New York: Hemisphere, 1991.
Uhrqvist, Ola. *Seeing and Knowing the Earth as a System: An Effective History of Global Environmental Change Research as Political and Scientific Practice*. PhD diss., Linköping University, Sweden, 2014.
VanDeveer, Stacy D. "Ordering Environments: Regions in European International Environmental Cooperation." In *Earthly Politics: Local and Global in Environmental Governance*, edited by Sheila Jasanoff and Marybeth Martello, 309–334. Cambridge, MA: MIT Press, 2004.
Velikhov, Evgenii. "Sovetskaia programma mira i zadachi sovetskikh uchenykh." In *Klimaticheskie i biologicheskie posledstviia iadernoi voiny*, edited by Evgenii Velikhov, 3–43. Moscow: Nauka, 1987.
Vidmer, Richard F. "Soviet Studies of Organization and Management: A 'Jungle' of Competing Views." *Slavic Review* 40, no. 3 (1981): 404–422.

Vieille-Blanchard, Elodie. "Les limites à la croissance dans un monde global: modélisations, prospectives, réfutations." PhD diss., École des Hautes Études en Sciences Sociales, Paris, 2011.

———. "Technoscientific Cornucopian Futures versus Doomsday Futures: The World Models and *The Limits to Growth*." In *The Struggle for the Long-Term in Transnational Science and Politics: Forging the Future*, ed. Jenny Andersson and Eglė Rindzevičiūtė, 92–114. New York: Routledge, 2015.

Volkova, V. N., and Denisov A. A. *Osnovy teorii sistem i sistemnogo analiza*. St. Petersburg: SPbGTU, 2001.

von Hippel, Frank. "Gorbachev's Unofficial Arms-Control Advisers." *Physics Today* 66, no. 9 (September 2013): 41–47.

Ward, Barbara, et al. *Science, Technology and Management: Who Speaks for Earth?* Edited by Maurice F. Strong. New York: W. W. Norton, 1973.

Waters, Malcolm. *Daniel Bell*. New York: Routledge, 1996.

Weale, Albert. *The New Politics of Pollution*. Manchester, UK: Manchester University Press, 1992.

Weick, Karl E. *The Social Psychology of Organizing*. 2nd ed. New York: McGraw-Hill, 1979. First published in 1969.

Wengle, Susanne A. "Engineers versus Managers: Experts, Market-Making and State-Building in Putin's Russia." *Economy and Society* 41, no. 3 (2012): 435–467.

Westad, Odd Arne. *The Global Cold War: Third World Interventions and the Making of Our Times*. Cambridge: Cambridge University Press, 2007.

White, Gilbert. "SCOPE: The First Sixteen Years." *Environmental Conservation* 14, no. 1 (1987): 7–13.

Wiener, Norbert, Arturo Rosenblueth, and Julian Bigelow. "Behavior, Purpose and Teleology." *Philosophy of Science* 10, no. 1 (1943): 18–24.

Wierzbicki, Andrzej P. *Technen: Elements of Recent History of Information Technologies with Epistemological Conclusions*. Berlin: Springer, 2014.

Wildavsky, Aaron. *Speaking Truth to Power: The Art and Craft of Policy Analysis*. Boston: Little, Brown, 1979.

Wolfe, Audra J. *Competing with the Soviets: Science, Technology, and the State in Cold War America*. Baltimore, MD: Johns Hopkins University Press, 2013.

Wynne, Brian. *Models, Muddles and Megapolicies: The IIASA Energy Study as an Example of Science for Public Policy*. IIASA Reports WP-83-127. Laxenburg, Austria: International Institute for Applied Systems Analysis, 1983.

Yates, JoAnne. *Control through Communication: The Rise of System in American Management*. Baltimore, MD: Johns Hopkins University Press, 1993.

Zagladin, Vadim. "Programmnye tseli KPSS i global'nye problemy." *Voprosy filosofii* 2 (1986): 3–15.

Zagladin, Vadim, and Ivan T. Frolov. *Global'nye problemy sovremennosti: nauchnye i sotsialnye aspekty*. Moscow: Mezhdunarodnye Otnosheniia, 1981.

Zaleski, Eugène. *Planning Reforms in the Soviet Union, 1962–1966: An Analysis of Recent Trends in Economic Organization and Management*. Translated by Marie-Christine MacAndrew and C. Warren Nutter. Chapel Hill: University of North Carolina Press, 2012. First published in 1967.

Zen'kovich, Nikolai. *Samye sekretnye rodstvenniki: entsiklopedia biografii*. Moscow: Olma Media Group, 2005.

Zhiritskaia, Ekaterina. "O kodekse zhizni na Nikolinoi Gore." *Nezavisimaia gazeta*, February 15, 2008.

Zubok, Vladislav M. *A Failed Empire: The Soviet Union in the Cold War from Stalin to Gorbachev*. Chapel Hill: The University of North Carolina Press, 2007.

Zubok, Vladislav, and Constantine Pleshakov. *Inside the Kremlin's Cold War: From Stalin to Khrushchev*. Cambridge, MA: Harvard University Press, 1996.

Zuckerman, Solly. *Men, Monkeys and Missiles*. New York: W. W. Norton, 1989.

Zvorykin, Anatolii, A. "Material'no-tekhnicheskaia baza kommunizma." *Voprosy filosofii* 4 (1960): 26–40.

———. "Nauka i proizvodstvo." *Kommunist* 4 (1962): 37.

———. *Sozdanie material'no-tekhnicheskoi bazy kommunizma v SSSR*. Moscow: Sotsekgiz, 1959.

Index

acid rain project, 181–203; nuclear winter project, comparisons to, 191–192, 202–203; objectivity of, 188–191, 192, 195, 203; origin of, 181–90; secrecy/security issues, 186–187, 188, 199–200; setup of, 190–202
Ackoff, Russell, 82, 126
Aleksandrov, Vladimir, 161–169, 171–172, 175, 177, 211, 256n49, 256n51, 257n79
Ambio (journal), 164, 169
Ansoff, Igor, 73, 124
Anthropocene, 23, 152–153
applied systems analysis, 78–79
Arbatov, Georgii, 89, 157, 254n27
Aron, Raymond, 29, 109
Arrow, Kenneth, 66, 82, 126–127, 236n74, 239n36
Arthur, Bryan, 117–118
Ashby, Ross, 82, 85, 88, 240n56
assembling/assemblage, 10–11, 75
atmosphere sciences, 186–187, 256n49, 256n51

Badash, Lawrence, 151, 157, 164, 253n5
Barth, Kai-Henrik, 165–166
Barthes, Roland, 8, 209
Bator, Francis M., 54, 55, 60, 67
Beer, Stafford, 71–72
Bell, Daniel, 29, 109
Berg, Aksel, 86
Bernal, John Desmond, 28, 30, 83, 240n45
Bertalanffy, Ludwig von, 78, 82, 86, 87, 88, 90
Bierly, Eugene, 161, 163–164
Bigelow, James, 109
biosphere: definition, 78; models/studies on, 126, 141–142, 161, 163, 170–171, 200; Vernadskii/Moiseev's work, 23, 140, 153, 171, 173, 175, 177–80. *See also* acid rain project; nuclear winter project
Blackett, Patrick, 30, 38, 73, 83
Bockman, Johanna, 214–215, 223n36
Bogdanov, Aleksander A., 78, 87
Bondi, Hermann, 123
Bower, Joseph, 66, 67, 234n38
Brezhnev, Leonid, 17, 35
Brezhnev era, 21, 24
Britain, 30, 84, 122, 123, 126, 174, 209

Brown, Thomas, 108
Brundtland, Gro Harlem, 185
Bukharin, Nikolai, 17
Bulganin, Nikolai, 30
Bundy, McGeorge, 54, 55, 58–59, 60, 67, 69, 71, 122, 232n6, 232n14

Canada, 70, 184, 189
Casti, John, 73
CERN, 54, 64, 110
Chakrabarty, Dipesh, 152
China, 144
Clark, William, 201
Clemens, Walter, 209, 229n62
Club of Rome, 37, 50, 57, 129, 132, 133, 248n14. *See also Limits to Growth* report
CO_2 emissions, 163–164
Cohrs, Patrick, 108
Cold War: epistemology of, 6; policy sciences and, 12, 15
Collier, Stephen, 79
common problems, 109–112, 206–207; proactively shaped, 112
communities. *See* networks
computer-based modeling. *See* global modeling
Computer Center (Soviet Academy of Sciences), 131, 158–159, 160–167, 175, 177, 216
computer technology: global modeling and, 22, 129, 130–132, 176, 181–182; at IIASA, 101, 119–120; in nuclear winter project, 169; Soviet Union and, 46–49, 61–63, 69, 84–85, 119–120, 173
control, 10, 127, 179, 207, 208
Cooper, Chester, 122–123, 124
coproduction, 10, 12–15, 208, 223n41; IIASA as, 5, 53, 117–121; modeling as, 130–131, 147
cost-benefit modeling, 190, 202
Cowles Commission, 81, 82, 214
critical loads, 202
Crutzen, Paul, 23, 152, 158, 164–165, 166, 175, 179, 200
cybernetics, 2–3, 6, 8–11, 44, 48, 85, 91, 158, 207–208, 222n26 *See also* system-cybernetic governmentality; systems analysis

287

INDEX

cybernetization, 29
cyborg sciences, 78–79
Czarniawska, Barbara, 33
Czechoslovakia, invasion of, 60

Darst, Robert, 182–183, 187
Dean, Mitchell, 12
de Jouvenel, Bertrand, 54, 83–84
depoliticization and neutrality: acid rain project and, 188–191, 192, 195, 203; in global modeling, 139–140; IIASA and, 63–71, 91–92, 110–113, 126, 184–185, 188–189, 191; in policy sciences, 73–74; of systems analysis, 14, 68, 71–72, 91–92, 107–113, 205
development, 139–140, 143–144 See also modernization theory
disarmament, 156–157, 172, 174
disarmament movements, 151, 155, 165
Djelic, Marie-Laure, 202
Dorfman, Robert, 68
Dorodnitsyn, Anatolii, 160–161, 163, 165, 200, 216
Dror, Yezhekel, 80, 237n5
Dr. Strangelove, 94

East-West Institute. *See* IIASA
ECE/UNECE (Economic Commission for Europe), 138, 182, 189–190, 193, 196, 197, 200
Eden, Lynn, 170, 203, 253n5, 259n129
Edwards, Paul, 94, 151, 206
Efremenko, Dmitrii, 148
EMEP, 185, 196, 200, 261n32
ENUWAR, 174
environment: acid rain and, 184–188; economic growth and, 131–134, 137–147; Gaia hypothesis, 23, 80, 177–178; human impact on, recognition of, 152–153; nuclear war and, 152–153, 170–172, 174; Soviet positioning and, 185. *See also* biosphere
environmental sciences, 78, 158–160, 175, 187
Evangelista, Matthew, 157–158, 168, 209, 229n62, 253n13, 255n39
Eyal, Gil, 214–215

Fedorenko, Nikolai, 138, 233n22
Fiat, contract with Soviets, 44
Fischer, Frank, 16, 25, 77
Ford Foundation, 44, 49, 60, 66, 73, 84, 101, 138
foreign diplomacy and policy: Soviet, 32–33, 44, 48, 50, 61–62, 185; US, 4, 50, 56, 59, 62, 71, 82–83, 107–108, 122

Forrester, Jay, 58, 132, 133, 135, 140–141, 248n19
Fortescue, Stephen, 50
Foucault, Michel, 7–8, 11, 79, 210, 221n20, 222n26
France, 70, 83–84, 123
Frolov, Ivan, 177
Future of the World Economy, The (report), 139–140
future studies, 54

Gaia hypothesis, 23, 80, 177–178
Galison, Peter, 130
Gates, Lawrence, 142, 162, 163–164, 166, 251n64, 256n70
Gelovani, Viktor, 90, 133, 141, 142, 143, 251n61, 252n84
Gemelli, Giuliana, 49, 219
general systems theory, 86
Geneva Convention, 118, 182, 184, 189, 195, 196, 199
Gerovitch, Slava, 6, 9
Gieryn, Thomas, 14
Gilman, Nils, 27, 94
GKNT (State Committee for Science and Technology): IIASA and, 56, 69, 70, 89, 99, 104–105; operations research at, 143; role of, 40, 46–49, 56, 210; senior managers at, 26, 40–42, 45, 46, 163, 188, 210, 231n114; technology transfer as aim of, 48–49, 62
Glassboro Summit, 21, 36, 39, 55, 59–60
globalism/global, use of terms, 132
global modeling, 129–149; on acid rain, 181–203; business games, 118–119; on climate, 161–164; computers and, 22, 129, 130–132, 176, 181–182; as coproduction, 130–131, 147; cost-benefit, 190, 202; definition and role of, 129–130, 132; depoliticization of, 139–140; development of, 129–137; of economic growth and its consequences, 131–134, 137–147; at IIASA, 134–137; impacts of, 147–149; on nuclear winter, 164–180; resource simulation, 118; socio-organizational process of, 182; in Soviet Union, 131–134, 138–139, 140–149, 150, 161–163, 168–180; at UN, 129, 137–140
global problems, 3, 64, 106, 111, 148, 186
global warming, 152
Golitsyn, Georgii, 168, 173
Gorbachev, Mikhail, 17, 157, 175, 210
Goskomgidromet, 159, 186, 187, 188
Gosplan, 27, 35, 73, 141, 144, 147
Gouré, Leon, 179

governmentality: concept of, 7–8, 221n20; shifts in, 126–128, 176–179, 203, 204–205
governmentality studies, 8, 12, 13–14
Graham, Loren, 14–15, 17, 20, 22
Gvishiani, Aleksei, 35, 40, 41
Gvishiani, Dzhermen: in acid rain project, 200; connections and contacts, 18, 37, 39–41, 57, 141, 229n73, 230n97; family and career, 36–45, 210, 228n50; at GKNT, 26, 40–42, 46, 47, 231n114; Gorbachev and, 210; IIASA and, 55–56, 59–63, 64, 68, 70, 89, 100, 105, 134; in rescue of, 122, 123; interests and supported areas: international publications, 73, 133; management, 42–44, 49, 63, 123–124; modeling, 133, 135, 143, 150, 233n27; oil/gas industry, 49; STR theory, 32, 33, 50, 212; systems analysis, 205; international role of, 26, 50–51, 105, 133, 141, 200, 212; *Limits to Growth* report and, 58, 133, 233n27; in VNIISI, 43, 89–90, 141, 143, 216, 230n97, 251n74
Gvishiani, Mikhail, 37

Habermas, Jürgen, 80
Hacking, Ian, 8
Handler, Philip: on Gvishiani, 38; NAS and, 235n60, 236n81; in setup of IIASA, 55, 57, 60, 61, 62, 65, 67, 70fig
Hevly, Bruce, 130
Hewlett Packard, 48
Heyck, Hunter, 6, 74, 239n33
high modernist approaches, 6, 16–19, 207, 208
Hitch, Charles, 154
Holling, Buzz, 99, 184–185, 190, 192, 200
Holloway, David, 103, 168
Hoos, Ida, 74, 75
Hordijk, Leen, 193–200, 202
human rights, 126, 185, 213
Humphrey, Hubert, 57

ICT. *See* computer technology
IIASA (International Institute of Applied Systems Analysis): acid rain project, 181–203; construction and staffing of, 63–71, 81–93, 98–100; coproduction at, 5, 117–121; crisis at, 121–125; culture of, 75–77, 95–106; depoliticization/neutrality of, 63–71, 91–92, 110–113, 126, 184–185, 188–189, 191; "family" metaphor, 96–97, 100, 101–102, 127; negotiations for, 58–63; origin of, 3–5, 21–22, 52–58; in post-Soviet era, 207, 209, 215, 217; secrecy/security issues, 98, 104, 120–121

IKSI (Institute for Concrete Social Research), 32, 43, 90
infrastructural globalism, 159
input-output studies, 138–139
international technology transfer: soft *vs.* hard technologies, 48, 50; Soviet desire for, 33, 48, 50, 61–63
Ishii, Atsushi, 202
issledovaniia operatsii, 87
Italy, 44, 70, 84, 123, 201, 209
Izrael', Iurii, 159, 163, 165, 173, 187, 188, 197, 200–201

Jasanoff, Sheila, 13
Johnson, Lyndon B., 3, 21–22, 53, 54, 56, 62–63, 107–108
Josephson, Paul, 22, 74

Kahn, Herman, 154–155
Kaplan, Fred M., 155
Kaysen, Carl, 58, 60, 66, 67, 83, 135, 234n38
Keldysh, Mstislav, 40, 45, 61, 105
Kendall Foundation, 172
Kennedy, John F., 109
Khrushchev, Nikita, 35, 37, 39, 44, 151, 154, 226n11
Kirillin, Vladimir, 45, 46, 105, 210, 231n115
Kondrat'ev, Nikolai, 118
Koopmans, Tjalling, 66, 82, 91, 98–99, 135, 188, 235n72, 244n56
Kosygin, Aleksei: arms reductions, opposition to, 59, 229n56; family and career, 18, 21, 26, 34–36, 44, 228n50; GKNT, and, 42, 46; IIASA and, 53, 59–60, 63; international role of, 36, 44; Khrushchev and, 35, 226n11; oil/gas industry, promotion of, 49, 228n52; retirement, 210; VNIISI and, 145
Kosygina-Gvishiani, Liudmila, 34, 39, 59
Kovda, Viktor, 161, 200
Kreisky, Bruno, 122
Krige, John, 55
Kurchatov, Igor, 168

Latour, Bruno, 11, 13–14, 19, 25, 223n44
Lavrent'ev, Mikhail, 17
Ledeneva, Alena, 217
Leontief, Wassily, 29, 56–57, 69, 71–72, 85–86, 138–140, 144, 233n22, 250n44, 250n46, 250n49
Letov, Aleksandr, 56, 70, 89
Levien, Roger, 59, 91–92, 232n6, 235n56
liberal governance, 207

290   INDEX

Limits to Growth, The (report): IIASA and, 58, 134–135; models and predictions of, 58, 118, 132–135, 189–190; Soviet reaction to, 22, 132–134, 140, 142, 145, 233n27; UN agenda, impact on, 137–138

l'Institut de la vie, 170–171

Livermore Laboratory, 161, 162, 168, 177, 256n70

Lovelock, James, 23, 80, 177, 178

MacCracken, Michael, 158, 163, 164, 166

MAD (Mutually Assured Destruction) strategy, 154, 156

Malone, Thomas, 173, 258n103

Margulis, Lynn, 80, 177

mathematics, 136, 139. *See also* global modeling

McNamara, Robert, 59, 107, 122, 151, 154, 215

Meadows, Dennis: models of, 58, 118–119, 132, 135, 140, 141, 145; Soviets and, 90, 133, 141

Meadows, Donella, 58, 101, 118

Men'shikov, Stanislav, 139, 144, 250n59, 251n82

Mesarovic, Mihajlo, 88, 134

Meynaud, Jean, 16

Mintz-Arakawa model, 161, 162–163

Mirowski, Philip, 78–79, 126, 238n20

MIT, 49, 58, 124, 216

modeling. *See* global modeling

modernization theory, 27–33, 41, 50, 63, 108, 137

Moiseev, Nikita: on anthropogenic change, 142, 153, 205; geophysical modeling, promotion of, 140–141; on limitations of modeling, 141, 147, 148, 250n57; in nuclear winter project, 157–163, 169, 171–172, 177–180, 254n31, 255n48; in post-Soviet era, 211, 213; travels internationally, 105–106

Mumford, Lewis, 79–80

NAS (National Academy Of Sciences), 158, 174; IIASA and, 61, 65–66, 121–122, 190, 192; nuclear war studies, 155, 164

NATO, 195

NCAR (National Center for Atmospheric Research), 161–162

neoliberalism, 213–217, 223n36

Netherlands, 193–194

networks: in acid rain project, 183–184, 192–194, 201–202, 203; of Gvishiani, 18, 37, 39–41, 57, 141, 229n73, 230n97; at IIASA, 81–93, 96, 101–103, 106, 117, 122–128; modeling and, 130, 144, 147; in nuclear winter project, 158, 159–160, 162, 163–164, 165–167; in post-Soviet era, 183–184

neutrality. *See* depoliticization and neutrality

nonknowability, 207–208

nonmodern technocracy, 16–19

noosphere, 23, 78, 140, 141, 153, 176–179, 211, 258n119

Norway, 142, 185, 189, 195

nuclear security, 113, 115

nuclear winter project, 150–180; as East-West bridge, 154–155; impacts of, 22–23, 151–153, 157, 172, 174–179; misperceptions of as failure, 156–157; Moiseev, role of, 157–163, 169, 171–172, 177–180, 254n31, 255n48; networks in, 158, 159–160, 162, 163–164, 165–167; origins of, 152–156, 160–167; overview, 150–152; in post-Soviet era, 211–112; public dissemination of, 170–177; Soviet involvement in, 164–180

objectivity. *See* depoliticization and neutrality

OECD, 181

Oltmans, Willem, 52

operations research (OR), 74, 78–79, 81, 85–88

Optner, Stanford, 73

Oregon State, Climatic Research Institute at, 162, 163

path dependence, 117

Patt, Anthony, 202

Peccei, Aurelio: Club of Rome and, 57–58, 132; IIASA and, 57–58, 60, 64, 84, 134, 233n28; Soviets, cooperation with, 44, 133, 134. *See also* Club of Rome

performativity of system-cybernetic governmentality, 10–11, 80–81, 203, 207–208

Pestre, Dominique, 110

Pickering, Andrew, 80, 207–208

Poland, 196, 201

Polanyi, Karl, 10

policy analysis, and neoliberalism, 213–217

policy sciences, 5, 8, 65–66, 73–74, 83–84, 238n20; in Soviet Union, 15, 25–27, 78

political purification. *See* depoliticization

pollution, 181. *See also* acid rain project

Polytechnic Museum, 217

Porter, Theodore, 14, 168

Pugwash meetings, 64, 69, 156, 157, 167, 254n22

Putin, Vladimir, 216

Quade, Edward S., 92, 238n20

qualitative approaches, 207

INDEX

Radin, Beryl, 107
Raiffa, Howard: on Gvishiani, 38, 68, 70, 100, 232n14, 233n27; IIASA and, 60, 66, 68–69, 70, 97–102, 111, 112, 122–123, 135, 243n51
RAINS project (acid rain), 181–203
RAND Corporation: IIASA as parallel to, 3, 56, 59; nuclear strategies and, 153–154; Soviet admiration for/imitation of, 27, 43, 64, 89, 94–95, 242n3; specialists from, in IIASA, 55, 66, 67, 71, 81, 82, 92, 125; studies by, 59, 60, 64, 65, 66, 68, 82
Reagan, Ronald, 151, 175
Richta, Radovan, 31–32
Rose, Nikolas, 14
Rostow, Walt Whitman, 27, 31, 50, 54, 55, 107, 232n10
Rowen, Henry, 59, 232n6. *See also* RAND Corporation
Royal Society, 122, 123, 174
Runca, Eliodoro, 189, 190, 193, 195
Russia. *See* Soviet Union

Sadovskii, Vadim, 86
Sagan, Carl, 163, 165, 166, 167, 172, 173, 259n129
Sagdeev, Roald, 165–166, 167, 173
Sahlgren, Klaus, 193, 196
SALT II treaty 156
Schmitt, Carl, 108
Schneider, Stephen, 158, 162, 164, 167, 168, 173, 174, 177
Schwartz, Thomas A., 54, 55, 220n12, 232n3
scientific-technical revolution (Soviet), 24–51, 71; discourses on, 32–33, 50–51; Kosygin/Gvishiani, role of, 26–27, 33, 37, 40–49; theories on socioeconomic change, 27–33, 49–51
SCOPE, 160–161, 173–174, 255n40, 258n103
Scott, James, 18–19, 74, 208
secrecy/security issues: in acid rain project, 186–187, 188, 199–200; IIASA and, 98, 104, 120–121; modeling and, 133, 144, 146–147
Shell (company), 195
Shils, Edward, 29, 109
Silk, Leonard, 28–29, 30
Simon, Herbert, 58, 65–66, 67, 117
Skriabin, Georgii, 165
Smolian, Georgii, 86
Snow, Charles Percy, 28
social issues and systems analysis, 110–111
sociology, 43
Sociology of Business (Gvishiani), 42
Sokolovskii, Valentin, 187–188, 197, 199, 201

Soviet Academy of Sciences, 46, 61, 85, 131, 138, 168, 174, 176; Computer Center, 131, 158–159, 160–167, 175, 177, 216; TsEMI, 89, 124, 138, 145
Soviet Union: acid rain project and, 185, 196–197, 199–201; computerization and, 46–49, 61–63, 69, 84–85, 119–120, 173; IIASA and: integration at, 100–106; in negotiations/setup, 56, 60–63, 68–70, 88–89, 99–101; secrecy/security issues, 98, 104, 120–121; modeling in, 131–134, 138–139, 140–149, 150, 161–163; nuclear winter project, 168–180; secrecy/security issues, 133, 144, 146–147; policy sciences in, 15, 25–27, 78; post-Soviet era, 209, 210–17; scientific governance in, 9–11, 14–15; secrecy/security issues, 133, 144; systems analysis in: government support of, 69, 85–86, 209; impacts of, 127, 145–149, 176–179; legitimacy of, 89, 90–92, 205, 207, 209; liberalizing effects of, 14–15; rise of, 84–93; technocracy in, 17–18, 24–27; West, willingness to learn from, 63, 73–74. *See also* scientific-technical revolution
Staples, Eugene, 60
Stenchikov, Georgii, 163, 168, 169, 173, 175, 212
Stone, Diane, 4
STRATEGEM-2 game, 118–119
Strategic Defense Initiative (SDI), 156, 167
Svedin, Uno, 189
Svirezhev, Iurii, 161, 163, 168, 169, 211–212
Sweden, 164, 181
system, definition, 79
system-cybernetic governance, definition, 2
system-cybernetic governmentality: as avant-garde and mainstream, 208–209; as coproduced, 10, 12–15, 53; definition, 7; depoliticization/neutrality and, 73–74; as performative, 10–11, 23, 80–81, 203, 207–208; as reflexive, 10–11
systems analysis: as art of governance, 8, 14; construction of problems by, 75, 206–207; decline of, 210–212; depoliticization/neutrality of, 14, 68, 71–72, 91–92, 107–113, 205; global governance, role of in, 204–209; intellectual/social organization of, 75–77; international appeal of, 74–75; neoliberalism and, 213–217, 223n36; overview of, 77–81, 92; process of, as important, 205; role of in global governance, 204–209

Tarko, Aleksandrov, 163, 168, 171–172, 177, 212
technics, 79–80

technocracy, 16–19, 223n34
technocratic discourse, 112
technoscience: neutrality of, 50, 204; as performative assemblage, 10–11
Timofeev-Resovskii, Nikolai, 140, 161, 250n53
Tinbergen, Jan, 138, 193
TsEMI, 89, 124, 138, 145
TTAPS group, 165, 168, 173
Turco, Richard, 158, 164–165

UNECE (Economic Commission for Europe), 138, 182, 189–190, 193, 196, 197, 200
United Kingdom, 30, 84, 122, 123, 126, 174, 209
United Nations, 137–140
universal problems, 3, 64, 111, 139, 148, 186
USSR. *See* Soviet Union

Van Horn, Richard, 49
Veblen, Thorstein, 16
Velikhov, Evgenii, 165–166, 167, 173, 175, 177, 211, 257n72, 257n80
Vernadskii, Vladimir, 23, 78, 140, 153, 171, 173, 178, 281n112; discussions of ideas of, 23, 171, 173, 177, 178, 258n119, 259n124

Vidmer, Richard, 20
VNIISI (Soviet Institute of Systems Research), 43, 89–90, 124, 141, 143–146, 200, 230n97, 250n58, 251n74
VNIPOU, 47
von Hippel, Frank, 157, 167
Voprosy filosofii, 31, 176

war room imagery, 94–95
Washington, Warren, 162
Weick, Karl, 53, 166
Weinberger, Caspar, 155
Wengle, Susanne, 216
Wiener, Norbert, 29, 81, 85, 86, 178, 237n8
Wiesner, Jerome, 38, 45
Wilson, Carroll, 45
Winter, S.G. Jr., 59, 232n6, 235n56
Wolfe, Audra, 64
WORLD3 model, 118

Zagladin, Vadim, 177
Zubok, Vladislav, 44
Zuckerman, Solly, 30, 57, 60, 70fig, 83, 134, 135, 232n8, 240n45
Zvorykin, Anatolii, 30–31, 32, 227n29

www.ingramcontent.com/pod-product-compliance
Lightning Source LLC
Chambersburg PA
CBHW021850230426
43671CB00006B/335